Prosperity Decade

FROM WAR TO DEPRESSION

1917–1929

THE ECONOMIC HISTORY OF THE UNITED STATES

Edited by Henry David, Harold U. Faulkner, Louis M. Hacker,
Curtis P. Nettels, and Fred A. Shannon

Curtis P. Nettels: THE EMERGENCE OF A NATIONAL ECONOMY, 1775-1815

Paul W. Gates: THE FARMER'S AGE: *Agriculture, 1815-1860*

George Rogers Taylor: THE TRANSPORTATION REVOLUTION, 1815-1860

Fred A. Shannon: THE FARMER'S LAST FRONTIER:
Agriculture, 1860-1897

Edward C. Kirkland: INDUSTRY COMES OF AGE:
Business, Labor, and Public Policy, 1860-1897

Harold U. Faulkner: THE DECLINE OF LAISSEZ FAIRE, 1897-1917

George Soule: PROSPERITY DECADE:
From War to Depression, 1917-1929

Broadus Mitchell: DEPRESSION DECADE: *From New Era Through New Deal*

PROSPERITY DECADE

From War to Depression: 1917-1929

By GEORGE SOULE

VOLUME VIII

The Economic History of
the United States

M. E. SHARPE, INC.

Armonk, New York   London, England

Cover photo courtesy of North Castle Historical Society.

This book was originally published as volume VIII of The Economic History of the United States series by Holt, Rinehart and Winston in 1947. It is here reprinted by arrangement with Holt, Rinehart and Winston, Inc.

Library of Congress Cataloging-in-Publication Data

Soule, George Henry, 1887-1970.
    Prosperity decade : from war to depression : 1917-1929 / by George Soule.
        p.   cm.—(The Economic history of the United States ; 8)
        Reprint. Originally published: New York : Rinehart, 1947.
        ISBN 0-87332-098-0 :
        1. United States—Economic conditions—1918-1945. 2. United States—Economic conditions—1865-1918. 3. Reconstruction (1914-1939)—United States. I. Title. II. Series.
    HC106.3.S654   1989   89-10694
    330.973'091—dc20   CIP

Printed in the United States of America

ED   10   9   8   7   6   5   4   3   2   1

Foreword

WHEN this series of nine volumes on the economic history of the United States was first conceived, the nation's economy had reached a critical stage in its development. Although the shock of the depression of 1929 had been partially absorbed, the sense of bewilderment which it produced had not yet vanished, and the suffering and the bitterness of its first years were being transformed into less substantial, though still anguished, memories. Reform measures, either in operation or proposed, were being actively debated, but with less sense of urgency than earlier.

To the Editors of this series a fresh consideration of America's economic history was justified by more than the experiences of the recent past or the obscurity of the future. Rich contributions to the literature of American history had been made through cooperative series dealing with the political, social, and cultural aspects of American life. Numerous single-volume surveys of the country's economic development had been written. But, as late as the end of the fourth decade of the twentieth century, the world's foremost economic power had not yet produced an integrated, full-length, and authoritative treatment of its own economic history.

Scholarly concern with American economic history has been constantly growing during the past half century, and chairs of economic history have been established in leading universities. A more profound understanding of the role of economic forces in the nation's history has not only been developed by historians and economists, but has also won some measure of popular acceptance. The earlier thin trickle of monographs has broadened in recent years into a flood of publications. At present, such specialized studies, the many collections of documentary materials, and the mountains of government reports on different facets of American economic life are staggering in their richness and scope.

This series has been planned to utilize these available sources in the preparation of a full-scale, balanced, cooperative, and readable survey of the growth of American economy and of its transformation from one of primitive character to world pre-eminence in industry, trade, and finance. Clearly, in nine volumes all aspects of the nation's economic life cannot be treated fully. But such a series can point the way to new fields of study and treat authoritatively, if not definitively, the main lines of economic development. Further, the series is intended to fill a present need of those professionally concerned with American economic history, to supplement the economic materials now available in general school and college histories of the United States, and finally to provide the lay reader with the fruits of American scholarship. If these objectives are attained, then the efforts which have gone into the creation of this economic history of the United States will have been amply repaid.

Contributors to the series have been chosen who have already established their competence in the particular periods they are to survey here; and they are, of course, solely responsible for the points of view or points of departure they employ. It is not intended that the series represent a school of thought or any one philosophical or theoretical position.

In PROSPERITY DECADE, volume VIII in *The Economic History of the United States,* George Soule deals with a period that opens with the crisis of war and closes with the catastrophe of depression. Between these terminal points there fall developments of unusual significance, which bristle with difficulties for the economic historian. The fumbling organization of a war economy, the issues and course of peacetime reconstruction, the boom and depression that followed the war, the expanding economy of the twenties, the collapse in 1929—these are among the problems that Mr. Soule handles with uncommon skill and success. In large part this happy result follows from his fruitful utilization of economic theory in posing and approaching his historical problems. His analytical account points up the degree to which the prosperity of the twenties was limited. In making clear the causes of the bursting of the bubble, Mr. Soule also indicates the larger implication of the history of that fabled period. Quite properly he deals fully, and with rare clarity, with the place and role of the United States in the world economy. His employment of larger institutional patterns enables Mr. Soule to treat with equal clarity such diverse problems as the impact of governmental behavior upon the economy, the sources of the depression in agriculture, the consequences of financial policy, concentration in ownership and control, the status of workers, and modifications in the labor movement. The economic developments with which Mr. Soule is concerned—and to the long-term meanings of which he is far from indifferent—encourage the display of bias and the writing of polemics in the guise of history. Happily, Mr. Soule's volume is singularly free of both.

THE EDITORS.

Preface

WHILE I alone am responsible for the text of this book, it is for the most part based on the work of others. I am particularly indebted to the National Bureau of Economic Research and the members of its staff for many of the figures and statistical tables, as well as to all the others cited in the footnotes. Extensive improvements in the manuscript have resulted from the careful work of the Editors of this series, who have twice gone over it in detail, offering suggestions and pointing out omissions. Though they did not attempt to influence my point of view or approach to the subject, much of the credit for any merits the work may have is due to them.

GEORGE SOULE

New York
May, 1947

Contents

ix

List of Illustrations

List of Tables

Prosperity Decade

FROM WAR TO DEPRESSION

1917–1929

Introduction

THE story of the period that this book covers might be told in a number of different ways. It was the time of prohibition, speakeasies, flappers, and petting parties. James J. Walker, the playboy mayor of New York, typified its geniality and irresponsibility. H. L. Mencken made fun of its boobs and yokels, and was a demigod to the smartly sophisticated. The Ku Klux Klan for a time built a tremendous organization on the aimless unrest, foreshadowing the Nazi movement in Germany by mobilizing hostility against Jews, Negroes, and Catholics. Serious literary men like Dos Passos and Hemingway gave more pointed expression to postwar disillusionment. Americans were excited by the succession of yearly models of automobiles; radios made their first public appearance and invaded nearly every home. Technology produced countless new gadgets in increasing numbers while it added to the insecurity of employment. Rich material exists in these years for the social and political historians.

The primary concern of this volume is the economic background of all this froth and turmoil. The period between 1917 and 1929 followed years that were characterized by criticisms of the American economic order and reforms undertaken to improve it. It was ended by a depression that was one of the worst ever experienced. Within this frame of time occurred the changes in American society wrought by the World War I, a subsequent attempt to forget these changes, to isolate the United States from the rest of the world, and to proceed as if nothing had happened. The consequent inflation and deflation, and the climb back to prosperity, which at the time seemed so sound that many thought it would last forever, led to disastrous collapse. This period was mainly characterized by a flowering of what is commonly known as private enterprise, with a minimum of governmental interference and a maximum of governmental encouragement.

Freedom under private enterprise is, as these words are written, generally regarded in America as a desirable goal. The experiences

3

of World War II are uppermost in most minds; behind them loom the contentious years of the New Deal and the tragic bewilderment of the Great Depression. Less is remembered about the last time private enterprise and prosperity reigned, under a business administration. What were its achievements and its failures? Were there weaknesses that foreshadowed the fate which we now know overtook it? What did bring about that misfortune? What happened, during the course of the war, the postwar period, and the subsequent expansion, to wage earners, farmers, businessmen, and others? What were the courses of important industries? What changes took place in industrial organization, banking, and the general anatomy of the economic order? A picture of these matters would not provide anything like a complete understanding of the United States during those strange thirteen years, but without some sense of the economic undercurrents the rest of the story is like the phantasmagoria of a dream.

Part of the reason for telling the story now is that again the United States has engaged in world war, again it has struggled with reconstruction, and again it seems to have set its face against any program but the utmost possible degree of "free enterprise." As will be observed by the judicious reader, many parallels with earlier experiences already have become apparent. The present, however, never repeats history exactly, and there are differences also. One may learn from both likeness and unlikeness. Whatever happens in the near future, the changes of the former period will influence America for years to come.

Now the essential economic characteristics of the 1920's may be viewed more coherently than they were at the time. During World War I regular statistical records were greatly extended, and after it they were currently kept and augmented. In recent years this quantitative material has been put in order and given meaning by careful and systematic research. It is possible therefore to see the main currents of the economy of the "New Era" more fully than any previous period of American history. I have attempted to make use of this new material. Those who dislike figures should remember that without relative quantities, emphasis may be distorted. It is important to know not only what and how, but how much. Indeed, without knowing how much, the what and the how may often be unknowable. The statistics, however, are not abstractions unrelated to human life. To look at them may add some comprehension of the broad forces within which contemporaries were borne along, exultant, careless, or baffled.

A brief preliminary outline of the story to be told may help the reader to follow the narrative as it develops. It is necessary to begin with the participation of the United States in World War I, for two reasons. First, this was the immediate source of the events that followed the war. Second, the war organization was a fumbling, but on the whole successful, attempt to use planning and economic management for a national purpose—an experiment on which the nation turned its back as soon as the war was over. The immediate result was inflation, great labor conflicts, and a sharp economic reaction, with unemployment and agricultural distress. Industry and its wage earners quickly revived, though union organization was set back for a decade. The farmers did not fully recover for years. Movements for reform were held in check while private business had its way, economically and politically. The Harding-Coolidge regime was marked by an almost continuous upsurge of production and profits, culminating in a triumphant climax of self-congratulation, with wild speculation for the rise in finance and real estate. Meanwhile, the American people did not all enjoy the ride. Miners, textile workers, and the unemployed, as well as many of the farmers, suffered, and registered their futile dissents. The end of the "New Era" came with the panic on the stock market in 1929, which signalized the onset of the Great Depression. Within the main stream of this narrative there are, of course, many crosscurrents and eddies that it is worth while to pause and examine.

No history can be completely objective, much less all-inclusive. The emphasis of this volume is upon the pattern of economic forces, though exceptions are noted and the effects upon the lives of individual Americans are briefly indicated. The treatment does not leave much scope for those sketches of personalities or of picturesque incidents that are ordinarily regarded as the dramatic material of history; nevertheless, the broader forces have a unity and a tragic irony of their own. I can offer no pretense that I have arrived at a final explanation of why so spectacular an advance was cut off by so sudden a nemesis. My opinions are frankly expressed, so far as knowledge seems to warrant opinions, but the major facts are here also, for the benefit of those who might interpret them differently. Nobody who cares about the future of America or of the world of which it is so large a part can afford to be indifferent to what happened in the United States between 1917 and 1929.

CHAPTER I

Organizing for War

FOR about two years before the declaration of war by the United States against Germany on April 6, 1917, the American economy had been stimulated by the sale of goods to the European belligerents and distorted by the changes brought by the war in the accustomed patterns of trade and finance.

The money borrowed in the United States by the Allies, plus the amount realized by the sales of their securities, resulted in the injection of at least $5 billion of purchasing power into the American economy between January, 1915, and April, 1917. This was a substantial percentage of the total national income at the time, and there is little wonder that it brought about a tremendous boom. The boom was not confined by any means to manufacturers of guns, shells, or other munitions of war. During the three years ending June 30, 1917, the Allied countries bought in the United States nearly seven times as great a value of wheat as during the three prewar years. They bought twice as much wheat flour, nearly two and a half times as much meat, nearly four times as much sugar, and thirty-seven times as much zinc.[1]

While the neutrality policy of the United States favored this economic expansion and the banking system readily offered credit to finance it, there was no governmental attempt to control or organize the agencies of production and distribution. The heavy demands of war had been imposed upon economic institutions that

[1] Cleona Lewis, *America's Stake in International Investments* (Washington: The Brookings Institution, 1938), p. 352.

had developed under the varied stimuli of private enterprise. There
was no system of priorities for scarce raw materials, no mobilization
of labor supplies, and no price-control machinery. The Allies had to
pay whatever the producers asked, except in so far as their agents
were able to moderate the exactions by business bargains. J. P.
Morgan & Co. then held a pre-eminence in the American economy
that has never been achieved by any private organization either
before or since. As sole purchasing agents for Great Britain and
France it was parceling out orders beyond the wildest dreams of
great American manufacturing corporations. These orders exceeded
$3 billion. For instance, Bethlehem Steel received within three
months two orders for ammunition totaling, respectively, $83 million
and $64 million.[2]

The confusion caused by the immense pressure of this demand
on an unplanned and unregulated economic system may well be
imagined. In spite of their elation over the enormous profits being
made, businessmen were harassed by the scramble for raw materials,
machinery, and labor. Executives of railroads and port facilities were
at their wits' end in devising means of handling the unwonted flood
of traffic to the eastern seaboard. Prices and the cost of living began
to shoot upward. Labor shortages and strikes multiplied. The Allied
governments, in turn—for whom the war was not going any too well
at the time—looked at the high prices they were paying, the enormous amounts of materials they required, the growing difficulties in
delivery of orders, and their dwindling credit resources, and became
seriously concerned about the future of their American base of supply if the war should last much longer.

Preparations for hostilities had, of course, begun in the United
States before 1917, but for the most part, to the Allies' demand for
production they simply added the requirements of a growing American navy and army, without doing anything to make headway
against the existing turmoil. It was therefore natural that, as soon
as the declaration of war made possible the exercise of the necessary
legal power, the nation turned its attention to the organization of
control.

ECONOMIC PLANNING FOR WAR

In the months following the declaration of war, Americans
probably learned more about the structure and operation of their

2 *Ibid.*

economy than they ever had known before. For the first time in the history of the nation it became necessary to understand this sprawling and confused giant as a whole, to tame it and direct it toward consciously reasoned purposes. In previous wars, nation-wide planning and coordination of production had been unnecessary. It is true that during the Civil War, the government in Washington took over the transportation and communication systems, and the Confederacy controlled even more of its economy, but at that time warfare was not highly mechanized and did not pre-empt the services of so technically advanced a manufacturing system. The function of fighting had been delegated to the armed forces; Congress had supplied them with funds, and they had gone out into the market and bought whatever they required or could get. The Army and Navy had always competed freely against each other in the markets for goods, and even the separate bureaus of each of the services had acted as if they were independent business enterprises. Congress was in the habit of making specific and detailed appropriations for each of the bureaus, and funds appropriated for any one of them could not be transferred to another. Many had never even grasped the idea that in modern warfare economic preparations ought to be made before the outbreak of hostilities. All these habits persisted until the United States declared war on Germany in 1917, and were difficult to eradicate even during the following months.

The story of how the necessity of planning and organization became evident and of how the wild horses of economic and governmental particularism were eventually bridled and driven as a team is a fascinating one. Agencies of control were created in confusing array, altered, brought into conflict with one another, coordinated and recoordinated, until finally, when the war was over, something like order had emerged. These agencies were more numerous and covered a larger sphere of economic life than anyone could have ventured to predict at the beginning. It was inevitable that they should do so, however, in a war which required not only a large contribution to the implements and the supplies employed by the British, French, and Italians, but the creation and sustenance of an American navy that became the largest in the world and an army of four million men. Altogether the war effort at its peak absorbed about one quarter of the national income.

There had been a few who had a glimmer of understanding

that civilian cooperation with the Army and Navy would be required. As far back as 1910 a confidential report on the military situation from the General Staff of the Army to the House of Representatives had included a recommendation for a Council of National Defense. A bill to effectuate this recommendation was introduced into Congress by Richmond Pearson Hobson but was never passed. The original idea, however, was merely to coordinate efforts of the Army, the Navy, and Congress.

The germ of the idea of industrial coordination had arisen in 1915. As a result of President Wilson's message to Congress of December 7, 1915, this nation started building "a navy second to none" and a huge merchant marine. A Naval Consulting Board, previously created to deal with the industrial requirements of the contemplated program, consisted of two members each from the various scientific societies and was headed by Thomas A. Edison. This board in turn set up in August, 1915, a Committee on Industrial Preparedness that included in its thinking the possible requirements of the Army as well as of the Navy. The committee was not primarily a governmental organization, being supported by private contributions. Its chief work was to draw up an inventory of manufacturing plants that could make munitions. About 20,000 supplied the data requested; these data covered only products, but not the processes used in producing them. The chairman of this committee, Howard V. Coffin of Detroit, was educated by this experience to see the need for more industrial preparedness and was one of those instrumental in creating subsequent agencies for this work.[3]

COUNCIL OF NATIONAL DEFENSE

As a result of conferences, including Mr. Coffin and others, among whom were a scientist, Dr. Hollis Godfrey, the Secretary of War, Chief of Staff General Leonard Wood, and Dr. Henry E. Crampton, another eminent scientist, the Military Appropriations Act of August 29, 1916, created a Council of National Defense. This was composed of a number of cabinet officers, but its main work was performed by an advisory commission consisting of leaders outside the government. The first director of the council was Walter S. Gifford, chief statistician of the American Telephone & Telegraph

[3] Grosvenor B. Clarkson, *Industrial America in the World War* (Boston: Houghton Mifflin Company, 1923), p. 13.

The American War Council

Front row: Robert DeForest, President Wilson, Ex-President Taft, Eliot Wadsworth; *back row:* Henry P. Davidson, Grayson Murphy, Charles Norton, Edward N. Hurley. (*Brown Brothers*)

Selective Service

Secretary of War Newton D. Baker drawing the first number from the goldfish bowl, June 27, 1918. (*The Bettmann Archive*)

Bombing Plane

World War I planes had open cockpits. Their frames were made of spruce, and the wings were covered with cloth. (*Brown Brothers*)

American Soldier with Equipment

This shows the World War I uniform, with its high collar, baggy breeches, and canvas puttees. For overseas service, the stiff brimmed hat was replaced by an unvisored cloth cap. Equipment shown: pack, canteen, cartridge belt, and service rifle. (*Brown Brothers*)

Company, who later became the head of that corporation. The first members of the advisory commission were Daniel Willard, president of the Baltimore & Ohio Railroad, Bernard M. Baruch, the Wall Street operator who was later to become the chairman of the War Industries Board, Mr. Coffin, Julius Rosenwald, president of Sears Roebuck & Co., Dr. Godfrey, Samuel Gompers of the American Federation of Labor, and Dr. Franklin Martin of the American College of Surgeons.

The legal authority of the Council of National Defense was derived not merely from the Military Appropriations Act, but from the National Defense Act of June 3, 1916. Section 120 of this law gave the President power to place orders for war material directly with any source of supply, to commandeer plants if necessary, and to appoint an industrial mobilization board. In the same section, the Secretary of War was instructed to prepare a complete list of all privately owned plants equipped to manufacture arms or munitions.

The pioneering work that had to be done by the Council of National Defense may be understood from the fact that as late as six weeks before war was declared, the Army did not even have plans for the organization and equipment of a large military force. The general understanding was that the United States did not intend to send soldiers to Europe. The unpreparedness of the Army itself may be attributed partly to the limitations of personnel and funds placed by Congress on the General Staff. It was only at the instance of the advisory commission that a rough estimate of what would be required for a large army was made by a retired officer, then submitted to the War College for review. This report became available three weeks before war was declared.

The public attitude toward advance preparation for possible military action may be inferred from the fact that a member of Congress demanded and received the early minutes of the advisory commission and reported to his committee a "startling disclosure of the secret government of the United States."[4] He stated with horror that even before war was declared the commission had thought of many eventualities, which later became the subject of congressional legislation. It had discussed such things as daylight-saving, conscription, the selection of Herbert Hoover to direct food control, the organization of industry for selling to the government, and the fixing

[4] *Ibid.*, p. 24.

of prices. Commissioner Willard had taken the first step toward what later became the Railroad Administration. Commissioner Baruch had taken the initiative in forming committees representing management in numerous industries, so that their resources could be surveyed and mobilized for action. Mr. Baruch was also particularly concerned with the existing and impending shortages of raw materials.

When war was declared, various bureaus of the Army proceeded to submit to Congress estimates of what it would require to raise and equip an army of a million men. These estimates, little more than guesses, varied widely. The War Department finally gave up in despair the attempt to coordinate them and asked for a lump-sum appropriation. In an attempt to get the buyers together, the advisory commission induced the Army and Navy to create first a Munitions Standards Board, then a General Munitions Board consisting of the chiefs of the main purchasing bureaus and of representatives from itself. This board, however, resulted in little more than a proliferation of the same kind of industrial committees that the advisory commission already had set up, while the separate bureaus persistently went their own ways. What was needed was a central source of information and central executive authority.

THE WAR INDUSTRIES BOARD

Noting the failure of the General Munitions Board, the Council of National Defense voted on July 8, 1917, to establish the War Industries Board, consisting of five civilians and one representative each of the Army and Navy. The War Industries Board itself, however, at first had no executive authority, and while it created an administrative machinery for contacts with industry and other important sectors of the national life, it failed to coordinate government purchases. The first chairman, Frank M. Scott, was broken by the strain, and his successor, Daniel Willard, resigned because of the fact that the board had no power.

During this period a spirited agitation arose for the creation of a separate governmental department, a Department of Munitions, to take charge of ordering military supplies at least for the Army, and possibly for the Navy as well. It was argued that in this way it would be possible to place this gigantic business enterprise under civilian control and trained business direction. In addition, such a department could, within the scope of its own executive authority, arrange the multitudinous orders, giving the necessary priority to each. It thus would not have to face the obstacles with which the War Industries Board had been vainly contending in the attempt to coordinate the activities of other governmental agencies over which it had no executive power.

The idea was suggested by observation of what had taken place in England, where in the early stages of the war, the purchasing of munitions had been as chaotic as in the United States. The British had solved the difficulty by establishing a Ministry of Munitions to take charge of the ordering, and placing at its head David Lloyd George.

Although the proposal was backed by some of the civilians who had been commissioned by the military to assist in the services of supply, it was vigorously opposed by the higher authorities in both Army and Navy, who desired to keep control over their purchasing policies. The opposition came not only from military conservatives but also from engineers and liberal experts in labor relations, who had been brought into the Ordnance Bureau of the War Department and were engaged in reforming its practices from the inside. Because they were making headway and expected to conquer the existing confusion within a short time, they thought it would be wasteful to start all over again with a new organization. Furthermore, the War Department under its newly appointed liberal Secretary, Newton D. Baker, was maintaining excellent relations with labor, and it was feared that the business interests pushing the proposal for a Department of Munitions would fill it with anti-union employers and disorganize the labor situation. President Wilson, persuaded by these views, did not set up the proposed department.

In this connection it is interesting to note the influence which the British and to some extent the French exerted over the American organization for war. To them it was a vital matter that the effort should be conducted as efficiently as possible and that the ambitions of the American army and navy should not lead this country to prepare merely to defeat the Germans with its own forces at some later date, rather than give the Allies the utmost possible aid in the field at this critical moment. If they had had their way, the United States might not have had a separate army in

France at all, but American soldiers would have been brigaded with the British and French. It was months before close cooperation between the several general staffs was achieved, and it was not until the final campaign in the summer of 1918 that there was a single Allied commander in chief in the field. The British were equally concerned that this country's industrial mobilization should profit as early as possible from their mistakes and the remedies that they had discovered. "British experience" became almost a byword in Washington, and though the British were tactful about telling Americans what they ought to do, mission after mission crossed the Atlantic to spread information concerning vital problems among those most concerned.

In the spring of 1918 President Wilson finally took action to bring order into the sectors of the war economy that were supplying the military forces. He retained the War Industries Board, but reorganized it and gave it a specific executive mandate to coordinate war industry. Bernard Baruch was appointed chairman of the board, with final authority over everything except the fixing of prices, which was delegated to a separate committee within the board responsible directly to the President. This exception was made because it was believed that Mr. Baruch would be better able to handle the rest of the job if he were freed from the delicate responsibility of price fixing, and because the resistance to fair maximum prices was so great on the part of business interests that the authority of the President himself was thought necessary to enforce them. Even under this new dispensation, however, the board never did any actual buying except for the Allies. Its chief functions were advisory, informational, and organizational.

The job that the board had to do may easily be imagined. Under the stress of enormous purchases by the Allies and the United States, many raw materials were insufficient in quantity. Their production had to be increased and the amounts available had to be allocated to the most necessary uses. The same principles had to be applied to manufacturing and transportation facilities. The requirements of the various governmental departments and bureaus had to be balanced against one another in view of the limitations of supply, and all these in turn had to be compared with the wants of the Allies. Finally, the needs of the civilian population had to be considered. While production was being stimulated, prices had to be kept as far as possible under control. All this had to be done by an agency that, in order to be effective, had to act through other governmental bodies, since, for the most part, it never executed a contract or disbursed any governmental money except for the maintenance of its own offices.

A letter from the President to Mr. Baruch of March 4, 1918, outlined the board's functions and procedures.[5] It was, first of all, to create new facilities and open up additional sources of supply. Wherever necessary, it was to convert existing facilities to new uses. It was to conserve resources and facilities by any possible economies in their use. It was to determine priorities of production and delivery, and allocate the available quantities to the various purchasing agencies whenever a shortage arose. Finally, it was actually to make purchases for the Allies. The board was to act in an advisory capacity to the chairman, who was to have within it final executive authority. A committee on priorities was to be formed, with representatives from the Food, Fuel, and Railway Administrations, the Shipping Board, and the War Trade Board.

The real basis of the board's authority, aside from its presidential instructions, lay in the detailed knowledge it accumulated concerning the amount and locations of the various supplies that could be obtained, and of the demands being made upon them. Thus it could help purchasers find what they wanted. At the same time it could demonstrate to purchasers competing for scarce goods what the actual situation was and convince them that adjustment was necessary. Through its committees, routine methods of making these adjustments came to work more smoothly. Private industry on the whole recognized its authority and cooperated with it, largely because otherwise the confusion created in trying to fill conflicting governmental orders would have been beyond human endurance.

Two principal police powers were exercised, but another lay in the background. One power was the use of priorities and clearance orders, which gave the right of way to the most needed articles in the order of their need. The second was price fixing. Finally, plants could be commandeered if necessary. These measures could legally have been enforced under the broad war powers of the Chief Executive. Like most police measures adopted to bring order out of

[5] *Ibid.*, p. 49.

confusion, however, priorities and fixed prices were in the end for the most part voluntarily obeyed. Commandeering, when utilized, was by order of the Army or Navy, rather than by the War Industries Board. The Army issued 510 requisitions for goods and 996 orders for compulsory production. The board, eventually given this power, used it only as a threat.[6]

In the early months of the war the issuance of priorities had caused almost as much trouble as it had prevented. The priority order was designed to give the right of way to the manufacture and shipment of the kinds of goods that were most needed. Since, however, there was then no carefully integrated production program governing the war economy as a whole, and correlated with the scarcities of raw materials and equipment, high priorities were issued much too frequently and were attached to a large proportion of the orders issued by the Army and Navy. The natural result was that priorities almost lost their significance. It was impossible to fill promptly all the orders having priority status; hence the goods that were really needed first were often delayed in delivery. On the other hand, many materials or goods in process were shipped before those plants that had to handle them were ready to receive them. Railroad yards were clogged with goods that the consignees did not take away, since because of limited storage space, they preferred to leave the shipments in the freight cars until they could use them.

One of the first tasks of the reorganized board was to reduce the issuance of priorities and to issue the various grades according to their genuine rank of importance. A Requirements Division coordinated the programs of the several purchasing agencies. A still more effective measure was the creation of clearance committees to take charge of the distribution of scarce materials. These materials were listed, the quantities available were inventoried, and any order involving their use had to be passed by the clearance committee concerned before it could be filled. The Clearance Division itself, under the chairmanship of an able businessman, contained representatives of the various purchasing bureaus. Day by day it examined the relative needs of these bureaus and gave the right of way to the most pressing.

Much criticism was originally directed at the Council of Na-

6 *Ibid.*, p. 177.

tional Defense because its committees, which were supposed to regulate industry, were composed of dollar-a-year men who were themselves industrialists. Mr. Baruch modified this situation by placing in control of each commodity section a man not connected with the related industry and thus representing the government only, and by retaining the industry committees as bodies to deal with the governmental spokesmen on behalf of the business interests concerned.

One of the most effective ways of increasing quantities of necessary manufactures was found to be the standardization of products and the reduction in number of styles and designs. This was done first of all with weapons and other munitions by the Munitions Standards Board, which under the title of the Advisory Committee on Plants and Munitions, became a part of the War Industries Board at the time of its reorganization. For instance, the British model of the Enfield rifle, also used by American troops, was redesigned to shorten the process of manufacture and to use the same ammunition as the American Springfield. Within ten months the United States was turning out service rifles twice as fast as Great Britain.

The War Industries Board itself instituted many savings in the civilian sectors of the economy. Retail customers were asked to carry their own purchases home, cooperative deliveries were encouraged, and the number of deliveries was reduced. It was estimated that the substitution of paper wrappers for pasteboard cartons and packing cases in the hosiery and underwear trade alone saved the space of 17,312 freight cars a year. Women, who at that time were still wearing boned corsets, were compelled to help the war effort by sacrificing the steel which went into them. Three hundred tons of tin were obtained by prohibiting the use of this metal to give weight and rustle to silks used for women's dresses. Wood and transportation were saved by increasing the yardage of thread in each spool. The number of colors of typewriter ribbons was reduced from 150 to 5, and 395 tons of steel were saved by ceasing to pack them in metal boxes. The number of sizes and styles of plows was reduced from 376 to 76. Everything from baby carriages to coffins was standardized and simplified. Altogether, 1,241 savings of this kind were effected.[7]

In addition, entire industries were greatly restricted by the cut-

[7] Ibid., pp. 216–224.

ting down of their supplies of materials. This measure applied mainly to building for nonessential purposes and to automobiles, which were eventually and for a short period in 1918 produced at only 25 per cent of their former quantity.

The price control that was applied was subsequently criticized because it was so generous to private business as to leave contractors with large war profits. Much of it was done not according to any scientific formula, but by a bargaining process in which the industry committees were not always modest in their demands. In some cases private business even threatened to cease production unless its exactions were met. There were, however, a number of extenuations for the price-control authorities. In the first place, prices had risen considerably when the war controls were established. In April, 1917, the United States was in the mid-course of an inflationary boom. The government's method of financing the war, as will subsequently be explained, did nothing to weaken this inflationary tendency, but instead distributed enormous amounts of credit-created purchasing power. This was well understood by those in charge of price control, and they looked upon a certain amount of rise in the price level as unavoidable.

Another ruling consideration was the fact that the chief concern lay in expanded war production. In almost every industry some producers have much higher costs than others. If a flat price is set for all units of a given product, a price high enough to keep the marginal units in production will usually yield large profits to the more efficient establishments. There are ways around this difficulty, such as offering differential prices that have a relationship to the costs of the individual producer, but these methods are difficult to apply, especially when, as at the time of World War I, good cost accounting was not widely employed. Flat maximum prices were therefore set. The board was satified if it could provide the governmental war agencies with what they needed without allowing prices to obstruct the war effort.

Price fixing by agreement began even before the War Industries Board had been organized. In March, 1917, the Army needed 45 million pounds of copper, which was already selling as high as 37 cents a pound. Mr. Baruch and Eugene Meyer, Jr., appealed to the copper producers for a more reasonable price, and they consented to charge, for this order, the average for the ten years preceding the war, or 16⅔ cents. This example, however, was not consistently followed in the case of other requirements. By July, 1917, the average price of metals was almost three and one half times higher than in 1913, and the index was 86 points above March, 1917. Between March and July, pig iron rose from $32.25 a ton to $52.50. Steel plates jumped from $4.33 to $9.00. The steel producers agreed to deliver a half million tons at one third less than the market price, but this was a specific concession, and steel prices continued to rise.[8] The Federal Trade Commission instituted an investigation of costs in the steel industry, and the chairman of the Shipping Board threatened to commandeer steel mills if prices were not adjusted in accordance with its findings.

The War Industries Board finally took control of the situation. On September 21, 1917, it held a meeting with sixty-five representative iron and steel producers. Judge Elbert H. Gary, chairman of the United States Steel Corporation, opened the meeting by inquiring of Judge R. S. Lovett of the War Industries Board, "May I ask by what authority the War Industries Board has undertaken to fix these prices?" After a moment of ominous silence, Judge Lovett replied, "A gentleman of your eminent qualifications in law requires no information from me on that point."[9] There followed a grim and long battle in which the board, armed with figures from the Federal Trade Commission and reinforced by the steel experts on its staff, at length induced the industry to fix the basic prices of coke, steel, and iron. Before the board's separate Price Fixing Committee was established in March, 1918, the board itself had dealt with prices for many other raw materials, including copper, aluminum, zinc, lumber, hides and skins, wool, and sulphuric acid.

The price controls were applied mainly to raw materials or intermediate products like steel. There was little check on prices at levels closer to the consumer, and many manufacturers, wholesalers, and retailers made huge profits. The Price Fixing Committee revised prices every three months to take account of new requirements. Though the stabilization of materials undoubtedly had some effect in holding down prices at retail, the inflationary tendencies consequent to the enormous market demand began to disrupt the whole price structure. At the end of the war, economists of the

[8] *Ibid.*, pp. 162–164.
[9] *Ibid.*, p. 177.

board were engaged in work preparatory to the control of prices all the way to the consumer. Statistics indicating what actually happened to prices are contained in the next chapter.

The price-fixing authorities were influenced by the fact that Congress had passed excess profits taxes at high rates, and they believed that these taxes would return to the Treasury any gains arising from unduly high prices. That they were at least partially justified in this belief is shown by the fact that in 1918 corporate profits after taxes were considerably smaller than in either of the preceding two years.

The Revenue Act of October 3, 1917, imposed taxes on all profits that exceeded the average net earnings of 1911, 1912, and 1913. The tax rate was graduated from 20 per cent to 60 per cent, according to the rate of the excess profit to invested capital. The corporate taxpayers were allowed exemption from this tax equivalent to not less than 7 per cent or more than 9 per cent of their invested capital for each taxable year. This provision was supposed to guarantee a "reasonable" return on the amount actually invested. There was also a penalty tax on undistributed earnings.

Excess-profits taxes, although they seem high under war conditions, are far from being a precise instrument with which to prevent private enterprise from earning more in war than it would in peace. In spite of the exemption allowed these taxes operated unequally on concerns that had had different fortunes during the test period. Those that had been in the early stages of their growth, and would normally have expanded even if war had not intervened, were penalized. On the other hand, those that had been prosperous during the test period, and had had a large volume of business could, during the war, make substantial profits not subject to the excess profits tax. This was true, for instance, of large steel companies. Furthermore, recovery of profits by the Treasury does not serve the same purpose in a war economy as a sufficiently rigorous regulation of prices, since the latter can stop inflation at its source.

THE FOOD ADMINISTRATION

A control agency of almost as much importance as the War Industries Board was the Food Administration, created at the suggestion of the Council for National Defense, and directed by Herbert Hoover, who was recalled from the Belgian relief agency for the purpose. This administration, unlike the War Industries Board, rested upon specific congressional legislation. It had charge of the industries producing and distributing food both for war purposes and for the civilian population of the United States.

The demands of the Allies on American food production had been even larger than their demands upon mining and manufacture. Normally the United States has always produced a surplus beyond the amount necessary to feed its own population, with the exception of a few commodities such as sugar, vegetable oils, and coffee. Production of food in the European nations, however, was sharply decreased by the war, and their enlarged demand for imports was concentrated on the United States because of the ravages of the German submarine campaign against shipping and the consequent necessity to eliminate long ocean hauls. The demands made on the food supply in this country by the Allies may be indicated by the fact that whereas the food exports of the United States for an average of the last three prewar years were 6,959,055 tons, they rose to 12,326,914 tons in 1917–1918 and 18,667,378 tons in 1918–1919. These figures include exports of sugar from Cuba to Europe because these exports limited the American supply. The normal stock of bread grains in the United States had been reduced from 153,000,000 bushels on July 1, 1916, to 43,800,000 bushels a year later, and the hog population was also seriously depleted.[10]

Competitive bidding by the Allies and civilian consumers had increased the average price of farm products 135 per cent above the level of 1913 by July 1, 1917. At the same time profits in the food business had become munificent. Even the farmers benefited, the price of wheat per bushel having much more than doubled inside a year. Consumers were paying in turn $2.50 a barrel more for flour than was warranted by the price of wheat. To add to the difficulties, the 1916 and 1917 harvests suffered from drought and were below normal. The irregularity of transport caused violent fluctuations of prices and stimulated speculation. Finally, a substantial amount of American food exports was finding its way to the enemy through neutral nations.[11]

Soon after the declaration of war, Mr. Hoover returned from

[10] William C. Mullendore, *History of the United States Food Administration, 1917–1919* (Stanford University: Stanford University Press, 1941), pp. 13, 5.
[11] *Ibid.*

Belgium to the United States, at the cabled request of the government, to investigate the food situation. On May 19, the President announced a program of food control and Mr. Hoover made a statement summarizing his conception of the task. The President's program included increasing production, voluntary conservation through elimination of wasteful practices and the substitution of more plentiful for less plentiful foods, protection of the consumers against high prices through regulation of distribution, and the elimination of speculation. Mr. Hoover enunciated five cardinal principles, embodying his conviction that the task was one not for a dictator but for an administrator, that it was to be done through regulation of existing distributive agencies, that conservation should be voluntary, that the proposed agency should be staffed so far as possible by volunteers, and that it should be directly under the President, cooperating with the Department of Agriculture, the Department of Commerce, the Federal Trade Commission, and the railway executives.

Since it might take many weeks to frame and pass the necessary legislation, it was decided to begin at once the organization of conservation on a voluntary basis. A letter from President Wilson to Mr. Hoover instructed him to undertake this task and asked for the cooperation of the women of the country. Mr. Hoover quickly proceeded to set in motion the organization of the consumers for conservation, which characterized a large part of the work of the Food Administration throughout the war. He also enlisted the aid of specialists in studying the problems that would confront the Food Administration when it was established. Since the new wheat crop was already beginning to move, a definite program for wheat was mapped out in conferences with the millers and grain trades.

The food control bill, to become known after its passage as the Lever Act, was promptly passed by the House but was continuously debated in the Senate for five weeks. Opponents of control were vociferous. Attempts were made to include in the bill control of steel, cotton, and many other commodities. Even the Prohibitionists tried to use it for their own purposes. Personal attacks on Mr. Hoover were made. As passed by the Senate, the bill contained provisions for control not only of food but of fuel and fertilizers, provided for administration by a board of three, and limited the licensing power. Most of the changes made by the Senate were eliminated in conference except the addition of fertilizer and fuel control, and the bill became a law on August 10, 1917. On the same day the President created the United States Food Administration and appointed Herbert Hoover its food administrator.

The power conveyed by the bill rested not only on the interstate commerce clause of the Constitution but on the general war powers of the President. The control of the administrator was bulwarked by three specific powers: first, to make voluntary agreements; second, to license and to prescribe regulations for concerns operating under license; and third, to buy and sell foodstuffs. Penalties for violation were provided, but only in two or three cases was anyone charged with violation of its provisions. In addition to the powers exercised under the Lever Act, the Food Administration could influence the export and import of foods through the War Trade Board.

The Food Administration began its work by setting up a number of divisions corresponding to the various types of food and to the administrative functions with which the agency was charged. It also had a large number of volunteer workers distributed widely throughout the country.

The administration at once set to work to increase production. It did so by guaranteeing a minimum price on wheat and stabilizing prices on other products, thus assuring to the farmers a market for all that they could raise at prices which, though not so high as they might have received from the continuance of competitive bidding, gave them a substantial profit of which they were sure for a whole crop year. This control of prices was achieved by the centralization of Allied purchasing in the Food Administration and by the establishment of a United States Grain Corporation, with a large capital, for the purchase and sale of grain.

The United States Grain Corporation was an interesting innovation in the technique of governmental control. It did not supplant any existing private agency, nor did it operate for profit. It had an authorized capital of $150 million and used this money to bring security and order into the marketing and distribution of grain. For instance, in 1917, it made allotments to the mills of the available wheat on a proportionate basis determined by the average grind of each mill for the three prewar years. It obtained control of country shipments by agreements with over 20,000 country grain elevators,

guaranteeing them against any decline in the price of their wheat
below that set by the government and paying them a fixed charge
for storage and carrying. This largely eliminated competitive buying at the terminal elevators and permitted prompt and efficient distribution of the available supply. The stabilization of price, in turn,
encouraged the farmers to bring their grain to market without waiting for possible future price increases. The Grain Corporation also
exercised control over transportation in such a way as to eliminate
unnecessary burdens on the railroads and to minimize delay. This
it did by bringing about adjustment of freight rates and by insisting
upon the maximum utilization of cars, boats, docks, and storage
facilities. Adequate reserves were kept in storage and these reserves
were properly distributed.

In addition, several hundred agreements dealing with production, prices and profits, and the elimination of waste were made
with other farm and business organizations. Another widely used
method of influencing prices was the establishment of fixed margins, for the various sections of the food trade, between cost of
materials and the price of the finished product. The power underlying these activities, aside from the economic pressure exerted by
centralized purchasing, was the legal right held by the administration to establish a licensing system in any part of the food trade
and to deny licenses to anyone who violated its mandates.

In dealing with sugar the Food Administration likewise employed a business form of organization. Sugar was insufficient in
supply, and difficulty was experienced in restricting price increases
while encouraging production. There were four main sources, and
in view of the scarcity of the product, it was necessary to obtain
the utmost possible output from each. Yet the costs of production
differed widely among these four sources. Cuba, which normally
furnished 49.8 per cent of the sugar sold in the United States,
needed in 1918 a price of 5.55 cents per pound in order to stimulate
production. The domestic beet sugar industry, which furnished
15.97 per cent of the American supply, needed at least 9 cents a
pound. The Hawaiian industry, normally supplying 13.66 per cent,
also required about 9 cents. The cane sugar industry in Louisiana,
producing 6.27 per cent of the American total, required about 10
cents a pound. The rest of the supply for the United States came
from Puerto Rico, which furnished somewhat less than Hawaii, the

Philippines, and miscellaneous foreign sources. Each had its price requirement. Under market conditions, a high enough price would have had to be paid for the whole supply in order to bring into the market the output of the producers with the highest costs. As Mr. Hoover pointed out, such a price would have meant that the American people were paying the Cuban producers over $20 million more than was necessary for their crop. The Allies, who also bought from Cuba, would likewise have had to pay about $20 million extra to Cuba. On the recommendation of Mr. Hoover, the President therefore approved the formation of the Sugar Equalization Board by the Food Administration. It was created on July 11, 1918, with Mr. Hoover as chairman, George M. Rolph as president, and a board of directors including Professor F. W. Taussig of the Tariff Commission and other prominent men. It had a capital of $5 million from the emergency funds of the President, was authorized to buy and sell sugar, and was intended to equalize "the cost of various sugars and secure better distribution." [12]

The Sugar Equalization Board arranged to purchase raw sugar from the producing regions at the price necessary in each region. At the same time, the price for Cuban sugar to be exported to Europe was fixed. The American refiners agreed not to purchase any raw sugar except from the Equalization Board, and the board engaged to supply their requirements at a fixed price per pound—7.28 cents—which represented a weighted average of the prices paid by the board, so that it could come out even. The price to be charged by the refiners was fixed at a margin of 1.54 cents a pound above the cost of the raw sugar to them. The board purchased the entire Cuban crop and resold one third of it to Great Britain, which, in turn, handled the requirements of France and Italy. The portion bought by Britain was refined in the United States at an agreed price. [13]

One of the most interesting instances of the use of price control to stimulate production was the action of the Food Administration in the case of hogs. The war was characterized by a shortage of fats and a consequently heavy demand for pork products. For three prewar years the exports of pork products had averaged 994,000,000 pounds, while for the year 1918–1919 they were 2,669,000,000

[12] *Ibid.*, pp. 259–269.
[13] *Ibid.*

pounds. When the Food Administration took hold of the situation in 1917, the receipt of hogs by the principal slaughtering centers of the country was running from 7 to 10 per cent below the corresponding weeks of 1916. This occurred in spite of the fact that the farmers were led to ship all available hogs to market, because prices were the highest in history, and the price of corn was also so high that it did not pay to keep the hogs for further fattening.[14]

Something had to be done to induce the farmers to increase the hog population and continue feeding until the product was of the best size for slaughtering. Whatever action was to be taken must be prompt in its effect. Investigation showed that the amount of pork production had in the past varied in accordance with the ratio of the price of hogs to the price of corn, which was the chief ingredient of their feed. When the price of corn had been high in relation to the price of hogs, it had been more profitable to sell the corn on the market than to employ it for feed. The reverse was also true. The Food Administration appointed a committee of leading producers, who reported that in order to stimulate production, the price for 100 pounds of hog must be so fixed as to equal the value of 14.3 bushels of corn.[15] The ordinarily profitable ratio was 10; an excess profit of 43 per cent was thus recommended.

The Food Administration had no legal authority to fix the prices either of hogs or of corn. It did, however, handle the purchases of the Allies as well as those of the Army and Navy, Belgian relief, and the Red Cross. These buyers consumed between 30 and 40 per cent of the pork products raised in the United States, and the prices they paid largely determined the price for the entire product. They agreed to pay whatever price was set by the Food Administration. The packers agreed to pay the farmers whatever price the Food Administration should determine, if they themselves should receive a sufficient margin. These arrangements enabled the Food Administration to maintain the price of hogs in fairly close relationship to the predetermined ratio of hog prices to the price of corn. The task was not easy, and modifications eventually had to be made in the agreements, but production was substantially increased.[16]

[14] *Ibid.*, pp. 259–269.
[15] *Ibid.*
[16] *Ibid.*

Another activity of the administration, pursued largely by voluntary methods, was the conservation of scarce foods and reduction of consumption on the part of civilians. Foods were not rationed, except by compelling consumers to buy substitutes for wheat and rye flour, since the scarcities were temporary and applied to relatively few commodities. Certain restrictions were imposed on the processing of food, such as the distillation of grain and the manufacture of candy and sweets. Speculation was discouraged by control of the speculative markets, and by rationalization of the channels of distribution to prevent dealers from buying more than they needed in order to profit from an increase of price. Various other activities assured the United States of the necessary food imports and rationed the neutrals in such a way that they could not continue to supply the Central Powers.

Mr. Hoover was opposed to direct price control in the retail markets. While Congress might have given him this power, he did not request it and the law did not include it. He believed that it had been a failure where tried in Europe and would inevitably lead to extensive black markets. Nevertheless, although the cost of food to the consumer rose during the activity of the Food Administration, its rise was held in check by the measures applied to the food industries.

The chief criticism made of Mr. Hoover at the time was that he unduly limited the returns of farmers by placing what amounted to maxima on prices of farm crops. Mr. Hoover replied that no maximum prices had been established, but that only minimum prices were set. While this was literally true, the activities of the administration undoubtedly prevented increases that might have occurred without it. A better defense would have been that the prices were high enough to call forth the required production, and that still higher prices would only have intensified the deflation from which the farmers eventually suffered.

There was more substance in the criticism made at the time, and repeated later with greater knowledge of the facts, that although he had the legal power to control profits, many of the food industries made an enormous amount out of the war. This applied with particular force to the big meat packers. Mr. Hoover defended his action on the ground that it was necessary to be generous in order to stimulate production. It is difficult to believe, however, that it was necessary to permit the packers to earn as much as 9 per cent —the limit he established—on the capital they employed in the food business, including borrowed money, especially in view of the fact that a large and profitable part of their business—that not destined for food products—was not under control at all. By its control of margins the Food Administration did considerably narrow the previously existing spread between what the farmers received and what the retail consumers paid. The measures of rationalization applied in the flow of food from producer to consumer helped to make this result possible, and would have been capable of much further extension if applied on a permanent basis.

Wholesale food prices at the beginning of 1917 were 50 per cent above the 1913 level. By the time the Food Administration began its operations in August, they had risen to 80 per cent above 1913. Though seasonal variations occurred after that, no important price increases were registered until the midsummer of 1918, and even in November, when the armistice was signed, the wholesale index was 100 per cent above 1913. An index of retail prices of twenty-four principal foods shows an almost equally good record, although since retail prices normally lag behind wholesale, some rise was to be anticipated, to take up that which had already occurred in the wholesale markets. This index stood at 49 per cent above 1913 in August, 1917, and gradually rose to 81 per cent above in October, 1918. A study made by the Food Administration of the cost of principal foods per capita to indicate the margin between wholesale and retail prices shows that although retail prices were 47 per cent above wholesale in 1915 and 1916, they were 39.6 above in the fourth quarter of 1917, and for the greater part of the control period the margin was held below 40 per cent. [17]

This achievement enhanced Mr. Hoover's reputation among those who hoped for a more orderly economic system that would yield better livings to farmers and those of small incomes in the cities, and would make less necessary the profits of middlemen and speculators. For these reasons there arose a hope that the Food Administration would be continued after the war. This hope, however, was not shared, to say the least, by the regulated trades or by Mr. Hoover himself. The majority of the population had so little under-

[17] *Ibid.*, pp. 319–320.

standing of the issues involved that political pressure for permanent reforms of the sort did not prevail.

TRANSPORTATION AGENCIES

Ocean shipping was the bottleneck of America's economic aid to the Allies, as well as of her own military effort. The greater part of the available cargo space had for years been owned and operated under the British flag. In 1914, the United Kingdom had 9,240 ships with a gross tonnage of 100 tons and upward and a total gross tonnage of 19,257,000. The United States had one third as many ships with about one quarter of the tonnage, and most of these were operating in coastwise traffic.[18] During the war, Britain's tonnage was sharply reduced in two ways: in 1915 and 1916, she was able to build scarcely more than one third of the tonnage launched annually in peacetime; and the German submarine campaign sank much of what she had. By the second quarter of 1917, the Germans had sunk 5,360,000 tons or nearly one fourth of the British merchant fleet. They sank 1,360,000 tons in that quarter alone.[19]

Agitation for building up the American merchant marine had begun, for commercial and military reasons, long before the United States entered the war. American merchants and manufacturers who customarily had depended upon British cargo space to carry their foreign sales and purchases often found their trade interrupted because the ships were commandeered for war supplies. Those businessmen who were engaged in profitable war sales also had an interest in enlarging the means of shipment. Without any specific governmental action, American shipyards turned out in 1916 more than twice as large a tonnage as previously, partly in response to orders from abroad and partly for American shipping companies that wished to enlarge their share of the immensely profitable ocean trade. Their total output in that year was, however, only 384,899 tons.[20] When war was declared, the United States had about sixty shipyards with 215 ways, and all of these were busy.[21]

In September, 1916, Congress finally passed a bill, signed by the President on September 7, establishing the United States Ship-

[18] *Lloyd's Register of British and Foreign Shipping* (London), 1933–1934.
[19] Frederic Logan Paxson, *American Democracy and the World War* (Boston: Houghton Mifflin Company), II, 67.
[20] *Lloyd's Register,* 1933–1934.
[21] Paxson, *American Democracy and the World War,* II, 67,

ping Board to control shipping in behalf of the government, and providing $50 million for investment in a subsidiary corporation that was to build new ships. The board could not be organized as a going concern before the end of that year. William Denman of San Francisco was appointed its chairman. Ten days after the declaration of war, a subsidiary, the American Emergency Fleet Corporation was chartered in the District of Columbia with Major General George W. Goethals as its general manager. General Goethals was selected for this job, which at the time was conceived as the most important confronting the nation, because of his success in constructing the Panama Canal. The Fleet Corporation had to be organized out of nothing. As Major General Goethals put it, "A separate corporation was formed and I am it." [22]

Naturally enough, the major task to be done was thought to be building new ships. The slogan was that Americans must build "a bridge of ships" across the Atlantic. Almost everyone entertained exaggerated hopes as to the speed with which this complex undertaking could be accomplished. Persons who knew little or nothing of shipbuilding put forward a host of suggestions. It was proposed to build vessels by filling molds with concrete. A vociferous faction argued for the construction of wooden ships. Still another idea was to apply to shipbuilding the technique of mass production, so that standardized parts and materials could be fabricated by plants that had never built a ship, to be forwarded from the interior and assembled at the coast. Conservatives argued that all such ideas were fantastic and that the job should be entrusted to the existing shipbuilding companies.

Mr. Denman, as chairman of the Shipping Board, also occupied the post of chairman of the Emergency Fleet Corporation. In the haste and pressure of the undertaking, General Goethals fretted under this authority, and at the end of May made a speech before the Iron and Steel Institute in New York in which he said, "All boards are long, narrow, and wooden." [23] As friction between the two men grew, public dissatisfaction with lack of results was vigorously expressed. The services of both were ended in July. Edward N. Hurley, a Democratic politician from Chicago, who had been chairman of the Federal Trade Commission and a member of the board of

[22] *Ibid.*, pp. 76, 68.
[23] *Ibid.*, p. 70.

the American Red Cross, was appointed chairman of the Shipping Board and remained in that post until the end of the war.

The Shipping Board with its subsidiary soon became a huge organization, with very little to show for its efforts. By June, 1918, it had to move to Philadelphia, because of lack of space in Washington, with 2,400 central office employees and 200 truckloads of equipment. It did, however, have an ambitious program. Fifteen million tons of shipping were to be built—1,700 ships of steel and 1,000 of wood. New government shipyards were started in Wilmington, North Carolina, Newark, New Jersey, Bristol, Pennsylvania, and on the mudflats south of Philadelphia known as Hog Island. These yards were to contain 94 new ways. Most of the ships were to be mass-produced out of prefabricated parts and materials, according to standardized designs.[24]

It took the designers months to agree on the details of the standardization. The contract for Hog Island was let September 13, 1917, and the first keel in it was laid February 12, 1918. The first ship from this great undertaking was not delivered until December 3, 1918, after President Wilson had sailed for Europe to discuss the terms of the peace. Even this belated delivery might not have been made if Charles M. Schwab, the enterprising steel executive, had not been drafted to take over direction of the Emergency Fleet Corporation on April 16, 1918.[25] In spite of the criticisms of delay, confusion, and incompetence, and of highly paid "silk-shirted workers" who "loafed on the job," the Emergency Fleet Corporation did accomplish more than might have been expected in the short duration of America's participation in the war. In 1917, 821,115 tons were launched in American yards and in 1918, 2,602,153 tons.[26] The latter figure was twice the construction of Great Britain and Ireland. After the war, the soundness of the mass-production technique was proved by the launching of a large amount of tonnage, which, though not well adapted to the commercial requirements of peace, would have contributed greatly to victory if the war had lasted longer.

In the meantime, the Shipping Board itself took other measures that, though less spectacular than the plans of the Fleet Corpora-

[24] Ibid., p. 265.
[25] Ibid., pp. 73–74.
[26] Lloyd's Register, 1933–1934.

tion, probably did more to meet the emergency need. On August 3, 1917, it commandeered all hulls under construction in American yards—431 in number with a total of 3 million dead-weight tons. It also took over the 97 interned German vessels, repaired the sabotage that had crippled them, and put them into service. In March, 1918, it seized 87 Dutch ships laid up by their owners on account of fear of submarine damage. The Dutch objected loudly to this action, largely in order to avoid German reprisals, but they were handsomely compensated. Finally, the board took over all American ships of 2,500 tons and over that were fit for use, with the understanding that they were to be operated by their owners under charter. By September 1, 1918, the Shipping Board had control of the use of 8,693,579 dead-weight tons of shipping.[27]

Periodic announcements of the figures of government-controlled ships were at the time ridiculed by critics, who pointed out that most of the ships had been in existence before the government took them over, and that the total cargo space was not being greatly increased. This criticism overlooked the fact that the elimination of competition, both among government agencies and private owners, was increasing the effective capacity of the ships so that cargoes delivered were greatly augmented. Urged by P. A. S. Franklin, president of the International Mercantile Marine, who was the executive in charge for the Shipping Board, the War Department and the British were induced to cooperate, and all the ships were pooled so that they could be used to best advantage. The average "turn-around," that is, the time occupied by a ship in unloading and taking on new cargo, was cut in half. More economical packing methods were worked out so that little space was wasted.

All this was done with the expert aid of a Division of Planning and Statistics, the director of which was Edwin F. Gay, the economic historian and dean of the Harvard Graduate School of Business Administration. It was from this type of experience that the possibilities of governmental planning were first learned in the United States. The more economical use of existing facilities through public direction and unified control, rather than the ambitious scheme to increase shipbuilding, was what enabled the United States to break the shipping bottleneck.

[27] Paxson, *American Democracy and the World War*, II, 71, 72, 265.

Hog Island Shipyard

A forest of derricks and ways stretching to the horizon was employed for building wooden ships. (*Brown Brothers*)

Railroad Artillery

Heavy naval and coast-defense guns were mounted for railroad use. Note camouflage—then a new art. (*Underwood–Stratton*)

Troopship Leaving New York

The *Mauretania*, great liner, converted for troop carrying and camouflaged against submarines. (*Brown Brothers*)

Troops Returning Home

Aboard the *Leviathan*, formerly the German liner *Vaterland*. (*Brown Brothers*)

Railroad transportation was in the end placed under the control of a United States Railroad Administration (December 28, 1917). Secretary of the Treasury William G. McAdoo was head of this body until after the armistice, when he was succeeded by Walker D. Hines, a prominent railroad executive.

At the beginning of the war, while still under their private managements, many of the railroads were suffering from capital structures overburdened with mortgages and loans, did not enjoy good credit in the money markets, and were underequipped and technically backward. They also constituted a prominent example of the over-all inefficiency of competition in a field where there is a large measure of natural monopoly. This competition was manifested in unnecessary crosshauls, in the maintenance of wasteful competitive terminal facilities, and in underuse of freight cars, resulting partly from the fact that while these cars traversed the whole railroad network of the country, each railroad regarded its cars as private property that must be returned to its own lines as soon as possible.

The railroads early showed signs of breaking down under the strain of war traffic. They had long been overburdened in busy seasons. Now the difficulty was increased by the fact that a large number of shipments consisted of goods consigned from the interior to the eastern ports and piled up there before ships were available to take them away. There was no coordination between the control of shipping and that of railroads. Also, the military authorities issued priority orders so freely that little distinction existed between goods needed immediately and those which the consignees were not prepared to handle. So confused did the situation become that there was an almost complete stoppage of movement at critical points.

During most of 1915 there had been a net surplus of freight cars, which in the early months of that year exceeded 300,000. A freight car shortage developed early in 1916, and during the fall assumed large proportions. It continued throughout the whole of 1917, seldom falling below 100,000 and sometimes rising above 150,000. In 1917, the railroads had the largest traffic in their history, consisting of 12 per cent more passenger-miles and 9 per cent more ton-miles of freight than in 1916, their heaviest previous year.[28] An example of the congestion existing in the East was in the terminals about Philadelphia: the sidetracks for miles westward were filled with freight cars loaded with material for the Hog Island shipyard long before there were any railroad tracks or unloading facilities at Hog Island itself.

It was obvious from the first that order could be restored only if the railroads ceased to act as independent units and their facilities were pooled. The railroads in 1917 made an effort to achieve this result by a voluntary organization called the Railroad War Board. The work of the organization was hampered, however, by the fact that there were no means of compensating any particular company for traffic diverted from its lines. Competitive individualism persisted. Also, the railroads as private companies could not deal effectively with the governmental agencies that had charge of priorities and the use of merchant ships.

By the end of 1917 their failure was so apparent that it was necessary to take drastic action, and the Railroad Administration was created. It guaranteed by contract to each railroad a standard return based on the earnings of a test period before the war (1914–1917), and so removed the financial obstacle to operation of the roads as a national unit. It also promised so to maintain the roads as to return them in as good a condition as when they were taken over. The task of running the railroads was given to skilled railroad men, many of whom sacrificed larger salaries in order to work for the government. The Railroad Administration was able to direct traffic by shorter routes, to employ cars and locomotives wherever they might most be needed, to enforce common use of terminals, to coordinate ocean shipping with railroad deliveries, and to limit the use of priorities to goods that might be removed by the consignees shortly after arrival. Thus the nation's freight was kept moving.

The Class I railroads, under the jurisdiction of the Railroad Administration, had in 1918 over 233,204 miles of track. The total net ton-miles transported were 440,001,713. This was an increase of about 10 million over the previous year, when, under the Railroad War Board, the roads had had their heaviest traffic hitherto. In 1918, the average carload was 29.28 net tons as against 27.01 in

[28] Walker D. Hines, *War History of American Railroads* (New Haven: Yale University Press, 1928), pp. 267–268.

1917 and 24.96 in 1916. The net tonnage of average train loads was also increased. In spite of the heavy traffic, the net shortage of freight cars rapidly disappeared during the year and was replaced by a net surplus approximating 300,000 by its end. This was the statistical evidence of the greater efficiency that unified operation was able to produce under the severe stress of war transportation.[29]

At the end of the war the railroads complained that their equipment had not been adequately maintained, and received from the government a limited extra compensation on this account. The complaints, however, were for the most part ill-founded, according to the reports as to the condition of the roads made by the regional directors, who were themselves railroad executives. Director General Walker D. Hines subsequently wrote, "The notion of a broken-down condition of the railroads' properties at the end of Federal control never had any foundation and has been clearly disproved by subsequent events and analyses." [30]

The government control of railroads was also criticized on the ground that it resulted in a large deficit, which had to be paid out of the national Treasury. For the entire period of federal control—twenty-six months ending March 1, 1920—the standard return paid to the railroad companies exceeded the net railway operating revenue by $628,502,000. During the period of control the Railroad Administration had access to a revolving fund of $500,000,000 appropriated by Congress. This enabled it to meet other expenses as well as pay rental to the railroads. For instance, in 1918, it loaned them $183,264,000, made investments amounting to $103,326,000, spent $445,500,000 for additions and betterments, and allotted $118,088,000 for an increase in materials and supplies.[31]

An increase of 25 per cent in rates was made shortly after the government took over. Mr. Hines pointed out, however, that with the rising costs of labor and materials, the railroads themselves could scarcely have achieved a better financial result without further substantial rate increases. Various considerations of policy prevented these increases at the time. It was not a matter of great importance to the people of the nation whether they paid for their transportation by means of higher rates or through subsidy, since

[29] *Ibid.*
[30] *Ibid.*, p. 120.
[31] *Ibid.*, pp. 216, 300.

in both cases the greater part of the cost was borne by the Treasury. But higher rates would have increased all other prices. As far as the railroad owners themselves were concerned, the money paid by the government assured them of the standard return promised. Soon after the Railroad Administration relinquished control, the Interstate Commerce Commission permitted much larger increases in rates than would have been advisable during the war itself.

One of the most interesting chapters in the history of American propaganda is the way in which government control of railroads was later interpreted to the public by the railroad managements. Many American citizens subsequently were led to believe that during the war the government actually owned the railroads. Others, better informed, understood that the government had merely taken over their general direction for war purposes, but still assumed that it had done so unnecessarily and had ruined them in the process. The railroads, it was said, were eventually turned back to their owners bankrupted and in deplorable physical condition. This argument was employed against any proposal for governmental activity in business. The facts on record, however, tell quite a different story.

The outstanding lesson of the experience was that when the railroads were operated as a unit and in the public interest, they succeeded in doing a difficult job of transportation that they were incapable of accomplishing as separate and competing properties.

SELECTIVE SERVICE

Conscription, although it was not primarily an agency of economic control, had important economic effects. It is impossible to create an army of 4,000,000 men even in a nation with as large a population as the United States without affecting industrial and agricultural man power. Soldiers are not removed from the market for goods, although they are removed from the factories and farms that produce those goods. As a matter of fact, even if one disregards the weapons and other military equipment of the Army, it is probable that many of the soldiers were, as individual consumers, better fed and clothed and even in some cases better housed than they had been in their peacetime employments. Naturally, their induction produced labor shortages.

The largest single classification of Army expenses was that devoted by the Quartermaster Corps to food, clothing, equipment, and miscellaneous supplies. For these purposes, the government spent during the war $6,243,000,000, or over $2,000,000,000 more than it spent for munitions. Indeed, the care and sustenance of the soldiers, excluding their pay, constituted between one quarter and one third of the cost of the war to the United States from April, 1917, through April, 1919. An example of the level of their consumption is the fact that Army blankets delivered in scarcely more than a year numbered 21,700,000, a figure equal to the normal consumption of blankets by 100 million American civilians for two and a quarter years. Clothing was ordered in much the same proportion. For many months preceding the armistice, the War Department was the owner of all the wool in the country. It purchased approximately 30,000 kinds of commercial articles.[32]

The Selective Service Act, signed by the President May 18, 1917, required the registration of all men between the ages of twenty-one and thirty inclusive. It was administered by Major General Enoch H. Crowder, who was given the specially created post of provost-marshal-general. Local boards were created in 4,557 districts throughout the country and were given the duty of examining registrants. On June 5, 1917, fixed as registration day, over 9.5 million young men were registered. This total was later raised to almost 10 million by late comers. Of these, 2,810,000 were inducted almost at once. Men of draft age were also allowed to volunteer for the various services for some time before their names were called.[33]

Several classes were established. Class I consisted of those who were physically fit and were not deferred because of the nature of their employment or the existence of personal dependents. Deferment was widely granted to those who had jobs in essential war industries, such as munitions, ships, steel, or lumber. Those who were classified as idlers or unemployed were given the choice between military service and effective employment, under the work-or-fight order issued by General Crowder May 17, 1918. This order also specified certain "nonuseful" callings in which deferment was not to be granted for occupational reasons. These occupations included waiters, operators of passenger elevators, domestic servants, theater ushers, clerks, and, later, professional baseball players. Although it

[32] Leonard P. Ayres, *The War with Germany* (Washington: Government Printing Office, 1919), pp. 49–52, 133.
[33] Paxson, *American Democracy and the World War*, II, 101.

eventually became necessary to extend the age limits of military service, the entire requirements of the armed forces were filled from Class I, plus the voluntary enlistments. This meant that many millions of workers were in fact exempt because of their employment in war industries.

The extensive exemption for occupational reasons gave rise to charges that draft dodgers were entering favored occupations where they could earn high wages while others were risking their lives at the front. The prevalent labor shortages and the occasional strikes prompted agitation for drafting men for industry. Labor spokesmen replied that it would be unfair to compel men to work for private employers making large profits, and that industrial conscription would be justified only if the government also conscripted wealth and took over the factories. In the case of one strike of munition workers in Bridgeport, Connecticut, the President finally did utilize the Selective Service machinery by ordering that the strikers be removed from preferred draft status unless they returned to work.

Although the most essential occupations were thus not seriously disturbed by the draft, the total labor supply was depleted by the diversion of about 16 per cent of the male labor force into the armed services. Unskilled labor was particularly affected. The housing of the Army in specially constructed cantonments also created a large though temporary pressure upon the supplies of building materials and labor. Sixteen camps and sixteen cantonments were built. Many other types of construction were also necessary. Army housing provided for 1.8 million men, or more than the contemporary population of Philadelphia. Total Army construction expenditures up to the time of the armistice were approximately $800 million and kept continuously occupied about 200,000 men, or more than the total strength of the Union and Confederate armies at the battle of Gettysburg.[34]

FUEL AND OTHER AGENCIES

A Fuel Administration was authorized by the same law that established the Food Administration—the Lever Act. The coal industry in the United States had long been in chaotic condition, although in normal times its chief difficulties were felt by the workers

[34] Ayres, *The War with Germany*, pp. 57, 58.

rather than by the consumers. Some of the mines had lower costs than others, and the high-cost mines were likely to come into production only at the peak of demand. Many of the mines were closely affiliated with the railroads, which took an interest in them, not only because of their own needs for fuel, but because coal provided a substantial proportion of their traffic. One consequence of this connection was that coal was often shipped by unduly long routes and there was a good deal of waste in transportation.

During the war the country suffered the unusual experience of a coal shortage. The demand was greatly increased by the need of industry, railroads, and shipping for fuel. In order to deal with this situation, the President established the Fuel Administration on August 23, 1917, and appointed as administrator Dr. Harry A. Garfield, president of Williams College. A price for coal was fixed high enough to bring into production the marginal mines, and there were attempts to protect coal consumers against extortion. The shortage of coal in the eastern part of the country continued, however, and winter storms, by interrupting transportation, finally made drastic action necessary.

Dr. Garfield accordingly ordered a coal holiday, beginning Friday, January 18, 1918, and continuing for the next four days. It applied to all industries east of the Mississippi River except the most essential war plants. On these days the affected establishments were to use only as much coal as they customarily did on Sunday. Thereafter, "heatless Mondays" continued for nine successive weeks. This action brought a storm of public criticism again the "Professor" who was supposed to know nothing about the coal industry, but it did serve to fill the bunkers of the waiting ships.

Later the Fuel Administration established a system of zone distribution so that each section of the country should be served by the mines nearest to it. This eliminated crosshauling, economized transportation, and augmented supplies in the markets. Eventually, the Fuel Administration set up control of oil, because the coal shortage had induced many consumers to substitute it for coal.

Effectual warfare demanded economic measures against the enemy as well as military action. This fact was recognized by the passage of a Trading-with-the-Enemy Act, under the authority of which on October 12, 1917, the President created a War Trade Board and appointed as its chairman Vance McCormick, a former chairman of the Democratic National Committee. Members of the board represented the Departments of State, Commerce, Agriculture, and the Treasury, and the Food and Shipping Administrations. The objectives were to obstruct the enemy's trade so far as possible, to obtain needed supplies for the United States, and to economize shipping space. A licensing system was established for exports and imports, and all who engaged in foreign trade were subject to careful investigation. The routes by which the enemy obtained necessary supplies were traced down, and the names of all concerns in neutral nations that facilitated enemy purchases were entered on a black list. Naturally, the Germans had sought to conceal their channels of commerce so far as possible by operating through dummy or neutral firms. The War Trade Board cooperated with the Allied agencies having the same function. By the end of the war, it had 2,789 employees.[35]

The Trading-with-the-Enemy Act also provided for the seizure and administration of all enemy property in the United States. In order to exercise this function, the President appointed as Alien Property Custodian A. Mitchell Palmer, a Quaker who might have become Secretary of War but for his religious convictions, and who subsequently was appointed Attorney General. To take charge of the large and miscellaneous assortment of properties under his jurisdiction, Mr. Palmer set up and administered more than 32,000 separate trusts, the value of which aggregated $502 million.[36]

It was discovered that German ownership had penetrated much more widely into the American economy than had previously been suspected. It included not merely securities, but direct control of many manufacturing establishments, particularly in drugs, chemicals, electrical equipment, and surgical instruments. Many of these properties had been protected by technical transfer of ownership for the period of the war, and careful investigation was required to ferret them out. Since it was necessary that the operations of most of them be continued for war purposes, Mr. Palmer asked and obtained an amendment to the law permitting him to sell German property to new owners whose loyalty would be unquestioned, and to invest the proceeds in Liberty bonds, which he held in trust for postwar negotiation.

[35] Paxson, *American Democracy and the World War*, II, 133.
[36] *Ibid.*, p. 131.

Among the most valuable items of German property were numerous patents, many of them covering dyes and chemicals. These were licensed to American producers. The sales of German property and the licensing of patents became an immense source of profit to numerous sections of American business. The American chemical industry, in particular, profited by acquiring a trade that before the war had largely been in German hands. The intervention of the United States government, through the authority of a single man, to convey such large favors upon private interests was sharply criticized at a later date. The critics did not question the military necessity of taking over German property, but argued that the government should have retained the gains and should have exercised more care for the interests of consumers.

A Committee on Public Information, under George Creel, was created to conduct governmental publicity. The newspapermen, jealous of the traditions of a free press, suspected it of imposing an unnecessary censorship and of substituting propaganda for news. Whenever possible they went behind the agency to tap original sources. In spite of much opposition and ridicule, however, it was the prototype in the United States of the agencies that in time of war were created to affect public opinion on the home front.

At the opening of the war, the aircraft manufacturing industry was in its infancy and the Army possessed few planes. On May 16, 1917, the Council of National Defense created the Aircraft Production Board, under the chairmanship of Howard Coffin, to cooperate with the Army in an advisory capacity. Like the Emergency Fleet Corporation, it attempted to facilitate production by standardization and mass-production methods. Probably its greatest achievement was the Liberty motor, which was designed within a few weeks and officially adopted June 4. The motors were not, however, produced in quantity until a year after the delivery of the first experimental model. Then production rose rapidly and over 30,000 were completed before the armistice.[37]

Even greater delay was occasioned in the manufacture of the planes themselves. At that time the frames were constructed of spruce, and the wings were covered with linen cloth. The spruce had to be cut in the forests of the Northwest, where labor difficulties among the lumbermen had to be resolved. The supply of the linen

[37] *Ibid.*, pp. 267, 112.

fabric customarily employed was now restricted by the needs of the Allies for their own plane manufacture. A special cotton fabric had to be designed, woven, and then chemically "doped." The supply of castor oil required for the lubrication of airplane motors was insufficient, for this lubricant had customarily been used mainly for medicinal purposes. The growth of castor beans had to be encouraged and manufacturing facilities provided. The first completed model of the new Army planes was not produced until April 8, 1918, and even at the time of the armistice most of the American flyers at the front were still using French and British planes. The delay in this part of the war program occasioned wide public criticism, and though corruption was charged, it was never proved. The facts seem to be that, as in the case of ships, an ambitious plan for mass production—which was to have provided 22,000 planes by June 30, 1917—could not be set going quickly enough to cope with the emergency.

Among the most important of the war agencies were those created to deal with the distribution and proper employment of labor, the avoidance of work stoppages, and the regulation of wages and hours. The performance of these agencies is inseparable from their effect on the lives of the workers; they will therefore be described in Chapter III, which concerns the consequences of the war to the main groups of civilians.

On April 5, 1918, Congress authorized the War Finance Corporation to supply capital that might be necessary for private establishments working on munitions. The same act set up a Capital Issues Committee to pass upon all new security issues and to protect the war economy against diversion of its resources to nonessential purposes by preventing loans that did not contribute to the war effort. A committee with the same name and function had previously been formed on February 1, 1918, under the Federal Reserve Board, but without specific legislative sanction.

Because of threatened strikes the telephone and telegraph companies were taken over by the Post Office Department. Many governmental bodies were created which, though of less magnitude than those previously described, were vital to the prosecution of the war, such as the Storage Facilities Committee, the Emergency Construction Committee, and the Automotive Transport Committee. Altogether, nearly five thousand governmental war agencies were set up at one time or another, though many of them were dissolved after serving their specific purposes or were subsequently merged with others. Before the war was over, Congress passed the Overman Bill, which gave the President wide powers to rearrange governmental bureaus or special administrations and to transfer funds from one to another. Though Congress was continually busy with legislation, it could not hope to keep up with the detailed and shifting administrative requirements of waging a modern war.

NATURE OF CONTROL

For the first time in history there was an approach to close cooperation among several great nations in the management of their economic affairs. There was established an inter-Allied shipping control, which attempted under great difficulties to mobilize as a unit the cargo space available to the several enemies of Germany. The Allied purchasing agents for munitions were brought together in an Inter-Allied Purchasing Commission, which operated through a special division of the War Industries Board. In this way their demands were coordinated with each other and with those of the American military establishment and the civilian population. Allied food purchases in the United States were centralized in the Food Administration. Liaison agents maintained contact between all the war agencies and the various Allied administrations concerned with their activity. It was thus demonstrated that, if sufficient need exists and there is unity of purpose, there could even be effective international mobilization of production and distribution.

Another development of the period significant in later years was the first extensive utilization of a new device—the government-owned corporation. Prominent examples were the United States Grain Corporation and the Emergency Fleet Corporation. These were agencies set up to do constructive jobs of a sort that hitherto had been handled mainly by private business, but on a scale and for purposes that private corporations could not attempt. They were organized much like business corporations, the government supplying the capital and owning the stock. The purpose and public control of the corporation thus having been assured, it could be operated with as much administrative efficiency as any private concern. It was necessary only to choose capable men as executives and set them to work. They were freed of bureaucratic red tape, of hampering civil service restrictions, and of detailed oversight by Congress over their income and expenditures. It was not necessary to obtain a separate appropriation every time an activity was to be launched. They were, of course, subject to general direction and accounting control by the President or his subordinates.

The same device has been used again and again in subsequent years, perhaps the outstanding example being the Tennessee Valley Authority. It provides a method whereby the administrative efficiency of business organization can be devoted to public purposes.

Finally some account must be given of the nature of the power that enabled this extensive and complicated war planning to operate. The period was characterized by a great expansion, not only in the powers of the President, but in the exercise of his initiative and discretion in prescribing the form and details of the administration. In peace, it had been the custom of Congress to legislate in great detail concerning the formation and functions of governmental bureaus or other administrative agencies, and to make separate appropriations for each bureau or agency. Detailed control of the purse strings had made many parts of the executive branch in effect more responsible to Congress than to the President. It had enabled members of the House or the Senate to control patronage in appointments and to influence spending to the advantage of their constituents. This kind of control would hopelessly have obstructed the war effort.

It is true that some of the more important emergency administrations, like the Food and Fuel Administrations and the Shipping Board, were created in accordance with congressional enactments and derived some specific legal powers from the laws that authorized their establishment. Others, however, like the War Industries Board, were set up by the President without specific congressional authorization and rested upon general grants of power conveyed in such omnibus bills as the National Defense Act. Much of their activity might have been brought into question under a strict interpretation of these laws, and could have been justified mainly by the constitutional war powers of the President. Appropriations, too, were made in large lump sums, specific allocations of the money being left to executive discretion. The ability of the rapidly developing and complex war administration to act effectively did not depend to any large extent either on specific grants of power by Congress, accompanied by customary penalties for failure to observe the law, or on the fact that the Supreme Court would probably have upheld the President's authority.

Many writers have emphasized the important role played by the fact that this government and others were doing so much of the buying. American industry and agriculture naturally had to follow the pattern prescribed by their chief customers.

It is also asserted that the heightening of patriotism during the war influenced people to accept much in the way of regulation and cooperation that they would resist when the lives of soldiers at the front were not at stake. Certainly it is more difficult to express the national interest so vividly and dramatically at times when there is no threat from a foreign enemy. Nevertheless, the force of the patriotic motive in inducing acceptance of the war organization can be exaggerated. Those who remain in civil life are inclined to continue their customary pursuits in their customary ways, no matter how concerned they may be about the battles being fought. Something that affects them more practically than abstract sentiments of patriotism is required to change economic and business habits.

Even patriotism and the mobilization of purchasing power were probably not the strongest influences at work in the acceptance of war planning. Almost everybody concerned understood at the time that without planning there would have been intolerable confusion and duplication of effort. Those in charge of affairs, even the smallest, needed a scheme of action that would not result in frustration of their energies. Planning was accepted as an operational necessity. There had to be leadership, and this leadership had to be exercised by government. It fulfilled the function of the traffic officer at a congested road intersection. Though people may resent his authority, they cannot get along well without him.

CHAPTER II

The War Economy

THE war agencies that administered the economy were devised and altered to deal with specific and pressing needs. Few of them possessed current information about the behavior of the total economic order—the type of information subsequently dug out and arranged in a meaningful manner. Even the broad concepts useful to show the entire picture were little developed at the time and were not known to most of those exercising authority.

Basically, the economic pattern of the war years may best be interpreted in terms of the effect of the demand for goods and services upon the supply. What was the total demand and how was it expressed? How did the nature of this demand differ from that to which the nation was accustomed in peace? What was the effect of demand on total production and on the various kinds of production? What was its effect on prices? What, in the setting of this demand, did war planning accomplish? What were the real costs of the war, and what economic gains flowed from it?

THE MONETARY EMBODIMENT OF DEMAND

The urgent requirements for war goods and services were embodied in purchases by governments. These purchases were, of course, the principal origin from which all other economic consequences flowed during the war. Before the entrance of the United States into the hostilities, purchases were made chiefly by foreign governments. They were evidenced by a net gain of the American export surplus during the three years prior to the declaration of war, amounting in all to between $4.5 and $5 billion.[1] Payment for these war exports virtually canceled the permanent net foreign debt of American citizens. In addition, it stimulated American economic activity. Enough was saved and invested in the United States greatly to expand the equipment for production, and at the same time to leave more for consumption per capita of the population than ever before.

The cost of the participation in the war by the United States, calculated by the Treasury by subtracting from the expenditures of government the estimated normal expenses of peacetime, was, between April 6, 1917, and June 30, 1920, approximately $24 billion. The expenditure by the Allies in the United States during this period, almost entirely covered by the United States government loans to them, was about $9.5 billion. The expenses of the American government included slightly more than $1.75 billion paid in interest on the domestic debt, which must be subtracted in calculating the effect of the war demand on the economy. The grand total of the demand was thus slightly less than $31.5 billion.[2]

According to an estimate by the National Bureau of Economic Research the American expenditures for war in 1917 were $9.5 billion, or between one fifth and one sixth of the total national income estimated at $54 billion, and were in 1918 $14.6 billion, or nearly one fourth of a national income estimated at $62 billion.[3]

Of the total fiscal outlay, $10,703,000,000 was raised by taxes in excess of the estimated normal budget, and $23 billion by government borrowing. The war debt reached its peak in August, 1919, at approximately $24,500,000,000.[4] This division between taxes and loans had effects of the greatest importance on prices. Broadly, it may be stated that when the government spends money that it takes from the current income within the country, it does not increase the total of demand, but merely shifts it from those goods and services that the citizens might have bought, if they had retained the money, to those goods and services that the government requires. When, on the other hand, the government spends money not taken from the

[1] John Maurice Clark, The Costs of the World War to the American People (New Haven: Yale University Press, 1931), p. 24.
[2] Ibid., p. 30.
[3] Ibid., p. 34.
[4] Ibid., p. 31.

current income of the citizens, it increases the purchasing power in circulation and thus the total demand for goods and services. This may call forth increased production. In so far as it does not do so, it will result in some increase in prices. Tax revenue is, of course, withdrawn from the current income of the population. Government borrowing may be withdrawn from that income, but it may also rest upon an expansion of bank credit, as was largely the case in this instance.

Oliver M. W. Sprague, in an article in *The New Republic*, February 24, 1917, entitled "Conscription of Income," advocated that after the first war loan, all necessary revenue be raised by taxation. In the same journal, July 14, 1917, Mr. Sprague wrote that this proposal "has received the approval of a very large number of economists throughout the country. The position which they have taken found expression shortly after the Declaration of War in a Memorial to Congress in which they urged the immediate imposition of heavy taxation, especially on incomes and excess profits." Professor Seligman of Columbia and Professor Bullock of Harvard opposed this policy. The economists' document was interesting not only because of its contents, but also because it was probably the first occasion in American history when economists as a group, speaking only for themselves and out of their professional knowledge, attempted to influence governmental policy. Their object was, of course, to avoid inflation of prices.

In raising revenue for the war, the government relied on drastic increases in the income tax, on the excess profits tax (described in Chapter I), and on various special and excise taxes. The income tax in effect at the beginning of 1917 exempted all married persons with incomes below $4,000 and single persons below $3,000. The normal rate was 2 per cent. Surtaxes did not apply under a net taxable income of $20,000, and their rates rose in slow stages from 1 per cent only to 13 per cent in the highest bracket. The Revenue Act of October 3, 1917, reduced the exemption to $2,000 for married persons and $1,000 for single persons. It increased the normal rate to 4 per cent, applied surtaxes to all incomes above $5,000, and introduced a far more steeply graduated scale of rates that ended at 63 per cent in the highest bracket. Income taxes were increased again by the act of February 24, 1919, but this did not take effect until after the war was over. Excise taxes were levied on beverages and tobacco and on numerous luxury articles such as furs. Taxes were placed on theater admissions, club dues, and sales by public utilities and insurance companies.[5]

Excess profits taxes yielded a large share of the tax revenue. In the fiscal year ending June 30, 1918, they amounted to $2,227,569,818. Income taxes in the same year yielded $663,184,588. Of this, more than $48 million was derived from the regular corporation income tax. The various excise and special taxes yielded somewhat more than the personal income tax.[6]

The borrowings of the government were in the first instance from the banks, but a series of bond issues was floated to fund the short-term debt as rapidly as it grew. Great publicity campaigns were staged to sell these Liberty Bonds. Rates of interest were moderate at first, but rose gradually as the war continued. Of the war bonds, about $7 billion, or 30 per cent, were sold to individuals with incomes of $2,000 or less, about $10 billion to individuals with incomes of $2,000 or more, and nearly $6 billion to corporations (including banks).[7]

It must not be supposed that the purchase of Liberty bonds represented in its entirety a drain on the current purchasing power of those who bought them. Not only were the banks permitted to lend money for the purchase of bonds, but this practice was even encouraged by the fixing of a lower rediscount rate for loans secured by government collateral. It was possible for both businesses and individuals to subscribe to the Liberty Loans and then retain their current incomes almost unimpaired by obtaining bank loans against the bonds they had purchased.

FEDERAL RESERVE AND CREDIT EXPANSION

In order to understand the part played by the banks in expanding purchasing power, it is necessary to describe the operations of the Federal Reserve System, which came into existence during President Wilson's first administration. Before the Reserve System had been established, there had been a controversy of many years' standing about the desirability of central banking in the United States. On the one hand, a central banking system had been advocated as

[5] Ernest Ludlow Bogart, *War Costs and Their Financing* (New York: D. Appleton-Century Company, 1921), pp. 271–274.
[6] *Ibid.*, pp. 281–289, 295.
[7] Clark, *The Costs of the World War to the American People*, p. 137.

a means of mobilizing reserves and providing greater stability for the country's banks. On the other hand, centralization was feared because of its power over credit and interest rates. Many citizens had long been hostile to the growth of any central money power and were jealous of the control already exercised by the Treasury Department and in Wall Street.

The Federal Reserve System was an attempt to compromise this controversy by gaining the benefits of central banking without incurring its dangers. The banking system was to be removed from Treasury control. The country was divided into twelve regions, and a federal reserve bank was set up in each. One third of the directors of these reserve banks were chosen from the banks of the region that became members of the system, one third from business or agricultural representatives of the various communities, and one third to represent the Federal Reserve Board, established to supervise the whole system.

The Federal Reserve Board was composed of the Secretary of the Treasury and the Comptroller of the Currency ex officio, and six members appointed by the President and confirmed by the Senate. The latter were to be made independent by being given a salary equal to that of cabinet officials and having a term of twelve years, one going out of office every two years. Not more than one of them could be selected from any federal reserve district and attention was to be paid to representation of financial, agricultural, and industrial interests of the country.

By this means it was hoped to regionalize the central banking function, and to separate what was supposed to be the needs of sound credit policy from the fiscal activities of the United States Treasury, which in former years had often dominated the money market. It was complained, for instance, that when the Treasury needed to borrow, it would customarily use its influence on the banks to keep interest rates down, although sound banking policy might require higher interest rates at that particular time.

The Federal Reserve System, however, hardly had a chance to establish itself before the abnormal conditions of war forced the government to borrow large amounts of money. Far from being an independent institution, the system became almost at once an accessory to the need of the Treasury to borrow and to hold down interest rates. Governor Harding of the Federal Reserve Board was quoted in the *Federal Reserve Bulletin* of January 1, 1919 (p. 2), as follows: "The only period when the FRB was able to exercise any control over the banking situation was during the last two or three months of 1916 and the first quarter of 1917."

Before the inauguration of the Federal Reserve System, paper money in the United States had consisted largely of bank notes, backed by the separate reserves of the issuing banks, and various forms of national paper money. If a bank failed, its notes, of course, depreciated or became worthless. The new system improved this situation by introducing a new form of paper currency—federal reserve notes—that was largely to displace the others. These notes were issued by the Federal Reserve Board. The reserves were made more efficient by being concentrated to a large extent in the reserve banks instead of remaining scattered in individual banks throughout the country. The notes had to be backed by a reserve of at least 40 per cent of their total value, the reserve consisting chiefly of gold.

The plan was also intended to provide greater elasticity of credit in response to the needs of business. When a member bank lends money to a businessman or farmer on the basis of commercial paper, it can send the note signed by its customer and endorsed by itself, to the reserve bank of its district and receive in return federal reserve notes or a credit on the books of the reserve bank. For this loan the member bank customarily pays a somewhat lower rate of interest than its customer has paid. Thus it can continue to make new loans to customers before the old ones are repaid. It was thought that by this process of "rediscounting," the total amount of currency and of commercial loans could automatically expand or contract according to the needs of business. The central authorities of the system, it was believed, also could either encourage the extension of credit or discourage it by changing the rate of interest paid by the member banks—the "rediscount rate."

There remained an upper limit somewhere on the issuance of currency and the expansion of credit, depending on the size of the reserve. According to the law, the reserve had to be not only at least 40 per cent of the federal reserve notes, but also at least 35 per cent of total deposits. When the lending bank does not pass out money to the borrower, it of course adds the proceeds of his loan to his deposit.

Early in the war, the Treasury took measures to enlarge the reserves by encouraging the import of gold. Later an embargo on gold exports was established. By these means a reserve was built up that would permit a large expansion of currency and credit. The possibility of increase was further enhanced by a law passed just after the United States entered the war, which permitted member banks to obtain reserve notes in exchange for gold deposited in the reserve banks, as well as in exchange for commercial paper, as before. The gold then became part of the reserve, permitting a further enlargement of the circulation.

The most striking change of all was made by an amendment to the law, passed in 1916, that permitted reserve banks to rediscount loans made on the collateral of government bonds, as well as those represented by commercial paper. This at once gave the Treasury a means of expanding credit almost at will, entirely aside from the demands of business, so long as the reserves were sufficient.

The more bonds were sold by the Treasury, the more found their way into the banking system, and the more credit the banks could issue. Thus it was possible for the Treasury to encourage expansion of credit whenever it might wish to do so. As a matter of fact, expansion of purchasing power became almost an inevitable accompaniment of any substantial enlargement of the government debt, and the restriction of purchasing power a result of reduction of the government debt, unless specific counter measures were taken. No such measures were taken during World War I.

The adequacy of the reserves is usually indicated by what is called the "reserve ratio," which is published weekly. This indicates the percentage of the reserve held by the reserve banks to their combined deposit and note liabilities. By watching the reserve ratio, it is possible to keep track of the amount of reserves in excess of legal requirements and consequently to estimate the possible expansion of federal reserve notes and credit available to the system.

During the months when the United States was at war, or from April 27, 1917, to November 29, 1918, the amount of federal reserve notes in circulation increased 500 per cent. So great was the expansion of currency and credit that the reserve ratio fell from over 80 per cent to 50 per cent. This occurred in spite of the fact that the gold in the reserve banks doubled. How large a part the issuance of war bonds played in this expansion is indicated by the fact that loans by the member banks secured by these bonds were tripled during 1918 alone, and that in addition their own holdings of United States securities increased almost one and a half times.[8] During the first eleven months of 1918 the discounts of the federal reserve banks aggregated $32.5 billion, and of these more than 80 per cent were against the collateral of government loans.[9]

Some expansion of bank credit was undoubtedly necessary to facilitate the operations of business in supplying a changing and expanding demand. The needs of business for working capital might have been adequately met out of profits and ordinary commercial borrowing. Nevertheless, many of the loans obtained on the basis of war bonds were employed in the course of business and trade. No data exist by which it is possible to separate loans required for war production from those which served merely to enlarge the total purchasing power without increasing the output of goods at the same time. The only possible measure of the effect of credit expansion on prices during the war consists in the figures of production and prices themselves.

PRODUCTION

The purchasing power poured out by governmental agencies brought forth some additional output in 1917, but in 1918 production as a whole fell off again almost to the level of 1916. The net increase for these two years was far less than the growth in the volume of spending expected to stimulate it.

The production of agriculture depends upon weather conditions fully as much as upon market demand. In any case, the effect of demand on the volume of crops cannot be rapid, since the plans of individual farmers must be made months, if not years, in advance. Poor growing conditions occurred in both 1916 and 1917. In the former year, the physical output of agriculture was 8 per cent below 1914, and while it recovered somewhat in 1917, it was still 4 per cent less than the base year. Another expansion in 1918 brought it 1 per cent above the level of the year when the European war broke out. The output of mining responded more readily to the demand. In 1916, it had been 26 per cent above 1914, and in 1917 it rose to

[8] W. H. Steiner, *Money and Banking* (New York: Henry Holt and Company, 1933), p. 871.
[9] *Federal Reserve Bulletin* (March, 1919), pp. 4, 84.

33 per cent above. Only a gain of one additional point in the percentage, however, was achieved in 1918.[10]

It is much more difficult to estimate accurately the growth of physical production in manufacture than in the output of raw materials. Manufactured products are highly varied and are subject to change, both in kind and in quality, from time to time. Statistics of the number of physical units produced exist for only a limited number of manufactured products. In many cases, it is necessary to estimate the physical production by applying an index of change in prices to the sales value of the output. These difficulties are particularly troublesome in estimating factory output during a war, when many of the products consist of munitions never made before, or made only in very small quantities, and there is no index of the course of their prices extending from prewar years. The best statistical estimates, however, indicate that there was no increase in the physical output of manufacture after 1916, but rather a decrease. In 1916, the index of the National Bureau of Economic Research, for instance, stands at 39 per cent above 1914, in 1917 at 38 per cent above, and in 1918 at 37 per cent above.[11]

Construction gained slightly during the war, but remained below 1914 throughout its course. Railroad transportation grew more than any other major factor of production, rising from the 1914 level by 24 per cent in 1916, 36 per cent in 1917, and 42 per cent in 1918.

In discussing the effect of war demand upon production, the

PHYSICAL PRODUCTION INDEXES, MAJOR INDUSTRIAL DIVISIONS
(1914 = 100)

Industry	1914	1915	1916	1917	1918
Agriculture	100	100	92	96	101
Mining	100	109	126	133	134
Manufacturing	100	117	139	138	137
Construction	100	89	91	93	94.5
Transportation—Railroad	100	107	124	136	142
Gross national product (1914 prices)	100	108	114	120	115

Source: Simon Kuznets, *National Product in Wartime* (New York: National Bureau of Economic Research, Inc., 1945), p. 148.

[10] For production figures in this paragraph and subsequent ones see accompanying table.

[11] Arthur F. Burns, *Production Trends in the United States Since 1870* (New York: National Bureau of Economic Research, 1934), p. 284, Table 44.

best means of expressing the output of goods and services for the whole national economy is the total known as the gross national product. This differs from the figure ordinarily known as the national income because it includes no deductions for depreciation or replacement of existing equipment. It merely indicates the total actually turned out in each year, regardless of the purposes for which it is used. The gross national product was, in 1916, 14 per cent above 1914. In 1917, it rose to 20 per cent above. In 1918, it fell back to 15 per cent. Thus, if the nation's output is regarded as a single whole, an increase of only about 5 per cent in total purchasing power would have been necessary to call forth, without any increase in prices, the additional war production achieved in 1917. The actual expansion of purchasing power was, of course, much greater than this.

It should not be assumed that the production of goods needed for war purposes followed the same course as that of manufacturing in general, or of the gross national product. The output of war supplies increased rapidly. For instance, the production of ships grew from 325,000 gross tons in 1916 to 664,000 in 1917, and 1,301,000 in 1918. Locomotives manufactured in 1916 were already about double the product of the previous year, and their output increased from 4,075 in 1916 to 5,446 in 1917, and 6,475 in 1918. The production of aluminum, which in 1916 was 110,200,000 pounds, or almost twice as high as the prewar level, grew to 132,300,000 pounds in 1917, and 143,300,000 pounds in 1918. The output of steel reached its peak in 1917 at 45,061,000 long tons, or about twice the prewar level. It did not further increase in 1918. But such gains in production were accompanied by a decline in industries serving mainly civilian needs. It is interesting that the output of cigarettes used both by soldiers and civilians, was tremendously boosted by the war, being, in 1918, 47,528,000,000 as compared with 26,203,000,000 in 1916, and 17,944,000,000 in 1914.[12]

It is clear that most of the gains in war production during the participation of the United States were made at the expense of the civilian economy. Between the outbreak of the European war in the second quarter of 1914 and American belligerency in the first quarter of 1917, the war component of the gross national product increased by only $100 million in terms of 1914 prices, whereas the nonwar component increased by $5.1 billion. Between the first quar-

[12] *Ibid.*, p. 298.

ter of 1917 and the fourth quarter of 1918, when the war ended, again in terms of 1914 prices, the war component increased by $11.2 billion, while the nonwar component *decreased* by $13 billion, or 31 per cent. In 1917, the nonwar output for the year was $39.6 billion, while the war output was $4.1 billion. In 1918, the nonwar output was $31.9 billion, and the war output $9.7 billion.[13]

PRICES

The fact that purchasing power grew much more rapidly than physical output of goods and services was naturally registered in a sharp increase in prices. The price controls exercised by the government curbed this increase somewhat, but were not sufficiently rigid or widespread to prevent it. Wholesale prices of all commodities stood at 29.1 per cent above 1913 in 1916 (1913 was slightly higher than 1914 because the latter was a year of depression). In 1917 the general index of wholesale prices had risen to 71.2 per cent above 1913, and in 1918, it experienced a further increase to 95.7 per cent above the base year.

The prices of manufactured goods followed a roughly similar course. In 1916, they were 29.4 per cent above 1913; in 1917, 69.4 per cent above; and in 1918, 98.4 per cent above. The index of prices of raw materials is particularly interesting because it reveals the effect of price controls exercised by the War Industries Board, which extended price regulation little beyond the raw material sector. In 1916 and 1917, this index was roughly parallel to those for general wholesale prices and manufactured goods, being 27.9 per cent above 1913 in the first of these years, and 74.4 per cent above in 1917. It thus had begun to rise more rapidly than prices in general. In 1918, however, it was 88.9 per cent above the base year, or from 7 to 10 points below the other two indexes.[14]

Prices of farm products rose more during the war than did most other wholesale prices. Raw farm products cost, in 1916, 25.4 per cent more than in 1913, 82 per cent more in 1917, and 106.3 per cent more in 1918. The prices of processed farm products rose more slowly at first, but in 1918 reached 110.1 per cent above the base

---

[13] Simon Kuznets, *National Product in Wartime* (New York: National Bureau of Economic Research, 1945), pp. 105, 134.

[14] Frederick C. Mills, *Economic Tendencies in the United States* (New York: National Bureau of Economic Research, 1932), p. 584.

year.[15] Retail prices, as recorded by the cost-of-living index of the Bureau of Labor Statistics, lagged somewhat behind wholesale prices, as is usual when prices are rising rapidly. In 1916 this index was 8 per cent above 1914 and rose to 28 per cent above in 1917 and 50 per cent above in 1918. All these figures are yearly averages and do not mark either the low or the high points of any given year.

ACCOMPLISHMENT OF WAR CONTROLS

The war planning did not substantially increase the gross national product, but such an increase was not its principal purpose. It was highly successful in achieving a rapid expansion of war production, doing so whenever necessary at the expense of the civilian economy. It did attempt to maintain an essential flow of civilian supplies, and its executives would have had no objection if civilians could have lived even better than before, so long as the necessities of war were fulfilled.

Various bottlenecks prevented a more rapid growth of output at various times and places. So many were the shifts in the accustomed patterns of production that seldom were all the required factors in balance. The difficulty of bringing about increases in the output of farms was one important cause of the lag in total product. The shortage of certain imported materials like tin was another. Railroad transportation before the reforms instituted by the Railroad Administration constituted a serious handicap. In the end, the most fundamental obstacle to expansion was probably the shortage of labor, combined with the effect on efficiency of employing new and untrained workers, and of absorbing into the productive system even the slowest and the least intelligent.

When the United States entered the war, there was no large reservoir of unemployment from which the demand for labor could be supplied. Yet the total of those gainfully occupied, excluding the armed forces, increased by approximately 700,000 from 1916 to 1917 and by another 600,000 from 1917 to 1918. In the latter year the employed labor force was about 40,600,000.[16] Part of the influx that offset the shrinkage of the labor force by conscription came from the natural increase of population. Another large part came from the

[15] *Ibid.*
[16] Kuznets, *National Product in Wartime*, p. 145.

entry into gainful occupations of women and others who had not previously been employed.

There was in these years no net gain in the employees of agriculture. While some took up farm work, others, including several hundred thousand southern Negroes, were attracted to industry from the rural South. Employment in mining increased by 100,000 from 1916 to 1917 and remained stable thereafter. Employment in manufacturing was a great gainer, growing by 300,000 from 1916 to 1917 and by another 600,000 from 1917 to 1918. In all, manufacturing employed 9,900,000 in the latter year. Construction contributed to the supply of labor by losing 200,000 men. Transportation gained about 300,000 in the two war years, and governmental employment, including arsenals and navy yards, was swollen by 3,100,000. Trade remained about stationary, while unclassified employees were diminished by some 2,000,000.[17]

In view of the difficulties, the record of productivity was fairly good. In manufacturing, the index of wage earners required for a unit of output had been 79 in 1914 (on the basis of 100 in 1899). This index fell to 69 in 1916, but rose again to 74 in 1917 and 77 in 1918. The index is based upon the number of wage earners employed, and its regressive tendency in the war years may have been due partly to reduction in the number of hours worked. Unfortunately, there are no reliable figures of man-hours for these years. Such figures exist only for the census years of 1914 and 1919. The index of man-hours per unit of output rose only from 73 in 1914 to 74 in 1919, whereas in the same period the index of number of wage earners per unit increased from 79 to 84.[18]

On steam railroads, the index of employment per unit of output decreased from 116 in 1916 to 111 in 1917 and then rose again to 113 in 1918 (base 1929=100). In agriculture, the number of workers per unit remained constant in 1916, 1917, and 1918. Man-days per unit in mining (base 1929=100) increased from 127 in 1916 to 132 in 1917, and remained at that figure in the following year.[19]

Without governmental planning and control, it would have been impossible to concentrate so much of the nation's energy and resources on war requirements. It is probable also that this control

[17] Ibid.
[18] Solomon Fabricant, Labor Savings in American Industry, 1899–1939 (New York: National Bureau of Economic Research, 1945), p. 46.
[19] Ibid.

minimized the inevitable loss to civilian consumers and did something toward equalizing its distribution.

How great the total civilian sacrifice was depends largely on the standard of comparison. If one should assume that without the war the economy would have remained in the depressed condition of 1914, or would perhaps have suffered still greater retardation, the conclusion would be that the people on the average gained from the war in levels of living. An estimate of total consumers' outlay in terms of 1914 prices indicates that it was $30.6 billion in 1914, $33 billion in 1916, $32.7 billion in 1917, and $30.9 billion in 1918.[20] If, at the other extreme, it is assumed that without the war there would have been in 1917 and 1918 as much employment as actually occurred, and the national product would have been as great as it was, then the consumers endured sacrifice to the extent of the total war cost. Neither of these assumptions, however, is realistic. It is probable that if the war had not occurred there would have been a business recovery and some net growth of the national product, but not so much as was evoked by the forced draft of war expenditure.

J. M. Clark, in estimating the cost of the war to the people, concludes that of the $31 billion of national resources used for war, $18 billion represented decreased civilian consumption, as compared with the rate per capita in 1915, $5.75 billion was derived from the increase of personal real income above the 1915 level—this amount being taken by the government in taxes and loans—and $7.25 billion represented increased productive efforts. These figures cover the three years 1917–1919.[21] He chooses the year 1915 as a base, because this seems a reasonable compromise between the two extreme positions outlined above. How the losses and gains were apportioned among the major groups in the population is summarized in the next chapter.

LASTING GAINS AND LOSSES

The war, of course, exerted effects on the economy that became manifest in subsequent years and will appear later in the narrative. Here some of the more important may be briefly noted. The movement for standardization of products and processes, the interchangeability of parts, and reduction in the number of sizes and styles made

[20] Kuznets, *National Product in Wartime*, p. 134.
[21] Clark, *The Costs of the World War to the American People*, p. 137.

rapid headway, and the attention of many was called to the savings that could thus be effected. Scientific management received governmental encouragement, and more attention began to be devoted to the arts of managing industrial personnel. The industry committees formed with the encouragement of the War Industries Board and the Food Administration constituted the basis of the subsequent growth of trade associations.

The war marked a great increase in the physical plant of American manufacturing. Expenditures for new buildings and equipment rose from $600 million in 1915 to $2.5 billion in 1918.[22] Some of these additions represented special-purpose facilities useful for war only, and some were devoted to industries like shipbuilding and aircraft production, which suffered a drastic shrinkage in the postwar period. Nevertheless, a fairly large proportion of the new investment provided plants and machinery capable of being turned back to peace production without difficult problems of reconversion. The war therefore occasioned a large and permanent increase in manufacturing capacity.

Naturally, some industries boomed while others were adversely affected. It is not easy in all cases to separate from the normal trend the effects of the war on a specific industry. During the period there was a rapid growth of the relatively new automobile industry. Production of passenger cars rose from 460,000 in 1913 to 1,750,000 in 1917.[23] In 1918, production was reduced by government order, but not eliminated. The adoption of this new method of transportation created a stimulus in many other directions. There was a proliferation of oil wells and refineries, pipe lines, filling stations, and garages. State and local governments built many miles of road, mostly on borrowed money. All of this naturally helped to accentuate the war boom.

It is possible to learn something about the relative growth of industries by changes in their physical output between 1914 and 1919. Neither of these years is ideal as a bench mark, because both were characterized by slumps of physical production. Nevertheless, they are chosen because they were years when the quinquennial census of manufactures was taken. The industry which showed the

[22] Paul A. Samuelson and Everett E. Hagen, *After the War—1918–1920* (Washington: National Resources Planning Board, 1943), p. 29.
[23] *Ibid.,* p. 20.

greatest growth of all in this period was motor vehicles, which more than quadrupled in output. Next in order came rubber goods, with an increase of 186 per cent, due largely to the demand for automobile tires. The only other industry that more than doubled was condensed and evaporated milk, with a growth of 134 per cent. Other heavy gainers were petroleum refining, linoleum, iron and steel, slaughtering and meat packing, explosives, soap, hats, motorcycles, canning and preserving, manufactured ice, paints and varnishes, woolen goods, silk manufactures, and pianos. Industries that declined during the period were largely associated with construction. They included brick, cement, clay products, lumber, cast-iron pipe, turpentine, and rosin. A few industries showed the effect of permanent declines in demand, like cotton lace goods. A few others, like fertilizers, cordage and twine, and jute and linen goods, reflected shortages of materials resulting from the war.[24]

The shrinkage of housing construction, while the population continued its growth, laid the basis for the future housing shortage and building boom. Those who enjoyed larger real incomes on account of the war constituted an active market for luxury goods and created higher standards of living that later affected wider circles of consumers. While the President and the Secretary of the Treasury during the war were asking people to curtail their expenditures for patriotic reasons, business interests conducted a nation-wide anti-thrift campaign with billboards and full-page advertisements urging liberal buying of consumers' goods.

Allied buying before 1917 virtually extinguished the net debt of Americans to foreigners, and the amounts loaned to their associates in the war consisted almost entirely of an expansion of the Allied debt. Approximately $643 million of Allied borrowing was used to repay the short-term notes obtained by the Allies through American banks before the entry of the United States into the war and interest before the end of the war period amounted to over $700 million more. The rest was paid for commodities and services in the following order of importance—cereals and food, munitions, cotton, other supplies, transportation and shipping, and miscellaneous.[25] The former debtor position of the United States was thus dramatically

[24] Mills, *Economic Tendencies in the United States,* pp. 194, 195.
[25] Lewis, *America's Stake in International Investments,* p. 364.

changed to a creditor one, and American producers became accustomed to a large export surplus financed on credit.

Few gave any thought at the time to the question how these loans were to be repaid or what would happen to exports when the stream of foreign lending stopped. It was not until later that people began to be aware of the difficult problem of transferring payments for the Allied debt. The controversy that subsequently arose concerning this matter and the long train of misfortunes set in motion by postwar readjustment were not foreseen.

The credit inflation that accompanied the governmental policies in financing the war, and the rapidly rising prices that resulted, naturally had a direct bearing on the economic history of the next few years.

Finally, the eyes of many who had participated in the war planning, or who had observed it with understanding, were opened to the possibilities of managing the economy for chosen ends. Whereas in previous years the behavior of the economic order had seemed like a series of unpredictable and uncontrollable natural phenomena, it now was analyzed with the aid of masses of new statistics and more detailed examination of cause and effect. It began to be possible to speak in terms of relative magnitudes and large aggregates, and to apply deliberate social controls by policies of priority and other devices. Toward the end of the war, a relatively few people began to ask why, if production and distribution could be governed even by a hastily improvised organization for war purposes, even better results might not be achieved over a longer period for purposes regarded as desirable in peace.

This attitude, however, did not at the time gain the adherence of those who held power, and failed to attract a wide popular following. The literature of reconstruction in the United States was far less voluminous and had a much smaller circulation than it did in England and other countries. No influential advocate of economic planning appeared. Mr. Hoover and Mr. Baruch had emphasized that everything being done was for the emergency only. They saw no peril in a rapid abandonment of controls. Planning even for demobilization and reconversion had made little headway within government circles when the end of the war arrived. Most of the war agencies themselves were staffed by volunteers who were eager to get back as soon as possible to their customary pursuits. The overcrowded and distracted atmosphere of Washington seemed to be an evil from which everyone would be glad to flee at the earliest possible moment. Nevertheless, the experience of war planning exerted a permanent influence on the thinking of the economists and engineers who participated in it.

CHAPTER III

The Army of Producers

THE demand for labor had already become insistent by April, 1917, because of the war orders of the Allies and the stimulus that they provided to the American economy in general. The hostilities restricted the supply of labor at the very time when the demand for it was increasing. Before the war, immigration had provided a large and continual source of new workers. In 1913, for instance, there was a net immigration of over a million persons. By 1916 the need of Europe for its own man power and the wartime restrictions on travel had reduced the excess of those arriving in the United States over those departing to 264,000. By 1917, the excess had shrunk to 81,000 and in 1918, it was only 41,000.[1] To this shrinkage of immigration was added the effect of the withdrawal of over 4 million men for the armed services. Unemployment in manufacturing and transportation—for which there were no accurate figures at the time—was estimated by Paul Douglas to have declined from nearly 13 per cent of the labor force in 1914 to 3.5 per cent in 1917 and 1918.[2] The latter figure comes close to being an absolute minimum required to account for those workers in the process of shifting from one job to another, especially in a period of rapid labor turnover.

[1] Harry Jerome, *Migration and Business Cycles* (New York: National Bureau of Economic Research, 1926), p. 124.
[2] Paul H. Douglas, *Real Wages in the United States, 1890–1926* (Boston: Houghton Mifflin Company, 1930), p. 460.

Naturally the war demand did not impinge equally on all industries. Shipyards, munitions plants, steel mills, and, after American entry into the war, clothing factories and textile mills were under continual pressure to expand their output. Railroad labor was scarce. On the other hand, building, printing, and similar peacetime industries were either affected adversely or were little enlarged The result was a confused and rapid shifting of labor from one industry or locality to another, coupled with an intense competition by employers for operatives of the types most in demand. It became a common complaint that one employer was "stealing labor" from another. In the areas of acute labor shortage, wages were increased rapidly to retain and attract employees. For instance, United States Steel raised wages seven times between January, 1916, and August, 1918, the aggregate increase being 75 per cent.[3]

Before the war, established trade unions had included only a small percentage of the industrial workers of the country and were largely concentrated in a relatively few occupations, such as transportation, building, printing, and clothing. Several factors now combined to increase manifestations of labor unrest, not only among those who were organized but also in establishments where unions had not been recognized. The demand for labor strengthened the workers' bargaining power, while the enlarged profits of business diminished the resistance of employers to increases of pay. The wage boosts given under little or no union pressure, for the purpose of attracting labor, stimulated demands for similar increases elsewhere. The rising cost of living compelled the workers to ask continually for more. At the same time, the pressure for production led to long hours, speed-up, and other working conditions that aggravated discontent. According to the United States Bureau of Labor Statistics, the number of strikes increased from 1,405 in 1915 to 4,359 in 1917, and the number of persons affected from 504,000 to 1,213,000.[4] Many of these strikes were spontaneous uprisings of nonunion workers or of workers whose union leaders had not authorized their action. The membership of trade unions themselves

[3] Gordon S. Watkins, *Labor Problems and Labor Administration in the United States during the World War* (Urbana: University of Illinois Studies in the Social Sciences, September, 1919), p. 63.

[4] *Monthly Labor Review*, U. S. Department of Labor (June, 1919), pp. 303, 325.

is estimated to have increased from 2,607,700 in 1915 to 3,104,600 in 1917.[5]

LABOR ADMINISTRATION

The administration of industrial man power for war production necessarily came to be one of the first concerns of the national government. It would have been stupid to strain every nerve to expand, allocate, and economize the material factors of production while remaining indifferent to wastes and inefficiencies in the utilization of the producers themselves. It was necessary to facilitate the redistribution of workers from areas of surplus to areas of scarcity. Newcomers had to be trained. Once men were employed at essential processes, it was desirable to keep them at their jobs rather than allow them to move about in search of higher pay or better conditions, thus interfering with full production and increasing its costs. Industrial managers came to realize that high labor turnover constituted a terrific waste of human resources. Interruptions of production resulting from industrial disputes had to be avoided so far as possible. At the same time, the health and good will of the workers had to be safeguarded in order to stimulate productiveness.

All these considerations were important for the military objectives of the nation, entirely aside from questions of social justice or long-term reform. Their importance, however, was not recognized by many employers or government purchasing agencies, themselves, especially at the beginning. Plans for labor administration and adjustment were developed during the course of the war, piecemeal and by a process of improvisation. Fortunately, the administration was liberal in its tendency and early called to its assistance experts in labor relations who had some understanding of the workers' problems.

The American Federation of Labor, under the strong influence of President Samuel Gompers, was a wholehearted supporter of the war and an opponent of socialist and other labor political movements, which the conservative trade-union leaders feared would divert the energies of the established unions to impractical revolutionary programs. Although traditionally in favor of peace, Mr. Gompers had early in the war become friendly to the Allied cause

[5] Leo Wolman, *The Growth of American Trade Unions, 1880–1923* (New York: National Bureau of Economic Research, 1924), p. 119.

and had carried on a long running battle against the pacifists and radicals in the labor movement. His stand reflected not only his personal sympathies but a deliberate policy of strengthening unions by enlisting governmental support.

A general trade-union conference called by him met on March 12, 1917, and not only pledged the labor movement to support the "democracies," but pointed out that the national effort would be weakened if labor's interests were sacrificed under the guise of national necessity. The government must enlist the wholehearted cooperation of wage earners by checking economic exploitation. The cornerstone of national defense, said the declaration, was economic justice, and the government should recognize the organized labor movement as the agency through which cooperation with the wage earners must be carried on. Safeguards of labor standards were demanded, as well as direct representation for labor on all defense agencies. Although this representation was granted on the Advisory Commission of the Council of National Defense and, later, on the War Industries Board, labor for the most part had to be satisfied with representation on agencies for the adjustment of industrial disputes.

WAR LABOR AGENCIES

The first governmental agency created during the war to deal with the labor situation was the Cantonment Adjustment Commission. It was organized on the basis of an agreement of June 19, 1917, between Secretary of War Baker and President Gompers of the American Federation of Labor. In a general sense it set the pattern for the many adjustment bodies that followed. It contained a representative of the Army appointed by the Secretary of War, a representative of labor appointed by Mr. Gompers, and a representative of the public, who, for a time, was Walter Lippmann. The commission was to use as basic standards the union wages, hours, and conditions in force in the various localities and was to make such adjustments as were required by circumstances. Its decisions were to be binding. The War Department could enforce upon the employers observance of the rulings of the commission because the contracts made with the private constructors placed all questions of wages, hours, and conditions under the jurisdiction of the quartermasters.

Implicitly, this arrangement carried with it recognition of the unions, which were prevalent in the building industry, as the representatives of the employees. In spite of pressure from organized labor, however, the commission refused to require the closed shop. Decision concerning the maintenance of the closed or the open shop was left to the individual contractors. The commission did exclude the closed nonunion shop by ruling that no contractor could discriminate against an employee because of his membership in a union. No important stoppage of production occurred under its jurisdiction. So extensive was the construction work of the War Department that the commission was eventually given authority over all of it under the name of the Emergency Wage Adjustment Commission.

The necessity for rapid production of uniforms under sanitary conditions soon led to the establishment of another labor agency. On July 20, 1917, the Secretary of War appointed a committee to study conditions in the clothing industry. This industry had long been suffering from cutthroat competition and had been characterized in large part by unsanitary sweatshops. The committee decided that better deliveries and decent standards should be safeguarded in contracts let by the department, that these contracts should be supervised and enforced by inspectors, and that preference should be given to manufacturers operating under collective agreements with unions. A Board of Control for Labor Standards was set up to carry out these recommendations. Sidney Hillman, President of the Amalgamated Clothing Workers of America, was active in urging these reforms and helped to carry them out. After the board had completed its preliminary work, its functions were turned over to an administrator of Labor Standards in Army Clothing. This post was eventually filled by Professor William Z. Ripley of Harvard University.

Other special agencies followed in rapid succession. They included the National Harness and Saddlery Adjustment Commission, the Arsenal and Navy Yard Wage Commission, and the Shipbuilding Wage Adjustment Board. The policies of the War Department in relation to labor were almost from the beginning guided by a special assistant to the Secretary—a post occupied in succession by Felix Frankfurter, Walter Lippmann, and Stanley King, a former manufacturer who subsequently became president of Amherst College. Franklin D. Roosevelt served on both the Arsenal and Navy

Yard Board and the Shipbuilding Adjustment Commission, as representative of the Navy Department.

At first, the special boards were exceptions to a general policy of referring the adjustment of disputes to conciliators of the Department of Labor, who had been accustomed to performing this function in time of peace. The exigency of the demand for Army supplies, however, soon forced the abandonment of this policy. Neither employers nor employees were under any compulsion to reach agreements through voluntary mediation, such as the Department of Labor could offer. The War Department itself could exercise much stronger pressure, not only because of its military character, but also because as the purchaser, its power to enforce its decisions was undoubted.

Systematic administration of personnel problems by the War Department became the accepted policy. In Ordnance, for instance, there was an Industrial Service Section, with district offices in twelve principal centers of manufacturing. At its Washington headquarters, branches were established for adjustment of disputes, supervision of the employment of women (who now entered heavy industry in large numbers), information, procurement of labor, housing, community organization, safety and sanitation, and employment and training methods. Industrial Service Sections with less elaborate organization were also formed in the Construction Division of the War Department, Aircraft Production, and the Quartermaster Corps. Since the several purchasing agencies often faced similar problems and tapped the same supply of labor, their policies had to be coordinated. The guidance given by the office of the Secretary of War was formalized on June 14, 1918, by an order centralizing in the office of a special assistant the control of wages, hours, and conditions of work on all War Department projects.

The Railroad Administration which, on account of its direct control of the railways, was for the time being itself an employer, determined labor policies on the railways, and set up its own adjustment machinery.

On April 8, 1918, the President established the National War Labor Board as a sort of court of last resort for disputes that could not be settled by any of the separate adjustment agencies or other authorities having jurisdiction. The composition of this board and the principles governing its procedure had previously been agreed upon unanimously by conferees representing unions and management. The board consisted of five representatives of labor and five representatives of employers, with two chairmen representing the public. One of these was former President William H. Taft, and the other was Frank P. Walsh, who had achieved a reputation as a liberal on the prewar Commission on Industrial Relations.

It was believed that this was a fair arrangement, since one of the two chairmen was a conservative who could be counted upon to give weight to the employers' point of view, while the other was regarded as sympathetic to labor. No doubt this type of joint chairmanship was arrived at because a previous suggestion for an arbitration board, which was to have contained representatives of the public equal in number to those respectively of employers and employees, aroused strong objection upon the part of labor. Union officials feared that the public representatives would be biased in favor of the employer, since the interests of the "public" had been so often appealed to by opponents of organized labor during industrial disputes.

The principles of the board registered the agreement that there should be no strikes or lockouts, recognized the rights of union organization and collective bargaining, approved the *status quo* as to the existence of union and nonunion shops (without forbidding the organization of labor where it did not exist), specified that women should have equal pay for equal work, approved in principle the basic eight-hour day, and as bases for the fixing of wages referred to those prevailing in the locality affected and to the right of labor to minimum living standards. The War Labor Board found its field of greatest usefulness outside the industries under direct governmental control where efficient adjustment machinery had already been established. According to the Department of Labor, about 6,000 strikes occurred during the nineteen months of war, but most of them were brief and voluntarily ended by labor.[6]

In the early months of the war, there was no national system of coordinated employment exchanges to aid in making contacts between job opportunities and workers qualified to fill them. Some states had systems of public exchanges, but the principal part of this important task had been left to profit-making employment bureaus or to employers themselves. Much of the hiring was done at the gates

[6] *Monthly Labor Review* (June, 1919), pp. 303, 325.

of industrial establishments from applicants who were attracted by information or rumor. To remedy this confusion, a United States Employment Service was established in the Department of Labor. It made little headway for a time, because of insufficient funds. In the early summer of 1918, it received a large appropriation and established branch offices all over the country. On June 17, the President issued a proclamation urging all employers engaged in war work to use it exclusively in filling their vacancies. It was most successful in effecting a more rational distribution of unskilled labor, which was particularly short on account of the draft, the opportunities for obtaining semiskilled jobs after brief training, and the virtual cessation of immigration.

An attempt to coordinate the numerous labor activities of the government was made in May, 1918, by the appointment of the War Labor Policies Board in the Department of Labor. Felix Frankfurter was the chairman, and the board contained representatives of all the various departments and agencies dealing with labor matters. It did not undertake detailed administration, but served as a clearinghouse through which policies might be unified. It investigated such matters as central recruiting of labor, standardization of wages and conditions of work, dilution and training, employment of women and children, and other current problems. In addition, a conference committee of the various adjustment agencies was established in September, 1918, because of the need for standardizing wages and hours. Each agency agreed not to make any changes without first consulting this committee. It had hardly begun the task when the armistice ended most of the complex structure of labor administration.

HOURS AND CONDITIONS OF WORK

The actual effect of governmental labor policies on the welfare of labor during the war has been a subject of much controversy. That hours were reduced and money wages were increased is incontestable. Some, especially in the more radical ranks of labor, contended that greater gains could have been registered if the American Federation of Labor had not renounced strikes and if union organization had been vigorously pressed in traditionally anti-union industries, such as iron and steel. On the other hand, it was argued that cooperation of labor with the government gave the union spokesmen power and status, and enabled them to win more than would have been likely if widespread industrial conflict had broken out and drastic measures of repression had been invited.

One permanent gain, at least, was established in most industries—the basic eight-hour day with, in many cases, a Saturday half holiday, so that the working week was forty-four hours. In numerous cases this gain had been won by strikes or collective bargaining before the United States declared war on Germany. The labor shortage, combined with the urgent demand for production in manufacturing industries and the large profits being made, led employers to grant the concession in the form in which labor asked it: a standard or basic limitation of hours with extra pay for overtime. Since overtime was customarily worked, the change seemed to the employers in substance an increase of wages rather than a reduction of hours.

After the United States became a belligerent and governmental labor adjustment agencies were set up, there developed a national policy not only of installing the basic eight-hour day, but of limiting the hours actually worked as well. Various studies and experiments had indicated that longer hours over any considerable period did not result in larger production, and it was thought that the natural tendency of employers to lengthen the working day in order to fill war orders was defeating its own end. While this reform did not extend to the steel industry and others where collective bargaining was not established and industrial disputes did not threaten production, the average working week for manufacturing industries approximated fifty by the end of the war.

One of the main causes of this reduction of hours was a law that had been passed in 1912 making the eight-hour day mandatory for those engaged on government contracts. At the time of its passage, this law affected a very small percentage of businessmen and workers. The war economy, however, made government contractors out of a substantial part of the nation's industrial establishments. Though the law permitted the President to waive its provisions during time of war, the Naval Appropriation Act of March 4, 1917, provided that in this event time and a half must be paid for all work in excess of eight hours daily. Aside from the requirements of these laws, it became the policy of all government purchasing agencies to require the basic eight-hour day wherever their authority extended, and the War Department as well as others discouraged working hours actually longer than ten.

On the railroads, the train employees had gained the eight-hour day by the Adamson Act in 1916. The workers in railroad shops and offices and on the rights of way had been far less well organized than the engineers, firemen, conductors, and trainmen, but under the Railroad Administration, which practiced collective bargaining, the same basic working hours were extended to all railway employees.

The federal government supported such state legislation as protected employed women or forbade the employment of children. It also exerted all its available power and influence to prevent the exploitation of women and children working on government contracts. Efforts were made in numerous directions to improve the conditions surrounding work for men as well. Better sanitation was insisted upon, red light districts in munition boom towns were abolished, and various activities were inaugurated to moderate the acute housing shortages that arose in these localities. In the latter months of the war, the government actually built model housing in the neighborhood of shipyards and munitions centers. If the war had continued, this first experiment in public housing in the United States might have made a substantial contribution to better living conditions. The armistice, however, interrupted the progress of public housing, and the experiment left its mark principally in the minds of architects and city planners, to be revived at a later date.

A somewhat broader interest in the political and psychological aspects of labor unrest was expressed by the President's Mediation Commission under the chairmanship of Felix Frankfurter, which traveled about the country visiting scenes of acute labor conflict, adjusted disputes, and rendered a report that called widespread public attention to aggravated cases of injustice. For instance, in Bisbee, Arizona, the Industrial Workers of the World had called a strike of copper miners in the hitherto ununionized company town of Calumet. The result was that 1,186 men were forcibly deported from the town in violation of their elementary civil rights. The Mediation Commission investigated this outrage and restored industrial peace. It also called attention to the Mooney case in San Francisco, in which a labor leader had been tried and convicted on perjured evidence, under questionable legal procedure, on the charge of causing a bomb explosion in a Preparedness Day parade.

WAGES AND LIVING LEVELS

It became the policy of the wage adjustment authorities to permit increases in wage rates equivalent to increases in the index of the cost of living compiled by the Department of Labor, and to allow somewhat larger rises than this for the more poorly paid workers, on the basis of the principle that everyone should be able to afford a family budget representing a "minimum of health and decency." This policy, however, failed to assure that no wage earner should lose in purchasing power because of the war. It was applied, not as rapidly as prices rose, but only when disputes had to be adjudicated. Wage adjustments usually were based on the cost-of-living index of several months previous to the decisions, and in the meantime more price increases had occurred. Uneven gains were registered among the various occupations.

Statistical measures of wages rest on the rather slender and uncertain data available for the period. When it comes to estimating the earnings actually received, hourly or daily wage rates have to be modified by dubious estimates taking into account overtime and the volume of employment. All this, in turn, leaves out of account the effect of additional income in some families through the entrance into industry of new members, and the subtraction of income through the conscription of family members.

Estimates by Paul Douglas place the average annual earnings of all employed wage earners in 1916 at 11 per cent above 1914. The increase above 1914 became 30 per cent in 1917 and 63 per cent in 1918. When modified by the index of the rise in the cost of living, to obtain figures of real earnings or purchasing power, these increases over 1914 are 4 per cent in 1916, 1 per cent in 1917 and 4 per cent in 1918. It must be remembered that 1914, the base, was a year of depression. Annual real earnings, according to Douglas, had been as high as in 1917, or higher, in 1905, 1909, 1910, and 1913.[7]

Another calculation by Douglas covers the workers attached to manufacturing, transportation, and coal mining only, all of which were expanded by the war. It makes an allowance for the effect of employment. When employment is high, average annual earnings of the whole labor force will be greater at the same wage rates. Accord-

[7] Douglas, *Real Wages in the United States*, p. 391.

ing to this estimate, average annual real earnings in 1916 were 15 per cent above 1914, fell to 14 per cent above in 1917, and rose to 20 per cent above in 1918. In no previous year (except 1916) were real annual earnings as high as in 1917, according to this index. It must be noted that, if these figures are approximately correct, most of the gain in income arose from full employment rather than from increases in wage rates greater than the rise in the cost of living.[8]

These averages conceal a wide divergence in the fortunes of those engaged in the various occupations. According to Douglas, the increases in hourly wages between December, 1917, and December, 1918, ranged from 6.4 per cent in newspaper printing to 32 per cent in the metal trades and 42.5 per cent in meat packing, though the majority of the trades were grouped between 20 and 27 per cent. In the same year the cost of living rose 31 per cent. An example of the effect of fuller employment was the cotton textile industry, where hourly earnings increased 26 per cent, but annual earnings rose 41 per cent. Hourly earnings in the union building trades rose only 21 per cent from 1914 to 1918, while the cost of living went up 50 per cent, and employment was curtailed.[9]

Among railroad workers the gains were unevenly distributed because sectional differences were ironed out—southern wages being raised more than northern—and the lower paid received larger percentage increases than the more highly paid. Average hourly earnings on railroads were, in 1916, 8 per cent above 1914; in 1917, 22 per cent above; and in 1918, 77 per cent above. The corresponding percentages of rise in the cost of living were 1916, 8 per cent; 1917, 28 per cent; 1918, 50 per cent. It was not until adjustments were made by the Railroad Administration, therefore, that the railroad workers on the average gained in purchasing power.[10]

These measures of gains in real earnings—gains which, on the average, were almost negligible for all occupations taken together— must be modified by two further considerations, almost impossible to estimate, if one is to guess at the effects of the war on the levels of living of the workers regarded as individuals. The statistics, in the first place, record the pay of broad classes of occupations. But many individuals climbed up in the scale as men were drafted and

[8] *Ibid.*, p. 460.
[9] *Ibid.*, pp. 96, 101, 120, 127.
[10] *Ibid.*, p. 167.

employment opportunities increased. The Negroes who moved from southern cotton fields to Chicago, Detroit, Pittsburgh, and other industrial centers (over 400,000 between 1916 and 1920)[11] probably could buy more with their cash incomes than ever before. Many of the women who poured into war industry had never previously earned money from an employer. Employees who had previously had jobs were promoted.

On the other hand, a mere comparison of wages with the price statistics gives an inadequate impression of how people actually fared. Many who previously were exempt had to pay income taxes. Shortages existed of sugar, meat, coal, and other things; money in the pocket means little when goods desired are not available. Nor do prices fairly measure the many declines in quality.

Many bought war bonds rather than spending all their money. But these were far from being true savings in all cases. Some of the economic sacrifices of the war, less visible at the time, later demanded the expenditure of the money laid aside. The diversion of energies and materials from house building later turned up in an acute shortage of living space and in soaring rents. Out of the total sales of Liberty bonds, it is estimated that $7 billion or 30 per cent went to persons with incomes of $2,000 or less. This bracket included virtually all the wage earners.[12]

If the gains of wage earners in living levels during the war were largely illusory, the experience of salaried workers was one of unmitigated misfortune. They did not engage in collective bargaining, and there were no boards to alter their compensation as the cost of living rose. In government service, where their salaries were fixed by law, few changes were made during the war. The purchasing power of the annual earnings of those in government service (federal, state, and local) dropped steadily after 1915; the fall by 1918 is estimated as more than 32 per cent. Salaried workers in industry had a similar experience; the purchasing power of their pay probably dropped 25 per cent between 1914 and 1919; a 22 per cent drop occurred in the last three years of the period between 1916 and 1919.[13]

[11] Clark, *The Costs of the World War to the American People*, p. 256.
[12] *Ibid.*, p. 137.
[13] Willford I. King and others, *Income in the United States* (New York: National Bureau of Economic Research, 1922), II, 215. Also Douglas, *Real Wages in the United States*, p. 364.

FARMERS' GAINS

The farmers, as a whole, made substantial gains in real income during the war. Their numbers scarcely increased, but the prices paid for their products did, and their total output was maintained. Prices of raw farm products rose steadily after 1913, being 82 per cent above that year in 1917 and 106 higher in 1918.[14] Production of farm products was almost the same in all these years. The purchasing power of the realized income (that is, the net income available for spending after paying income taxes) of all those drawing incomes from agriculture was, in 1918, 25 per cent above 1915. Note that this was an increase in *real* income, that is, it takes account of all increases in prices paid by the farmers. This average includes both farm operators and agricultural wage earners. The gain of the former in real income was 29 per cent; of the latter, 2 per cent.[15]

Another way of demonstrating the effect of the war on farmers' incomes is the estimate made by King of the National Bureau of Economic Research that, in 1913, 143,000 farmers had incomes of over $2,000, whereas, in 1918, 1,861,000 had risen above this level. Those with incomes under $2,000 in 1913 numbered 6,245,000 and in 1918 had dropped to 4,571,000. Thus the percentage of all farmers earning $2,000 or more grew, during the war in Europe, from 2 to 29. In round numbers, the average income of those in this bracket increased during the same period from $2,400 to $3,100. The fact that the average income of those earning $2,000 or less rose from $620 in 1913 to $1,020 in 1918, or by approximately 65 per cent, indicates that many marginal farms prospered as well.[16]

The gains, of course, were unevenly distributed. Cotton growers suffered from the war, since the foreign markets of British cotton mills were seriously diminished. Though 1916 was a good year for them, cotton consumption declined in 1917; and in 1918 fell nearly a million and a half bales below 1916—though not to the low level of 1914.[17] Wool growers profited from the heavy demand, though in the United States wool is not a major crop. Hog raisers benefited more than most; wheat growers and cattlemen also profited. Since

[14] Frederick C. Mills, *Prices in Recession and Recovery* (New York: National Bureau of Economic Research, 1936), p. 39.
[15] Clark, *The Costs of the World War to the American People*, p. 153.
[16] King, *Income in the United States*, II, 313.
[17] Burns, *Production Trends in the United States since 1870*, p. 283.

farming was regarded as an essential occupation, the labor shortage was not so acute in the country as in the city, though the expansion of acreage brought its demand for additional help.

The net income of the farmers as a whole, in terms of current dollars, more than doubled between 1914 and 1918, growing from $4 to $10 billion.[18] Whether the farmers actually developed a higher level of living commensurate with their monetary gains is, however, open to serious question. Some sold out at the high land values, moved to California, and lived on their incomes. More invested their surplus in farmland, often supplementing their own capital with mortgage loans to do so. This may have seemed like a sound investment at the time; it had long been the habit of farmers to expand their landholdings with their savings. As subsequent events proved, however, it was a disastrous speculation. In consequence, much of the apparent gain in real income was illusory.

THE GAINS OF BUSINESS

The more strategically placed business corporations were the greatest gainers from the war in current money income. Examples of tremendous war profits are commonly cited. The profits of United States Steel, for instance, grew from $76 million on an average for 1912 to 1914 inclusive, to $478 million in 1917. These figures of the Federal Trade Commission show an expansion of over sixfold; the reports of the corporation itself indicate a fivefold increase. The profits for ten steel mills in 1918 ranged between 30 per cent and 319 per cent on their invested capital. Twenty-four copper companies made, after paying taxes, 12 per cent in 1913 and 24 per cent in 1917. Also after taxes, forty-eight lumber companies netted 17 per cent in 1917, while oil companies made about 21 per cent on their investment in the last six months of 1917 and the first quarter of 1918. The four principal meat packers, which in the three years 1912–1914 had made profits aggregating $19 million, registered an additional $36 million in 1916, and an extra $68 million in 1917.[19]

A combination of influences rendered these figures conservative, to say the least. Excess-profits taxes made it good business to inflate costs wherever the corporation or those who had power in it could thereby derive any advantage. Great sums were spent for advertis-

---

[18] King, *Income in the United States,* II, 313.
[19] "Profiteering," *Senate Document* No. 248, 65 Cong., 2 Sess., pp. 9–13.

ing on the assumption that it would build up good will. Large salaries were often paid to executives. Huge bonuses were also bestowed on highly placed individuals. Four officers of Bethlehem Steel divided among themselves $2.3 million in 1917 and $2.1 million in 1918.[20] The common government practice of awarding contracts on a cost-plus basis also led to a generous treatment of costs, since the profit allowed was a percentage of the cost of production. It is largely a matter of guesswork how many gains were concealed under cost items.

The figures for business profits as a whole show much less spectacular, but still substantial gains. In the most prosperous year immediately preceding the war, 1913, the total net earnings of American corporations were about $4 billion, according to the National Bureau of Economic Research. By 1916, they had almost doubled, the estimate being $7 billion. In 1917, they were very slightly larger. In 1918, they dropped back to $4.5 billion because of income and excess-profits taxes, and governmental price controls.[21]

The real gains of the great majority of owners of American business were, however, far less than the figures of profit would seem to indicate. While some companies increased their dividend payments substantially—United States Steel dividends being 18 per cent in 1917 and 14 per cent in 1918 as against 5 per cent before the war —the greater part of the war profits was retained in undistributed surpluses. For example, forty-six typical manufacturing corporations increased their dividend payments from $209,250,000 in 1913 to $284,750,000 in 1916, $383,510,000 in 1917, and $342,960,000 in 1918. Their corporate savings, however, grew from $120,410,000 in 1913 to $580,430,000 in 1916, $469,070,000 in 1917, and $319,000,000 in 1918.[22]

King estimates that the total disbursements to owners in manufacturing, including rents, royalties, interest, and profits, had a purchasing power that scarcely increased at all between 1913 and 1916, when it stood (in terms of 1913 prices) at $1.46 billion. This estimate of the purchasing power of property income shows a gain of about $400 million in 1917 over the previous year, or less than 30 per cent. In 1918 it fell back again to $1.52 billion.[23] Nor was this

[20] Ibid.
[21] King, Income in the United States, II, 328.
[22] Ibid., p. 96.
[23] Ibid., p. 239.

increase in money received by any means clear gain. About seven eighths of the taxes on personal incomes came from the owners of business and other property, who were responsible for about three fifths of the personal subscriptions to government loans.[24] In addition, they invested a great deal of money in the expansion of production facilities required for war work. J. M. Clark comes to the conclusion that when all these offsets are taken into account, the recipients of income from property, taken as a whole, actually had a diminished outlay for personal purposes during the war.

Some individuals naturally did make substantial gains, particularly in the higher brackets. In 1914, the number of persons reporting taxable incomes between $30,000 and $40,000 was about 6,000, while in 1918 there were 15,400 in this bracket. Those with taxable incomes between $50,000 and $100,000 increased in number during these four years from 5,000 to 13,000. It was estimated that at the end of the war there were 42,000 millionaires in the country.

It may be contended that the corporate savings plus individual savings and investments constituted real gains to the owners as did their personal expenditures during the war years. In many senses this is true. Though some special-purpose machinery for munitions production had to be scrapped, and industries like shipbuilding suffered a postwar contraction, a good deal of the new investment made during the war formed the basis of future profits. The huge undistributed surpluses permitted the distribution of dividends and interest in almost undiminished volume two or three years later, when both wage earners and farmers were suffering loss of apparent war gains. Nevertheless, not all the accumulated business profits resisted the tides of change. As will appear in a subsequent chapter, they were greatly diminished by postwar price deflation.

[24] Clark, *The Costs of the World War to the American People*, pp. 130 ff.

CHAPTER IV

The Postwar Boom

WHEN the armistice was signed on November 11, 1918, there were 4 million men in the armed services and 9 million persons, or about one fourth of the civilian labor force, engaged in war industries. Few in authority had given any serious thought to the problems of demobilization or to the reconversion of industry to civilian demands. The eyes of almost everybody were on Europe and the future peace terms. Dollar-a-year men in Washington rose from their desks, locked the doors of their offices, and went to Florida for a vacation before resuming their peacetime jobs. On November 12, the day after the German surrender, the telephone wires from Washington were overburdened with calls canceling contracts. The War Department had $6 billion worth of contracts outstanding, of which one third had already been completed. Considerably more than half of the remainder were canceled within four weeks. These orders for cessation of production usually included no more relief than allowance for a month's further operation at the current rate. Two days after the armistice the War Industries Board began to end price control. Within little more than a month no more priority orders were issued. Early in December, Congress instructed the United States Housing Corporation to stop work on all buildings not more than 70 per cent completed. Some Washington offices closed so suddenly that the executives had to lend money to the stenographers to get home.[1]

[1] Samuelson and Hagen, *After the War*, pp. 5, 6.

DEMOBILIZATION AND BOOM

Although somewhat more moderation was exercised by the Army in returning soldiers to civilian life, the demand to go home was so strong that 600,000 men were released almost immediately, and by April of the following year nearly 2 million had been discharged. Monthly releases from the Army averaged over 300,000, and almost the entire force had been demobilized a year after the armistice.[2]

In October, 1918, the War Department Committee on Classification of Personnel, in cooperation with the War Labor Policies Board, had begun to draw up plans for demobilization of the armed forces. In order to effectuate a smooth transition, it was the policy of these agencies, approved by Secretary of War Baker, to discharge first those men trained for jobs in which vacancies existed and to minimize unemployment by holding in the Army those who would be unlikely to find jobs when they came out. The Chief of Staff, however, ordered that the Army be demobilized by military units without regard to employment possibilities. The policy favored by Secretary Baker would in any case have encountered strong popular disapproval, since almost every soldier wished to doff his uniform as soon as possible and his family wanted to have him home.

The War Industries Board attempted to plan for the placement of returned soldiers, but failed to elicit the necessary information from employers. The task was then delegated to the United States Employment Service, which placed representatives in every army camp and set up special bureaus for veterans in towns and cities throughout the country, to coordinate local and voluntary bodies like the Red Cross and the Y.M.C.A. But Congress, in January, 1919, at a time when it was placing 150,000 men a week, curtailed the appropriation for the Employment Service by 80 per cent. Many of its staff then volunteered to work without pay, and it appealed for private funds to go on with the job. The agency managed to continue with 490 offices out of the 750 that had previously existed. On July 1, Congress appropriated enough more for it to continue until October on a still smaller scale.[3] Eventually, the whole function

[2] *Ibid.*, p. 8.
[3] E. Jay Hovenstine, Jr., "Lessons of World War I," American Academy of Political and Social Science, *Annals*, CCXXXVIII (March, 1945), 180–187.

was turned over to an unofficial Emergency Committee on Employment for Soldiers and Sailors, which sent boy scouts to employers to ask them to promise to rehire servicemen, and attempted to suppress peddling and panhandling by unemployed men in uniform.

A large federal program of public works had been advocated to stimulate employment after the war, but Congress made no appropriation for the purpose. A conference of governors and mayors, which President Wilson called to ask them to undertake more local building, met in Washington, March 3–5, 1919, but because of the lack of federal stimulation, the local governments did not respond to this appeal. The public works division of the Department of Labor set in motion a "Build-Your-Own-Home" publicity campaign. The Emergency Committee on Employment inaugurated a "spruce-up" drive to urge people to make necessary repairs to their houses. The net result of all these activities was a construction index that in 1919 was 11 per cent below the prewar level of 1910–1913.[4] The only effectual governmental aid for returned soldiers was a plan sponsored by Secretary of the Interior Franklin K. Lane to settle them on reclaimed farmland, but this opportunity was necessarily narrowly limited.

Why, in these circumstances, did not the country at once experience a severe crisis of unemployment? It is true that production fell sharply in the last quarter of 1918 and in the first few months of 1919. Unemployment was reported from numerous sections of the country, but because no statistical measurement of it existed at the time, nobody knows exactly how great it was. It is estimated that in February, 1919, the total was 3 million.[5] In spite of lack of any advance provision for these eventualities, however, production and employment turned upward in the second quarter of 1919 and a boom followed that lasted well into 1920. Some would now call this recovery sheer good luck, in so far as it was wholesome at all. Others might allege that it gave testimony to the recuperative powers of private enterprise when government controls were removed.

Industrial production, which in the third quarter of 1918 had reached its peak for the year at 17 per cent above the 1914 level, fell abruptly in the last three months of the year and continued downward, reaching its trough in the second quarter of 1919 at

[4] *Ibid.*
[5] *Ibid.*

12 per cent above the base year. In the third quarter of 1919, it suddenly jumped to 19 per cent higher than in 1914 and remained substantially at this level, which was above that of 1918, until the second quarter of 1920.[6]

Prices continued to rise during this entire period, suffering a slight reduction only in the first quarter of 1919, and thereafter shooting up even more rapidly than they had risen during the war. The index of wholesale prices (1913=100), which in 1918 had been 195.7, averaged 203.4 for the year 1919, and 227.9 for 1920. In the two-year period, prices of raw materials rose from 188.9 to 202.2, of manufactured goods from 198.4 to 239.5. Prices of raw farm products reached their peak in 1919, rising from 206.3 in the previous year to 221.9. Their decline began earlier than that of most other prices and was registered in the figure for 1920 at 212.5. Prices of processed farm products, however, reflected the general inflation, going from 201.1 in 1918 to 224.9 in 1919, and 241.9 in 1920.[7] The cost of living rose to 77 per cent above 1914 in 1919 and to 105 per cent above it in 1920. These figures are annual averages and do not indicate the highest point of the year.[8]

The gross national product of goods and services, even in terms of 1914 prices, was slightly higher in 1919 than in 1918, being $41.8 billion as against $41.6 billion. It was greater than any in the history of the country hitherto, except that of 1917. Even in 1920, the latter part of which saw the beginning of the depression, it was $40.1 billion. The rapidity of reconversion is indicated by the fact that the war output decreased from $9.7 billion in 1918 to $5.3 billion in 1919 and $1.1 billion in 1920, whereas the nonwar output in these three years was $31.9 billion, $36.5 billion, and $39.0, respectively. All these figures are in terms of 1914 prices.[9]

What economic forces were actually at work to bring about this surprising result?

One influence of moderate importance was the fact that the Emergency Fleet Corporation, which had barely begun to finish ships, continued its program. Many in the United States cherished the hope of restoring the country to prominence in the ocean-carrying trade, and ships might be used as well in peace as in war. More

[6] Federal Reserve Bulletin (January, 1921).
[7] Mills, Economic Tendencies in the United States, p. 39.
[8] Monthly Labor Review (March, 1921).
[9] Kuznets, National Product in Wartime, p. 134.

than twice as much shipping tonnage was completed in the two years following the armistice as had been built before. Other agencies were also retained somewhat longer than the majority. The Railroad Administration was continued because of a widespread belief that a new type of organization and control was required for the transportation system, and Congress was not yet ready to enact new legislation. A minor influence contributing to recovery was the fact that every discharged soldier was given transportation home and $60.

A factor diminishing unemployment was that two or three million persons had been drawn into war industry who did not desperately need jobs and who retired from wage earning when the war was over. Among these were many women, and persons from agricultural regions who could go back and live on the farm. Moreover, most industries did not have a difficult technical job in turning back their plants and machinery to civilian production, while there was still a considerable amount of civilian purchasing power available to buy the goods that they could make. Automobile production, for instance, began to increase again. Output of passenger cars, which in 1917 had been 1,750,000—the highest volume in history—had during 1918 dropped to less than a million. In 1919 it came back again to 1,650,000 and in 1920 was 1,900,000.[10] Returned soldiers bought civilian clothing and so increased activity in the clothing and textile industries.

Consumers' demand for goods that had been scarce during the war was probably not, however, an important factor in the boom. Civilians had been deprived of relatively few goods and only for a short period. Many of the shortages occurred in perishable commodities like food or coal for heating, and these cannot subsequently be made up. At that time, with the sole exception of automobiles, there had not developed a large market for consumers' durable goods such as electric refrigerators and other mechanical household equipment, while radios had not been offered for sale; hence the war economy had demanded little cessation in the output of such commodities. Furniture and house furnishings do not wear out in the space of less than two years, and the demand for them depends to a great extent on the construction of new houses, which was still at a low level.

Careful studies indicate that although some of the war bonds

[10] Samuelson and Hagen, *After the War*, p. 20.

were redeemed, few persons were spending their war savings in the retail stores, and individuals continued to save an unusually high proportion of their current incomes. It is estimated that there were 22.8 million separate subscriptions to the Fourth Liberty Loan. Of the $21 billion of Liberty bonds outstanding in 1919, about $17 billion were held by others than business corporations and banks. Income payments to individuals averaged, for the years 1919 and 1920, $63.8 billion. Of this $58.4 billion was spent and $5.4 billion, or 8.39 per cent, was saved. This percentage of saving compares with the average of 5.57 for the years 1922–1929. It is true that by June 30, 1920, about $1.6 billion worth of bonds of $50 and $100 denominations had been returned to the Treasury for conversion into bonds with a higher face value.[11] This, however, does not indicate an equivalent volume of redemption by small holders for the purpose of acquiring spending money. Many of the bonds had been bought on bank credit, and many of the purchasers merely sacrificed them by failing to repay the loans.

A factor of some importance in the recovery was the resumption of private building after the wartime restrictions on use of materials were removed and labor became available. A severe housing shortage had developed, and rents were going up rapidly. This offered a stimulus both to speculative builders and to prospective homeowners. It is estimated that, in the cities, monthly construction in 1919 averaged four times as much as in 1918. A still further increase occurred in 1920. The levels reached, however, were far below those attained later when the construction boom began in earnest. The dollar volume of building in 1919 was less than 40 per cent of the average for the following decade. The recovery in building therefore cannot account for more than a minor part of the immediate postwar boom.[12]

A far more important influence was the continuation of exports at a high level. The government was still lending money to the Allies, and this money was, as usual, spent mainly in the United States. Exports were also stimulated by the fact that government control of foreign exchange was ended after the armistice, and the price of the dollar in terms of some foreign currencies fell. About $3.3 billion

11 *Ibid.*, pp. 16–19.
12 *Ibid.*, p. 21.

net was spent for American exports in 1919.[13] Although the purchase of weapons of war had been ended, there was a brisk demand for other manufactured goods. The bulk of the purchases, however, consisted of the products of American farms. Farm prosperity was thus a substantial element in the postwar boom.

Exports were augmented during this period by a renewal of private lending to finance sales by American manufacturers of goods needed for reconstruction. There was, for instance, a shortage of rolling stock on European railroads. The Baldwin Locomotive Works and the American Locomotive Company sold over $11 million worth of locomotives to Belgium in 1919 and also made substantial contracts with Poland, Rumania, Argentina, Mexico, China, and Colombia. The foreign governments concerned usually paid by short-term obligations. In the case of Rumania, oil was taken in exchange. American engineering and contracting companies also did a large amount of work not only in Europe but in South America and even in China.

Still another factor that stimulated American exports was the immediate postwar need for relief of European populations. In Britain influential opinion held that the inter-Allied agencies built up during the war to control shipping and the purchase and distribution of commodities ought to be preserved and utilized for the relief work. Herbert Hoover, who was the natural choice of the United States government to supervise relief, opposed this plan and advised the President that the inter-Allied war control agencies should be dissolved. Since the relief would be financed mainly by American credit, he believed that it should be administered by a purely American organization. This attitude on his part occasioned regret in England, and the charge was subsequently made that the demobilization of the Allied controls and the necessity of building up a completely new organization caused a delay of several months in the distribution of food to the starving. Mr. Hoover has vehemently denied this charge.

At any rate, the American Relief Administration was set up under Mr. Hoover and was empowered by act of Congress in February, 1919, to sell relief supplies on credit. Later the same power was given to the United States Grain Corporation. The two agencies

[13] *Ibid.,* p. 27.

together made sales and loans aggregating $141 million and thus served to swell exports of foodstuffs.[14]

Many of these separate influences were recognized at the time, but very few understood how temporary their effect was likely to be and why. A major factor behind them had not yet been cogently stated in terms of theory, as later elaborated in the volumes of J. M. Keynes in Great Britain, Alvin H. Hansen in the United States, and other leading economists. This central influence was the fact that the government had long been spending very large amounts, and was spending much more money than it took from current incomes of the citizens. It continued to do so well into 1919. Because of the fact that the deficit was financed largely on the basis of bank credit, the stimulation to the general purchasing power was reinforced.

It was after the armistice that the government floated the final war bond issue or Victory Loan. Although the excess of expenditures over receipts was not so great in 1919 as it had been in 1918, and declined throughout the year, it still amounted to considerably over $4.5 billion. Because the money continued to circulate through private hands, the indirect effects of this deficit financing, of course, persisted beyond the time when the amounts were actually spent by the government. This basic influence not only served to expand spending at home, but also financed a large part of the Allied purchasing in the United States during 1919. Loans by the United States government to the Allies aggregated $1.75 billion in that year.[15]

CREDIT INFLATION AND PRICES

The effect of the governmental deficit was registered not only by the expenditure of this government and its associates in the war, but also by the expansion of private credit, which it facilitated. As during the war, loans by the banks to business and agriculture were encouraged because of the fact that government bonds could be used as collateral for such loans, which could be rediscounted by the federal reserve banks. This practice made it easier for traders and businessmen to expand their activities freely. The total of bank loans and of money in circulation continued to rise as long as the boom

[14] Lewis, *America's Stake in International Investments*, pp. 364–365.
[15] Samuelson and Hagen, *After the War*, p. 23.

lasted. The easy credit conditions also made it possible to finance exports, particularly of agricultural products, far beyond the point that the governmental loans to the Allies would by themselves have permitted. The unfunded foreign trade balance increased nearly $3 billion in 1919 and 1920.[16]

Of course, the bank loans were for short terms and could not be indefinitely renewed. Most people did not understand that the time was near at hand when banks would have to go slow in making new loans or even stop renewing those that had already been made. Of the two forces certain to bring about this cessation of credit expansion, the first and most important was that the bank reserve was not increasing, and the limits fixed by law for the minimum percentage of reserves to currency and deposits were rapidly being approached. As a matter of fact, when exchange controls were demobilized, the United States began to lose gold. The other factor was that, with the cessation of governmental bond issues, the available collateral for bank loans would stop growing.

Public resentment at high prices, combined with uneasiness over the orgy of speculation, influenced Congress on several occasions to adopt resolutions regarding the current inflation. One, introduced in the Senate in July, 1919, directed the Banking and Currency Committee to report whether new legislation was needed to bring about a reduction of the money in circulation. The Federal Reserve Board was also worried about the situation, although for a long time it believed that rising prices were created by the shortage of commodities, and it regarded the monetary expansion as the result of high prices rather than the reverse. Nevertheless, it did take several ineffectual steps to curtail credit.

In June, 1919, the board sent a letter to the chairman of each reserve bank warning against the issuance of loans for speculation in the stock market, and it published a similar statement in the *Federal Reserve Bulletin*. The New York Reserve Bank explained the nature of the Federal Reserve Act to its members, and tried to persuade those that seemed to be borrowing too much to reduce their rediscounts. Throughout the system, member banks were advised to curtail nonessential credits and especially to discriminate against speculative loans. The member banks, however, failed to respond, partly because speculation had become an accepted business prac-

[16] *Ibid.*, p. 28.

tice, and partly because it was difficult to distinguish between loans needed for production and loans to finance the holding of materials and inventories. Finally, the central authorities conducted a drive to reduce the loans secured by government bonds. Although this endeavor met with some success and the banks disposed of a large amount of federal securities, they did not use the proceeds to reduce their indebtedness to the reserve banks, but instead increased their commercial loans and investments.

The principal barrier to effective restriction of credit in this period was the need of the Treasury for additional funds. Both the funded debt and the short-term loans to the government kept on increasing until the beginning of 1920, and the Treasury feared that restrictive measures would not only embarrass this financing but would hamper the increase of production and the provision of jobs for returned soldiers. Therefore the rediscount rates were held relatively low, and preferential rates for war bonds were maintained.

Loans and investments of banks that were members of the Federal Reserve System increased about $2 billion between June, 1919, and June, 1920. Federal reserve notes in circulation rose almost 20 per cent during this period, and the reserve ratio fell to less than 41 per cent.[17]

The expansion of credit not only had the general effect of a rapid increase in prices, but also financed a widespread speculation for the rise that usually appears when prices soar. This occurred in trade and industry generally as well as in the speculative markets proper. Businessmen bought liberally in expectation of higher prices when the goods were sold. The estimated increase in the value of business inventories during 1919 was $6 billion, an increase almost four times as large as that in any year of the succeeding decade except 1923, and almost twice as large as that in 1923. About two thirds of the gain in value was due to increase in the physical volume of stocks, and one third to the rise in prices. Between May, 1919, and April, 1920, department store inventories alone were increased by more than 50 per cent.[18] The vicious spiral of speculative inflation was boosting prices even more rapidly because prices were rising, through the increased demand of business. This was a far more important factor in the boom than demand by ultimate consumers.

[17] Steiner, *Money and Banking*, pp. 872–873.
[18] Samuelson and Hagen, *After the War*, p. 33.

Profits were swollen on the books merely because of the rise in inventory value. Many business purchasers in the rush to buy placed duplicate orders with several firms in the expectation that all the orders could not be filled. This practice made the market demand appear even higher than it was. The eagerness of purchasers was increased when factories began to fall behind in their deliveries by the third quarter of 1919. A shortage of freight cars reappeared at the same time.

There was a contemporary belief that the apparent shortage of goods was caused by the strikes that characterized the year. Wage earners were attempting to catch up with the soaring cost of living, and the war adjustment machinery had, for the most part, been abandoned. About 4 million workers were involved in more than 3,600 strikes during 1919.[19] The greatest of these were the steel strike beginning in September and the strike of bituminous coal miners starting in November. The wage earners managed to gain less than 1 per cent in annual real earnings, which averaged for 1919 about 5 per cent above 1914.[20] It is probable that the strikes were a minor factor in restricting output, but the major cause of the shortage was the speculative expansion of business demand, rather than any diminution in the supply. Business was buying many more goods than could eventually be sold in consumers' markets at the prices asked.

Manufacturers were stimulated by the speculative demand to increase their investment in plant and equipment by about $3 billion in 1920. This was larger than the new investment in manufacturing in any subsequent year, including even 1929 and the years of preparation for military production in World War II.[21] Manufacturing investment, however, is not a major component of total investment, and this expenditure represented in part the higher cost of materials and labor.

Another phenomenon which influenced the postwar situation was the fact that both during the war and after it the relationship of various groups of prices to one another that had existed before the war was upset. Some prices fell while others rose, and among

[19] *Ibid.*, p. 31.
[20] Douglas, *Real Wages in the United States,* p. 391.
[21] Lowell J. Chawner, "Capital Expenditures for Manufacturing Plant and Equipment—1915 to 1940," *Survey of Current Business,* XXI (March, 1941), 9–15, Table 1.

those that rose, some went up much more rapidly than others. This development was a reflection partly of changes in demand for the several kinds of commodities and partly of the fact that some producers were in a stronger position than others to control the prices charged. Its natural effect was to increase uncertainty about the future and to encourage speculation. When prices have a more stable interrelationship, producers know what to expect and are likely to bend their energies toward improving their position by increasing their output and reducing their unit costs. These activities benefit the entire economy. When, however, prices both of raw materials and of finished products change rapidly and often go in opposite directions, the attention of the business community tends to be diverted to shrewd trading, speculating, and boosting prices. These activities may benefit the more fortunate or the more farsighted individuals, but they do not increase production or consumption, and in the long run they are likely to undermine confidence in the future.

The prices of raw materials are in normal times much more variable than those of manufactured goods. The war further increased their price variability. What is more striking is that during the war years the monthly variability of prices of manufactured goods was more than doubled. At the end of the period, the prices of factory-produced articles had risen much more than those of raw materials. This situation, of course, increased profit margins and was a powerful factor in the inflation that took place.

A measure of price dispersion, which indicates the degree to which prices of individual commodities depart from their common average from year to year, ranged in the decade before the war between 5.7 and 10.2. In the war years it was somewhat higher. After a decline in 1919, it rose in 1920 to 15.7 and in 1921 to 18.3.[22] In no previous year of which there is record had price dispersion approached anywhere near these high levels. Wide divergences appeared even between the prices of broad classes of goods. Raw material prices, for instance, had doubled in 1920, while manufactured goods had risen 39.5 points more than raw materials. In 1921, the corresponding index numbers were 125.0 and 162.7. A similar divergence occurred between the prices of raw and processed goods used by producers. Among goods bought by consumers, processed foods

[22] Frederick C. Mills, *Behavior of Prices* (New York: National Bureau of Economic Research, 1927), p. 259.

rose much less than processed nonfood products. In 1921, processed foods had dropped to 146.9, and other consumers' goods to 187.2. All these are wholesale prices with the base 1913 = 100.[23]

A dramatic illustration of the confused movement of prices in the postwar period is that of cattle, leather, hides, and shoes. These, of course, represent commodities in the various stages from raw materials to final product. While the prices of all rose during the war, they moved within a relatively narrow range of one another through 1918. In 1919, the prices of all but shoes turned downward, while shoe prices continued their upward course. By 1920, the price of shoes was nearly three times the 1913 level, although the other commodities which enter into shoe manufacture had fallen to about 60 per cent above that level. By 1921, hides were about 25 per cent below 1913, cattle were about 8 per cent above it, leather was some 25 per cent higher than in the base year, and shoes cost approximately 120 per cent more than in 1913.[24] The disturbances caused in the various markets by such a wide dispersion may well be imagined.

THE ORDER OF THE FORCES

If these various influences are rearranged in some order so that their interrelationships may be seen, it is well to begin with the fiscal policy of the government. Though war contracts were canceled, the Treasury continued for a year after the armistice to spend more than it received out of the current incomes of the citizens. This spending consisted partly in the continuation of shipbuilding and other activities not demobilized, partly in current military expenses and dismissal payments to soldiers, partly in settlement of business contracts, and to a considerable extent in reconstruction loans to the Allies. By one path or another these government expenditures flowed into the hands of businessmen, farmers, and wage earners, as they had during the war, though now in diminishing volume. In spite of transitional unemployment caused by the shift of war industries to civilian production and in spite of the demobilization of the armed forces, consumers were thus enabled to spend in retail markets as much as they had been spending before the armistice. There is no evidence, however, that they produced the boom by the satisfaction of deferred demands. To summarize the effect of governmental def-

[23] Mills, *Economic Tendencies in the United States*, pp. 584–585.
[24] Mills, *Behavior of Prices*, p. 255.

icit spending in this period, one may say that while it was a major
factor in cushioning the shock of demobilization and in maintaining
employment and production at a level sufficient to satisfy the more
urgent wants of the consumers, it was not directly responsible for
the boom itself in the sense of necessitating rising prices and run-
away speculation.

The next group of forces to consider are those in the private
sector that might have been capable of carrying on a stabilized prosperity when government deficit spending tapered off. Although the
expenditures of business necessary for reconversion were not large,
they helped to maintain employment in the transition period. The
revival of automobile production and sales was an industrial factor
of importance, which might have continued without interruption
if other circumstances had been favorable. The same may be said
of building construction, which began to grow in order to satisfy a
real demand. Neither of these trends, however, had reached very
high levels before the boom ended.

The chief force that facilitated the change from a desirable
recovery to an unwholesome boom was the continued expansion of
bank loans to private borrowers. This, combined with a relaxation
of price control, resulted in rapidly rising prices and speculative
activities in almost every sector of the economy. It led
businessmen to create an artificial activity and an appearance of
shortages of goods by bidding against one another for supplies in
order to profit from the rise in price they expected before the supplies could be sold. It diverted credit to speculation in the stock
and commodity markets, and so helped to create a shortage of
mortgage funds that might have sustained building. Speculative
purchases of crops concealed the developing agricultural surpluses
and so eventually aggravated them. The rapid rise in the cost of
living caused labor troubles and so contributed to the shortage of
supplies. Disparities among prices of various kinds, which had already occurred during the war, were exaggerated by the inflationary forces at work. These, in turn, encouraged speculation at the
expense of regularized production.

The roots of this inflation lay in the four preceding years, in
the sense that during that period there had occurred price increases
which probably could not have been sustained when the credit-
financed demands for extraordinary war supplies should cease. But
a correction of these prices would have been less difficult and pain-

ful if the excessive extension of bank credit could have been avoided. This expansion was deliberately fostered by the Treasury, partly on the mistaken assumption that it would increase total production and partly in order to sell the war loans.

It is possible that the Federal Reserve System might have succeeded in checking the inflation if the Treasury had not resorted to bank credit to float the final Victory Loan. There may seem to be a contradiction between this statement and the earlier conclusion that the continuation of governmental spending was a desirable factor that helped to moderate the shock of transition to a peace economy. It is necessary, however, to draw a careful distinction between governmental spending as such, and the private spending that resulted from public bond issues. Their seeming inseparability at the time was largely because of the prevailing practice that encouraged the use of war bonds as collateral for bank loans.

The expansion of purchasing power that continued after the war probably would not have resulted in speculative inflation if it could have been accompanied by an equivalent increase in physical production. The productive facilities of the country, however, were already being used virtually at their full capacity, and little further increase in output could occur in the confusion of demobilization and reconversion. Since all price controls had been abolished, a sharp upturn of prices was the inevitable accompaniment of the continued expansion of purchasing power and the failure of physical production to increase appreciably.

At the time, no comprehensive theory of the influence of fiscal policy upon the total economy had been elaborated. There was little definite quantitative information about either the amount being added to purchasing power or the course of production as a whole. If the problem had been correctly visualized and the necessary facts had been marshaled, it might have been possible to organize a relatively smooth transition from war to peace that would have avoided the inflationary boom of 1919–1920. Some readjustments of production and price would, of course, have been necessary. In particular, it would have been impossible to maintain agricultural exports at the war level. Nevertheless, if these readjustments had been foreseen, if the necessary governmental controls had been continued until the crisis was passed, and if the implications of fiscal policy had been better understood, the outcome might have been more fortunate.

CHAPTER V

The Postwar Depression

IN SPITE of the rosy anticipations of farmers and businessmen
—perhaps partly because of them—the postwar boom began to
collapse in 1920. Business slid at first gradually downhill, and by
1921 ended in one of the most violent crashes of prices that the
nation has ever experienced. The index of wholesale prices of all
commodities fell from 227.9 in 1920 to 150.6 in 1921 (1913 = 100).[1]
Raw materials and farm products dropped considerably more than
this, while manufactured goods fell somewhat less. Retail prices,
as represented by the Bureau of Labor Statistics index of the cost
of living, which had never risen as high as wholesale prices, fell
between 12 and 13 per cent in the two years.[2] Industrial production also declined, but not so much as wholesale prices. It had
reached its high point in the third quarter of 1919 at 19 per cent
above the 1914 level. At the low point of 1921 in the second quarter
of that year, it was 2 per cent higher than in 1914. The gross
national product in terms of 1914 prices was reduced from $40.1
billion in 1920 to $37.6 billion in 1921.[3] Though no accurate figures
of unemployment exist for the period, it is estimated that in 1921
there were 4,754,000 out of work.[4] The crash brought about more
than 100,000 bankruptcies. Before the reckoning was finally complete, 453,000 farmers had lost their farms.

[1] Mills, *Prices in Recession and Recovery*, p. 39.
[2] *Federal Reserve Bulletin* (October, 1945), p. 1049.
[3] Kuznets, *National Product in Wartime*, pp. 135–136.
[4] Hovenstine, "Lessons of World War I."

DEFLATIONARY FORCES

The fiscal policy of the United States government led to a sudden stoppage of the stream of purchasing power entering this country on European account, and also put an end to the stimulation of domestic purchasing power that it had been exerting. Whereas the government had been spending every year many billions more than it had extracted from the current income of the population, it now suddenly began to spend less than it received. This reversal took place in the last quarter of 1919, and in the first six months of 1920 the excess of receipts over expenditures on the part of the Treasury amounted to $831 million. This contrasts violently with the nearly $9 billion excess of expenditures over receipts in the last half of 1918.[5] Within the space of a little more than a year, therefore, the American economy had to absorb a net decline in purchasing power stemming from governmental sources that amounted to approximately one quarter of the total national income. This was perhaps the most fundamental influence of all in the deflation.

The change in fiscal policy was brought about not only by the cessation of war borrowing, but also by the fact that taxes were increased. The act of February 24, 1919, set the normal income tax on corporations at 12 per cent for the preceding year and 10 per cent for subsequent years. The normal tax for individuals was boosted to 8 per cent on all incomes of $4,000 and above. Additional revenues, as a result of this law, were received in 1919 on 1918 profits and incomes. Naturally, the inflation of 1920 also affected the tax receipts. Tax policy was governed largely by the belief that the budget must be balanced as soon as possible and a start made at reduction of the debt.

The reduction of government spending would not alone have brought deflation if the private sector of the economy had achieved a compensating increase in activity, and if this activity had been of a productive rather than a speculative nature. In that case, an expansion of bank credit for legitimate business purposes would have sustained the general purchasing power when government deficit spending was withdrawn. But the banks had already extended their business loans nearly to the legal limit while the

[5] Samuelson and Hagen, *After the War*, p. 23.

federal government still had a deficit, and these loans were being employed largely for speculative purposes. By 1920, the total of physical production was not so large as when the volume of purchasing power had been considerably smaller.

What occurred in federal reserve policy in 1920 was almost inevitable, given what had preceded it. The total of loans and discounts had risen so far that the legal reserve limit was rapidly being approached. Further expansion could not have been allowed without either an amendment to the law changing this limit or some action that would have increased the reserves. Either or both, though difficult, might have been possible. There is a real question, however, whether such action would have averted the crisis.

Bankers were well aware that speculative activities were increasing prices and that this speculation was being supported by credit. They knew from experience that all speculative booms must collapse sometime, and they knew that the higher the climb the harder the fall. They also observed, with justified concern, that most of the outstanding commercial loans were being renewed instead of being paid off. Thus a danger to the stability of the entire banking system was developing through frozen short-term credit. In these circumstances, the federal reserve authorities warned the member banks against renewal of loans and raised the rediscount rates. The total volume of credit and of purchasing power began slowly to contract. Merchants and manufacturers who could no longer carry their inventories by means of bank credit were forced to sell at reduced prices. The fall of prices in turn endangered more loans and induced further credit restrictions. The downward spiral of deflation was in process.

In the last months of 1919, the Federal Reserve Bank of New York had begun to raise its rediscount rates. At the end of that year, the rates stood at 4¾ per cent for all classes of loans except agricultural. Near the end of January, 1920, the general rate was advanced to 5½ per cent, and on June 1 it was raised to 7 per cent. Not all the reserve districts maintained the same rediscount rates. In general, those in agricultural regions held their rates lower in spite of the fact that in many of them reserves fell below the legal minimum and they had to borrow from other reserve banks.[6]

The high point of rediscounted loans by the reserve banks was

[6] Steiner, *Money and Banking*, pp. 873–880.

reached in three industrial districts—Boston, Philadelphia, and Cleveland—near the beginning of 1920. In some other districts the peak was not reached until the end of the year. For the system as a whole, rediscounts touched a maximum of $2.8 billion on October 29, 1920, and then fell steadily until they had declined to $397 million at the end of August, 1922. Federal reserve notes in circulation were reduced by more than $1 billion during 1921 alone.[7]

The rediscount rate of the New York Reserve Bank was first reduced from 7 per cent on May 5, 1921, and thereafter fell rapidly until it reached 4 per cent in June, 1922. This action was taken in an effort to cushion the fall of prices and credit that was well under way. It was justified on the grounds of narrower banking policy by the fact that reserves were being increased once more by the import of gold, consequent upon the refusal of further credits to foreign purchasers, and by the fact that the total of loans had been rapidly reduced.[8]

It has subsequently been discovered that increase of interest rates by the banks is a much less efficient instrument of credit restriction than was supposed when the Federal Reserve System was formed. At times when purchasing power is being poured into the economy, when production is active and confidence is strong, people do not care how high may be the interest that they have to pay as long as the profits they make or expect to make from the borrowed money are higher still. This experience suggests that the action of the federal reserve authorities in 1920 would not alone have been sufficient to cause a collapse. Other and more fundamental factors must have been at work.

FALL OF CROP PRICES

One of these forces was a reduction in demand for exports, especially of farm products. The dollar volume of exports was falling rapidly all through 1920, and agricultural prices began to drop sharply by the middle of that year. For instance, wool, for which farmers had been getting as high as 60 cents in 1918, dropped to 19.6 cents in the next two years. Corn, which cost at the farm $1.88 in August, 1919, fell to 42 cents before the end of 1921. Wheat, which had been selling at $2.50 or more a bushel, fell

[7] *Ibid.*
[8] *Ibid.*

below $1.00 in the fall of 1921. Agricultural prices in general fell almost to their prewar level during the deflation.[9]

What lay behind this disastrous collapse of agricultural prices? The first element was that the huge war demand at very high prices had led the farmers to expand their acreage and the numbers of their livestock to such an extent that production after the armistice was considerably greater than that which had been sufficient to meet the war need. The surplus of supply did not at once become evident because during 1919 it was moving into storage on the basis of speculative demand. Because of the shipping shortage, surplus stocks had been built up during the war in other regions of agricultural production such as Argentina and Australia. After the war, shipping space increased rapidly, and these more distant sources of supply came back into the market. The former belligerent nations in Europe also began to resume normal agricultural production. It is therefore not strange that supplies available to European consumers began to exceed the demand at the prices charged.

Those who opposed this explanation of agricultural deflation pointed out that during 1920 there was no decrease in the physical volume of crops exported to Europe, as there was in the volume of manufactured exports. How, they asked, could a reduction of demand explain a fall in price if a hungry Europe was importing and eating more than before? The answer is simple. There is no doubt that Europe needed the food and was glad to get it. There is also, however, no doubt that it did not have as much money as before with which to buy it. The market surpluses moved into consumption, but only at reduced prices. When supply exceeds demand, a new balance can be brought about in either of two ways—by a reduction of supply or by a reduction of price. Farmers, competing with each other both nationally and on a world market, find it difficult to reduce their output in a short period of time and traditionally do not do so. Manufacturers, on the other hand, find it much easier to curtail their production when prices fall and therefore limit the price reduction by diminishing the supply of goods for sale. As will be seen in more detail somewhat later, this was exactly what occurred in the postwar deflation.

[9] *Yearbook of Agriculture, 1928* (Washington: Government Printing Office, 1928), pp. 957, 714, 686.

CONSUMERS' DEMAND

One of the most widely accepted current explanations of the deflation was that of a buyers' strike by American consumers. The cost of living was seeking the clouds in early 1920. Retail consumers were unquestionably both inconvenienced and angry over their reduced purchasing power. The theory advanced was that they became so disgusted that they simply stopped buying anything they could possibly do without, and that this removal of consumers' support caused the whole inverted pyramid of inflation to tumble.

There is no statistical support for this theory. In so far as the figures are known, there is no evidence of a drop in sales at retail such as a deliberate strike by consumers would be expected to cause. As a matter of fact, consumer expenditures seem to have been larger in 1920 than in 1919. The outlay of consumers is estimated at $53.9 billion in 1919 and $62.9 billion in 1920. In 1921, it dropped to $56.1 billion. In terms of constant purchasing power (1929 prices), consumers bought $48.9 billion in 1919, $50.9 billion in 1920, and $53.6 billion in 1921.[10]

It probably is true, however, that something considerably less dramatic did take place in the stimulus which consumers' buying offered to production. While those with small incomes continued to spend as freely as they could, they did not have enough money to buy, at the high prices charged in 1920, so large a volume of physical goods as had been produced. The amount of goods that consumers bought was not so great, in 1920, as the amount offered for sale, and the effect was felt in an enlargement of stocks on hand. Businessmen, acutely conscious of the popular resentment of high prices, began to fear that they could not dispose of all they had ordered. This psychological influence, combined with the inventories, led to a sudden flood of cancellations of orders. The speculative boom in inventories thus collapsed at the very time that bank credit to hold those inventories began to be withdrawn. The consequence was distress sales and falling prices. The enlarged consumer outlay in 1921 (in physical terms) took place at a time that production of goods decreased and represents an absorption of the swollen inventories at reduced prices.

[10] Simon Kuznets, *National Income and Its Composition* (New York: National Bureau of Economic Research, 1941), pp. 137, 147.

This chain of events fails to provide evidence for the contemporary theory that the collapse was attributable to deliberate policy on the part of banking authorities. The theory was particularly prevalent in the agricultural regions, which had always suspected the motives of eastern banking control. The argument ran that the money power was mainly interested in its investments in bonds and other long-term securities. Income from fixed investments becomes worth much less in terms of purchasing power when commodity prices are high. It had long been a popular maxim that creditors gain by deflation, while debtors lose by it. Not only does the man of money profit by his increased purchasing power when prices fall, but he can, with his larger reserve, acquire more property by foreclosing mortgages and buying distressed businesses at a few cents on the dollar. Though the charge lacked substantiation, it was also alleged that prominent banking executives were on the short side of the stock and commodity markets.

No doubt those in positions of power in the financial centers sometimes have motives of this kind, and banking traditions give evidence that such motives may also have an unconscious effect. Nevertheless, the facts of the situation do not support this charge in the particular instance under discussion. As a matter of fact, during the preceding two years, banking policy had taken exactly the opposite course: rather, it had been too liberal in its extension of credit, and too optimistic about continued prosperity at the existing high price level. The Federal Reserve System is more to be criticized for its encouragement of inflation in 1919 than for its deflationary activity thereafter.

NO BUILDING EXPANSION

While manufacturing industry was contracting its output because it had produced more than could be sold at current prices, building was producing less than homeseekers demanded. The shortage created by the war years was still far from being made up. Rents were rising and did not suffer from the deflation as did other prices. Building costs were high also, but probably had not risen so much as rents. It therefore might have been expected that the building boom which had begun would continue to grow. If it had done so, it might have provided a substantial check to the depression. The construction industry is one of the largest in the country and normally provides an outlet for savings that would otherwise not be used. It not only directly provides employment and income to a large number of persons when it is active, but furnishes a large fraction of the demand for the output of other industries, such as lumber, steel, cement, brick, plumbing supplies, and the like. Building, however, after reaching a temporary peak in April, 1920, began rapidly to decline. Three months later it was less by one third, and kept going down until, at the end of the year, it approached the low levels of the war.[11] Never was the fact more clearly illustrated that the actual need of the population for even the basic essentials of life does not under all conditions of a private-enterprise economy call forth the production of those essentials.

Two reasons may be assigned for this failure of a useful activity at the moment of crisis. One is that buildings are long-term investments and, in order to repay the owner and mortgagor, must earn a profit over many years. Aware of the prevalent inflation, many of these were shrewd enough to foresee that the existing high rents might later fall and that the prices of materials were likewise due for a collapse. It was therefore the part of wisdom to wait until deflation had run its course. The other reason, more compelling, affected also those who were not so shrewd. During the boom so much money was being made in the stock market and in speculation of other kinds, and the interest paid for this money was so high, that mortgage loans were almost unobtainable. After the boom, the tightness of credit affected building. The chance of quick and transitory profits thus inhibited the legitimate productive activity of the country.

EFFECTS ON AGRICULTURE AND INDUSTRY

The effect of the price deflation was distressing to all elements in the national community, but injured them in different ways and with different degrees of permanency. The physical output of agriculture scarcely declined at all. Indeed, 1920 was a bumper crop year. The prices of agricultural products, however, plummeted almost to the prewar level. This decline caused a loss to farmers who had bought land at the inflated prices, and virtually wiped out their war profits. It left them, moreover, with expanded

11 Samuelson and Hagen, *After the War*, p. 21.

facilities for production that were to be employed for many years and were to keep crop prices down. Many of those who had borrowed money to buy land were in an even worse predicament when their mortgages were foreclosed and they had to make an entirely new start. Although efforts were made to provide easier credit to enable the farmers to meet their difficulties, these efforts were not effective on the whole and in the long run. The farmers could not look forward to a revival of their European market on anything like the war scale. The trend of agricultural exports had been downward even before the war, and was to continue so after it. Fundamental influences at work in producing this result included the slowly rising levels of cost in America, the competition of newer agricultural regions, and the shift of the United States from the status of a debtor nation to that of a creditor one.

Industry was affected in quite a different way. Instead of maintaining their production, manufacturing establishments cut it sharply, so that in 1921 physical output of manufactures was down almost to the prewar level. In consequence, prices of manufactured goods did not fall so far as those of agricultural products. They were still, in 1921, 66 per cent above 1913.[12] The price deflation of industrial goods was, however, sharp enough to cause financial difficulties to many business concerns, especially in view of the large inventories they had built up. Book profits arising from values of goods on hand were quickly wiped out. Bank loans based on this collateral were called or not renewed, and many a small business in a position to operate profitably at the new and lower levels of prices was forced into bankruptcy simply because of the drop in the value of its inventory. The number of failures was high, and the tendency of industry to become concentrated in the larger and stronger units was hastened.

Industrial labor, in turn, suffered unemployment as a result of this reduction in activity. The number of wage earners in manufacturing industries was reduced by almost one quarter between 1919 and 1921, and fell almost to the depression level of 1914. Those who did retain their jobs did not have so many hours of employment, the man-hours worked falling in the same period by about 28 per cent.[13] There was at the time no unemployment insurance

[12] Mills, *Economic Tendencies in the United States*, pp. 221–222.
[13] Fabricant, *Labor Savings in American Industry*, p. 46.

or organized governmental relief, and the unemployed had to sub-sist as best they could either on their savings or on charity. No doubt an unemployed worker at this period would gladly have exchanged places with the farmer who, though he had suffered financial reverses, still had a job and enough to eat.

The owners of big business were relatively little affected, as far as their current income was concerned, by this sharp cut in output and prices. The corporations had built up such huge sur-pluses during the war and the postwar inflation that they were able to keep on paying dividends and interest almost without interrup-tion. Dividends, of course, suffered, falling from $3.2 billion in 1920 to $2.9 billion in 1921. The latter figure was, however, larger than the total of 1919. The interest paid actually increased in the year of depression, largely because immediately after the war there had been a large flotation of interest-bearing securities by busi-ness, and there were few bankruptcies among the bigger concerns. The net result was a decline of not more than $32 million in divi-dends and interest together from 1920 to 1921; in both years the total exceeded 1919. If income from rent is also included, prop-erty income advanced steadily throughout the deflation, while farmers were being pushed to the wall and the earnings of those receiving wages and salaries were cut by about $9 billion.[14]

Both employers and wage earners were eventually benefited by the deflation as the farmers were not. Since crop prices had fallen more than other prices and remained at a low level when the deflation was over, the purchasing power of the farmers for the goods they bought fell about 25 per cent and did not wholly recover for many years. Manufacturers, on the other hand, came out of the deflation with a wider margin between the prices of the raw materials they had to buy and the prices received for their finished goods than had existed either during the war or before it. For instance, in 1921, the prices of raw materials were 25 per cent above 1913, while the prices of manufactured goods were 63 per cent above it.[15] This increased margin allowed the manufacturers more money for labor, overhead, and profits. Although the mar-gin was somewhat narrowed in the subsequent recovery, it re-mained a potent encouragement to industry.

[14] Kuznets, *National Income and Its Composition*, pp. 316, 318, 314.
[15] Mills, *Economic Tendencies in the United States*, pp. 210, 205.

Manufacturing labor, in turn, though it suffered from wage reductions, benefited by a steep decline in the cost of living, so that at the end of the period of deflation those who were still employed could buy more with the wages they received than during the war. The average annual real earnings of those who were employed rose from 6 per cent above 1914 in 1920 to 8 per cent above in 1921. This increase in purchasing power occurred in spite of the fact that their average money earnings were reduced from 118 per cent above 1914 to 91 per cent above it.[16] An entirely unpremeditated gain, it resulted from the fact that wage rates were more resistant to change than were retail prices. Naturally, the figure does not take account of the losses in family incomes and in the purchasing power of labor as a whole that arose from the unemployment prevailing in the year of depression.

[16] Douglas, *Real Wages in the United States*, p. 460.

CHAPTER VI

Recovery and Expansion

IN 1922, recovery from the postwar depression began. The American economy entered a period of expansion that continued with only minor interruptions until the crisis of 1929. The index of wholesale prices, which in 1921 was 97.6 (base 1926 = 100), became stabilized at about that level. It did fall to 96.7 in 1922 and rose again in subsequent years of prosperity, but it never went above 104 or below 95 in the postwar decade. Industrial production, according to the index of the Federal Reserve Board (1933–1939 = 100), evinced a remarkable and fairly steady rise from 58 in 1921 to 110 in 1929.[1] In the first year of recovery, it jumped from 58 to 73. Production at the end of the period was more than one third greater than in the boom year of 1920. The national income grew apace with the output of goods, being only slightly affected by changes in prices. In 1921, it was $56.5 billion and in 1929, $87.1 billion.[2] Eliminating the effect of price changes (1929 = 100), the income per unit of the population grew from $522 in 1921 to $716 in 1929.[3] It will be well to obtain a broad view of the course of the economy in its entirety during this period before examining its effect on the life of the nation in more detail.

[1] *Federal Reserve Bulletin* (October, 1945), p. 1049.
[2] Kuznets, *National Income and Its Composition*, p. 137.
[3] *Ibid.*, p. 153.

ECONOMIC GROWTH, 1921–1929

Year	Industrial Production	Wholesale Prices	National Income (*Billions*)	Real Income Per Capita (1929 Prices)
1921	58	97.6	$59.4	$522
1922	73	96.7	60.7	553
1923	88	100.6	71.6	634
1924	82	98.1	72.1	633
1925	90	103.5	76.0	644
1926	96	100.0	81.6	678
1927	95	95.4	80.1	674
1928	99	96.7	81.7	676
1929	110	95.3	87.2	716

Sources: For Industrial Production and Wholesale Prices, *Federal Reserve Bulletin* (October, 1945), p. 1049. For National Income and Real Income Per Capita, Simon Kuznets, *National Income and Its Composition, 1919–1938* (New York: National Bureau of Economic Research, 1941), pp. 137, 153.

PRICES AND RECOVERY

Why is it that business activities and employment start up again after a speculative boom has been ended by a deflation of prices and credit? The popular theory is that when prices rise "too high" they must necessarily fall, and that when they have fallen enough, the normal economic life of the country can continue. But this statement of the case begs the whole question. How does anyone know when prices are too high, and what does he mean when he says they have fallen enough? What is the correct level for prices, by comparison with which one can judge whether they are too high, or too low, or just right?

In a country which, like Great Britain, depends largely on foreign trade, prices may be too high to encourage the necessary exports. Theoretically, this situation could be remedied either by a reduction of the internal price level or by a devaluation of the monetary unit in terms of gold, so that the rates of foreign exchange would be more favorable to the country in question. The industrial economy of the United States, however, has never in peacetime been sufficiently dependent on foreign trade so that such considerations were matters of primary importance. They did not have much to do either with the business depression of 1921 or with the recovery that succeeded it. Although the decline of prices for crops undoubtedly prevented a drop in the volume of agricultural exports in 1921, this was hardly a case in point,

since the reduction of European demand for American grain after
the war arose from other factors than high prices.

Since the top limits of currency and credit are usually supposed to be fixed by adherence to a gold standard, it is also held
that prices can be too high in relation to the gold reserves of the
nation in question. The higher prices rise, the larger is the purchasing power necessary to carry on production and trade. If the
amount of this money and credit becomes so large that the gold
in the reserve will not support it, according to the legislation fixing the limits of circulation, there must be a reduction of credit
and currency, and prices must fall. After they have fallen to a
point where the gold reserve becomes ample again, economic
activity may be resumed.

This kind of limitation has played an important part in certain crises of inflation and deflation. After all, however, it is an
arbitrary one, established by law or custom. If there were no
consideration involved aside from maintaining a fixed relationship
between currency and gold, the gold standard might well be
modified or even abandoned. As a matter of fact, it has been made
far more elastic in the course of time, as a result of natural efforts
to release the needs of the people from so Procrustean a bed. But
in instances when the gold standard has been abandoned entirely,
and virtually unlimited issuance of currency has been permitted, the
results have been unfortunate. Inflation can be allowed to go on
until prices reach astronomical heights, but this is no guarantee
that major disturbances in economic life will not result. It is virtually a guarantee of the opposite. And if at any point the course
of inflation is stopped by a cessation of currency expansion, deflation and falling prices are likely to ensue.

These phenomena do not prove that there is any magic virtue
in the gold standard. What they do indicate is that there are other
reasons why a rapid increase of prices is undesirable, and why,
when such an increase has occurred, a drop to a lower level of
prices usually follows.

The disturbance caused by a rapid upward movement of
prices results in part from the fact that when this occurs, they go
up unevenly. It is more difficult to increase production of some
things than of others. Some kinds of prices respond more readily
to a heavy excess of demand over supply than do others. The

profits of those engaged in production and trade usually rise more
than wages and salaries, and speculators for the rise make the
greatest gains of all. The rapid shift in the customary distribution
of income upsets any balance that has been achieved in the flow
of purchasing power. Scarcities of goods are intensified in some
markets, while surpluses are built up at other points. Energy and
money are diverted from production to the passing of goods or
paper from hand to hand. Finally, the hope of speculative gain
becomes uncertain because the speculators are unable to dispose
of their holdings, at the prevailing prices, to purchasers who expect to keep and use the products or property. The bubble is
pricked, and monetary gains vanish through a fall of prices resulting from a sudden excess of supply over demand in important
markets. None of these consequences need occur if all prices and
incomes should, by some miracle, rise or fall by exactly the same
amount, or if the changes in the interrelation among prices and
incomes should take place more gradually.

WHY PRODUCTION EXPANDED

What, then, was the reason why production began to expand
again in 1922? Clearly it was not because prices as a whole had
fallen to any mathematically "correct" level. It is true that, partly
because of their fall, the gold reserve had now become more than
sufficient, and the reserve ratio had risen to a point where credit
could be freely extended. But this was a passive rather than an
active factor. Money is not always borrowed just because it is
available. The borrower must expect that he can make profitable
use of money before he will pay the interest on a loan. What was
it that gave businessmen this assurance? In part, the drastic fall
of prices may have provided what is called by economists a
"psychological motive," since businessmen shared the general belief that when prices had fallen sufficiently recovery was certain
to come. Nevertheless, no one of them could be sure the bottom
had been reached until after an upturn of prices had actually
occurred. Some more specific influence must have been at work.

The stimulus, whatever it was, must be sought in the private
sector of the economy. The excess of governmental expenditures
over receipts had been replaced by an excess of receipts over
expenditures. No more public loans were being made to foreign

governments; indeed, by this time these governments had begun to pay back interest and principal. Since the Treasury had ceased flotation of bonds on a large scale, there was no longer any impulse from this source leading to the expansion of bank loans to private borrowers. Nor had the new administration introduced positive measures of any kind to aid recovery or relieve unemployment, if one excepts removal of the excess-profits tax. Its avowed purpose was to withdraw as far as possible from exerting any influence on the economic life of the country except the encouragement that might be derived from a balanced budget and nonintervention with private enterprise. Although the standard Republican prescription for prosperity, the protective tariff, had been administered, it was incapable of producing recovery because there had been little competition from imports.

In the area of private enterprise itself, no important stimulus came from outside the country. While some effects of European reconstruction and relief expenditures were still being felt, and while a trickle of private credits flowed to foreign purchasers, the value of exports continued at about the same low level they had reached in 1921. In sum, an economic order that for about six years had largely been nourished by orders from abroad and huge governmental spending by the United States was now left to its own devices.

There is good ground for believing that the turning point was marked by nothing more substantial than changes that had taken place in figures on the books of business concerns. At the beginning of the deflation, many a manufacturing or distributing company had found itself in the following position: It had a large stock of goods on hand bought at high prices. While prices fell and this inventory was either being sold at a loss or revalued at the lower current prices, the mere change in value turned up on the books as an operating deficit. It therefore looked as if production and trade were unprofitable. Nevertheless, all through the period of deflation, there was a sufficient margin between the prices of materials and the prices of finished products so that the company in question could have made a profit on the purchase and sale of new goods at any given moment. When the inventory losses had been absorbed and the loans on the inventories had been liquidated, the possibilities of profit making in current production and trade became clear. They had existed all the time, but had been obscured by the fog of accounting and credit symbolism.

The size of the incubus that was rolled off the back of the business order may be judged by the estimate that during 1919 the value of business inventories had been increased by $6 billion, or nearly four times as much as that of any other single year in the ensuing decade except 1923. Of this increase about $4 billion was due to a growth in the actual quantity of goods on hand and $2 billion to the mere rise in prices.[4] These figures were enhanced in the early months of 1920 and then underwent a rapid reduction after the speculative boom cracked. Observation of this phenomenon has led many economists to describe the period as one of inventory boom and depression.

The question may be asked how businessmen could be sure, even though there was a sufficient margin of profit on each unit of production, that the goods could be sold. Doubtless they had little assurance except the perennial hope that rises in the breast of the seeker after profit. Nevertheless, at this time a number of substantial factors made certain the fulfillment of the hope. Study of economic statistics over a long period of years shows that consumers' demands, especially for perishable goods, are remarkably stable, varying less than any other element in the economy, even between full prosperity and extreme depression. Because of unemployment, wage reductions, and the difficulties of the farmers, the dollar volume of consumers' spending, of course, dropped somewhat during the depression. It did not, however, drop so rapidly as the prices of the goods that consumers bought. Actual expenditures by consumers fell, it is estimated, from $62.9 billion in 1920 to $56.1 billion in 1921, or about 11 per cent.[5] They remained about at this level in 1922. When, however, the effect of price changes is taken into consideration, and these spendings are expressed in terms of dollars of constant value (1929 = 100), there was an increase of $3.7 billion from 1920 to 1921 and a further increase of $3.2 billion from 1921 to 1922.[6] In the latter year, consumers were buying a volume of goods and services more than

[4] Simon Kuznets, *Commodity Flow and Capital Formation* (New York: National Bureau of Economic Research, 1938), Vol. I, Pt. VII, Table VII-6.
[5] Kuznets, *National Income and Its Composition*, p. 137.
[6] *Ibid.*, p. 147.

12 per cent larger than at the peak of the postwar boom. The purchasing power flowing into the retail markets from consumers thus constituted a steadily increasing reinforcement to the profit possibilities noted by businessmen.

One important element in this increase of purchasing power has previously been noted. During the deflation, wage rates had fallen less than the cost of living. For every hour's work, therefore, the average wage earner could now buy more than he had been able to purchase at any time during the war or the postwar boom. As production was resumed and the total hours of employment increased, a sharply augmented total of purchasing power in the hands of the wage earners sustained the advance. Thus the business community now profited from the resistance labor had offered to wage reductions when employers had been arguing that drastic reductions were necessary in order to stimulate recovery.

The average annual earnings of employed wage earners in terms of constant purchasing power (1914 = 100) according to Paul Douglas, was 8 per cent above the base year in 1921, 13 per cent above in 1922, and 19 per cent above in 1923. During the next two years, the figure remained about at this level and then increased again, reaching 32 per cent above in 1928.[7]

Aside from this increased consumer buying, the major factor adding to the stream of purchasing power was the revival of residential construction. A good estimate of the amount spent in this way indicates an increase of slightly more than $1 billion between 1921 and 1922. Every factor was favorable: the price of materials had fallen, rents still remained relatively high, plenty of money was available for mortgages, the labor supply was abundant, and a severe housing shortage was still to be made up. At the time, construction was the only outlet for savings, in which a considerable expansion occurred. Business construction increased between 1921 and 1922 only about $500 million.[8] There was an actual reduction between these years in the investment in other producers' durable goods, as well as in inventories and the foreign

[7] Douglas, *Real Wages in the United States*, p. 391; data for 1926–1928 from P. H. Douglas and F. T. Jennison, *The Movement of Money and Real Earnings in the United States, 1926–1928* (Chicago: University of Chicago School of Commerce and Administration, Studies in Business Administration), Vol. I, No. 3.
[8] Kuznets, *Commodity Flow and Capital Formation*, Vol. I, Pt. VI, Table VI–6.

balance. The government, of course, was paying off loans instead of borrowing. In subsequent years, savings found an outlet not only in residential building but in capital investments of business as well, and the building boom remained a powerful factor of expansion for five years.

The federal reserve index of value of construction contracts awarded (1923–1925 = 100) rose steadily from 56 in 1921 to 135 in 1928. A similar index of residential construction increased from 44 to a temporary peak of 124 in 1925, dropped slightly in the next two years, and finally attained its high point for the period at 126 in 1928.

THE COURSE OF RECOVERY

Recovery continued in 1923. In fact, activity rose so rapidly that a minor peak of the business cycle was reached and a moderate recession occurred in 1924. This time, inflation played little part in the variation of economic forces, since prices remained relatively stable, and their interrelationships changed much less than in the previous years. With the recovery in employment, the expenditures of consumers jumped nearly $7 billion from 1922 to 1923.[9] Each dollar could buy almost as much in the second year as in the first. Private investment kept on growing, and the construction boom continued. Financially, business was in a sounder condition than ever. How, then, can one account for the recession of 1924? Examination of the available figures reveals only one major factor that showed wide variation in these two years—the value of inventories. The dollar value of goods in business hands increased by over $3 billion in 1923.[10] Since the rise in prices was not great, this represented almost entirely an expansion of the quantity of goods on hand. Apparently, business was again producing or preparing to produce more than the purchasing power in the hands of the public would allow it to buy at the prices charged. This occurred in spite of the fact that consumers' purchasing power was rapidly increasing. The natural result was a correction of the "overproduction," in the form of a reduction in inventories, brought about by a decline in production and a slight decrease in prices. The recession was short, however, because consumers' outlay kept

[9] Kuznets, *National Income and Its Composition*, p. 137.
[10] *Ibid.*

on growing, though temporarily at a diminished rate, and the building boom made further progress.

The wholesale price level was 4 per cent higher in 1923 than in 1922, and during the recession of the following year it fell back to 1.4 per cent above 1922. The physical volume of industrial production, excluding building, increased 12 per cent from 1922 to 1923 and declined 6 per cent in the following year.[11] These figures do not indicate an important interruption in the general upward trend. The recovery that had already taken place had narrowed but had not eliminated the wide margin between cost of materials and price of finished products, which was acting as a bait to manufacturers. The total cost of materials used by representative manufacturing industries in 1923 was 134.6 per cent higher than in 1914, whereas the value of the products turned out by these industries was, in 1923, 149 per cent higher than in 1914.[12]

The minor boom and recession that took place in 1923 and 1924 was probably somewhat moderated by the first coordinated attempt of the Federal Reserve System to stabilize prices and reduce the swings in the business cycle. In June, 1922, the policies of the several federal reserve banks in the purchase and sale of government securities and bankers' acceptances in the open market were brought under unified control by the creation of an Open Market Committee covering all of them. They soon proceeded to sell government bonds, and by the middle of 1923 they had disposed of an amount totaling $525 million.[13] When the reserve banks sell securities, the effect is to restrict the expansion of purchasing power because the money paid for these securities is drawn out of circulation. Since the business community had been educated to understand the purpose of this activity, it also served as a warning and probably had some psychological effect. The New York Reserve Bank raised its rediscount rate early in 1923 in order to discourage credit expansion. After the decline of prices and production had begun, rediscount rates were reduced again in 1924 and the reserve banks renewed their buying of government bonds. The reserve bank authorities not only wished to curb busi-

[11] *Federal Reserve Bulletin* (October, 1945), p. 1049.
[12] Mills, *Economic Tendencies in the United States*, p. 221.
[13] Steiner, *Money and Banking*, p. 882.

ness fluctuations by these changes but, when rates were reduced, also desired to encourage foreign borrowing in the American market and so to stimulate exports.

In 1925, advance was resumed again with an increase of 7 per cent in the volume of physical production. In 1926 another 6 per cent gain occurred, bringing the output of industry about 24 per cent above 1922. Prices during these years varied little, remaining close to the 1922 level.[14] The expenditures of consumers continued to grow, and so provided a market for the increased output. Whereas in 1922 they had spent about $58 billion for goods and services, in 1926 they spent over $73 billion. Some of this increase went to the occupations supplying services, such as garages, purveyors of entertainment, transportation, beauty shops, and the like. About an equal amount of the increase was paid for perishable goods like food. Most striking of all, a 50 per cent increase occurred in the purchases of durable goods like automobiles, furniture, and household equipment. The dollar value of the increase in this category, however, was smaller than that for perishables and services, the amount spent on durable goods at the beginning of the period having been considerably less than that expended for other types of goods and services. The retail buying of semidurable goods like clothing increased very little.[15]

This distribution of consumers' purchases marked the growing importance of the market for the "durable goods" not used up every day or every week, the sales of which are financed to a considerable extent out of credit or savings, and the production of which consequently is likely to vary more from time to time than that of the daily necessities. While in the long run this factor added a substantial element of instability to the business order, for the time being the curve of prosperity floated upward on the increased output of automobiles, radios, electric refrigerators, and minor innovations in household equipment. If older kinds of durable goods like construction, house furnishings, and new productive facilities in private industry are also taken into account, the importance of this sector of the economy is revealed by the fact that the production of durable goods increased 51 per cent between 1922 and 1926, whereas the production of nondurable and semidurable

---

[14] *Federal Reserve Bulletin* (October, 1945), p. 1049.
[15] Kuznets, *National Income and Its Composition*, pp. 137, 285.

goods increased only 14 per cent in the same period. Between 1922 and 1929 the index of production of durable goods increased from 81 to 132; of nondurable, from 67 to 93 (1935–1939 = 100).[16]

THE CRITICAL ROLE OF INVESTMENT

This development leads directly into one of the most controversial issues of modern economic theory: the question concerning the critical factor that keeps production and employment expanding when it continues on the upgrade, and leads to a contraction when a major depression arrives. During the war it was easy to identify this factor. It was obviously the immense quantity of governmental purchases, first on the part of the Allies and then on the part of the United States. What could take the place of this stimulus when it was withdrawn? It has been shown that immediately after the war the upward trend of production was renewed by a speculative price inflation which did not last. It is also probable that after the collapse of the inflation and the liquidation of excess inventories, recovery was initiated by a change in the interrelationships of prices that set the profit motive at work again. But more than this was necessary to push the expansion forward for a period of several years.

An analysis of the figures indicates that the steadily increasing output of buildings, automobiles, and other durable goods was the most active element in this long-term expansion. This supports the inference that new investment in such durable goods is one of the principal requirements for long-continued prosperity and a high degree of employment. As a matter of fact, investment grew from about $11 billion annually in 1921 to $19 billion in 1926.[17]

The most widely accepted theory connected with this type of observation is an intricate one in its detail, but with some oversimplification its essence may be stated in a few words. If everybody always spent all the money he received, there could not be any decline in productive activity, because the total amount of purchasing power would be continually passing from hand to hand. In order to account for a decline in production and employment, therefore, it is necessary to locate a place in the stream of circulation where money that is received is not all spent by its recipients.

---

[16] *Federal Reserve Bulletin* (October, 1945), p. 1049.
[17] See table, page 120.

It seems clear that the only obstruction of this sort is where saving occurs. When individuals or business concerns save money, they obviously do not spend it.

Such saved money may be deposited in a savings bank or paid to a life insurance company or used for the purchase of stocks or bonds. If it is saved by a corporation, it may serve to swell the corporate surplus. In any event, it passes into the hands of the people who, if they return it to circulation, are likely to do so by investment in new buildings, machinery, or other capital goods. Thus a savings bank lends money on mortgages or buys bonds. A corporate surplus may be invested in new production.

The crux of the theory lies in the proposition that money is not necessarily invested as rapidly as it is saved. The decisions of banks and businessmen to invest in new production depend not on the amount that savers leave in their hands, but on the prospects for profit in investment. The habit of saving is a relatively stable one, and year in and year out people tend to lay aside about the same percentage of what they earn. New investment, however, does not proceed so regularly, since the anticipation of profit varies widely from time to time. If savings and investment grow apace, employment is stabilized and the economy expands. If, however, investment declines, an interruption in the flow of purchasing power and a drop in production and employment necessarily occur. This result leads to a reduction in income and a consequent diminution in the savings themselves. In such a crisis, three remedies are theoretically possible: first, an expansion of private investment; second, an increase in the percentage of current income spent; and third, an enlargement of governmental spending.

Whatever may be the truth of this theory, it is obvious at least that during the period under consideration, new private investment did seem to offer in large part a substitute for the stimulation that during the war had been provided by government spending. It did so largely because there was a considerable demand for building and machinery. Another important element was an active sale for automobiles, furniture, and other products of industries making durable consumers' goods, which are not ordinarily regarded as investments in the economists' discussions. The interrelationships of prices and costs were such as to render this activity profitable and so to provide an incentive for the investments.

No figures exist by which the Keynes hypothesis may be proved, since it is difficult, if not impossible, to infer from general statistics the actual sequence of cause and effect in economic fluctuations. It is impossible even to compare the course of total savings, in terms of the money withheld from current spending, with the course of money actually invested, because no good figures exist as yet for such withholdings on the part of individuals. All one can say is that the aggregate figures that are known are not inconsistent with the hypothesis. For instance, the accompanying table of gross capital formation reveals marked advances in this figure at the peaks of the business cycle, as in 1920, 1923, 1926, and 1929. It reveals decreases in years of depression or recession like 1921, 1924, and 1927. Gross capital formation does not include deductions for depreciation and hence is a better measure of the effect of capital expenditures on economic activity for short periods than net capital formation, which does allow for such deductions.

Within the total of gross capital formation, the widest fluctuations are found in business inventories and producers' durable goods. Public construction and claims against foreign countries are the least responsive to the movement of business cycles. In consequence, business investment is without question the most violently fluctuating element in the stream of purchasing power.

Purchases made by consumers fluctuate much less widely in terms of percentage change than do expenditures for capital goods. Consumers' spending, however, is a larger element in the total national income than is new investment. A minor percentage change in consumer outlay may therefore mean a considerable alteration in the amount of dollars contributed to the stream of spending. Interesting comparisons may be made between the annual changes of gross capital formation and consumers' outlay in the accompanying table. Thus, between 1920 and 1921, capital formation decreased by nearly $11 billion while consumers' outlay fell by nearly $7 billion. In the recovery from 1921 to 1923 capital formation grew by $6.5 billion, while consumers' outlay rose by $6.9 billion. A most interesting comparison is that for the 1924 recession. Capital formation dropped under the preceding year $2.9 billion (mainly because of reduction of inventories), while consumers' outlay actually increased $3.2 billion. There can therefore be no doubt which was the major element in this downward movement of the cycle.

Comparisons of such large aggregates, which rest on so many assumptions, cannot lead to any but rough conclusions. Above all, they cannot prove that the movement of either total resulted from the movement of the other. Over a series of years, these factors are

CAPITAL FORMATION AND
CONSUMERS' OUTLAY

(Current prices—billion dollars)

Year	Gross Capital Formation	Consumers' Outlay
1919	19.2	53.9
1920	21.9	62.9
1921	11.1	56.1
1922	12.2	56.2
1923	17.6	63.0
1924	14.7	66.2
1925	18.4	66.8
1926	19.0	72.3
1927	17.8	71.9
1928	17.3	74.3
1929	20.7	77.2

Sources: For the Gross Capital Formation, Simon Kuznets, *National Product since 1869* (New York: National Bureau of Economic Research, 1945), page 50. For Consumers' Outlay, the same author's *National Income and Its Composition*, p. 137.

interacting, since larger investment increases individual incomes, and larger consumers' outlay will probably, in the course of time, increase investments. Much more refined analysis would be necessary if light were to be thrown on the actual sequence of events.

In examining the sources of investment, it is interesting to note that over the years 1919 to 1928, corporate savings comprised less than 15 per cent of net capital formation, savings by unincorporated business comprised about 20 per cent, government savings contributed about 15 per cent, and individual savings 50 per cent.[18] It should be understood that this figure for individual savings refers only to those savings actually invested, not to the money withheld from circulation by individuals for the purpose of salting it away.

[18] Kuznets, *National Income and Its Composition*, p. 276.

RAPID ADVANCE IN PRODUCTIVITY

A development of critical importance in this period was a great gain in efficiency of production. For the decade between 1919 and 1929 the output per person employed, as well as the output per man-hour, increased with unusual rapidity. In manufacturing, the index of number of wage earners per unit of output was reduced from 84 in 1919 to 51 in 1929. The man-hours per unit fell in the same period from an index number of 74 to 42, or by 43 per cent (1899 = 100). There was little or no increase in productivity during the war. Immediately after it, however, immense gains were made, the index of man-hours per unit falling from 74 in 1919 to 55 in 1922, or by 26 per cent. Gains continued in the following years at a more moderate rate (see table below).

Increases in productivity were also registered in mining, in transportation, and even in agriculture. On steam railroads employment per unit of product decreased from 124 in 1919 to 100 in 1929. The index of the number of gainfully occupied per unit of product in agriculture fell from 84 in 1919 to 67 in 1929 (1900 = 100). The number of hours worked weekly did not fall as in manufacturing, and therefore the output per man-hour did not show such striking gains as in factories.

INDEXES OF EMPLOYMENT PER UNIT OF OUTPUT

Year	Manufacturing (1899 = 100)		Agriculture (1900 = 100) Gainfully Occupied	Railroads (1929 = 100) Man-Days	Mining (1929 = 100) Man-Days
	Wage Earners	Man-Hours			
1919	84	74	84	124	135
1920	78	67	83	120	128
1921	74	61	82	130	130
1922	64	55	81	119	119
1923	65	56	79	114	116
1924	64	53	76	114	118
1925	59	50	74	108	112
1926	57	48	71	105	112
1927	55	47	70	106	108
1928	53	44	68	102	103
1929	51	42	67	100	100

Source: Solomon Fabricant, *Labor Savings in American Industry, 1899–1939* (New York: National Bureau of Economic Research, 1945) pp. 43, 44, 45, 46, 50.

The first effect of an increase in efficiency is to reduce unit labor costs. The gain may be retained by the employer as a larger margin of profit. It may also be utilized either to pay higher wages or to reduce selling prices, or to do both at once. Increase of wages serves to enlarge the purchasing power of the wage earners, while reduction of prices naturally augments the purchasing power of all consumers. Thus the manufacturer may, through larger volume of sales, gain more in aggregate profits than he loses by cutting his widened profit margin.

If output and sales do not increase or do not increase rapidly enough, gains in productivity are likely to result in reduced employment. If the technical gains, however, are rapidly translated into increased production and sales, employment may not suffer or may even increase.

The nature and effects of the productive advances of this period will be considered in greater detail in subsequent chapters. Here it is sufficient to point out what actually happened to wages, consumers' purchasing power, employment, and the reward of capital in the aggregate.

DISTRIBUTION OF INCREASED PRODUCT, 1923–1929

Year	Employee Compensation (Million dollars)	Cost-of-Living Index	Consumers' Outlay (Billion dollars)	No. of Employees (Thousands)	Property Income (Million dollars)	Dividends (Million dollars)
1922	37,003	97.7	56.1	28,585	11,925	2,962
1923	43,339	99.5	63.0	31,351	13,211	3,745
1924	43,323	99.8	66.2	31,068	13,818	3,683
1925	45,019	102.4	66.8	31,680	14,469	4,270
1926	48,017	103.2	72.3	33,121	14,565	4,615
1927	48,433	101.2	71.9	33,201	15,065	4,918
1928	49,361	100.1	74.3	33,394	15,707	5,344
1929	52,214	100.0	77.2	35,059	16,822	6,117

Source: Kuznets, National Income and Its Composition, pp. 314, 145, 137, 318, 316.

In the accompanying table the figures for employee compensation include the effect of both the changes in wages and salaries and the changes in volume of employment, for all occupations in the country. They reveal a considerable advance during the recovery from 1922 to 1923 and then a slower growth to the peak of 1929, the gain for the entire period being about 40 per cent.

The dollars received changed little in their purchasing value throughout the period, as is shown by the cost-of-living index, which rose slightly, with a bulge in the middle of the decade. The figures for consumers' outlay include what was spent not only by employees, but also by all other members of the population. They exclude, however, that part of their incomes which people saved, as the figures for employee compensation do not. They indicate a rise in consumers' purchases for the period of slightly more than 37 per cent. The totals for numbers of employees offer a rough guide as to how much of the growth in employee compensation was due to expansion of the number employed. This gain was about 23 per cent, as compared with the 40 per cent increase in total compensation. The gain in earnings per capita was, thus, approximately 15 per cent.

Property income includes dividends, interest, and rent, as well as that part of the income of individual enterprisers which is not attributed to payment for their labor. Farmers, of course, bulked largely in this latter category. It shows a gain of something over 41 per cent, or slightly more than the gain in employee compensation. It should be remembered, however, that this total income was divided among a number of people which probably did not increase markedly during the period, as did the number of employees. While the number of stockholders grew, the number of farmers declined. The number of individual enterprisers grew about 5 per cent.

The column for dividends, which shows the gains in current income registered by the owners of corporations, takes no account of that part of the profits retained by corporations in surplus accounts. The total of dividends paid grew in the period by slightly over 100 per cent. Obviously, the corporation owners were the greatest winners from the increase in productivity. It is unlikely that their numbers increased more rapidly than those employed.

Wholesale prices reached their high point for the period in 1925 and then declined for the next two years. Though the decline was relatively moderate, the experience of an expansion of production while prices were falling was so unfamiliar that business spokesmen complained that this was a time of "profitless prosperity." Apparently investors and speculators did not regard it as profitless, however, because the stock market enjoyed a heavy increase in transactions during most of the period and the averages of stock prices had a rising trend.

In addition, the growth of profits led to a change in the methods of financing business. Many companies, especially the larger ones, accumulated enough working capital so that they financed themselves instead of resorting to borrowing, and the commercial loans extended by the banks declined. This development was, of course, accompanied by a corresponding retardation in the expansion of demand deposits. Business kept its surplus cash in time deposits, which grew almost three times as much as demand deposits between 1924 and 1927. Thus bank resources were released for collateral loans on securities, and these grew 40 per cent during the three years. This development facilitated activity in the stock market.

AGRICULTURAL DISTRESS

The prosperity of the industrial sectors of the community was not shared by the agricultural regions. It is true that the city populations increased their purchases of food, particularly of the higher grades, such as milk and other dairy products, fresh vegetables, fruit, and the better cuts of meat. This did not bring much relief to the growers of the great staples like grain and cotton. When standards of living rise above a certain point, individuals eat less bread rather than more. There was no permanent revival of the foreign markets for these crops. The average of farm prices, which had been more than double the 1913 level at the peak of the postwar boom, fell to only 16 per cent above it in 1921; although it rose slightly thereafter, it did not register a net gain of more than 10 per cent during the years of economic expansion. The prices received by farmers for their crops remained low in relation to the prices they had to pay for what they bought. In 1921, the relation of these prices was such that a farmer selling the same amount of produce that he had sold in 1913 could buy only three fourths as much with the proceeds. In 1922, he was still at a disadvantage of about 19 per cent. Although the disparity narrowed in subsequent years, it did not disappear during the whole period of industrial prosperity.[19]

Meanwhile, mortgage debts incurred during the years of high

[19] Mills, *Economic Tendencies in the United States*, p. 210.

prices were slowly and painfully being liquidated. The more fortunate farmers succeeded in retaining their property while paying the necessary charges, but a large acreage passed under the control of banks, insurance companies, and other mortgage holders.

The plight of the farmers was not, however, one of unrelieved gloom. The purchasing power of the money received for a single bushel of wheat or a bale of cotton does not tell the whole story of agricultural welfare. Output of the farms steadily increased, while the number of those engaged in agriculture slowly declined, so that there was more income to be divided among a smaller number of persons. The index of agricultural output (1900 = 100) rose from 126 in 1920–1921 to 144 in 1929, while the index of those gainfully occupied fell from 104 to 97. Farmers did, therefore, benefit from the general increase in productivity.[20]

THE BUDDING OF SPECULATION

While there were other shadows in the national picture, such as the difficulties in coal and textiles and the increase in the number of unemployed persons, the prevailing feeling was one of well-being and prosperity. Though commodity prices were no longer rising and no further speculation in inventories occurred in the business community, the rapid growth of liquid assets stimulated speculation of other kinds.

Speculation in land, which was an old American practice, broke out early in the neighborhood of the government property at Muscle Shoals, Alabama, when people thought it was about to be turned over to Henry Ford. Land booms had occurred in the agricultural regions, and southern California property enjoyed a large expansion of value as the population increased. A large share of the growth in income was channeled to those whose gains were derived from holding or dealing in real estate. (See page 170.) Although the Muscle Shoals speculation soon petered out, a much larger boom got under way in the promotion of Florida real estate. For a long time a few winter resorts in Florida had been playgrounds of the rich. Now with the advent of the automobile, the general prosperity, and increased leisure, thousands of people with moderate means were attracted to that state. Real-estate interests were not slow in exploiting this opportunity and raising

[20] Fabricant, *Labor Savings in American Industry*, p. 43.

it to larger dimensions. A large section of the public became interested in Florida, not merely for the purpose of their own enjoyment but also as a source of speculative gain. Land was sold and resold far above any value that it could permanently retain. Much of this land was unimproved and some of it was even under water. People of small means squandered their savings in the purchase of worthless tracts without ever seeing them and merely in the hope of making profits from resale. After a few years this speculative bubble burst, as its predecessors had always done. The amount of land offered for sale far exceeded the demand on the part of those who wished to retain and use it, and knowledge of the true situation gradually spread among the speculators so that they no longer wanted to buy from each other. When this occurred, prices naturally fell like a plummet, and those who had not retired from the market soon enough were left with their losses.

The incident was a significant forerunner of the speculation soon to seize the stock market. It indicated that large numbers of people were in a mood in which they believed that money could be made almost miraculously out of the mere growth of the country. Incidentally, the fact that the collapse of the Florida boom had little depressing effect on the nation's economy reassured many observers a year or two later when they observed speculative inflation in the financial markets. They assumed that the unwary would be caught when the market collapsed, but that the phenomenon was in some way insulated from legitimate business and would not affect it for better or for worse.

An account of the later years of the postwar decade, when expansion first wavered and then became converted into speculative boom and collapse, must be reserved for a later chapter. In the meantime, it is well to turn aside from the main current of the economy to see more in detail what took place in business and finance, labor, agriculture, and foreign economic relations.

CHAPTER VII

Industry, Business, Finance

BEHIND THE GAIN IN EFFICIENCY

THE rapid growth in production per unit of labor that underlay the rise in real incomes in the postwar decade resulted from a combination of many factors. The dramatic conception of the affair —that an inventor devises a new machine, that this in turn produces many more goods with fewer workers, and that as a result wages may be raised and prices reduced—is far from the whole story.

High wages may be a cause of technical advance as well as a result. In the northern blast furnaces after the war an expensive machine was introduced for casting pig iron, but in the South it was cheaper to continue the old method of sand casting because of the plentiful and relatively cheap supply of Negro labor. In consequence, productivity of blast furnaces increased less in southern than in the northern steel centers. In the decade after the war, wages in manufacturing increased about 17 per cent, while the prices of goods employed for capital equipment declined 3 per cent.[1] Since investment funds were available at low rates, this situation provided a strong financial incentive to save labor by spending more on capital equipment. The annual real earnings of the average employed wage earner jumped about 10 per cent from 1921 to 1923, and then made little further advance until the latter years of the decade;[2] it was in the immediate postwar period also that the most rapid gain in productivity occurred. It is prob-

[1] Harry Jerome, *Mechanization in Industry* (New York: National Bureau of Economic Research, 1934), p. 346.
[2] Douglas, *Real Wages in the United States*, p. 391.

able that the cost of labor stimulated improvements, improvements that in turn led to more income to be divided among the participants in production.

Another influence that facilitated gains in efficiency in this period was a delayed effect of measures inaugurated during the war itself, the full benefit of which could not be enjoyed while they were still unfamiliar and while workers shifted about rapidly and had to be trained. Mass-production methods in building ships, airplane motors, and many other goods proved themselves on a large scale at the end of the war and were later extended where volume of output was adequate to justify them and the product could be sufficiently standardized. The great addition to plant and machinery—much of it of new design—installed for war purposes now took effect in economies of peacetime production. Standardization of parts and processes, reduction of the number of styles and designs, and the methods of modern engineering management first introduced by Frederick W. Taylor, and developed by the engineers who learned from him, had been made familiar to many during the war and now were adopted on a wider scale.

A basic element in technical progress was the increase in the use of power as a substitute for human muscle, and the enhanced economy and flexibility in the employment of power itself. In earlier years the typical individual factory had bought its coal, made its steam in a hand-fired boiler, and carried the power to the workplaces by a series of steam engine, shafts, pulleys, and belts. The substitution of individual electric motors on the machines was a great advance in flexibility. In 1929 about 70 per cent of manufacture was electrified, against 30 per cent in 1914.[3] More factories now bought their power from the utility company; this in turn produced it more economically. The number of central stations decreased, while between 1917 and 1927 the power produced by them increased from 25 to 75 billion kilowatts. Oil, powdered coal, or water turbines often replaced the old sources of heat energy, and where coal was still used, mechanical stokers were introduced. The public utilities saved 47.5 per cent in their consumption of coal per kilowatt-hour between 1919 and 1929.[4] During the war their

[3] Edward C. Kirkland, *A History of American Economic Life* (New York: F. S. Crofts & Co., 1940), p. 645.

[4] Jerome, *Mechanization in Industry*, pp. 165–168.

man-hours per unit of output had already registered a remarkable drop—from an index number of 161 in 1917 to 121 in 1919, but it fell further to 100 in 1929 (the year on which the index is based).[5]

Meanwhile, improvements in efficiency were made in steam locomotives. The internal combustion engine made possible the use of trucks, tractors, and other machinery in transportation, on farms, in building construction, and in many other fields. Horsepower per worker increased, in the decade between 1919 and 1929, 49.5 per cent in manufacture, 62.2 per cent in agriculture, 60.3 per cent in mines and quarries, and 74.2 per cent on steam railroads.[6]

The shortage of unskilled labor consequent upon the virtual cessation of immigration led to a wide adoption of mechanical methods of handling materials and transporting partly finished products from one workplace to another. This technique in turn favored orderly planning of operations, facilitated further subdivision of processing, saved working space, and, through systematic routing and in other ways, cheapened and expedited production. Mechanical loading devices saved from 25 to 50 per cent of loading labor in the mining of bituminous coal; the finishing machine for cement highways saved between 40 and 60 per cent of the labor on finishing. Mechanical pavers spreading centrally mixed materials were a great advance over the roadside dump and wheelbarrow method.[7]

Finally examples of enormous savings may be cited in specific manufacturing machines. New glass machines reduced labor time 97 per cent in the production of electric bulbs; the productivity of labor in lamp assembly plants was multiplied four- and fivefold in the decade. Cigar machines reduced labor between 50 and 60 per cent; a warp-tying machine in textiles dispensed with ten or fifteen workers for each machine; new machines in clothing shops reduced pressing labor between 50 and 60 per cent; in mixing mills of automobile tire plants labor per unit was reduced about one half by the Banbury mixer; a new method of making inner tubes increased output per man about four times.[8]

[5] Fabricant, *Labor Savings in American Industry*, p. 47.
[6] Jerome, *Mechanization in Industry*, p. 225.
[7] *Ibid.*, p. 367.
[8] *Ibid.*, pp. 368–369.

The effect of increased productivity on employment, naturally more costly to labor in some cases and in some localities than
in others, will be considered in more detail in Chapter X. In terms
of large totals it has been estimated that between 1920 and 1929,
manufacturing dispensed with the labor of 32 out of every 100 men
required per unit of output, but reabsorbed 27 of them through
increases in the total produced. In manufacturing, railroads, and
coal mining it is estimated that in the decade the labor of 3,272,000
persons was made unnecessary for a given output, the actual increases in production required the addition of 2,269,000, leaving
a net decline of 1,003,000. Meanwhile, increases of employment
in trade and service industries offset the loss of employment opportunity in the basic industries but still left many without jobs.[9]

Taking output of goods and services as a whole, in all stages
from primary producer through distribution to the consumer, David
Weintraub estimates that the man-years per unit of output shrank
21 per cent from 1920 to 1929. The gain in productivity occurred
almost entirely in the basic industries, while productivity in the
service industries as a whole remained stationary. Of every 100
man-years of labor in 1920, 70 were engaged in the basic industries
and 30 in the service industries. But in 1929, when 79 man-years
could turn out the same product as did 100 in 1920, only 49 of
these man-years were in basic industries, while 30 were still in
the service occupations.[10]

No count or other official record of unemployment existed;
estimates that are rather uncertain must therefore be cited. Weintraub's estimate is that (in terms of man-years) 25 per cent of
the total labor supply was unemployed in 1921 and 11 per cent
in 1923. The total of unemployed man-years rose to 13 per cent
in 1924 and 1925, and never during the decade was below 10 per
cent, which it reached in 1929.[11] Although employment expanded
during the active period, so did the labor supply, and at about the
same rate. The persistent unemployment cannot be traced solely
to technical improvement, though this, combined with the failure

[9] *Ibid.*, p. 382.
[10] David Weintraub, "Unemployment and Increasing Productivity," in *Technological Trends and National Policy* (Washington: National Resources Committee, 1937), Part One, Section V, p. 75.
[11] *Ibid.*

of total production to increase more rapidly than it did, was undoubtedly an important factor.

From the time that President Harding entered office in 1921,
with his "return to normalcy," through the administrations of Calvin Coolidge and Herbert Hoover, the federal government was
more influenced by the attitudes of business than by any other
consideration.

The first legislation of importance to business was the passage
of the Fordney-McCumber Tariff Act in 1922, which increased
duties markedly above those in effect under the Underwood Act,
passed before the war. During the war itself, virtually all imports of anything that could be produced domestically had been
cut off, and American producers were under pressure to turn
out all that was demanded both at home and abroad. After it,
many of them feared foreign competition. The new act not only
raised rates but installed what was intended to be a "flexible tariff"
to equalize the cost of American and foreign goods to the domestic consumer. This device was unwieldy and resulted in few
modifications. In effect, the tariff gave little stimulation to most
of the industries that expanded rapidly after the war; it did not
apply to automobiles, and in any case there was virtually no foreign competition either for the newer industries or for building
construction. The new chemical industry was an exception; with
the German patents to which it had fallen heir, it grew rapidly.
The Chemical Foundation, formed in 1920, lobbied for high tariffs
and obtained prohibitive duties in the new bill. The tariff offered
a largely ineffectual protection to industries that did not share fully
in the general prosperity, such as agriculture and textiles.

The tendency of the Republican administration was well indicated by President Harding's choice of Andrew Mellon as Secretary of the Treasury. One of the two or three richest men in the
country, he had held consistently conservative views, not only on
finance, but on all economic issues, and his policy was to reduce
taxes as much as possible, especially in the higher brackets, while
maintaining a budgetary surplus and retiring the debt. This undertaking did not require much financial genius, because the steadily
rising national income kept tax yields relatively high and there

did not seem to be any need for extraordinary governmental expenditures. Mr. Harding's Secretary of the Interior, Albert Fall, became involved in a scandal and was subsequently convicted of accepting a bribe in connection with the disposal to private interests of naval oil reserves in Elk Hills and Teapot Dome. The facts of these transactions were brought out by a senatorial investigation, persistently and skillfully conducted by Senator Thomas J. Walsh of Montana. Though they created a national sensation, they did not become public until after President Harding's death in 1923. Vice-President Calvin Coolidge, who succeeded Mr. Harding, was not implicated in this scandal or others of the Harding administration, and though many felt that the Republican party should be held responsible for these delinquencies, Mr. Coolidge rode out the storm.

Coolidge's tendency was to resist proposals for governmental expenditure of kinds that business did not want, or for social reform, and thus to minimize the role of the federal government while business was growing in wealth and power. He retained Mr. Mellon as Secretary of the Treasury; the policy of tax reduction and "economy" continued. Nevertheless, a considerable increase in federal expenditures occurred in the decade 1920–1930.[12] The only major classifications reduced (in terms of stable purchasing power) were promotion of health and welfare, and interest on the debt. Law enforcement cost a great deal more, mainly because of prohibition. Shipping subsidies and other services to shipping consumed large funds. Services to business by the Department of Commerce under Herbert Hoover greatly expanded. These included elaborate statistical publications, promotion of exports and of foreign loans, aid in standardization and simplification, and aid to aeronautics and radio. On the other hand, public works and buildings decreased, with the exception of Mississippi flood control and federal aid for road construction by states.

Federal tax revenue, which in the fiscal year ended June 30, 1920, had been $5.7 billion, was reduced to $3 billion in 1925, and then started to rise again, reaching $3.5 billion in 1930. The reluctance of the federal government to undertake new functions, however, did not prevent a rapid growth in the need for governmental

---

[12] Carroll H. Wooddy, "The Growth of Governmental Functions," Chap. XXV in *Recent Social Trends* (New York: McGraw-Hill Book Company, 1933), p. 1278.

services, especially those supplied by state and local governments. It is estimated that the total burden of federal, state, and local taxes rose from $7.6 billion in 1922 to $10.3 billion in 1930, or from $68.9 to $83.71 per capita. Of the latter amount, more than 25 per cent arose from the costs of war, but 21 per cent went for education, 15 per cent for rural highways, and 14 per cent to pay the expenses of cities of over 30,000 (exclusive of education.)[13]

The contribution of state and local governments to economic activity is indicated by their borrowings for construction projects, which before the war had been about a third of a billion dollars annually, approached a billion in 1921, and ran regularly more than $1.25 billion from 1925 on, reaching their peak at $1.34 billion in 1927.[14] In the decade, public construction of roads and buildings absorbed more capital and employed more men than any single private industry. This counteracted the deflationary influence exerted by the fact that the federal government was spending less than it collected in taxes. Without it the growth of the automobile industry and the expansion of residential and commercial building would have been less impressive, while many contractors and manufacturers of supplies would have had far less business.[15]

On the negative side, the national administration and its conservative supporters in Congress resisted the agitation for farm relief, for measures to cope with unemployment, for labor legislation, and for extended controls over business and public utilities. A spirited progressive bloc, with several eminent leaders in the Senate, notably George W. Norris of Nebraska, kept these issues alive and was continually critical of the tendencies of the President, but it achieved little except to prevent the disposal of the government's hydroelectric plant at Muscle Shoals to private interests and to lay the groundwork for action in the subsequent Great Depression. The confidence of the business and financial community rested in part on the feeling that no obstruction would be interposed at Washington in the way of any of its activities.

[13] Clarence Heer, "Trends in Taxation and Public Finance," Chap. XXVI, *ibid.*, pp. 1334, 1336, 1346.
[14] *Ibid.*, 1351.
[15] Total governmental expenditures on goods and services grew steadily from $8.4 billion in 1921 to $11.0 billion in 1929. In this entire period there was not a year that did not show an increase. *Federal Reserve Bulletin* (September, 1945), p. 873.

The increasing concentration of industrial control will be discussed in the following section, but here it must be noted that during the postwar decade the antitrust laws were only mildly enforced, except in certain instances against labor. From 1917 to 1929 inclusive forty-eight fines were imposed under these laws; eight of these were against labor unions and one was against war spies. The most prominent company involved was the National Cash Register Company, against an official of which $2,000 was assessed in 1928. A higher court reversed all but $50 of this fine and the balance was remitted by the President. Most of the other cases were against building material rings and food racketeers and were initiated in the early years of the decade. In the same period eighteen equity suits instituted by the government under the antitrust laws were won in the lower courts. Three of these were against unions. The most important against business organizations—the Cement Manufacturers' Protective Association, the Maple Flooring Manufacturers' Association, and the Standard Oil Company of Indiana—were subsequently reversed by the Supreme Court.[16]

After the middle of the decade, court action was seldom resorted to. Of seventy-five antitrust cases started in the fiscal years 1925–1929, thirty-seven were settled by consent decrees, thirteen were ended by pleas of guilty or *nolo contendere,* and twelve were dropped. Of the consent decrees, Walton Hamilton writes: "The device lends itself to lax enforcement of the law. The parties meet informally behind closed doors; the negotiations leave no public records; groups who do not participate are left in the dark. . . . [The terms of the decree] can be understood only by the person who intimately knows the industry. As a result, the instrument is useful to a sympathetic administration in building up a paper record of accomplishment." [17]

Convictions carrying prison sentences for business executives were almost nonexistent. Of the eight sentences after 1921, five were against labor. Sentences were often suspended. One case of this kind occurred in 1926 and another in 1929, both of them against racketeering; otherwise the Coolidge-Hoover slate was clean.[18]

[16] *Antitrust in Action* (Washington: Temporary National Economic Committee, Monograph No. 16, 1940), pp. 122–134.
[17] *Ibid.,* pp. 30, 90.
[18] *Ibid.,* p. 121.

REGULATING COMPETITION

The Federal Trade Commission, created by Congress at the recommendation of President Wilson in 1914, had begun to function in 1915, but during the war had had little opportunity to exercise its legal duty to safeguard competition. It soon came to be occupied mainly with extensive investigations required by war agencies, concerning costs, prices, and profits in steel, coal, meat-packing, and other industries.

The theory which led to its establishment was that the antitrust laws had lacked full effect largely because they come into operation only after monopolistic practices have become entrenched, and can be enforced only by the cumbersome processes of litigation. The Wilson administration therefore set up the Federal Trade Commission to prevent "unfair methods of competition," such methods being defined in the law as those that involved "substantial lessening of competition or tendency to create monopoly."

The commission was empowered to investigate suspected cases, and if the facts warranted, and those accused of illegal action did not voluntarily consent to abandon it, to issue a "cease and desist order" outlawing the disapproved practices. Such orders were subject to review by the courts. The commission could also call "trade practice conferences," which could agree, subject to its approval, on those practices that were to be allowed and those that were to be forbidden. Finally, it was authorized to undertake investigations of business and publish the results, on the theory that publicity for the facts would have a wholesome effect on everyone concerned.

In the years 1915–1928 inclusive, 14,193 charges of unfair competition were lodged with the commission. Of these the great majority were summarily dismissed; and 3,081 out of the 4,830 filed for investigation were dismissed after further inquiry. Those thought by the commission to warrant more careful attention were continued; in these cases complaints were issued and trials of the accused parties were held before it. The trials resulted in dismissal of 546 cases, 857 cease and desist orders, and 350 stipulations by the offending parties that they would avoid the practices held to be contrary to law.[19]

Two general kinds of "unfair competition" can be identified. One

[19] T. C. Blaisdell, *The Federal Trade Commission* (New York: Columbia University Press, 1933), p. 39.

included acts previously forbidden under the common law—such things as inducing breach of contract, enticing away employees, betrayal of trade secrets, defamation, misrepresentation of products, intimidation, bribery, conspiracy to injure a competitor. The second type was added by the Clayton Antitrust Act—such practices as "tying contracts," which forced a buyer of one product to buy something else in order to get what he wanted; resale price maintenance; price discrimination based on trade status, as when special discounts were offered to wholesalers and denied to cooperatives or others who bought the same quantities; and exclusive dealer arrangements.

The commission's effectiveness was greatly hampered by the courts, to which appeal was taken in important cases involving large business interests. Its orders were reversed in more than half of the cases appealed. A majority of the Supreme Court held that while the commission's findings of fact had to be accepted, the Court itself was the judge of what constituted unfair competition. Brandeis and others in the minority usually contended that the commission was instructed by Congress to exercise this function also, and that the Court could pass only on the manner in which it administered its duties. The commission was somewhat more fortunate in reversals of cases involving the old principles of the common law than in those involving practices forbidden by recent statute. Of the former, the circuit courts sustained it in eighteen cases and reversed it in nineteen; of the latter, they sustained it in thirteen and reversed it in twenty-five. The Supreme Court itself sustained it in two cases involving the old common law and reversed it in one, but sustained it in only two cases involving the Clayton Act and reversed it in ten.[20]

The commission, therefore, made little progress in stopping unfair competition except in instances that would have been outlawed by the courts if the antitrust law had never been passed. And these cases had only a minor effect in preventing the growth of industrial concentration. More than half of the cease and desist orders themselves (427 out of 857) forbade misrepresentation, which had never been a major reliance of monopoly. Even here, the commission could legally protect only injured competitors; misrepresentation was held to be beyond its jurisdiction if only consumers were damaged. However, it did successfully outlaw boycotts, conspiracies, and commer-

[20] *Ibid.*, p. 40.

cial bribery. Contrary to the commission, the Court held that oil companies could compel retailers to sell only the products of the companies which supplied the pumps, that it was permissible for the Beech Nut Company to fix the prices at which its products could be sold at retail, that manufacturers could give lower discounts to wholesalers or chain stores than to others ordering the same quantities, that dealers acting as agents could be prevented from handling products competitive with those of their principals. All these decisions favored big business.[21]

The commission was also under repeated political attack. On October 20, 1919, Senator James A. Watson of Indiana charged on the Senate floor that eleven of its employees engaged in the investigation of the meat packers were guilty of "sedition and anarchy"; although a Senate investigation cleared them, all subsequently resigned or were dismissed. After the return of the Republicans to power in 1920, the commissioners appointed by President Wilson were not reappointed; their places were filled, when they resigned or when their terms expired, by men of more conservative views. V. W. Van Fleet, a friend of Senator Watson, was appointed in 1922. A majority of the five commissioners was gained by the administration in 1925 by the appointment of W. E. Humphrey, an attorney for lumber companies, of whom Senator Norris said, "He is known to be in favor of big business and to have little sympathy with the small business man."[22]

The commission then adopted the policy of keeping secret the charges against business interests, minimizing cease and desist orders, and relying mainly on trade practice conferences, in which business agreed upon its own rules. To these rules the commission gave approval—thus insuring against legal action those who complied with them. Certain of the rules the commission undertook to enforce. Subsequently, when the commission began to revise some of these rules because they might be in violation of the antitrust laws, business interests violently objected.

In October, 1924, just before the Republican administration gained a majority of the commission, it reported to Attorney General Harlan F. Stone that its investigation had revealed that the Aluminum Company of America was acting in a manner contrary to the

[21] *Ibid.*, pp. 23, 24.
[22] *The Nation* (September, 1925).

antitrust laws and had actually violated a decree by a federal court. Mr. Stone replied that the charge warranted consideration. No legal action could be taken, however, since the investigation did not proceed after 1922 and the statute of limitations applied after one year. The commission therefore renewed its investigation. When the Attorney General requested the results—after the change in the majority of the commission—the latter replied that it could not reveal the information without the written consent of the Aluminum Company because the company had supplied the evidence voluntarily. Mr. Stone was soon appointed to the Supreme Court, and his successor never instituted legal proceedings in this matter. Secretary of the Treasury Andrew Mellon was a large owner of Alcoa.

The investigatory powers of the commission were exercised in many fields, including milk, tobacco, cotton, farm implements, electrical power, electrical appliances, radio, meat packing, and aluminum. In some cases it had difficulty in obtaining desired information because of inadequate records; in some cases companies refused to supply certain facts and backed their refusal by interminable litigation. When recommendations were made to the Department of Justice, the latter usually failed to act. Though the published reports contain much valuable information, T. C. Blaisdell seems to be justified in concluding, "The influence of these studies on public opinion is hard to measure but there is no evidence that they have had far-reaching results in changing the structure of the industries involved."[23]

CONCENTRATION OF CONTROL

Traditional economic theory postulates that a substantial measure of competition must exist as a means of promoting the survival of the more efficient and as a basis for the maintenance of equilibrium among supply, demand, and price. In a period like the postwar decade, characterized by the rapid reduction of labor costs and the growth of new industries, flexible prices are especially desirable, if the economic order is to rely on automatic adjustment. If prices are deliberately maintained in any area of business while costs fall, production and employment will be restricted while monopoly gains are received, either by the owners and executives or by capital and labor in combination. Aside from economic theory, concentration of

[23] Blaisdell, *The Federal Trade Commission*, p. 255.

industrial control in the hands of persons not responsible to the citizens enhances the rewards and power of a few who may abuse their
prerogatives. It is dangerous to a democratic society.

Before the war numerous attempts had been made to prevent
monopoly by legislation. This effort had been partially successful in
curbing some of the more obvious monopolistic devices such as
mergers, pools, or agreements among competitors, formed for the
purpose of controlling markets and maintaining prices. It was impossible, however, to foresee in advance all the ingenious methods that
business organizations might use to increase their power, and it was
difficult to enforce unlimited competition without at the same time
restricting the efficiencies of large-scale operation and preventing arrangements that seemed to be reasonable and in the public interest.
For instance, the law did not forbid corporations to expand by purchasing the physical assets of others. The law, as interpreted, did
not place any limits on bigness as such. While it forbade holding
corporations formed with the aim of controlling competitors, it
permitted them for purposes of administering a single business or
enlarging its operations. Similar provisions existed with respect to
interlocking directorates. A wide latitude of discretion was necessarily left to the courts in interpreting such provisions, and the tendency of the courts was conservative.

The United States Steel Corporation, although it had been
formed by a merger and controlled at least half of the country's
output of steel, was held by the Supreme Court in 1920 not to involve any unreasonable restraint of trade. The test, the Court held,
was not whether restraint was exercised, but whether it was "reasonable." In other industries, particularly the newer ones, successful
corporations grew to giant size as a result of the reinvestment of
their own surplus profits. There were numerous areas of importance
in which the antitrust laws were not applied. One of these was the
industries in which monopoly rights were held to be legally con-
ferred by patents. Another was railroads and public utilities, in which
prices were supposed to be under public regulation. The Webb-
Pomerene Act permitted combinations to sell abroad. Legal monopoly also was possible through ownership or lease of limited deposits
of raw material.

Moreover, there were many reasons for the relative inflexibility
of prices in industries where large corporations occupied a dominat-

ing position, aside from any formal monopolistic control that might be legally forbidden. The heavy investment required in highly mechanized and mass-production processes retarded the entrance of new competitors into the field. At the same time the overhead charges occasioned by this investment often became a large element in the cost of production. Fixed costs were difficult to reduce except in the unlikely event that the corporation should go bankrupt and its capital obligations should be scaled down. An industry dominated by a few large concerns, even though they may be nominally competitive, is likely to follow the price policy set by its leaders in order to avoid uncomfortable consequences to all concerned. It is easily possible for these leaders to arrive at gentlemen's agreements or tacit understandings that are never put on paper and cannot be proved by legal evidence. As far as public utilities are concerned, the process of regulation is slow and cumbersome, and was conservatively exercised in view of the accepted principle that the investors must receive a "fair return." Flexibility of price change was out of the question.

Thus the laws directed against monopoly could be fully effective, even if vigorously enforced, only in the industries in which the growth of the giant corporation was prevented by other circumstances, and in which numerous competitors survived. The members of these industries naturally tried to protect themselves against cutthroat competition by devices through which they hoped to stabilize prices without running afoul of the antitrust laws. One of these was the open-price system, which required each member of a trade association to file with a central office the prices it was charging. Two instances of this system were declared illegal by the Supreme Court, one in the American Column and Lumber Company case in 1921 and the other in the American Linseed Oil Company case in 1923. In these cases the opinion of the Court seemed to depend to a large extent on the fact that the trade association circulated official interpretations of the price data, and exacted penalties for failure to adhere to the published prices.

Agitation arose in behalf of the trade associations, on the ground that their efforts to stabilize their industries were discriminated against in comparison with the industries already virtually under the control of big corporations. Later Supreme Court decisions, rendered in 1925 in the Cement Manufacturers' Protective Association case and the Maple Flooring Manufacturers' Association case, permitted the trade association to collect and publish statistical information that might furnish a guide to the pricing policies of its members. One of the most important of these types of collective action was the adoption of standard cost accounting systems; another was the use of uniform formulas for the figuring of costs in bidding for contracts.

The industry committees formed in connection with the War Industries Board during World War I had provided a great stimulus to the organization of trade associations. Herbert Hoover, as President Coolidge's Secretary of Commerce, used his influence to promote the trade association movement. By this means striking advances were achieved in the collection and publication of statistical information concerning prices, costs, and volume of production. The movement for engineering standardization and for simplification of the number of sizes, styles, and designs received a strong impetus. As a means of eliminating waste and providing better understanding and control of the economic order, these were highly praiseworthy activities. At the same time they were long steps away from the kind of competition visualized by the classical economists as an essential condition of price flexibility and automatic equilibrium.

As a net result of all these influences the concentration of industrial control proceeded almost unchecked, in spite of all academic theories and such few legal efforts as were made to prevent monopoly. Plants themselves increased in size as mass production made headway and heavy machinery was introduced. In 1923 4 per cent of the factories, each of which employed more than 250 workers, accounted for more than half the industrial wage earners.[24] Even where individual establishments remained small, this did not limit the possibilities of centralized management. In some cases small plants may be more efficient than large ones, but they still may be part of a corporate combination. An illustration of this is the chain store.

[24] The percentage of wage earners in these plants was 53.3. In 1929, the percentage had scarcely changed, being 52.8. Corresponding percentages of total wage earners in plants above 1,000 workers each were 1923, 24.1 per cent; 1929, 24.4 per cent. Alfred L. Bernheim and others, *Big Business, Its Growth and Its Place* (New York: Twentieth Century Fund, 1937), pp. 38–39.

THE EXTENT OF MERGERS

| Year | Manufacturing and Mining | | Public Utilities |
	Number of Mergers Recorded	Net Number of Concerns Disappearing	Number of Firms Disappearing
1919	89	438	22
1920	173	760	15
1921	89	487	74
1922	67	309	285
1923	67	311	426
1924	95	368	580
1925	121	554	402
1926	139	856	1,029
1927	207	870	911
1928	221	1,058	585
1929	—	1,245	—

Source: Reprinted by permission from *Recent Social Trends in The United States,* copyrighted, 1934, by the Research Committee on Social Trends, Inc., published by McGraw-Hill Book Company, Inc.

Between 1919 and 1930 more than eight thousand separate business establishments in manufacturing and mining disappeared as separate entities either by being combined with or acquired by another company. Before 1928 nearly five thousand public utilities so disappeared. By 1929 chain stores sold 27 per cent of the food of the country, 19 per cent of the drugs, 30 per cent of the tobacco, 27 per cent of the apparel, and 26 per cent of the general merchandise. The independents began to organize cooperative chains of their own. In 1930 ten groups of holding companies controlled 72 per cent of the electric power. By the same year, 20 per cent of the railway mileage was under holding company control. It was estimated that by the end of 1929 the two hundred largest business corporations possessed nearly half the corporate wealth of the country, 38 per cent of the business wealth, and 20 per cent of the total national wealth. They had been growing so much more rapidly than small business that if they continued at the same rate, they would by 1950 own 80 per cent of the corporate wealth and about 50 per cent of the total wealth of the United States.[25]

Concentration of control, which began to run far beyond any conceivable purpose of exercising influence on productive or mana-

[25] Adolph Berle and Gardiner C. Means, *The Modern Corporation and Private Property* (New York: The Macmillan Company, 1933), pp. 31–40.

gerial efficiency, was undertaken for financial gain to the promoters. An example in the automobile industry was that of Dodge Bros., Inc., bought by a banking house for about $146 million. The sale was financed by a public offering of bonds, preferred stock, and nonvoting Class A common stock totaling $160 million. The promoters not only made a handsome profit merely from this shuffling of paper evidences of wealth, but retained entire voting control through 500,000 shares of Class B no-par-value stock not offered for sale. Among commercial concerns controlled by holding companies or voting trusts were Kaufmann Department Stores in Pittsburgh, Stern Bros. in New York, Simmons Hardware, De Forest Radio, and Coca Cola. Industrial Rayon and Hires Root Beer were among the companies using the device of different classes of common stock to retain insiders' control while obtaining capital from the public. Most of this refinancing was to be found in the newer industries or those in trade.[26]

In general industry, out of the ninety-seven largest corporations at the beginning of 1929, twenty-one were purely holding companies, five were parent companies primarily for holding purposes, eight were parent companies devoted about equally to holding and operating, and fifty-nine were parent companies primarily concerned with operating. Only four of the ninety-seven were strictly operating companies. Prominent examples of the pure holding company were Allied Chemical & Dye, American Radiator and Standard Sanitary Corporation, Eastman Kodak Co., and United States Steel.[27]

The accounting practices of these great business units often gave little information either to the public or to their outside stockholders as to their actual condition or profits. Some issued no reports at all. Some made excessive charges to depreciation. Some lumped together capital and surplus as a device to make the balance sheet come out even. Some assigned arbitrary values to the capital stock, or employed unstandardized methods of valuing inventories. The bankers or promoters bought, sold, reorganized, or refinanced in order to profit from the transaction, with little regard to industrial policy. In regulated industries like railroads or utilities, the insiders were enabled to reap much larger gains than the return on invest-

[26] William Z. Ripley, *Main Street and Wall Street* (Boston: Little, Brown & Company, 1927), p. 85.
[27] James C. Bonbright and Gardiner C. Means, *The Holding Company* (New York: McGraw-Hill Book Company, 1932), p. 77.

ment allowed by the regulating bodies to the operating companies, and to escape public supervision altogether.

Investment trusts, originally formed with the idea of exercising central and expert management over the combined funds of many individuals, accumulated within ten years about $3 billion.[28] In some cases these funds were used to purchase corporate control.

Of course this does not mean that there were not still thousands of small corporations and partnerships or that bitter competition had disappeared from all branches of industry. It persisted, for instance, in textiles and clothing and in many branches of retailing. But the areas where relatively large numbers of competitors continued were in much the same disadvantageous position as the farmers. While they could not effectually restrict output and while the prices at which they sold were more flexible, they suffered from the controls exercised by the more firmly integrated sectors of the economy.

Producers of some raw materials that had been at a price disadvantage during most of the period attempted combinations of their own in order to hold goods off the market and increase prices. In the case of products sold in international trade, as many raw materials are, these valorization schemes often had the assistance of the governments directly concerned. The commodities affected included rubber, coffee, silk, sugar, Egyptian cotton, copper, nitrates, potash, mercury, sulphur, quinine, and camphor. A number of international cartels contributed to rigidity of prices on world markets though they did not directly affect the United States. These included steel, aluminum, rayon, and zinc.

The period between the two world wars was characterized by the formation of many cartels in Europe. Though participation in these schemes on the part of American business was restricted by the antitrust laws as far as domestic sales were concerned, the Webb-Pomerene Act, passed in 1918, which allowed American companies to combine for selling abroad, did encourage some participation on the part of business concerns in the United States. The legal monopoly provided by patents also opened a pathway for cooperation.

For instance, two corporations, the Texas Gulf Sulphur Company and the Freeport Sulphur Company, owned or leased virtually all the deposits in the United States. In 1922, they jointly formed the Sulphur Export Corporation, which made an agreement with an

[28] *Ibid.*, p. 7.

Italian cartel controlling the other chief source of world supply. The agreement divided the world market between the Italian and the American interests and though it specifically applied only to the markets outside Italy and North America, virtually no sales were made by either party in the country of the other.

German dye patents, seized by the Alien Property Custodian, were sold to Sterling Products Co., Inc., which in turn sold them to the Grasselli Chemical Co. In 1924, this company made an agreement with the original German owners of the patents. In 1925, the General Dyestuff Corporation was formed to handle the sales of Grasselli as well as those of American agencies of German companies that were being consolidated into I. G. Farben. The manufacturing activities of Grasselli were later acquired by Du Pont. Thus, through patent agreements and a common sales agency, American and German interests were united.

In 1928, General Electric made an agreement with Krupp giving the former the power to fix prices in the United States for all tungsten carbide sold in that country by either concern. Before the agreement, the prevailing price in the United States was $50 a pound, which was considered high. Following it, the General Electric subsidiary organized to conduct this business, Carbaloid Company, raised the price to $453 a pound. Tungsten carbide, a hard metal employed for cutting edges was of special usefulness in armament manufacture, cost much more in the United States than in Germany, and was used in Germany much more extensively.

Magnesite brick is used in metallurgical plants. In 1923 the two principal manufacturers in the United States made an agreement with the European producers of magnesia, dividing the world market with them and forbidding the European companies to sell any of the material or brick in North America except to the two American companies. Other international cartels in which American business interests participated at one time or another during the decade concerned titanium, soda ash, electric lamps, radio tubes, matches, copper, lead, zinc, and steel rails.

Where patent rights were involved, prices could be set or sales controlled even within the United States by such agreements. When the American producers participated in the international arrangements only through export associations formed under the Webb-Pomerene Law, which forbade monopolistic agreements in the home market, they were likely to develop such a community of interest that it was relatively easy to limit competition even inside the United States, without the use of formal contracts that would have been illegal.

According to the index of physical production of the National Bureau of Economic Research, between 1919 and 1929 a growth of 64 per cent occurred in the output of all manufactures. This average, however, conceals a wide variation among the fortunes of various industries. Some grew with extraordinary rapidity, others just about kept pace with the increase of population or the national income, while still others actually declined. Even the figures for large industrial groups indicate this divergence.

The petroleum and coal products industry heads the list with a gain of 156 per cent in production, due largely to consumption of gasoline and oil for automotive transportation. Though there are no adequate figures for the period covering the alcoholic beverage industry, this probably stands at the bottom of the list because of prohibition. One can only guess at the volume of manufacture of bootleg liquor. Even between 1914 and 1919, beverage output dropped about 30 per cent. Of the industries concerning which we have data, leather products showed the smallest gain—11 per cent. This was due mainly to the decreased demand for shoe leather, partly brought about by style changes in women's shoes and partly attributable to the fact that people in general did more riding and less walking.[29]

The output of forest products gained only 27 per cent in spite of the building boom. American forests were shrinking rapidly, substitute materials were more widely used, and much of the demand, especially for pulpwood, was being met by imports. Foods, tobacco products, and textile products were in the middle range, with gains of 54 per cent, 44 per cent, and 49 per cent, respectively. Output of rubber products grew 86 per cent, largely because of the demand for automobile tires, although this demand was dampened down by improvements in quality that led to longer tire life. Printing and publishing gained 85 per cent, while output of paper products rose

[29] Solomon Fabricant, *The Output of Manufacturing Industries, 1899–1937* (New York: National Bureau of Economic Research, 1940), pp. 60, 97, 110, 111.

89 per cent—a consequence not so much of higher literacy as of the tremendous growth of advertising.[30]

Transportation equipment grew by exactly the same percentage as total manufacturing, or 64 per cent. Although the output of automobiles increased more than this, the average was kept down because the group includes locomotives and ships as well. The percentage rise in automobile output for the decade was 255, while the production of railroad cars dropped 41 per cent; of locomotives, 69 per cent; and of carriages, wagons, and sleighs, 84 per cent. Iron and steel products, which were affected not only by the building boom and the expansion of the automobile and petroleum industries but by a declining demand for railroad equipment, showed a gain of 70 per cent. Chemical products, which included a number of important new materials, increased 94 per cent.[31]

Many of the industries that expanded most rapidly were those which made relatively new products. Automobiles are, of course, the outstanding example. Rayon had just come on the market before the outbreak of war, and in 1919 produced only 6.7 per cent of its output in 1929. No figure for output of radios appears until 1923. Between that year and 1929, the index number of production (1937 = 100) rose from 2.6 to 69.

In 1921, mechanical refrigerators were turned out at only 0.6 per cent of the rate of production in 1929. Canned milk and canned fruits and vegetables increased rapidly after the war because of changes in housekeeping and merchandising methods. Production of flour, on the other hand, actually decreased about 12 per cent, while lumber mill products gained only 3.[32]

Several minor items throw an interesting light on consumers' taste and style changes. As the sale of alcoholic beverages became illegal, the consumption of ice cream jumped. Men stopped smoking so many cigars, but cigarette sales soared as both men and women smoked more. People drank less tea but more coffee and more carbonated beverages. Men bought less clothing, perhaps because women multiplied the demand for dresses. Women stopped wearing cotton underwear and substituted silk and rayon. According to the United States Department of Agriculture, this tendency was more

[30] *Ibid.*
[31] *Ibid.*
[32] *Ibid.*

marked among single women than among married ones and more prevalent in towns and cities than on farms.

The output of furniture declined for every room in the house except the living room, where the increase was sufficient to counterbalance the losses in all the other items. This is a commentary on the decline in the number of rooms in dwelling places and perhaps on the size of families as well. Drug and toilet preparations spent as much on advertising in 1929 as did the food industry or the automotive industry. As the radio rose, the piano fell into disfavor. It suffered a 67 per cent loss in output and at the end of the period was being produced at the annual rate of four per one thousand families.[33] One unfortunate manufacturer gloomily reported that the bottom had fallen out of baby carriages.

The apparently accidental or capricious shifts in consumption produced one broad result of great significance for the behavior of the economy as a whole. As production and the purchasing power of consumers grew, people spent little more of their extra money for the perishable or semidurable goods ordinarily thought of as the staples of life. The output of foods, textiles, and boots and shoes increased comparatively little. Consumers did, however, spend greatly increased amounts on the more durable goods, such as housing, automobiles, furniture, electrical equipment, and the like. In several important respects, durable consumers' goods are more like business capital than they are like the necessities of life that are quickly consumed. Because of their longer life, they can be accumulated in one period, and bought in much smaller volume in another when for any reason demand for them decreases. Therefore, the larger they bulk in consumers' purchases, the larger is the element of instability introduced into demand. This effect is reinforced by the fact that purchases of durable goods are more extensively financed on credit than are those of perishable ones.

An activity important both in its own volume of expenditures and in its effect on the economy was advertising. Though figures are lacking to provide a comprehensive picture of the rapid growth of advertising, it is estimated that $1,782,000,000 was spent on advertising in 1929. The number of national advertisers grew from ap-

[33] Robert S. Lynd, "The People as Consumers," Chap. XVII in *Recent Social Trends*, pp. 903–905.

proximately 5,000 in 1925 to 8,500 five years later.[34] Advertising provided a direct stimulus to the printing, newspaper and periodical publishing, and paper industries. The chief means of promoting the sales of the new products that expanded so rapidly, it was also a powerful stimulant to the concentration of control in retail merchandising and in the manufacture of consumers' goods of older types. More and more people ceased buying commodities in bulk and turned to branded and packaged products. It is estimated that by 1930 more than half the families in the country were using packaged cheese, crackers, macaroni, butter, lard, coffee, and soap flakes. In 1919 packaged bacon, for example, was almost unknown, whereas by 1930 about 44 per cent of the families were using it. Whether branding and advertising resulted in improvement in quality is a matter of dispute. It is also uncertain whether it raised prices and the cost of living. There is no doubt whatever that it increased the degree of control by large manufacturing and distributing concerns over retail markets.[35]

One of the aims of advertising agencies and their clients was to stimulate sales by fostering frequent style changes. Obsolescence was a familiar fact in the production process itself, where machines were often replaced by better ones before they wore out. Now obsolescence in consumers' goods was deliberately sought. Consumers' interest in durability was not encouraged; desire for the latest thing was stimulated by all the arts of salesmanship. This technique was applied not only to wearing apparel, where it had long been an important factor, but also to automobiles, furniture, and other products that by their nature are supposed to be "durable."

In addition, advertising became expert in creating wants that did not before exist. In some cases the articles sold in this way were useful products or enhanced the enjoyment of life. In other cases they were nearly useless "gadgets" that cluttered up time and space. In far too many instances they were definitely harmful, especially in the toilet and drug field, where advertisers often stirred ungrounded fears of disease or personal unattractiveness, in order to sell a product that was worthless for the purpose in view and might even cause injury. Attacks on these practices were made in books and in noncommercial magazines, and led to the establishment of services to

[34] *Ibid.*, p. 871.
[35] *Ibid.*, p. 877.

protect consumer subscribers in quality and price—the first of these, founded by Stuart Chase and F. J. Schlink, being known as Consumers' Research.

It was often also charged that advertisers dictated the editorial policy of newspapers and periodicals. Attempts at such blackmail undoubtedly occurred, but on the whole the influence of advertisers was more subtle; the fact that most popular journals could not meet their expenses without a large volume of paid advertising made them sensitive to the interests or opinions of advertisers. One amusing incident that came to my attention concerned a weekly of wide circulation, which suggested to a young author that he write a story centered about a tank car, at a time when tank car manufacturers were about to launch a campaign of institutional advertising.

The combination of more leisure time and greater purchasing power led to a great increase in the facilities for recreation. This, in turn, had important economic effects for numerous industries and regions. It was partly responsible for the relative prosperity of Florida and California, and went far to offset the industrial decline of New England as well as to add to the wealth and income of wilder and less developed regions than any of these. There was a rapid growth of state and national parks and forests. Annual appropriations for the administration and improvement of the national parks grew in the decade from $1 million to $12 million, while in its second half alone, $22.5 million was spent for roads and trails within them. A Senate committee estimated that $750 million was spent yearly for equipment for fishing and hunting and for transportation to and from the areas of wild life.[36]

At the end of the decade, 218 cities had public bathing beaches with an annual attendance of nearly 40 million.[37] The number of registered motorboats, excluding those under sixteen feet in length, was in 1930 nearly 250,000, most of them being used for pleasure purposes. This marked an increase of 90 per cent in ten years. The number of golf courses grew 207.7 per cent between 1923 and 1930, reaching 5,856 in the latter year. The Census of Manufactures set the value of golf equipment manufactured in 1929 at over $21 million. By the end of the decade, college football, with an annual

[36] J. F. Steiner, "Recreation and Leisure Time Activities," Chap. XVIII in *Recent Social Trends*, pp. 919, 920, 924.
[37] *Ibid.*, p. 924.

attendance of approximately 10 million and gate receipts of over $21 million, had become a major industry.[38] The estimated annual cost of recreation, including travel, motion pictures, and commercial amusements, was more than $10 billion.[39]

The automobile, the growth of recreation, and the wider distribution of purchasing power led to an expansion of the occupations that rendered services rather than produced goods. The net income originating in these occupations grew from $6.1 billion in 1919 to $11.3 billion in 1929. The number of persons engaged in them (employees being included on a full-time basis) increased from 12.2 per cent of the total in the country in 1919 to 15.6 per cent in 1929. This category excludes transportation, trade, finance, and government employment, but includes such things as garages and service stations, professional employments, barber shops and hairdressers, and domestic servants.[40]

BANKING AND FINANCE

The institutions that act as the custodians of money and credit, receive deposits, make loans, and purchase and distribute investments are, in a sense, the central nervous system of the whole economic order. The importance of their functions has long been recognized, and hot controversies concerning their structure and manner of operation have been relatively frequent since the early days of the republic.

In the United States, this function has been delegated, as in most other capitalist nations, to profit-seeking enterprise. Unlike most other nations, however, the United States has been served by a very large number of banking units rather than by a few strong institutions. Though banking had become subject to government inspection and control, most of the legislation had sought to protect the public interest through measures against dishonesty or flagrantly unsound management rather than through coordination of banking policies as a whole. The historical development of banking under the federal political system, tempered by spasmodic reforms, had led to a rather haphazard and sprawling structure.

In 1921, the Comptroller of the Currency reported the existence

[38] *Ibid.*, pp. 925, 926, 930.
[39] *Ibid.*, p. 949.
[40] Kuznets, *National Income and Its Composition*, pp. 310, 346.

of 30,812 banks.[41] Of these, some were national banks subject to federal supervision and were members of the Federal Reserve System. Some were chartered by the several states and were subject to state supervision of varying types and stringency. Some state banks could become members of the Federal Reserve System, but many did not do so. This total includes only commercial banks and trust companies doing commercial banking business. There were, in addition, mutual savings banks owned by their depositors, savings banks owned by stockholders, and other financial institutions such as investment banks, insurance companies, building and loan associations, and a scattering of cooperative credit institutions.

Bank failures, an old defect of the American banking system, were not lacking during the years of prosperity. The number of banks suspended did not fall below 367 in any year—the low was achieved in 1922—and rose as high as 976 in 1926. In the latter year, 3.4 per cent of the banks in the country closed their doors, tying up more than $260 million in deposits.[42] Most of the banks that failed were small, and a majority of them were in country districts, which suffered from the collapse of agricultural prices and of the land boom following the war. This fact led to more complacence about bank failures than was later proved to be justified when general depression overtook the country.

A tendency toward concentration of control set in among the banks, as well as in other parts of the economy. The establishment of branches by large city banks grew rapidly after the war. National banks were forbidden by law to set up branches outside their home cities, and even the local branches could not conduct a complete banking business, but were restricted to teller windows for the receipt and disbursement of money. By the end of the decade nine states and the District of Columbia, however, permitted state banks to establish branches anywhere in the state. California was the first to do so, having passed the permissive law in 1909. It was far in the lead by 1930, with 853 branches out of a total of 1,308 state bank branches in the nation. Maryland ranked next with 129. The giant of branch banking was the Bank of America in California, controlled by Giannini interests, which flowered in the exotic California fashion.

Some national banks had branches outside their respective

[41] Steiner, *Money and Banking*, p. 275.
[42] *Ibid.*

cities. This occurred when state banks with branches converted themselves into national banks and carried their branches along with them, or when national and state banks were merged. It was even possible for a national bank to become a state bank, acquire branches, and then reconvert itself into a national bank. There was much doubt as to whether many of the branches had been lawfully acquired. The confusion of the situation, coupled with agitation for an expansion of branch banking, led to the passage of the McFadden Act, which became law on February 25, 1927. It attempted to remedy the discrimination between national and state banks as to branches, but still confined branches of national banks to their home cities. The total number of national and state banks having branches increased from 530 in 1920 to 763 in 1929, and the number of branches from 480 in 1920 to 3,350 in 1929. Of the latter number, 2,275 were in the city of the head office and 1,075 were outside that city.[43]

In favor of branch banking it was argued that coverage of a larger area would increase stability through diversification of credit risks, would raise standards of management, and would permit better mobilization and distribution of credit resources. Branch banking was resisted by those who felt that local management could better serve local needs, while centralization of financial power was dangerous.

Mergers also took place; the number of banks absorbed by mergers affecting members of the Federal Reserve System rose from 77 in 1920 to 343 in 1929. Although there were, of course, great banks with enormous resources in New York and other financial centers, the tendency to concentration was far from establishing any monopoly of credit. The total number of banks, taking account of both suspensions and consolidation, decreased to 25,330 in 1929.[44] Branch banking and mergers were advocated on the ground that they might provide the same safety against disaster enjoyed in other countries where a few large banking units exercised a virtual monopoly, but as subsequent events proved, the practices of many of the large banks offered no more immunity against misfortune than those of the small ones.

[43] Edwin F. Gay and Leo Wolman, "Trends in Economic Organization," Chap. V in *Recent Social Trends*, p. 244.
[44] Steiner, *Money and Banking*, pp. 610, 275.

The principal control of an administrative nature exercised in the public interest was that which the Federal Reserve Board sought to apply in order to influence the volume of credit. This control itself was indirect and lacked full effectiveness. The board had no power to instruct member banks either to expand their loans or to restrict them. It could inform them of the general situation and offer advice. The raising or lowering of the rediscount rate would, it was supposed by the originators of the system, respectively discourage or encourage the expansion of loans by member banks. This device, however, proved to be largely ineffectual unless accompanied by other measures. Banks having plenty of resources did not need to make so much use of the rediscount privilege, and when demand for credit was active, higher rates did little to discourage borrowing. A stronger instrument of control was the policy of the federal reserve banks in buying or selling government securities and bankers' acceptances in the open market. When the federal reserve banks bought these investments, they increased the money and credit available to member banks. When they sold bonds and acceptances, they withdrew money and credit from circulation. The open-market policy of the reserve banks was coordinated and was deliberately employed on numerous occasions to influence the total volume of credit.

The policies underlying credit control were given their first comprehensive statement in the annual report of the Federal Reserve Board for 1923. Many economists had argued that central banking management ought to seek to stabilize the price level by expanding credit when prices fell and contracting it when they rose. The experts of the board, however, held that this was not the main criterion of policy. When price statistics become known for any given period, they are an accomplished fact, merely registering the effect of forces with which banking policy ought to concern itself while these forces are operating. As long as production and employment were increasing, and goods were flowing freely through distributive channels to consumers, the function of the banks was to supply business with all the credit that it needed for these activities. When, however, production stopped growing, or goods were bought to enlarge inventories while consumer purchases lagged behind wholesale buying, further expansion of credit would merely finance speculation and induce unwholesome increases in prices. The aim of the policy was dynamic stabilization, not of prices alone, but of the whole economic process, including production, sales, and employment.

This policy, as is indicated in other chapters dealing with the course of business, seemed at times to be moderately successful. As later events were to prove, it could not force an expansion of credit when business suffered from deep stagnation. Even during the years when expansion was dominant, it soon began to be limited by fundamental changes in the financial situation. It was appropriate to an order in which the use of short-term commercial loans was the main influence in determining the flow of purchasing power, and in which business was generally dependent upon commercial banks for the financing of its current operations. This order, however, began to be drastically modified.

The profitability of many business concerns led them to depend much less than formerly on bank credit for their working capital. The amount of demand deposits, which reflect rather closely ordinary commercial loans, grew very little during the decade. For national banks, the figures were $8.7 billion in 1921 and $10.9 billion in 1930. Business concerns piled up their surplus cash in time deposits, on which interest was paid. These grew, in national banks, from $3.7 billion in 1921 to $8.7 billion in 1930. Even when expanding profits were not used to finance business operation, the rising stock market and the ease of issuing and selling securities led many of the larger business concerns to acquire capital in this way, not only for long-term investments in property but for current needs.[45]

The banks, in turn, finding that the demand for commercial loans was not sufficient to yield them a return on all the resources available for the purpose, had to look for other ways of using their funds. It was natural for them to turn to the investment and real-estate markets, since both were booming. They expanded their own investments in securities and increased their loans on security collateral (loans that toward the end of the period were used mainly for stock market speculation) and their loans on urban real estate. Member banks of the Federal Reserve System increased their investments by two thirds between 1921 and 1929, more than doubled their loans on securities in the same period, and expanded their

[45] *Ibid.*, p. 613.

loans on urban real estate about 3½ times. All other loans—mainly commercial—remained stationary in these nine years.[46]

Thus the Federal Reserve System, with its admirably conceived credit policy, had little influence in stabilizing the flow of "investment" capital, which came to be by far the most important part of the financial picture. Though from time to time concern was expressed about the diversion of bank credit to the financing of speculation, few understood the implications of the new development. It was not generally appreciated, for instance, how great was the danger to the banking system in tying up so large a part of its resources either directly or indirectly in long-term investments rather than in the much more liquid form of short-term loans. Indeed, at the time, high-class bonds and stocks were regarded as more liquid than commercial credit.

Not only did commercial banks act the role of savings banks by paying interest on time deposits, but many of the larger ones also set up affiliated companies that went into the business of investment banking on a large scale by underwriting and distributing new issues of securities. This was at the time a highly profitable business. In 1927 security affiliates of banks either sponsored or took part in the floating of $19 billion of issues.[47]

As long as all went well, few noticed the dangerous ambiguity inherent in these new activities of banks. The commercial banks that accepted large amounts of so-called savings did not segregate these funds from those employed in their ordinary banking functions, and were not subject to the legal safeguards or to the conservative traditions that surrounded the savings banks proper. The old distinction between banking that served the current needs of business and investment banking was virtually obliterated. The proceeds of long-term securities might be used for current necessities, and money that might have to be paid out on demand could be tied up in investments not necessarily liquid. Even more serious from an ethical point of view, banking interests made money by selling with one hand securities that they bought with the other. Thus, at the same time, they were acting as agents of both seller and buyer, al-

[46] Annual Reports of the U. S. Federal Reserve Board.
[47] Hearings before a subcommittee of the Committee on Banking and Currency, United States Senate, 71 Cong., 3 Sess., pursuant to Senate Resolution 71, p. 299.

though it is ordinarily supposed that these sometimes divergent interests need to be safeguarded against each other.

Other types of financial agencies also became deeply involved in the rapidly expanding capital markets. Life insurance companies decreased the proportion of their funds devoted to holding government bonds and railroad securities, while they greatly enlarged their investments in urban real-estate mortgages. Investment trusts were formed to collect the funds of individual investors and purchase bonds and stocks with them. Some of these trusts were created by investment bankers. Keane's *Manual* listed 360 general management trusts and 29 fixed trusts in existence by 1929. As long as security prices were rising, investment trusts were extremely profitable for their promoters. The speculative nature of many of them was concealed by the fact that while their holdings were largely of common stocks, they raised their funds to a considerable extent by the sale of bonds or preferred stock.

Still another remarkable financial development of the period was the rapid extension of consumers' credit by installment sales. This business was handled largely by finance companies devoted mainly to the purpose. The practice was widely used for distributing not only automobiles but also furniture, radio sets, and electrical equipment for the home. No accurate figures exist of the total volume of installment credit through the period, but there can be no doubt that its growth was rapid. It is estimated that in 1929 sales on installment approximated $7 billion.[48] Although experience proved that the companies making these loans ran a negligible risk of loss from default, except by purchasers of farm machinery, the injection of this new volume of credit to finance a type of sales subject to wide swings in demand added an element of instability to the economy as a whole. Rapidly increasing use of installment credit facilitated expansion of the industries making the products in question. As long as the incomes of consumers did not increase at the same rate, however, there was necessarily a limit to the growth of installment debt. When this limit was approached, effective demand for the durable consumers' goods sold on installment would cease growing at the previous rate, and the consequences would be felt by the entire economy.

[48] Lynd, "The People as Consumers," in *Recent Social Trends*, p. 862.

CHAPTER VIII

Important Industries

WITHIN the framework of such broad influences as have been described, the several industries and occupations worked out their fortunes. Many expanded; some declined. Each had its own history, its own problems. Although all were interwoven in the same network, their experiences were far from parallel. Some of the more important industries will be briefly covered in this chapter.

RAILROADS

After the war the interest in laying the foundation for a better economic system led to an attempt at governmental planning in only one major industry—the railroads. For decades in the past, railroads had offered one of the chief outlets for investment, and their expansion had been almost synonymous with the growth of the country. Before the war their network had penetrated all important areas of production and trade, and the era of the extension of mileage of line had come to an end by 1916. Their monopoly of transportation was in many regions absolute, being threatened only to a minor extent by canals, coastwise and river shipping, and interurban electric railways.

A combination of powerful forces produced a reluctance merely to dissolve the Railroad Administration and return the roads to the type of management and regulation that had existed before the government took them over. It was clear that unified management had increased operating efficiency and had eliminated many of the wastes and inconveniences of competition. If some way could be found to preserve and enhance this gain, those who used the railroads and the workers who operated them could both be benefited. Some, therefore, revived the proposal for government ownership. The railroad unions advocated an ingenious scheme for effectuating it known as the Plumb plan, which will be described in more detail in the chapter on labor. This plan, however, never received serious consideration by Congress, because those who exerted the most influence over public opinion were strongly opposed to nationalization.

Many students of the subject advocated consolidation of the railroads into a smaller number of large systems under private ownership. Some favored regional consolidation; others were fearful that large combinations, each covering a given territory, would exploit the public, and wished to consolidate the roads in such a way that a substantial measure of competition would be retained, the competitors in any region having more equality of size and resources than had previously been the case.

A powerful interest at work was that of the holders of railroad securities. For many years, railroads had largely been financed by mortgage bonds or similar instruments bearing a fixed rate of return. These securities had been a favorite form of investment, not only for individuals but for great insurance companies and other financial corporations. In many cases, the capitalization had been grossly inflated and the railroad companies were in financial difficulties. This was true, for instance, of the New York, New Haven and Hartford and the Erie Railroad in the East, and of the Chicago, Milwaukee and St. Paul and the Missouri Pacific in the West. Other roads like the Pennsylvania, the New York Central, and the "Hill Roads"—the Northern Pacific and the Great Northern—were in a sounder position. Some of the roads regarded as weak suffered from inferior routes, poor management, or the decline of the territory they served. Security owners in the weak roads naturally wished to safeguard their investments, and thought this result might follow from a system of consolidation that would attach these roads to stronger systems.

Financial inequality provided still other reasons for consolidation. Unprofitable lines might have to be abandoned, and the populations of the territories they served strongly objected to such proposals. In the setting of rates, decisions had to be made that would cover both strong and weak roads at the same time. If rates were set high enough to protect the solvency of the unprofitable properties, they would provide unnecessarily large earnings for the strong companies. Some kind of pooling might therefore permit more rational rate regulation. In addition, it would assist the weak roads to attract the capital necessary for their improvement.

After long discussion of the proposals, Congress passed the Transportation Act of 1920, representing an attempt to please all the interests involved. The Interstate Commerce Commission was instructed to prepare a plan for railroad consolidation that would strengthen the weak roads, retain competition, and not interfere with customary routes of transportation. The railroads, in turn, were to be permitted voluntarily to propose consolidation plans and to proceed with them, provided the plans were in accord with the general scheme to be laid down by the commission.

The commission engaged Professor William Z. Ripley of Harvard to help prepare a tentative national plan, which was made public in August, 1921. This report contained a long and detailed study of the requirements of the situation and proposed that most of the railroads be embodied in eighteen or twenty systems.

Hearings held by the commission on this plan developed the fact that the instructions contained in the Transportation Act were mutually inconsistent and that it would be difficult to reconcile the various interests at stake. There was little evidence to show that important operating economies could be achieved if competition were to be retained. One of the most wasteful competitive practices was, for instance, the ownership of independent terminals by railroads entering the same city, and yet competition seemed to imply the continuation of this practice. Nevertheless, where, as in New England, Mr. Ripley recommended a unified regional system, the local interests feared that they would lose the competitive advantage of playing off the trunk lines to the west against one another. The strong roads evinced great reluctance to taking over unprofitable companies that might be a financial drain. Instead, they proposed consolidations that would increase their strength or bring them more traffic. For instance, it was urged that the Great Northern and the Northern Pacific be combined into a single system, although they were already largely connected by ownership, and in the interests of competition might have been separated.

The Interstate Commerce Commission never prepared its final plan. In 1927 its chairman asked Congress to be relieved of this duty. It would have been impossible to carry out the intent of the legislation in all its details. Even if a rational plan could have been formulated under the law, the interests in control of the railroads would not voluntarily have followed it. This situation brought support for a proposal for compulsory consolidation, which never met with the favor of Congress. The opinion of experts and of the commissioners themselves gradually veered to the conclusion that the ends sought, so far as they were feasible under private ownership, could be achieved as well without consolidation as with it. Terminals might be unified and cars could be pooled without combining whole railroad systems. The law had already provided for the recapture of earnings in excess of a "fair" return. The best way to deal with overcapitalization was financial reorganization that would reduce it. Poorly managed roads needed better management, which might be provided as well without consolidation as with it.

The Transportation Act of 1920 did result in the prompt termination of the Railroad Administration and the turning back of the roads to their private owners. The commission was instructed by law to fix rates that would provide an average "fair" return on the "value" of the properties. What constituted the actual value had long been in dispute. The commission was engaged in valuation studies that were about one quarter completed, and it now estimated that the value to be used as a rate base was $18.9 billion, as against the book value of $20 billion. It decided that 6 per cent would be a fair return, and in 1920 granted increases in rates averaging about 35 per cent for freight and 20 per cent for passengers, on the theory that this would accomplish the object in view. The 1921 depression, however, prevented the earning of 6 per cent, and freight rates were reduced again in 1922. The "fair" rate was then set at 5¾ per cent. The average return thereafter never reached this amount, but it is doubtful whether higher rates would have increased it, since they would have discouraged traffic.

Though railway traffic did not markedly increase in the postwar decade (passenger traffic actually declined), the roads improved their position somewhat by large investments in better equipment and by operating economies. These investments were principally charged to costs or met out of the earnings of the more profitable companies. Most of the companies were not in a position to attract outside capital. Net railway operating income grew from $608,000,000 in 1921 to $1,068,000,000 in 1927, while the investment was increasing; the return on this investment, however, exceeded 5 per cent only in 1926, when it reached 5.2.[1]

A few acquisitions were proposed by railroad managements and approved by the Interstate Commerce Commission, but these were not of the sort envisioned in the Transportation Act. Actual consolidations could be sanctioned only if they conformed with a general plan, and no plan had been approved. Financiers and promoters employed the holding company device to concentrate control of numerous roads and reap profits in the marketing of securities, but this activity was outside the jurisdiction of the Interstate Commerce Commission. A notable case was that of the Van Sweringen operations, which will be described in a subsequent chapter. Some of the weaker systems passed into receivership and underwent financial reorganization.

During the decade new forms of competition severely limited the railroads' monopolistic position. Motor busses and trucks, combined with the extension of good highways, deprived them of a share of both freight and passenger traffic. Private passenger cars as well supplied an alternative means of transportation, which in many cases was cheaper and more pleasant, even for long distances. Airlines were developing and offered greater speed. Railroad passenger-miles declined from 47 million in 1920 to 34 million in 1927. At the end of the period, although marked improvements in railroad service and efficiency had been made, the problem was far from solved.[2]

SHIPPING

The ambitious program of shipbuilding undertaken by the Emergency Fleet Corporation as a war measure was far from com-

---

[1] *Recent Economic Changes in the United States*, Report of the Committee on Recent Economic Changes, the President's Conference on Unemployment (New York: McGraw-Hill Book Company, 1929), I, 269, 294–296.

[2] *Ibid.*, pp. 294–296.

pleted when the armistice was signed. The government did not terminate it, as it did almost all other war production, because there was a strong agitation in favor of regaining the high place in sea transport that the United States had held earlier in its history, and military authorities believed that a large merchant marine was a necessary adjunct of the Army and Navy. Of the 2,602,153 gross tons of merchant vessels launched in 1918, many were not completed before the end of the year. In 1919, American shipyards launched 3,579,826 gross tons, and in 1920, 2,348,725. The net result of the combined building and losses of the United Kingdom and the United States, the two chief maritime powers, was an increase of the ships of 100 tons and upward of both nations from 24,570,000 gross tons in 1914 to 34,327,000 gross tons in 1920.[3] Meanwhile, there had been an actual decline in ocean freight, and the extraordinary war requirements for shipping space had disappeared. The result was an excess capacity that depressed freight rates and had a ruinous effect on the shipbuilding industry in both countries.

The United States was the sole gainer in terms of shipping space, since the gross tonnage under the American flag had increased from 5,323,000 in 1914 to 15,997,000 in 1920, while the gross tonnage of the United Kingdom had shrunk from 19,257,000 to 18,330,000.[4] Much of the prewar American tonnage had been used in lake and coastwise traffic. In peacetime competition, Britain held the advantage because its capital costs and operating expenses were lower than the American; it had long experience in this difficult and somewhat speculative business and it had better banking and insurance connections. With a few exceptions where the ships were a part of a well-established business, as in the case of oil tankers or the special-purpose vessels of the United Fruit Company, it was obvious that most American private companies engaged in ocean shipping could not remain solvent under the existing conditions without governmental aid.

Many of the ships built for war purposes were unsuited for economical operation in peacetime trade and had to be laid up. It was impossible for Americans to compete for the occasional and special cargoes customarily carried about the world by tramp

[3] *Lloyd's Register*, 1933–1934.
[4] *Ibid.*

steamers. The Shipping Board, formed just before the war, now established a number of government-owned lines with regular sailings, carrying both passengers and freight. Ships designed for this traffic were built in the early postwar years. Some of the liners taken from the Germans were also utilized for this purpose. The United States Lines, for instance, operated regularly between New York and European ports. The losses involved were met at governmental expense. Some lines were sold to private companies at a heavy sacrifice, thus subsidizing their capital costs. Subsidies for mail carrying were paid to these lines, and liberal loans for shipbuilding were authorized in addition by the White-Jones Act in 1928.

The experiment did not reduce costs of transportation for American trade or bring it any other important advantages. Its main effect was to impose upon American taxpayers the losses of uneconomical operation. The subsidy system was continually under fire.

AUTOMOBILES

The automobile industry, unlike railroads and shipping, was a relatively new and still expanding sector of the economy, which during the postwar decade was not only prosperous itself but contributed largely to the prosperity of the nation. The number of passenger cars produced annually rose from 1,518,061 in 1921 to 4,794,898 in 1929. The number of motor vehicles registered increased in the same period from 10,463,000 to 26,501,000. Of these, about 23 million were passenger cars, so that the entire population, which numbered somewhat less than six per car, might, if equally distributed among the vehicles, all have been speeding along the roads at once.[5]

The economic importance of the industry is revealed by the fact that in 1929 the value of its product was 12.7 per cent of the total of all manufactures. It employed 7.1 per cent of the manufacturing wage earners and paid 8.7 per cent of the manufacturing wages. The motor industry accounted for 15 per cent of steel production, being the most important purchaser of strips, bars, sheets, and malleable iron, and occasioned larger purchases than

[5] *Facts and Figures of the Automobile Industry*, National Automobile Chamber of Commerce, 1931 ed., pp. 4, 16

Calvin Coolidge and Warren G. Harding

The political symbols of the "New Era." (*Harris & Ewing*)

Henry Ford and Thomas A. Edison

The leading industrialist and the leading inventor, who typified America's faith in industry and technology. (*Underwood–Stratton*)

Assembly Line of Model T Fords

The symbol of mass production in the 1920's. (*Brown Brothers*)

Great Turbine Generator

The rapid growth of electric power was dependent on such units as this, which was installed in New York, and was capable of generating 80,000 horse power. Its dimensions were 60 × 26 × 47 feet. (*Underwood–Stratton*)

any other industry of gasoline, rubber, plate glass, nickel and lead.[6]

It is probable that by 1918 the number of persons owning automobiles was approaching an upper limit. Several changes, however, increased the demand in the succeeding years. One was the growth of the national income, and especially the increase of purchasing power in the hands of wage earners. Another was the production of closed cars at a price sufficiently low so that people with relatively modest incomes could buy them. In 1923, for the first time, the sales of closed cars equaled those of open models and in subsequent years many more closed than open cars were sold. The wider use of the self-starter increased the ease of operation, while the cord tire diminished tire trouble. Later improvements, such as the balloon tire and four-wheel brakes, provided additional attractions, and the motor of higher compression first used by the new Chrysler in 1923 added to power and gasoline economy.

The most effective innovation in promoting the sales of cars to persons of moderate income was the wide introduction of time payments, through installment loans made by finance companies on the basis of chattel mortgages. This device did not, of course, in the long run increase the purchasing power of a given income; rather, it had the reverse effect because it added interest to the price of the car. Nevertheless, families unlikely at any given time to accumulate enough savings to pay the full cash price were induced to mortgage their future earnings. By 1925, 68.2 per cent of new cars were sold on time payments. This percentage dropped to 58 in 1927 and 1928.[7]

It has been contended that the enlargement of production stimulated by installment purchases made possible a sufficient drop in costs and prices so that in the end purchasers were compensated for the loss of the interest. It is difficult to prove this point, since it is almost impossible to trace the course of automobile prices. The product itself changed rapidly from year to year, and what was acceptable at a given price in one year could not have been sold several years later for the same amount. A continuous series can be obtained only by the use of some abstraction like

[6] *Ibid.*, pp. 10, 82, 86.
[7] *Facts and Figures of the Automobile Industry*, 1929 ed., p. 32.

the price per pound, and this has little meaning in terms of utility to the consumer.

The industry had from the beginning been highly competitive, and it remained so throughout the period of its expansion. Only one successful merger of numerous companies was made during its history—General Motors. This corporation produced about 15 per cent of the total in 1921 and nearly 30 per cent in 1926. Ford was, of course, its principal rival. Walter Chrysler, an executive of long experience in motors, entered the field with his own company in 1923. Of approximately 181 companies that had been in the business between 1903 and 1926, only 44 remained in the latter year, and only 11 of these survived during the entire period. In this calculation a change of name or ownership is not taken into account.[8]

In large part, the industry remained under the control of practical manufacturers or engineers who had grown up in it, and was not subject to the influence of investment bankers or other outside financial interests. The greater part of its capital was accumulated by the reinvestment of corporate profits rather than from the sale of securities. General Motors provided the chief exception to this rule, having fallen into the hands of the Du Ponts on account of its need for financing. Even General Motors, however, reinvested in its business about 47 per cent of its profits between 1909 and 1926.[9]

Although the motorcar industry was never monopolized as a whole, the competition among the dwindling number of companies was of a nature very different from that which obtains where there are thousands or even millions of competitors, as in agriculture. General Motors and Ford between them made a substantial percentage of the sales. Their leadership was approached during the latter part of the decade by the Chrysler Corporation. A few other well-established independents such as Studebaker, Packard, Nash, and Hudson shared most of the rest of the sales, while smaller manufacturers maintained a precarious hold on life. Each company knew well in advance what the plans of the others were. The processes of mass production made necessary the tentative sched-

[8] Ralph C. Epstein, *The Automobile Industry* (Chicago: A. W. Shaw Co., 1928), pp. 163, 164, 176, 221.
[9] *Ibid.*

uling of output for a year ahead. Prices were also fixed by administrative decisions for each model year, and were not often altered with variations in demand for any particular car, at least until new models were offered.

All the companies except Ford were members of the National Automobile Chamber of Commerce and rendered to it monthly reports of their sales, which were accessible to members. While each of the competitors attempted to convince the consumers that it was offering the best value for the money, the competition was based fully as much upon attractiveness and mechanical features as upon price. Until 1925 no company maintained a monopoly of any mechanical improvement, except "revolutionary" changes, since new patents were regularly pooled and licensed without cost to members of the association. In that year the practice was ended, except for patents already in the pool, because the larger concerns had built up great research departments of their own. The consequence of all this was that whenever any insufficiency of demand occurred, it was felt to a much greater extent in curbing of output than in reduction of prices. Relative success was as dependent upon good salesmanship and distribution as upon any marked difference in essential quality at a given price.

Though the trend of production was upward from 1921 to 1929, the annual changes in output were extremely irregular, especially in passenger cars. The number of these produced shot up 55 per cent from 1921 to 1922 and 58.4 per cent from 1922 to 1923. In the following year, however, a drop of 12 per cent occurred —the first important decline in production since the birth of the industry except that enforced by the government in 1918. Since the depression of 1924 was relatively mild, this decline gave a clear indication that production was close to the saturation point of demand at the existing distribution of purchasing power. Output for 1925 again registered an increase, this time of 17.2 per cent, but in 1926 the gain was only 2 per cent. In 1927, the next year of cyclical depression, output fell again, and by 22 per cent. At the time, this drop was attributed largely to the fact that Ford was off the market. His Model T had suffered severely from the competition of other low-priced cars and he was changing over to the brand-new Model A. It is probable that many prospective buyers were waiting until they could see what he had to offer, and this in part accounted for the gain of 30 per cent registered in 1928. Nevertheless, if the advance in output for the two years is considered as a whole, it is only 1.6 per cent. The final burst of prosperity in 1929 brought a gain of 19 per cent, but output began to fall off several months before the stock market crash.[10]

Profits of the automobile manufacturers for the ten years 1919 to 1928 inclusive were, on the whole, ample, though fluctuating with the fortunes of the industry. Thirty-two corporations existing throughout the period had an aggregate net income that was 11.5 per cent of their total sales, and 19.7 per cent of their capitalization. Ford profits never fell below 20 per cent until after 1923, and the company lost money for the first time in 1927, when the sales of Model T's ceased. The year of highest profit for these firms taken together was 1919, when 38.8 per cent was earned on capitalization; the lowest was 1921, when 8.4 per cent was earned. In other years, the rate of profit ranged between 25.3 per cent in 1922 and 16.1 per cent in 1927 and 1928. It is interesting that the profit for 1928, which was a year of large volume, was actually lower than that for 1924, when a marked recession occurred and many firms wound up their affairs.[11] This would suggest that the industry was entering a phase of diminishing returns.

Productivity increased with extraordinary rapidity in the automobile industry, the labor-hours per unit of product falling, on the average, 7.4 per cent a year between 1919 and 1929.[12]

The effect of the automotive industry on the economy is not to be measured by the materials it consumed or the numbers it employed. It reinforced the demand for good roads and inaugurated an era of road building that enlarged public expenditure and continually stimulated expansion. It facilitated the growth of metropolitan regions at their outskirts by the building of suburbs, and thus was interlocked with the housing boom. It provided expanding markets for the petroleum industry, and caused a rash of filling stations, hot-dog stands, cabin camps, and advertising billboards to break out over the countryside. Country clubs, golf courses, and roadhouses multiplied to serve the more prosperous;

[10] *Facts and Figures of the Automobile Industry*, 1931 ed., p. 4.
[11] Ralph C. Epstein, *Industrial Profits in the United States* (New York: National Bureau of Economic Research, 1934), pp. 290, 291.
[12] Solomon Fabricant, *Employment in Manufacturing, 1899-1939* (New York: National Bureau of Economic Research, 1942), p. 69.

farmers found it easier to get to villages or to visit one another, and many began to market their produce through roadside stands. Hordes emigrated on wheels to Florida or California, while wilderness regions were invaded by millions of sportsmen with rod and gun. So important became the fishermen's vote that even Calvin Coolidge was persuaded, much against his will, to cast trout flies, dressed uncomfortably in waders, a stiff collar, and a ten-gallon hat.

Meanwhile other pursuits and regions suffered. The railroads could no longer compel everybody who must travel to stifle in antiquated coaches; trolley lines folded up except in crowded cities. The population of slums dwindled and left behind blighted urban areas and a knotty problem in municipal finance, but new slums were created in the centers of motor manufacture. Book publishers met greater sales resistance when people spent their leisure hours in traffic jams or at motion pictures. The demand for shoe leather diminished and the sale of men's shoes declined, but the women's shoe industry was revolutionized by a shift to rapid style changes of insubstantial creations made for appearance rather than utility on sidewalks. Combined with prohibition and "speak-easies," the automobile had an effect on morals and manners, especially of the young, that undermined family life and worried their elders and the preachers. Gunmen pursued their calling with the aid of long black limousines in which their victims were taken for a last ride, while "highjackers," stopping shipments of illicit liquor on country highways, sped off with their booty in motor trucks. Malefactors of all types were pursued by motorcycle police or police cars whose wailing sirens disturbed the calm of the virtuous. Traffic courts became an important source of income to rural towns.

The ingrained interest of Americans in any mechanism and their predilection for adventure in private enterprise found an unexcelled outlet in the motor industry. Every year some new feature was expected and the new models constituted an absorbing topic of conversation. Throngs visited the shows, discussing the merits of sleeve valves, free wheeling, air cooling, the number of cylinders from fours to twelves and sixteens. The falling star of W. C. Durant, who had before the war organized General Motors and later lost it, or the rising one of Walter P. Chrysler, who broke suddenly into the duel between Ford and General Motors with an attractive new car, gained almost as much attention as the innumerable stories about Henry Ford—how, for instance, when one of his staff had urged the offering of a color choice to meet the growing competition for his "tin lizzies," he was said to have replied, "The customer can have a Ford any color he wants—so long as it is black." Those interested in labor problems had much to say about the loss of craftsmanship in mass production and the soul-killing monotony of the production line, but the mechanical advances in the productive process attracted world-wide wonder and admiration.

CONSTRUCTION

As a stimulant of economic activity, the expansion of construction in the decade after the war ranks even higher than that of automobiles and other durable consumer goods. Building as a whole does not customarily follow the shorter cycles of business but pursues a somewhat independent course; it is active or depressed for longer periods. When building is large and increasing, any retarding influences in other parts of the economy are minimized. The estimated value of construction at current prices, derived from the value of materials used, rose from $12,158,000,000 in 1919 to a peak of $17,385,000,000 in 1928. The 1929 total of $16,207,000,000 was below any of the three preceding years.[13]

That part of the national income arising directly from construction was $2.1 billion in 1919 and rose to $4.2 billion in 1926, thereafter declining slowly, the 1928 figure being $4.0 billion. These totals were larger than those of any single group of manufacturing industries except metals and, for the first three years of the period, textiles and leather. Construction income was larger also than the income attributable to mining, including mining of coal and metals. It was smaller than the income of agriculture, trade, railroads, the various occupations grouped under service, or government employment. It was also smaller than the income of finance, but by far the largest item under the head of "finance" was real estate, which is closely associated with building. Real-estate income (composed largely of rent and interest) was, at its high point, larger than the income of agriculture, any group of manufac-

[13] Kuznets, *Commodity Flow and Capital Formation*, I, 375.

turing industries or railroads, and was nearly as large as the income from trade, service, or government employment.[14]

As an employer, construction ranked somewhat higher than as a source of income, having, at its peak in 1926, 5.7 per cent (full-time equivalent) employees out of a total of 33.1 million in the nation. Payments of wages and salaries by construction were in that year 7.5 per cent of a national total of $47.4 billion. As an employer, it was almost equal with railroads or agriculture, and was not far behind the metal group of manufacture or textiles.[15]

The influence of construction activity on the economy cannot be measured so completely by the statistics of its income or employment as is the case with manufacturing industries, since its function is mainly that of assembling in given locations a wide range of building materials and supplies manufactured or prepared by others, and transported by rail, truck, or ship. It furnishes a large part of the market for steel, electrical equipment, and glass, and is almost the sole outlet for such materials as brick, stone, cement, lumber, plumbing supplies, and hardware. Shipments of building materials comprised about one sixth of all railway ton-miles.

Because of the restrictions that had been imposed upon it, the demand for building was urgent after the war. So severe was the housing shortage that returning veterans had difficulty in finding places to live. Rent controls imposed for a while by New York State applied only to old structures and not to newly completed ones. There was no federal rent control except in the District of Columbia. Controls of some sort were adopted in thirteen states either by legislatures or by municipal authorities. Several of the rent-fixing laws were declared unconstitutional within a few months after their enactment.[16]

Construction costs soared; in 1920, the *Engineering News Record* index of the combined costs of lumber, steel, cement, and common labor (1926 = 100) reached 120.8 as against 44.5 in 1915. High cost coupled with shortage of mortgage funds halted the incipient building boom. In 1921, however, the index of costs fell to 97 and to 83 in 1922, when money became readily available. During most of the rest of the decade the index of costs remained

[14] Kuznets, *National Income and Its Composition*, pp. 310, 326–327.
[15] *Ibid.*
[16] *Housing after World War I* (Washington: National Housing Agency, National Housing Bulletin No. 4, December, 1945), p. 31.

stable in the neighborhood of 100. The demand was increased after 1921 by the rapid growth of the national income, including the purchasing power of wages, and by the expansion of business, giving rise to commercial and industrial building.[17]

Residential construction was the largest single classification of building—the value of residential contracts in twenty-seven states after 1921 ranging between 40 and 48 per cent of the total. Commercial and industrial buildings varied between 22 and 25 per cent, while public works and utilities were third. Industrial construction being more responsive than residential to short-run business cycles,[18] industrial building fell sharply after the postwar boom of 1919–1920, but residential building increased.

The peak of the boom in construction of one-family houses, usually built for sale or by owners who expect to occupy them, was reached in 1925, and that of multifamily apartments in 1926. The latter year also marked the high mark of employment in the industry, and of payment of wages and salaries. Commercial and industrial building, however, was active in 1928, and made a final spurt in 1929.

Changes in the practices and organization of the industry occurred during the decade, though on the whole it remained outside the trend toward concentration of control or management. In the earlier history of the industry the typical prospective home-owner would buy his land and engage an architect or at least a contractor, who would then proceed to erect the house. If the owner did not have enough ready cash, he might borrow on mort-gage from an individual or a savings bank. Building and loan companies also offered mortgage financing.

"Developers" and speculative builders in the 1920's took over a larger share than formerly in the building and sale of houses. This change was due partly to the rapid expansion of suburban regions consequent upon the automobile and rapid-transit sys-tems, and partly to the large profits to be made in selling houses to persons who had neither the time to wade through the morass of title searching, financing, building codes, contractors, and sub-contractors involved, nor the money to make at any one time more than a modest down payment.

[17] Kuznets, *Commodity Flow and Capital Formation*, I, 332–335.
[18] *Recent Economic Changes*, pp. 220–222.

A realty operator, with access to abundant credit, would buy a large tract of land in an outlying section; induce the municipal authorities to lay out streets, and perhaps install water mains and sewers; employ architectural and engineering services on a large scale; engage building contractors, who in turn would engage subcontractors; and sell finished houses to the house hunters on the basis of a small down payment and monthly installments. The "owner" was then left to meet possible city assessments and rising taxes, plus the relatively high capital costs involved not only in first mortgages, but often in second and sometimes third mortgages as well. In the cheaper developments quality often suffered, too large a percentage of the land was occupied by the house, the standard rectangular street layouts involved an unnecessarily heavy cost for utilities, aesthetic values were ignored, and the ultimate price to the purchaser was often exorbitant.

The industry was under a continual fire of criticism because of what were regarded as antiquated methods. Building workers remained handicraftsmen while possible mass-production by prefabrication of large sections was blocked by union rules and local building codes, supported by both unions and contractors' associations. Jurisdictional disputes among the unions frequently interrupted production, apprenticeship regulation restricted the labor supply, and working customs interfered with efficiency. Rings of material suppliers who attempted to hold up prices or monopolize local markets were responsible for the frequent charges of graft and racketeering.

By way of defense it was pointed out that many of these complaints were ill-founded, since some building laws or union rules protected workmanship, safety, or health, and others arose from the highly competitive and irregular character of the industry. A worker who had no single, steady employer, one who might be out of a job the moment a structure was finished, and who was subject to wide swings of seasonal unemployment, had good reason to try to protect his craft and gain the highest hourly pay attainable while he worked.

In any event, the actual cost of building materials and labor bulked much smaller in the whole housing picture than most people realized. Costs of financing were also important, as were costs of streets and utilities, resting ultimately on the dweller in the form of taxes and assessments. Experiments in large-scale construction, with careful advance planning, moderate financing cost, and limited profits were able to offer much better value at a given price, though they employed union labor. Pioneering efforts of this kind were Sunnyside in the Borough of Queens, New York City, and a model village in New Jersey named Radburn. Both were, unfortunately, overtaken by the depression before their costs were fully amortized.

No method was devised, however, by which city dwellers in the lower brackets of income could be enabled to enjoy new housing, and they continued to occupy—and overcrowd—slum tenements or the castoff dwellings of others. The housing boom tapered off through lack of sufficient effective demand long before decent living quarters were provided for a substantial percentage of the population.

In industrial and commercial building, as in the monumental skyscraper, real advances in technology and management practices were made. Materials were improved and standardized, portable machinery driven by electricity or compressed air was introduced, and good scheduling reduced time of construction, so that finishing operations would be in process on lower floors while the steel frame was still being erected on the upper.

Toward the end of the decade, speculative promoters of commercial buildings in the large cities, amply financed by the bank credit now flowing freely into real estate, pushed construction ahead of demand, in the general atmosphere of optimism. It was stated at the time that banks and other financial institutions were pressing builders to accept loans with little relation to the value of the building; in certain cases builders were known to have received on first mortgage more than enough to cover the entire cost of construction, so that they had no equity whatever to protect. Who would not continue operations with so little risk? The banking houses of issue in turn frequently passed on the risk to the public through real-estate mortgage bonds, which had now become a common means of financing large projects. Thus building became deeply involved in the speculative financial practices of the period.

BITUMINOUS COAL

The mining of bituminous coal was one of the more prominent of the "sick industries" of the postwar decade. It was not a declining industry in the sense that it was becoming obsolete; coal was used for house heating and, in spite of the increasing competition of oil and water power, remained the chief source of industrial energy. The growth of the use of mechanical power, which above all characterized the "plateau of prosperity," provided an ever-expanding demand for the various sources of energy. Coal mining was, however, an industry that not only did not share in the general prosperity but had a declining, uncertain, and for the most part inadequate income to share among its participants; bankruptcies were frequent, and the discontent of the miners with their lot was brought to the nation's attention by repeated interruptions of production. Most of the miners lived in squalid and insanitary houses, and the incidence of accidents and diseases was high. By the same token, the numerous population of the bituminous coal regions failed to provide a good market for the increasing quantity of goods produced.

The net income of the bituminous coal industry as a whole shrank steadily from 1.7 per cent of the national income in 1920 —a year of high coal prices, shortage, and tremendous profits—to .73 per cent in 1929. Wages and salaries paid by the industry shrank from 2.6 per cent of the national total in 1920 (and again in 1923) to 1.2 per cent in 1929. There was an absolute shrinkage of wages as well as a relative one, the decline from 1920 to 1929 approximating $500 million.[19]

The sales of bituminous coal moved irregularly from year to year, according to business conditions. In 1920, 569 million short tons were sold; though the ensuing year of depression brought the sales down to 416 million tons, they recovered to 564 million in 1923. The following year again evidenced a recession, but 1926 topped the 1920 peak with 573 million tons. Smaller sales in 1927 and 1928 were followed by recovery to 535 million in 1929. The price paid for the coal showed a steadily declining trend for the decade, alike in years of prosperity and depression, falling from $3.75 a short ton in 1920 to $1.78 in 1929. The number of men

[19] Kuznets, *National Income and Its Composition*, pp. 326, 332.

employed rose from 639,300 in 1920 to 704,600 in 1923, and then fell gradually to 502,800 in 1929.[20]

Demand for bituminous did not increase with the growing need of railroads, industry, and power stations for energy, because of the tremendous gain previously noted in efficiency in the use of coal. The industrial demand could not be spurred by any reduction of coal prices, because the cost of power was already so low as to be a minor factor in the costs and prices of the ultimate product. The sales of coal were fixed by production schedules of business customers; the demand for it is not, as the economists say, markedly elastic. Prices fell because the potential supply continually exceeded demand. For many years the industry had had a capacity in excess of its sales; production would have been at least a third greater than it was if all the mines had operated steadily.

If the industry had been monopolized, it might have abandoned the excess capacity and balanced supply with demand. Even if it had been dominated by a few large companies, like automobiles, the losers in the race might have left the field and the capacity might have been reduced. But it was competitive more as farming is competitive: it contained thousands of operators, small and large. No force except government could bring it under control, and government did not act.

Naturally, some mines were more efficient than others. Some seams were richer or less costly to excavate. Nonunion mines had lower costs, and the South was not unionized. Coal-cutting machinery and mechanization of other types had been growing in use. Secretary of Commerce Hoover recommended installation of better methods as a cure for the industry's ills. Costs were reduced in many mines by such methods. Mechanical cutting accounted for 60.7 per cent of the underground output in 1920, 78.4 per cent in 1929. Toward the middle of the decade, mechanical loading began to be introduced; in 1927, 7.4 per cent of the tonnage was mechanically loaded. In spite of the fact that management was often backward and the old-established "room-and-pillar" method of mining hampered efficient mobilization of work processes, the

[20] Harold Barger and Sam H. Schurr, *The Mining Industries, 1899–1939: A Study of Output, Employment and Productivity* (New York: National Bureau of Economic Research, 1944), pp. 284, 312.

productivity of the industry as a whole did rise—though less than in other types of mining and less than in manufacture. The index of output per man-hour rose from 90 in 1920 to 100 in 1929.[21]

But, contrary to the textbook rules of competition, the more costly mines were not promptly abandoned. They simply ceased operation except for periods of peak demand, standing by with their equipment and labor forces. To sell some of the coal in the ground seemed better to their owners than to sell none of it. Unemployed miners cost them nothing. When a mining company went bankrupt the mine did not disappear; many were not abandoned but turned up again, perhaps under new ownership, with lower capital charges. Coal deposits were so abundant that there was little natural limit on the possibility of ventures in mining, and the expenses of starting operations were not unduly heavy. Expansion took place whenever the market temporarily increased or when strikes created a shortage. Under such circumstances, a mine more efficient from the engineering point of view might be the very one to suffer from higher money cost to the operator.

The bituminous coal industry was assailed by a sea of troubles, other than the fundamental discrepancy between demand and potential supply. Steel companies owned mines—"captive" mines they were called—to be assured of a supply of high-grade coking coal. Sometimes, when business was active, they bought other coal as well, but when business was dull, they might dump their coal on the market. Railroad companies, too, owned captive mines and favored their own properties in distribution and traffic. A railroad would frequently encourage the opening of new workings, unnecessary for the total supply, to increase the traffic on its own lines. Governmental efforts to remedy this situation by compelling the allotment of coal cars according to mine capacity did not help matters; it kept open too many mines at less than full operation.

The older workings in Pennsylvania, Ohio, and Illinois were unionized in the main, but newer mines in West Virginia and Alabama drove out the union and paid lower wages. Therefore the nonunion section of the industry expanded while the union fields grimly held on and suffered unemployment. Mining unemployment does not mean, as a rule, the discharge of men who promptly try to find jobs elsewhere; it means fewer days of work for the same

[21] *Ibid.*, pp. 174, 346.

force. The diminution of the labor force attached to bituminous coal mines is a long and painful process.

The industry was assailed by engineering experts on the ground of waste of natural resources; it was stated that 150 million tons of coal were left in the ground every year in the pillars or in walls between competing properties.[22] In spite of safety laws, it was highly dangerous and wasteful of human life through preventable accidents. Other human wastes, such as unemployment, miserable living conditions, and industrial conflict, sometimes violent and bloody, prevailed. On the whole, it was an example of the fact that the competition, so dear to economic theory and so necessary if automatic equilibrium is to be maintained under private enterprise, was not pleasant for those immediately subject to the competition. Consumers, indeed, gained through fall in price, except when revolt of the oppressed interfered with their supply. But even consumers had little assurance of standard quality or even uniform prices at a given time.

So great were the difficulties in the industry that the United States Coal Commission was set up to investigate and make recommendations. Beginning its work toward the end of 1922, it was active for nearly a year, employing at one time more than five hundred persons and spending almost $600,000. Its reports covered many phases of the problem and filled several printed volumes. Though the technical quality of its work was excellent, its recommendations were ineffectual in reforming the industry. It urged better management, the avoidance of strikes, purchase and storage of coal by consumers in off seasons, and similar desirable reforms that were difficult to effectuate under the prevailing conditions.[23]

TEXTILES AND SHOES

Another important industry which did not share in the general prosperity was that engaged in the spinning, converting, and weaving of textiles. Both woolen and cotton establishments suffered; silk and rayon were somewhat more fortunate. As with bituminous coal and agriculture, the reason cannot be sought in

[22] F. G. Tryon and Margaret H. Schoenfeld, "Utilization of Natural Wealth, Chap. II in *Recent Social Trends*, p. 86.
[23] Edward E. Hunt, F. G. Tryon, and Joseph H. Willits, *What the Coal Commission Found* (Baltimore: The Williams & Wilkins Co., 1925), p. 416.

any marked diminution of demand for the products; people still bought clothing, sheets, blankets, and the many other woven products, and they had more money than ever with which to do so. Style changes, of course, injured the market for certain types of goods, but could scarcely have brought great difficulty to the industry as a whole, in view of new uses such as the strengthening of automobile tires with cotton cord.

Cotton and woolen manufacture, like coal mining and agriculture, were old industries rather than newly expanding ones like automobiles or electrical equipment. Traditions rather than modern management were therefore prevalent in them, though far from universal. The crust of custom was probably responsible for some of the trouble. Their outstanding characteristic, however, was that competition (within the tariff wall) ruled almost without check. While numerous large corporations existed, they could not be dominant in so extensive a market, and the pressure of supply on a demand that was not insatiable exerted a depressing effect on prices.

The total value of the factory sales of sheetings, drills, and the like fell from $180 million in 1923 to $134 million in 1929; of print cloth and other varied cotton products, from $381 million in 1923 to $272 in 1929; of thread and cotton yarns, from $332 million in 1923 to $239 million in 1929. The value of woolen and worsted woven goods (except blankets) fell from $630 million in 1923 to $469 million in 1929. Though some sections of the industry, such as dyeing and finishing, did better, the census group of textiles and their manufactures as a whole showed a steady decline after the peak of 1923, the value of its products falling from $3,893,000,000 to $3,576,000,000 at the end of the decade.[24]

This decline was not due to any general drop in the output of textiles; the index of physical production for the entire group actually increased from 82 in 1923 to 100 in 1929. Even cotton goods increased from 93 to 100. The physical output of woolen and worsted goods did fall about 20 per cent, while silk and rayon output rose from 73 to 100. Rayon, a new material, shared the expansion of new industries. In general, therefore, the decline in value of output after 1923 was due to falling prices fully as much as to any shrinkage in physical volume. Falling prices in turn were

[24] Kuznets, *Commodity Flow and Capital Formation*, I, 106, 107.

the consequence largely of competition in a market in which demand did not grow rapidly and in which the supply was not limited by human design or by nature.[25]

Prices of worsted goods per unit of product fell 2.3 per cent between 1923 and 1929; of woolen goods, 6 per cent; and of cotton goods, 24.4 per cent. In the same period the cost of materials for worsted goods rose 2.9 per cent per unit of product, while the unit of cost of woolen goods materials fell 3 per cent. Cost of materials of cotton goods per unit of product dropped 26.2 per cent. The course of prices therefore reflected rather closely the changes in the cost of materials. Total cost of fabrication per unit, plus profits, fell for woolen goods 9.6 per cent between 1923 and 1929; for worsted goods, 10.2 per cent; and for cotton goods, 11.7 per cent.[26]

Installation of better machinery and methods resulted in some gain in productivity in this industry, as elsewhere throughout the economy. The advance, however, was less than the average for manufacture as a whole. Physical volume of production per wage earner gained 15.2 per cent in cotton goods between 1923 and 1929, 6.5 per cent in worsted goods, and 6.6 per cent in woolen goods. The fact that unit labor costs fell by a considerably larger amount than the gain in production per wage earner reflects the falling wages and, at least in cotton, the increases in working hours.[27]

One of the most striking industrial changes of the decade was the migration of cotton textile production from New England and other northern states to the southeastern section of the country. Many new mills were built in North Carolina, Georgia, and Virginia, particularly. Northern mills, except those with unusually good management or other special advantages, reduced their operations or were completely abandoned. In many cases, northern capital and management moved south, though labor did not. The advantage of the southern location did not arise from proximity to the source of raw cotton, since possible freight savings were not more than 2 or 3 per cent of the value of the product and were offset by the additional cost of shipping finished goods to finishers or markets. The principal saving was in labor cost, which averaged

[25] Fabricant, *The Output of Manufacturing Industries*, p. 169.
[26] Mills, *Economic Tendencies in the United States*, pp. 297, 381, 382, 388, 389, 392, 405, 406.
[27] *Ibid.*

about 55 per cent of the value added by manufacture. There was an abundant supply of cheap labor in the South, and hours were not so fully restricted by state laws. Hourly earnings in the industry were between 25 and 60 per cent lower in the southern states than in New England. While the number of wage earners in the country as a whole fell about 2 per cent between 1919 and 1929, it increased 39 per cent in the southern Appalachians outside the coal plateaus. This gain was due largely to the growth of the textile industry in that region. Aside from cheap labor, the southern location was advantageous because of favorable climate and a supply of soft water. The competitive pressure on costs in the industry was thus borne chiefly by northern labor.[28]

Since the textile group was a larger employer of labor than any other class of manufacturing industries, and cotton textiles were its largest single component, the effect of this development on popular purchasing power was considerable.

Another old industry manufacturing consumers' goods which suffered changes as a result of virtually unlimited competition was that producing boots and shoes. Its physical output increased only 12 per cent in the decade 1919–1929.[29] The chief gains were in women's shoes, in which style changes were important. There was a considerable gain in efficiency, labor hours per unit of product falling 3.7 per cent annually, on the average, between 1923 and 1929, in the shoe factories.[30] A marked shift occurred in the geographical distribution of the industry. In 1919, its principal center was in Massachusetts, where it employed 80,000 wage earners comprising 38 per cent of the total in the industry. By 1925, the number employed in Massachusetts had shrunk to 57,000, or 28 per cent of the total.[31] The principal gainers were St. Louis and other midwestern centers. In this case the cause of the migration was probably not the search for cheaper labor as in the case of cotton textiles, but rather the advantage of proximity to markets. The geographical balance of population had changed since the

[28] Carter Goodrich and others, *Migration and Economic Opportunity* (Philadelphia: University of Pennsylvania Press, 1936), pp. 116–117, 377–378, 598.
[29] Fabricant, *The Output of Manufacturing Industries*, p. 192.
[30] Fabricant, *Employment in Manufacturing*, p. 68.
[31] Leo Wolman and Gustav Peck, "Labor Groups in the Social Structure," Chap. XVI in *Recent Social Trends*, p. 809.

establishment of the industry and competition finally caused this proximity to affect the older center.

PUBLIC UTILITIES

The group of industries furnishing services under public regulation, such as traction, gas, electric light and power, and telephones, experienced a rapid growth in the postwar decade. Traction companies virtually ceased expanding because of automobile and bus competition, and many of them got into financial difficulties. Growth was marked, however, in the case of electric light and power, the output of which virtually trebled between 1919 and 1929. Production of manufactured and natural gas increased by about 50 per cent, while the output of telephone communication expanded about 70 per cent.[32]

These industries were not so important as a source of income or employment as most of those previously discussed. The rapid growth of electric light and power, however, is indicated by the fact that whereas in 1919 it produced .48 per cent of the national income and paid .38 per cent of the total wages and salaries, in 1929 it produced 1.6 per cent of the national income and paid .84 per cent of the total wages and salaries.[33]

The horsepower of installed capacity in electric generating stations grew from 20 million in 1922 to 43 million in 1930. About two thirds of this was in steam plants, one third in water power. Internal combustion engines accounted for a small proportion of the total. All three grew in about the same ratio during the period.[34]

The principal cause of this expansion was the increased use of power by industry. Rapid technical advances in generating the power brought economies that reduced its selling price and contributed to the expanded use. There was also a gain in consumption by retail consumers, but the retail prices of electricity did not fall so rapidly as those charged to industrial users. The basic reason usually assigned for this difference is that large industries had the alternative of generating their own power, while most domestic customers were without this competitive potentiality.

[32] Fabricant, *Labor Savings in American Industry*, pp. 47–49.
[33] Kuznets, *National Income and Its Composition*, pp. 327, 332.
[34] A. A. Potter and M. M. Samuels, "Power," in *Technological Trends and National Policy*, Part Three, Section V.

A long and intricate controversy was carried on about proper methods for fixing rates, which, for the most part, had to be approved by state commissions. It was the accepted constitutional theory that rates should be so set as to allow a "fair return" on the value of the property utilized in the business. Commissions could not accept as a final criterion the book values declared by the utility companies themselves because of possible differences in accounting methods or watering of capital accounts. Some held that the proper basis was the original cost of the investment or, as Justice Brandeis expressed it, "the prudent cost." Others maintained that the rate base should rather be the cost of reproduction new at the time of the decision. In a period of rising prices, the use of original costs would result in lower rates, while in a period of falling prices, reproduction costs would favor the consumer. The companies and the consumer interests opposed to them argued accordingly. Other possible elements of value were also brought into the controversy, such as market value. There were also disagreements about what ought to constitute a fair rate of return.

Rate cases were continually before the commissions and were frequently appealed from them to the courts. No consistent doctrine was at the time evolved, but the strong influence of the utility companies on both commissions and courts undoubtedly prevented a more rapid reduction of rates than might otherwise have taken place. Whether this influence actually protected the profits of the industry is open to question, because lower rates might have led to sufficiently larger volume of sales to increase aggregate earnings, especially in the case of sales to household consumers.

Technical progress not only reduced the generating cost by economizing coal and labor, but made it practical to transmit power over longer distances. This in turn led to interconnections among companies serving local regions, so that pools of power were created and peak loads could be carried by drawing on the surplus capacity of wide territories rather than by adding to the capacity of small generating stations. Large economies arose in this way. This whole development, called "superpower," was the subject of comment.

The stable and growing earnings of this expanding industry led to the development of a high degree of concentration of control through the device of the holding company. Since the industry was, in any case, a "natural monopoly" under public regulation, those who for any reason wished to combine its units were in little danger from the antitrust laws. In numerous cases, holding companies were pyramided one on top of another so that the ultimate control was exercised at a level three or more steps above the operating companies. By the end of the decade of the twenties, ten groups of systems, controlled either by holding companies or by parent operating companies, sold approximately 75 per cent of the electric power produced in the nation. Sixteen gas systems controlled 45 per cent of the gas output, while American Telephone & Telegraph controlled all but a small fraction of telephone communication.[35]

Unlike the holding companies formed in industry and trade, those in electric and gas utilities were not for the most part motivated by a desire to exercise a dominating influence in a competitive field or to build up a well-rounded establishment from the operating standpoint. Frequently the operating companies within a single system were not logically connected in any geographical sense, but rather were widely scattered. It was argued that this dispersion was an aid to the stability of the parent company because it constituted a distribution of risk, but on the whole it was probably accidental.

Concentration of utility control through the holding company device began before World War I. In some of the early cases the motive was the sale of equipment or processes to the operating companies. Thus the United Gas Improvement Company was organized to promote the sale of a new method of gas manufacture. Similarly, General Electric acquired the securities of operating utilities in order to finance their purchases of electrical equipment. Its early control of these companies was limited and incidental. Later it organized the Electric Bond & Share Company, which built up an extensive system through minority stock ownership. In 1924 this company was legally divorced from General Electric when it took over the latter's utility interests and distributed its own shares pro rata to General Electric stockholders.

In their later development, utility holding companies served as a means not only of concentrating control, but of making fantastic profits out of financial promotion. Thus, a holding company

[35] Bonbright and Means, *The Holding Company*, p. 91.

would buy a controlling interest in numerous operating companies, pass a large part of the cost on to public investors by the issuance of bonds, preferred stocks, or nonvoting common stock, and retain control with only a small equity in the investment. If, as was usually the case, the earnings derived from the operating companies were at a higher rate than the interest or dividends that had to be paid on the holding company's securities sold to the public, the controlling interest would earn a large percentage on its actual investment, besides whatever profits it made on the financing. The same operation could be repeated by the pyramiding of holding companies, with a corresponding concentration of profits for the promoters at each upward step.

One of the most striking examples of a utility empire was that built up by Samuel Insull of Chicago. The Insull group consisted of five great systems, with combined assets in 1930 of $2.5 billion, which supplied 4.5 million customers with electricity or gas and produced nearly one eighth of the electric power in the country. The principal systems in this aggregation were Middle West Utilities with 111 subsidiaries, People's Gas, Light & Coke with 8 subsidiaries, Commonwealth Edison with 6 subsidiaries, Public Service Co. of Northern Illinois with 1 subsidiary. These four holding companies in turn jointly controlled Midland United Company with 30 subsidiaries. Above all of them were two top holding companies, Insull Utility Investments, Inc., with an investment of $285 million, and Corporation Securities Company of Chicago, with an investment of $157 million. These two companies were connected with each other by a 28.8 per cent interest in Corporation Securities on the part of Insull Utility Investments and a 19.7 per cent interest in Insull Utility Investments on the part of Corporation Securities. Samuel Insull was chairman of the board of both top companies, as well as chairman of each of the five major holding companies under them. Samuel Insull, Jr., was president of both top companies, vice-chairman of the boards of four of the subsidiary holding companies, and president of the fifth. This outline is merely a crude picture of the intricate corporate relationships in the Insull empire at one stage of its career. It was constantly developing and shifting.[36]

Another large utilities group was Cities Service Co., con-

[36] *Ibid.*, p. 109.

trolled by Henry L. Doherty, which in 1924 served 330 communities in 16 states, and at the end of the decade controlled 65 utilities
serving over 1,000 communities in 20 states. An example of mush-
room growth was the Associated Gas and Electric System, which
at the end of 1924 controlled properties with a book value of less
than $53 million, and at the end of the decade had a consolidated
balance sheet listing property and franchises worth $753 million
and investments of $123 million.[37]

So lucrative was the business of combining and refinancing
utilities that rival financial interests engaged in competitive bidding for operating companies and paid extremely high prices for
the properties. Although this inflated capitalization was not technically a part of the rate base of the operating companies themselves, it undoubtedly exercised an influence on the fixing of rates
because of the reluctance of commissioners to endanger the financial stability of the industry. The holding companies derived
income not only from the dividends and interest received on their
investments, but from payments received from the companies under
their control for management, construction, financing, and the like.
While the regulating commissions had the power to inquire into
these costs and disallow them if they were adjudged to be excessive, there is little doubt that in many cases they served to boost
prices to consumers for the benefit of the utility magnates.

[37] *Ibid.*, pp. 113–114.

CHAPTER IX

Labor in Inflation and Deflation

SOCIAL FERMENTS

THE labor movement emerged from the war with enlarged membership, full union treasuries, a temporary governmental guarantee of the right of collective bargaining, and numerous agencies for adjustment and arbitration which had adopted the principle that the lowest wage earnings should be sufficient to support a family in decency and that wage rates should be increased as the cost of living rose. The workers had been benefited by a high level of employment which, in spite of the fact that in many cases wage rates lagged behind the cost of living, brought their earnings somewhat above the prewar level. In 1919, the average annual earnings of those employed were 87 per cent above 1914, and the purchasing power of their earnings was 5 per cent higher than it was when Germany invaded Belgium.[1]

There were, however, serious weaknesses in the position of the union. It had not gained a foothold in basic mass-production industries like steel and automobiles. Many of its new members were in munitions and metalworking plants, which were being demobilized. It was weak even in such a great industry as textiles. The newly organized members were unfamiliar with union traditions and union discipline, while many employers had accepted collective bargaining only as a war necessity imposed by government, and were awaiting an opportunity to escape it. The

[1] Douglas, *Real Wages in the United States*, p. 391.

187

main strength of the unions lay in building, printing, railroads, and other occupations where the workers were organized, not by industrial units, but by crafts or trades, which were jealous of their respective jurisdictions and unprepared to organize the industries in which the skilled trades were in a minority and craft demarcations were confused. Most of the leaders of the American Federation of Labor were conservatives who looked with disapproval on mass labor movements that might challenge their authority. It was customary in labor circles to speak of the newly created unions as "war babies"—the same term used for the stocks of war industries in which huge speculative profits had been made.

It is estimated that the total membership of American trade unions, including not only the American Federation of Labor, but the Railroad Brotherhoods and other independent organizations, nearly doubled between 1914 and 1919, growing from 2,716,900 to 4,169,100.[2] Even the latter figure was not much more than one eighth of the wage-earning population. While some of those added to the rolls represented impermanent and unreliable gains, the extension of unionism among the unskilled and semiskilled and into new fields such as clothing brought into the movement a ferment and a progressive point of view unwelcome to President Samuel Gompers and most of the craft union officials. Aggressiveness in the rank and file had been stimulated by the virtual disappearance of unemployment and by the increased bargaining power resulting from a demand for labor in excess of the supply. At the same time, imaginations had been fired by the spirit of millennialism that was abroad.

The Bolsheviks had seized control in Russia only two years before and were proceeding to build a new society. This gave rise in other countries to interest and hope on the one hand and intense fear and hostility on the other. Germany was in the midst of a socialist revolution. A Bolshevik overturn had occurred in Hungary. Perhaps more influential in the United States than any of these events was the eloquent Nottingham program of the British Labor party, which declared, among other things, for the nationalization of coal and other basic industries and for the establishment of a national minimum that would abolish poverty

[2] Wolman, *The Growth of American Trade Unions*, p. 119.

and insecurity. Trade unions had enhanced their status throughout the Western world.

In the United States, there was neither an important revolutionary movement nor a political party representing labor. The Socialist party, whose influence had been growing for many years, had suffered defections of some of its leaders when it decided not to support the war and as an organization had lost much of its influence because of its pacifist stand. The split with the Communists further weakened it. Nevertheless, there was a good deal of discussion of economic and social reconstruction. More immediate pressures also stimulated activity. The brief unemployment crisis that accompanied demobilization and the abolition of war controls, including much of the labor adjustment machinery, gave rise to a feeling of insecurity. At the same time, the cost of living went on rising more rapidly than ever, and the patriotic inhibition on strikes no longer affected labor.

Early in 1919 the country was startled by the occurrence of a general strike in Seattle, Washington, where the leaders attempted to stop all activity and tie up the entire city, which was thoroughly unionized. Naturally such an attempt could not long endure and was violently denounced by all organs of public opinion. The Mayor of Seattle, Ole Hanson, won a short-lived fame by his suppression of the strike and his invective against its leaders and motives.

Another incident that particularly aroused the conservatives was a strike of policemen in Boston. The members of the police force had no radical aims; they were merely seeking better wages and working conditions, together with recognition of their union, but the very fact that police officers would go on strike was so frightening that their action was bitterly condemned by the general public. It was argued that no one had a right to strike against the government, least of all officers of the law. It was for his supposed part in quelling this strike that Calvin Coolidge, then Governor of Massachusetts, achieved a national reputation that led to his nomination for the Vice-Presidency in 1920.

During the war there had developed an alarming tendency to suppress civil liberties and carry on campaigns of vituperation against minority groups. At first the subjects of this campaign were mainly those suspected of being in sympathy with enemies in the war. Americans of German blood, conscientious objectors, and pacifists were the first victims, but it was not long before the adjective "disloyal" began to be applied to labor groups or others thought to be hostile to the vested economic interests. This practice grew when the second Russian Revolution had aroused the fears of the conservatives, especially since it was regarded by many as a German plot to take Russia out of the war. President Wilson's Attorneys General and the Federal Bureau of Investigation were not immune from this application of the patriotic motive, and turned suspicion against many loyal American citizens. Postmaster General Burleson was active in preventing printed matter that he disliked from being carried in the mails.

The most important organization of veterans formed after the war—the American Legion—was controlled by conservatives who were concerned lest the soldiers fall under leadership that would have a leftward tendency. Although most members of the Legion had little share in controlling it and played no part in its direction, the organization soon came to be employed in the campaign to suppress civil liberties and its members were even used in some cases against strikers. In those turbulent times the Legion was one of the chief exponents of the identification of patriotism with an opposition to social, political, or economic change of any sort.

THE 1919 STRIKES

Probably not so much attention would have been devoted to the Seattle general strike or the Boston police strike if industrial conflict of a more conventional nature had not been at high tide. Some of the more firmly established unions achieved wage increases to match the rise in the cost of living and, by collective bargaining or arbitration, made other gains. Strikes broke out, however, all over the country and in numerous important industries, including textiles, clothing, food, transportation, steel, and coal.

One of the earliest and most successful of these was that called by the Amalgamated Clothing Workers, an unaffiliated and progressive industrial union in the men's clothing industry, led by Sidney Hillman. Threatened by unemployment because of the cancellation of orders for uniforms immediately after the armistice, it shrewdly struck for the reduction of working hours to forty-four weekly. When the returning soldiers began to demand civilian clothing in large quantities, the employers were compelled to concede this demand.

During the war, the Railroad Administration had encouraged collective bargaining and had made it a practice to sign agreements with unions. As a result, railroad employees mainly engaged in the shops and in the maintenance-of-way departments, who hitherto had been unorganized, succeeded in establishing their unions and achieving recognition. The employees in train service had long been firmly organized in the Big Four Brotherhoods—the Engineers, Conductors, Firemen, and Trainmen. In the spring of 1919 the shop crafts became very restless, largely because of the fact that the cost of living had advanced much more rapidly than their wages, but also because they wished to obtain a national agreement that would bring uniformity in hours, seniority, and working rules. After negotiations had dragged along for months, unauthorized strikes broke out involving about a quarter of a million men. The government allowed a small wage increase and asked the shopmen to be patient, saying that measures would soon be taken to reduce the cost of living. It also signed national agreements of the sort requested. This action ended the unofficial walkout.

During 1919 the first serious attempt in many years was made to organize labor in the steel industry, which was traditionally antiunion and had broken the only labor organization in its field years before in the violent Homestead strike of 1892. During the war the American Federation of Labor had let it severely alone. It was overripe for organization, however, because of the working conditions that prevailed. Considerably over one third of the steelworkers had a twelve-hour day for seven days a week. Since blast furnaces have to be operated continuously as long as they are operated at all, there was no possibility of a gradual reduction from the long day, such as workers in many other industries had won. If hours were to be shortened for this group, they would have to go at once to eight. Another large fraction of the steelworkers still had the ten-hour day, while only a small minority had achieved the forty-eight-hour week then prevalent throughout the country. Although some of the more highly skilled men received comparatively good wages, the great majority did not. The work, moreover, was heavy and dangerous.

Most of the populations of the steel towns consisted of immigrants of a dozen different nationalities. Men working on blast furnaces had not only a seven-day week and a twelve-hour day, but an eighteen- or twenty-four-hour shift every two weeks. Because of their long hours and the primitive state of civilization in these towns, many of the workers had never learned English and some of them could not even read and write their own languages. Housing and sanitary conditions were often deplorable, many of the workers' houses being mere unpainted shacks without running water or plumbing.

The towns and counties in western Pennsylvania, where the heart of the industry was situated, were governed by representatives of political machines, supported and controlled by employers. The workers had no political organizations of their own and most of them seldom took the trouble to vote. Because of the power of the steel bosses over both government and press in this region, there was not a semblance of free speech, especially in periods of labor unrest. Persons who might convey to the workers ideas regarded by the employers as dangerous could not obtain halls or permits to speak. Union organizers were frequently ejected from town by the local or state police or by county authorities. With good reason, therefore, the steel empire—and especially its largest unit, the United States Steel Corporation—was regarded by labor as a feudal institution in its employment relations and as the strongest bulwark of antiunionism in the country.

The regular labor movement, as represented by the American Federation of Labor, was poorly prepared to challenge this industrial giant. No single organization held undisputed union jurisdiction over the steel industry, but twenty-four craft and trade unions claimed the right to enroll the various occupations in it. No one of them had the resources to carry on a successful strike of the small minority of the workers over which it had jurisdiction. The workers themselves would have looked with distrust upon such piecemeal penetration of the mills. No action could possibly succeed in organizing the masses of the workers except a general appeal to all occupations that would invite everybody to join at once. The few exceptions to this rule were workers in some of the more highly skilled crafts, whom the employers satisfied with relatively high wages. The employers were also adept in exploiting the prejudices of those of older American stock against the "foreigners."

In order to cope with this situation, the Federation's convention in 1918 passed a resolution introduced by William Z. Foster to form a Steel Workers Organizing Committee, consisting of the presidents of each of the unions claiming jurisdiction in the industry. A substantial fund was contributed by these unions. It was understood that the organizing campaign would be conducted by this committee as a whole and that not until after workers had joined the movement would they be sorted out into their various craft divisions. The chairman of the committee was John Fitzpatrick, an honest and veteran leader, who was president of the Chicago Federation of Labor. Its active executive, William Z. Foster, was a believer in syndicalism, who thought that by this method of organization the Federation might be induced to accept at least an approach to industrial unionism.

The committee started its organization work in September, 1918, with a high degree of success in the Chicago district, Indiana, and Ohio, where the War Labor Board prevented the discharge of union members. Later, when it went on to the Pittsburgh district, it encountered much greater difficulty, for the War Labor Board had ceased functioning. Yet, because of the spontaneous interest in the movement on the part of the workers themselves, it made more headway than the employers suspected. On July 20, 1919, the committee asked the United States Steel Corporation to confer about its demands, chief among which were the abolition of the twenty-four-hour shift, one day's rest in seven, wage increases, and the eight-hour day. Judge Elbert H. Gary, chairman of the corporation, refused to meet the union leaders or discuss the matter. It was obvious that he did not intend to make any concessions or to recognize the unions as bargaining agencies for the employees. The result was the calling of a strike, which began on September 22. Though it was not unanimous, the response of the workers to the strike call was sufficient to reduce the production of steel materially. The union estimated that 279,000 workers went out, and that later 376,000 were involved.

All the immense resources of the steel industry were summoned to defeat the strike. Prominent among these was expert publicity.

Certain New York newspapers, for instance, carried stories that the more luxurious New York hotels expected an influx of striking steelworkers who would use the occasion to take a vacation and spend their "high wages." The extent of the strike and its effect on production were carefully concealed, the corporation maintaining that most of its employees were hostile to the union and remained at work. Judge Gary argued that the eight-hour day would so increase costs of production that it was impractical. Particularly effective was a campaign against the responsible leader of the strike, William Z. Foster, who was charged with being a revolutionary. Quotations from his earlier writings were employed to discredit the entire movement of hundreds of thousands of workers. Mr. Foster replied that whatever he personally might believe, this was not a revolution but a perfectly orthodox strike for trade-union objectives. Certainly the organizers and leaders did not use revolutionary language, and the strike was singularly free from violence.

On the field of action itself, the employers resorted to more drastic methods. Labor espionage agencies reported working leaders to the bosses and strove to create disunion and discouragement among the rank and file. Mounted state troopers rode their horses through the streets of the steel towns in western Pennsylvania, dispersing groups of strikers with their clubs and pushing people off the sidewalks. The sheriff of Allegheny County issued an order that no meetings or gatherings of more than three people were to be allowed. An investigating committee sent by the Senate into the region censured the employers for long hours and for their failure to bargain collectively, but deplored the "Red" leadership. The Interchurch World Movement, an organization of the Protestant churches, studied the strike, held hearings, and later (in 1922) published a voluminous report revealing the abuses on the part of management. The press generally, however, was hostile to the strikers. So the battle wore on for weeks until the slender resources of the men were exhausted and they began to drift back to work. With its huge surplus profits, the corporation could afford to wait. Called off on January 8, 1920, the strike was not in vain, since it ultimately exerted such an effect on public opinion that several years later the United States Steel Corporation installed the eight-hour day.

While the steel strike was in its last stages, the soft coal miners

Auction of Unemployed

In the 1921 depression Urban J. Ledoux, "Mr. Zero," reproduced a slave auction, placing an unemployed man on the block in Boston Common. (*Press Association, Inc.*)

Steel Strike Headquarters

Union office in Pittsburgh of the 1920 strike. (*Brown Brothers*)

The Progressive Candidates

In 1924 Senators Robert M. LaFollette of Wisconsin and Burton K. Wheeler of Montana ran on a national third party ticket, with farmer and labor support. (*Harris & Ewing*)

The Gastonia Strike

In 1929 southern cotton–mill workers expressed their grievances by industrial action. (*Press Association, Inc.*)

also walked out. Many of them had for years been organized, and the United Mine Workers union was strong in Pennsylvania, Ohio, Indiana, and Illinois. The miners complained about unemployment and the high cost of living, and asked for a 60 per cent wage increase and a thirty-hour week. The Fuel Administration had ceased to control coal prices in February, 1919, and had become inactive in June. The mine operators declined to negotiate with the union at all, on the ground that a strike order had been issued to go into effect if no agreement could be reached, and they would not bargain under threats. The union therefore set the last day of October for the beginning of the strike. Just a week before that date the President proclaimed that the country was still legally at war and that a coal strike interfering with aid to the Allies would be unlawful. This position shocked and angered the miners, who did not understand how the war could be over for the employers but not for them. Since the prices of coal had risen sharply after the removal of control, they saw no reason why they could not pursue their usual course in seeking higher wages.

President Gompers of the American Federation of Labor on October 29 telegraphed President John L. Lewis of the miners that if the strike were postponed a conference with the operators would be possible. Simultaneously, the Attorney General of the United States, A. Mitchell Palmer, made a public statement that the act creating the Fuel Administration was still in force and that under it a strike would be illegal because of clauses forbidding combinations to restrict production and transportation. At the time of the passage of the act in question, labor had been assured that these clauses were not intended to cover union activity. Nevertheless, Mr. Palmer threatened that all the resources of the government would be used to prevent a cessation of mining operations. If it had not been for this threat, the strike might have been postponed, but the union officials decided that the rights of labor were at stake and that they could not compromise them by retreating before what they regarded as an unfair and unjustified procedure.

On October 30, President Wilson renewed the wartime regulation of coal prices, and on this legal basis, the Attorney General persuaded Federal Judge Albert B. Anderson to issue a drastic and detailed restraining order preventing the union or anyone else from doing anything in aid of the strike. Judicial interdiction of union liberty could scarcely have gone further. Nevertheless, on the following day over 400,000 miners failed to report for work. A deadlock ensued because the union would do nothing to facilitate a settlement as long as the court order stood, while neither the government nor the employers would make any promises until the strike order was recalled. On November 8 the court made permanent the restraining order and ordered the union to cancel the strike order by November 11. Even the conservative American Federation of Labor Executive Council denounced the government for breaking faith with the miners in its interpretation of the law, and urged all affiliated organizations to support the miners' union. On November 10, however, the leaders of the United Mine Workers surprisingly surrendered and called upon the miners to support the government. Though Mr. Lewis called the strike off, the miners refused to return to work. The unauthorized strike continued for several weeks until, on December 9, the renewed Fuel Administration granted a 14 per cent wage increase and the union agreed to the President's proposal that a commission be created to adjudicate the other demands.

The coal strike caused temporary shortages of fuel for both industry and railroads and created further difficulties for railroad transportation, which was already suffering from inadequate equipment. The steel and coal strikes together caused a temporary drop in the curve of industrial production and probably contributed something to the increase of prices already resulting from the excess of demand over supply. They also frayed the nerves of those who were apprehensive about revolutionary trends abroad and the unrest of labor in the United States.

POLITICAL PROPOSALS

The war had revealed the disorganization of the coal industry and had given rise to a demand for its reform. Of the many proposals made, none was carefully worked out in detail. Among labor progressives, the most popular called for nationalization of the mines—a demand that was in part a reflection of the program of British labor.

It was in 1919 that a remarkable proposal came from the Railroad Brotherhoods. Everybody realized that railroad reorganization of some sort was necessary, both in order to improve transportation and to rescue the carriers from financial instability. Many schemes were suggested and discussed, most of them emanating from financial circles. The Railroad Brotherhoods now came forward with a plan of their own, drafted by Glenn R. Plumb, a lawyer engaged by them to put their ideas in workable form.

The Plumb plan, as it came to be known, suggested that all the railroads of the country be unified and owned by a corporation, which in turn would be owned by the government. This corporation would be controlled by a board of directors, one third representing the managements, one third the government, and one third the employees. The corporation, after squeezing the water out of railroad capitalizations, was to pay off with securities of its own the owners of stocks and bonds at the value thus determined. Railroad rates were, as before, to come under the supervision of the Interstate Commerce Commission, and were to be so adjusted as to permit the corporation to earn 5 per cent. The existence and rights of the unions were to be safeguarded under the law, and an adjustment machinery of a neutral nature was to be set up to decide disputes about wages and hours.

The announcement of this plan created a sensation. It was widely denounced as a scheme for turning the railroads over to labor, few newspapers taking the pains to explain its detailed provisions in an impartial way. Its ideas were not adopted by either of the major parties, and it never found much support in Congress. Nevertheless, it became for a time a rallying cry for those who sympathized with labor's interest in economic reconstruction.

In 1919 the Railroad Brotherhoods applied for affiliation with the American Federation of Labor, in the hope of obtaining the support of the entire labor movement in their struggle for the type of railroad reorganization they desired. The move toward unity did not succeed, however, because of jurisdictional disputes with some of the Federation's unions.

Among union members and sympathetic persons in white-collar and professional occupations sentiment was strong for the creation of a national labor party. Local labor parties were formed in Chicago, New York, and other cities, and even a number of state federations of labor endorsed the idea, although most officers of the national unions in the American Federation of Labor were opposed to independent political action and did their utmost to discourage it. The local labor parties, without practical organization, funds, or experience, and run by amateurs, had little success at the polls.

There was, however, continued agitation within the labor movement for a new orientation in both political and industrial action.

Mr. Gompers and his followers were thus between two fires. On the one hand, they had been rebuffed by a formerly friendly administration and were fearful of the increasing hostility of employers to the traditional practices of the trade unions. On the other hand, they were menaced by the tide of the more radical ideas within the labor movement that threatened to capture it for independent political action and to reorganize the Federation on the lines of industrial unionism. There was a flood of reconstruction programs. For instance, the Chicago Federation of Labor called for an international league of labor to complement the League of Nations, a broad program of public ownership of industry in the United States, and the stabilization of employment through a flexible program of public works.

The Federation convention had in June, 1918, appointed a committee to draw up a reconstruction program of its own. This program, approved by the Executive Council on December 28 of the same year, concentrated on trade-union gains while throwing a few sops to those who wanted more general measures. Its legislative demands included a law making it a criminal offense for employers to interfere with the right to organize; government ownership of "public and semi-public utilities"—without any specific mention of railroads or mines; protection of women and children in industry; guarantee of the right of public employees to organize; federal and state development of water power, with rates to consumers set on the basis of cost; federal regulation of corporations; tax reforms; public housing; public employment exchanges; limitation of the power of the Supreme Court to declare legislation unconstitutional; guarantees of freedom of speech; and a two-year suspension of immigration. It favored a living wage, an eight-hour day, and a five-day week with prohibition of overtime, all to be achieved by trade-union action. It had a good word for consumers' cooperation, but conspicuously omitted endorsement of social insurance or independent political action. The subject of industrial unionism was, of course, taboo.

The storm on which conservative unionism was being tossed did not subside. As an aid in riding it out, the Federation called a union conference that met in Washington in September, 1919. The conference did not plan for action of any kind, but satisfied itself with adopting a report entitled "Labor's Bill of Rights." This declaration, besides reiterating labor's traditional program, demanded deflation of the currency and publicity for corporate accounts, endorsed scientific management, and supported the League of Nations and the International Labor Organization.

An account of this disturbed period would not be complete without mention of the futile attempt by the President to establish the basis for cooperation between capital and labor under peacetime conditions. He called a National Industrial Conference consisting of seventeen representatives of employers' organizations and bankers, twenty-one individuals supposed to represent the public (a group which, strangely enough, included John D. Rockefeller, Jr., and Elbert H. Gary, chairman of the United States Steel Corporation), and nineteen representatives of the unions. The conference split on labor's demand that the steel strike be arbitrated, and could not reach an agreement on collective bargaining with autonomous labor organizations. The employers wished to leave the door open to employee representation plans and "company unions" that were not affiliated with the national labor movement. Labor correctly interpreted this attitude as preliminary to a declaration of war on the trade-union movement, a development that came during the subsequent depression. The labor delegates left the conference and it dissolved without reaching any conclusions.

President Wilson attempted to save the situation by appointing a commission without labor representatives to work out an industrial policy. This commission showed its conservative temper by recommending an elaborate system of tribunals to decide labor disputes and the prohibition of strikes in industries affected by the public interest. The report received little attention and had no result.

The national administration was not, on the whole, deeply concerned with these domestic ferments. President Wilson had gone to Versailles, and had negotiated the peace treaty and the Covenant of the League of Nations. He returned to face a hostile Congress and the Senate irreconcilables. In spite of a speech-making tour of the country, he lost his fight for the League and became a defeated and broken man. The Democrats nominated for the presidency in the 1920 election James M. Cox of Ohio, who aroused little enthusiasm. The Republicans nominated Warren G. Harding of the same state, who genially tried to be all things to all men and advocated a return to "normalcy." The adherents of political activity on the part of labor, satisfied with neither of these alternatives, tried, with the support of the Nonpartisan League and left-wing farmer elements, to start a national Farmer-Labor party. The name of its candidate for President will probably now be remembered by few—Parley P. Christensen. Its platform was mildly socialistic, demanding national ownership of monopolistic industries and natural resources, as well as liberal reforms. Since it had the backing of no political machine and very little money, its vote was small. Mr. Harding was elected in a landslide a few months after the postwar boom had begun to crack, and prices had started to slip rapidly downhill.

DEFLATION AND OPEN SHOP

While prices continued their rise in the first half of 1920 and little unemployment existed, labor as a whole was successful in gaining wage increases commensurate with the rise in the cost of living. Annual money earnings of those employed are estimated to have been 118 per cent above 1914 for the year 1920, while their real earnings were 6 per cent above. This represented a gain of slightly less than 1 per cent over the previous year.[3] Some of the wage increases were won by collective bargaining or arbitration on the basis of contracts negotiated during the war or shortly after its close; others resulted from strikes.

Many employers, however, were preparing for a war of extermination against organized labor. They seized their opportunity the moment production and prices began to fall and unemployment reduced the bargaining power of the workers. The rallying cry of the anti-union employers was the "open shop." By this term they meant not merely an establishment in which they were relieved of the obligation to hire only union members, but one in which they were not compelled to bargain collectively with an autonomous labor organization. A number of important unions had never attempted to establish the closed shop, and many conducted successful collective bargaining without ever having won it. In the eyes of unionists, the campaign for the open shop was designed to achieve shops closed against union members.

The aim of the movement was well expressed by a resolution

[3] Douglas, *Real Wages in the United States*, p. 391.

adopted at a meeting of the National Conference of State Manufacturers Associations in Chicago on January 21, 1921, in which it was declared that workers "have the right to work when they please, for whom they please, and on whatever terms are mutually agreed upon between employee and employer and without interference or discrimination on the part of others." This was referred to as "the American plan of employment," and the meeting resolved to safeguard it "by the maintenance of the open shop." It should be noted that in the resolution the word "employee" is singular. The intention of the manufacturers to carry on individual as opposed to collective bargaining was emphasized by a representative of the Indiana Manufacturers Association, who, in speaking for the resolution, declared: "We will not employ an individual in any part of the plant that does not sign an individual contract in which it is expressed that he is not and will not become a member of a labor organization while in our employ." [4]

The open-shop drive was fostered by employers' associations that had a long record of opposition to organized labor. These included the National Metal Trades Association, the National Founders Association, the National Erectors Association, and the National Association of Manufacturers. Large companies engaged in labor espionage participated in the drive, in which nation-wide advertising and publicity were employed. Offices set up under such names as the National Open Shop Association enlisted the cooperation of local employers' organizations. According to the *Iron Trade Review* of November 11, 1920, open-shop associations were active in 240 cities of 44 states.

The objective was not merely to limit the power of unions but also to invade their strongholds. Labor organizations in the building trades were among the oldest and best organized in the country. President Eugene G. Grace of the Bethlehem Steel Corporation was quoted in an Associated Press dispatch in the New York *Times* of December 16, 1920, as follows: "The Bethlehem Steel Corporation will refuse to sell fabricated steel to builders and contractors in the New York and Philadelphia districts to be erected on a union shop basis." On being questioned, Mr. Grace asserted that his decision would not be altered even if building operations were suspended

[4] Savel Zimand, *The Open Shop Drive* (New York: Bureau of Industrial Research, 1921), p. 6.

entirely because of this action. He further declared that if 95 per cent of his employees belonged to a union, he would not recognize them as union men.

The open-shop drive was vigorously prosecuted in other important cities, such as Seattle, Indianapolis, Milwaukee, Detroit, Dayton, and Louisville. A bitter struggle was carried on in Chicago to break the unions in the building trades as well as in other organized occupations.

Because of the housing shortage and the high rents the building trades were a particularly vulnerable point for an attack which needed the support of public opinion. It was charged that the high cost of building was due to the wages paid and to the restrictive union rules and practices of the various craft unions engaged in construction. This campaign temporarily installed the "open shop" in a number of cities, but in the long run it had little influence on the membership and status of the building unions, and it made the basic troubles of the industry worse.

Assaults were also made on old established unions in other occupations such as printing. On the whole, however, union membership was diminished most in industries where expansion had been more recent and which were suffering more severely from the postwar readjustment. Decline was marked, for instance, in metal, machinery, and shipbuilding. The estimated total union membership dropped from its peak of 5,110,800 in 1920 to 3,592,500 in 1923.[5]

Some of the employers, while refusing to deal with the established national labor organizations, paid lip service to the idea of collective bargaining by encouraging and financing unions of their own within each plant. The scheme of employee representation had some years before been adopted as an inoculation against unionism by the Rockefeller-owned Colorado Fuel & Iron Company. With these "company unions," the employers in question often signed contracts, attempting to remedy grievances so that unions with outside affiliations could not gain a foothold.

Probably the major strike resulting in loss of union membership was that by the railroad shop crafts in 1922. The Transportation Act of 1920 established a system of adjustment for labor controversy with a tripartite board, entitled the Railroad Labor Board, to deal with nation-wide disputes. It contained three representatives of the

[5] Wolman, *The Growth of American Trade Unions*, p. 119.

unions, three of the employers, and three of the public, appointed by the President. Under this system, if collective bargaining did not achieve an agreement, resort to arbitration was compulsory. Labor objected to wage fixing by governmental agencies, however, and nothing in the law compelled either side to accept a decision of the board. It was believed that the support of public opinion would be enough to assure the acceptance of its decisions, but technical freedom of collective bargaining was retained.

In July, 1920, at the very peak of the boom, the Railroad Labor Board awarded a 22 per cent increase to the shop crafts, thus at last bringing their wage rates abreast of the rise in the cost of living. Scarcely had the award been made, however, when prices started downhill and railway traffic diminished. Railroad managements in turn lost no time in attacking the recent gains of the unions. They carried on a vigorous publicity campaign against the rules of the shop crafts, which, they asserted, restricted output and increased costs. The public, accustomed to similar charges in the building trades, accepted these statements uncritically, although there was less substance in them than in the case of the building industry. Since the working rules were embodied in the national agreements, the employers demanded the abolition of these agreements, and shortly thereafter asked for wage reductions as well.

President Harding failed to renew the appointments of public representatives on the Railroad Labor Board whom Mr. Wilson had named, and put in their places men looked on with more favor by railroad executives. In April, 1921, the Railroad Labor Board did abrogate the national agreements in the railroad shops and instructed the railroads and unions to negotiate new separate agreements by systems. Under the existing conditions of depression and unemployment, the shop unions on many of the roads were unable to preserve their gains, and on some of them—for example, the Pennsylvania Railroad—the managements succeeded in disorganizing the workers altogether. In July of the same year, the Railroad Labor Board ordered a 12 per cent reduction that caused further discontent. It is probable that a strike would have occurred at this time if the Big Four Brotherhoods had not been granted concessions by the managements.

On June 5, 1922, the Railroad Labor Board ordered another wage reduction that completely canceled the advance gained in

1920. The result was a nation-wide strike of the railroad shop crafts, which began on July 1 and involved about 400,000 men. Most of the newspapers opposed the strike, alleging that it was a revolt against the legally established labor adjustment machinery in the industry. President Harding issued a proclamation warning the strikers against interfering with the United States mails. The unions replied that it was not illegal to reject an award of the Railroad Labor Board and that the wages set by the board were too low to maintain a decent standard of living, the minimum being only 23 cents an hour. The President attempted to mediate the strike, and on July 27 reached an agreement with the heads of the unions covering all points at issue. Although they accepted most of these terms, the railway managements refused to agree to restore seniority rights to strikers. The unions declined to call off the strike as long as the managements retained this position, since it would mean discrimination against the strikers in favor of the strikebreakers. From long experience they had learned that ending a strike on such terms often results in the disappearance of the union.

Negotiations continued but they were futile, and the funds of the strikers began to give out. At this psychological moment (September 1, 1922) Attorney General Daugherty obtained an order in the Chicago Federal Court restraining the unions from doing anything in support of the strike. The order was based upon alleged conspiracy to violate the antitrust laws and the Transportation Act of 1920. The unions argued in vain that organized labor had specifically been exempted from the antitrust laws by the Clayton Act, especially when it was engaged in a direct dispute with employers about wages and hours. They also pointed out that the Transportation Act did not make strikes illegal. A substantial body of authorities versed in labor law upheld their position. Nevertheless, Judge James H. Wilkerson, who presided over the court in question, made the injunction permanent. The strike was ended by agreement on eleven important systems, more friendly to the unions than the others. On the remainder of the country's railroads, it was lost, and nonunion conditions prevailed in their shops for a considerable period.

The Baltimore agreement, signed on September 15, 1922, which ended the strike, was followed by an interesting development on the most progressive of the union roads, the Baltimore & Ohio. Here the shop craft unions made a cooperative arrangement with the management to assist in eliminating waste and in increasing efficiency, provided the management for its part would share with the workers any resultant benefits. The chief immediate benefit in view was the return to the railroad shops of the work of rebuilding locomotives, which had been recently sent to outside concerns because of lower costs. This experiment in "union-management cooperation," one of the first of its kind in American industry, was later taken over by other railroads, notably the Canadian National system, and was practiced extensively in manufacturing industries during the Second World War.

According to the arrangement, rank-and-file committees, whose members were not those handling union grievances and union demands, were to confer with management representatives about methods of improving work practices and shop organization. By this means the management not only tapped the extensive knowledge of the workers who had intimate contact with the processes involved, but created an atmosphere of interest in the results obtained and thus greatly improved morale. Subsequent comparisons of productivity between the shops of the union and those of the nonunion roads showed no advantage for the open-shop employers who had made such a vehement argument about the high cost of restrictive union rules.

During the war and the immediate postwar period labor suffered a number of reverses in the courts, in addition to the nation-wide injunctions against the coal and railroad strikes. In 1917, the United States Supreme Court, in *Hitchman Coal and Coke Company* v. *Mitchell et al.*, had held that a union could not lawfully interfere with an individual contract between an employer and his employee binding the employee not to join a labor organization.[6] This was a validation by the highest court in the land of an anti-union device called by labor "the yellow dog contract," which some years later was outlawed by federal legislation. It permitted an employer having a nonunion shop to protect it against labor organization by making an individual contract of this nature a condition of employment.

In April, 1919, a federal court of appeals, in the case of *United Mine Workers* v. *Coronado Coal Company*, upheld a judgment for

[6] 245 U. S. 229.

triple damages under the Sherman Antitrust Act against the union for calling a strike.[7] Labor had been assured during President Wilson's first administration that its legitimate activities were exempted from antitrust laws. In the same year, the courts held invalid a child labor law that Congress had attempted to enforce by forbidding products of child labor to enter interstate commerce. The Supreme Court in 1921, in *Duplex Printing Press Co.* v. *Deering*, held that a boycott by the International Association of Machinists to force unionization of a factory making printing presses was illegal under the antitrust law.[8] In 1921 also the case of *American Steel Foundries* v. *Tri-City Central Trades Council* sustained the view that the courts could limit picketing to "peaceful" picketing and that in order to do so they might require that no more than a single picket be stationed at each entrance of a plant.[9]

Legislatures, too, were busy. Under the so-called Criminal Syndicalism Laws they attempted to outlaw unions having radical aims. The Kansas legislature in 1920 forbade strikes in industries that were supposed to be affected with a public interest, and set up an industrial court to regulate wages, hours, and conditions of work in these industries.

Although wage reductions were generally demanded by the employers during the deflation and were widely enforced, wage rates did not drop so rapidly as the cost of living. The resistance of organized labor played a considerable role in limiting the fall of wages. The fact that many employers were trying to destroy unions probably had some influence in moderating wage reductions, since the leaders of labor contended that the open-shop drive was merely a cover for enforcing lower standards of living, while the employers argued that the worker would benefit from the absence of organization. In a sense, the employer was competing with the union leader for the loyalty of his employees, and this fact sometimes led to the payment of relatively high wages in nonunion establishments. In 1921, the average annual earnings of employed wage earners fell 9 or 10 per cent below 1920, but the purchasing power of the money received actually increased slightly. In 1922, though money earnings fell a little more, real earnings showed a sharp rise. When larger em-

[7] 259 U. S. 344.
[8] 254 U. S. 443.
[9] 257 U. S. 184.

ployment was resumed in 1923, wage earners came out of the deflation with the greatest increase in real earnings they had enjoyed for many years. Their gain over 1914 was by this time approximately 19 per cent.[10]

[10] Douglas, *Real Wages in the United States*, p. 391.

CHAPTER X

Labor in Prosperity

POPULATION MOVEMENTS

THE fortunes of labor in the postwar decade were affected by a number of influences. One of these was the restriction of immigration. Before the war the excess of aliens arriving over those who departed was over a million annually. Some settled on the land, but the great majority remained in the cities and augmented the labor supply. Unskilled labor and domestic service thus received new recruits continually, but many immigrants before long obtained jobs demanding a somewhat higher degree of skill. Workers of foreign origin were numerous in the clothing and garment industries and in textile mills, steel mills, shoe factories, railroad construction and maintenance, the building trades, and many other branches of manufacturing and trade.

The excess of arrivals over departures shrank rapidly during the war, until in 1919 it reached the low point of 5,000. In 1920 the number of arrivals jumped again, becoming 908,000. But the number of departures also increased, so that the net gain, or 495,000, was about half the prewar level.[1] Many went back to the countries of their origin to set themselves up with savings they had accumulated in America. If there had been no further obstacles to immigration, however, it is probable that the large net influx from Europe would have been resumed in subsequent years.

The increased nationalism stimulated by the war produced a strong movement to curb immigration. Formerly industry had sup-

[1] Jerome, *Migration and Business Cycles*, p. 124.

208

ported unrestricted immigration because it supplied a large stream of cheap and usually docile labor, while liberals opposed restriction on account of their wish to keep open the opportunities of the new country to the politically or economically oppressed of other lands. Now employers were frightened by the labor unrest in the United States and the revolutionary spirit in Europe, which they supposed had a large share in causing it. As is usual in a period of social ferment, strike leaders and those who proposed changes in the economic order were widely denounced as "un-American" or "alien agitators." Prejudice against the foreigner, always latent, but particularly strong where large numbers had come to communities formerly dominated by the native born, became more vocal than ever. Conservatives in the trade-union movement, who had long opposed immigration because of the competition in the labor market offered by the new arrivals and because they regarded immigrants as difficult to organize, supported restriction. Unions like those in the garment and clothing trades, which were composed largely of immigrants, argued for the traditional policy, as did many liberals, but restriction won.

In June, 1921, the law went into effect restricting immigration in any one year to 3 per cent of the number of a given national origin already in this country in 1910. This law was, in substance, a discrimination against migrants from southern and eastern Europe, from which the mass immigration of the prewar years had largely been derived. The national origin of the majority of Americans was English, Irish, German, or other northern European, rather than Russian, Polish, Hungarian, or Italian. The law did not apply to Canada or Mexico. Partly because of the current depression, and partly because of the legal restriction, net immigration fell in 1921 to 280,000. It remained about at that level in 1922, but in 1923 renewed employment opportunities brought the excess of arrivals to 707,000. A more drastic law in 1924, basing quotas on the population of 1890, reduced the flow to a negligible component of the American working force.[2]

The economic effect of large immigration on the one hand and of its restriction on the other was probably overestimated by most of those who took sides on the matter in the current debate.

[2] *Ibid.* For 1921 law, see Chap. 8, 42 Stat. 5, as amended and extended by resolution May 11, 1922, 42 Stat. 540. For 1924 law, see Chap. 190, 43 Stat. 153.

Some thought of additions to the population mainly as increases in the number of consumers, who would augment the demand for the products of industry and agriculture and would sustain rising land values. Others saw the new arrivals not in the light of additions to the nation's wealth, but as competitors for jobs. Immigrants were, of course, both consumers and producers and, broadly speaking, added to the demand for economic products about as much as they added to the supply. Where immigrants were concentrated, labor standards probably remained lower for a considerable period than they might otherwise have been.

An analysis by Harry Jerome for the National Bureau of Economic Research concluded that, under normal conditions, variations in immigration corresponded closely to variations in employment opportunities in the United States. Yet immigration frequently lagged behind changes in employment and "even in periods of low employment, net immigration was sometimes steadily adding to the supply of workers." In periods of prosperity, an ample labor supply made possible rapid expansion of production and tended to keep wages down, thus checking a rise in costs that might have dampened down the boom and minimized the severity of the subsequent depression. Whatever the truth in this theory, it must be noted that one of the most severe depressions in the nation's history occurred after immigration had been restricted and labor standards had risen.[3]

A relative shortage of unskilled labor during and after the war led to the introduction of new machinery and methods that in many occupations replaced human muscle by mechanical power. As one engineer remarked to me during the steel strike of 1919, "We do not intend to improve the condition of unskilled labor; we intend to abolish it." This tendency had momentous economic and social results, but competition for jobs in the labor market was probably increased as much by the introduction of engineering improvements as it was diminished by the cutting off of immigration.

Those who expected that stopping the influx of immigrants would check the spread of "un-American" and radical ideas were mistaken; there is little evidence that the majority of the new arrivals ever carried such ideas with them. While radical movements and even trade-union membership languished in the twenties, it is likely that the gradual assimilation of the foreign born made the task of

[3] Jerome, *Migration and Business Cycles*, pp. 239–244.

union organizers somewhat easier in the subsequent decade. Workers of one nationality are probably no more resistant to participation
in the labor movement than those of any other, given the economic
and political setting that favors organized activity. Nationalistic or
racial prejudices, however, often flourish among workers as in other
elements of the population, and may set up barriers against unity.
Such barriers are lowered as differences of language and custom disappear.

Growth of population as a whole had been slowing down for a
considerable period. The percentage increase from 1890 to 1900 had
been below that of any previous decade. Another decline was registered in the decade from 1900 to 1910. Between 1910 and 1920 the
war intensified the trend, and the rate of increase was only 15.4 per
cent. From 1920 to 1930, the rate recovered slightly, to 15.7 per
cent.[4] Without the limitation of immigration, it might have been
somewhat larger than this, although the chances are that the long-
term downward trend of growth would not have been reversed.

The population growth in the postwar period was very unevenly
distributed, being affected by strong currents of internal migration.
The population of California grew 66 per cent and that of Florida
52 per cent. Here favorable climate attracted many, as it did also in
the cases of Arizona and Oregon. Four other states that gained more
than 20 per cent in population—Michigan, New Jersey, North Carolina, and New York—enjoyed a rapid industrial or commercial development. Texas, the only other state whose population grew more
than one fifth in the decade, experienced an expansion of cotton
farming and an oil boom. At the other extreme, the population of
Georgia remained almost stationary, and that of Montana actually
declined.[5]

The growth in population occurred largely in urban communities. Cities and towns of over 2,500 gained 14.6 million between 1920
and 1930, while the rural nonfarm population increased only 3.6 million, and the farm population declined by at least 1.2 million.[6] In
1930 the rural population was less than 44 per cent of the total,
though it had been 60 per cent in 1900.[7] In the cities themselves, the

[4] Warren S. Thompson and P. K. Whelpton, "The Population of the Nation,"
Chap. I in *Recent Social Trends*, p. 1.
[5] *Ibid.*, p. 6.
[6] *Ibid.*, p. 8.
[7] *Ibid.*, p. 9.

most rapid growth occurred in metropolitan regions outside the big
city centers. People from the country were drifting into the city, and
people from the city were spreading out into the neighboring suburbs or satellites.

An index of population movement computed by subtracting the
number of persons born within a state who are living outside it,
from the number born outside it who are living within it, confirms
the inference that these shifts resulted largely from internal migration. This index, covering the native white population from 1920 to
1930, shows large gains for New York, New Jersey, Ohio, Michigan,
Illinois, Florida, and California, and minor gains in Connecticut,
Maryland, Virginia, Indiana, New Mexico, Arizona, Nevada, and
Washington. Losses were registered in all other states. Population
was drifting to Florida, California, and the industrial regions and
away from the older agricultural regions. Something of the same
tendency existed in previous decades, but was not so consistent or
marked.[8]

More detailed studies indicate movement from regions of low
living standards. The population of the southern Appalachian coal
plateau was too large for the resources of mines, forestry, and agriculture, and many of its inhabitants found industrial employment
north of the Ohio River. The old cotton belt in the Southeast was
impoverished by worn-out soils, tenancy, the competition of cotton
in Texas and westward, and the decline of exports. The birth rate
was high. Negroes drifted from this region to northern cities. The
disappearance of timber in the cutover region of the Great Lakes,
coupled with declining employment in mining and woodworking,
resulted in an outflow from that area. In 1927, no taxes were paid
on nearly one fourth of the cutover area of Wisconsin. In northern
Minnesota, accumulated unpaid taxes in 1930 often exceeded the as-
sessed value of the property.

Exhaustion of other natural resources, combined with the discovery of new fields, led to population shifts. The number of oil well
operatives declined during the decade in Ohio, Indiana, Illinois, West
Virginia, Kansas, Louisiana, and Wyoming, but very large increases
occurred in Arkansas and California and the previous increase in
Oklahoma and Texas continued. Those employed in the milling of
lumber decreased in the Great Lakes region, in the Northeast, and

[8] Goodrich, *Migration and Economic Opportunity*, p. 676.

in the South, but increased on the Pacific coast. The number of miners in Michigan copper mines declined and minor reductions occurred in Mississippi Valley lead and zinc mines and in western metal mines. In the last case, however, the result may have arisen from more efficient methods of production.

The decline of employment in New England cotton mills and shoe factories has already been mentioned. It was accompanied by a growth of cotton-mill employment in the South and of shoe employment in the Middle West. There was also a tendency on the part of the clothing and printing trades to seek cheaper labor by removing their establishments from the large cities to smaller centers. The clothing and garment trades particularly made use of the families of unemployed coal miners in Pennsylvania.

These shifts appear in the regional distribution of wage jobs in manufacturing. In 1919, New England had offered 14.9 per cent of the manufacturing employment of the country; in 1929, 12.4 per cent of the factory wage earners were located there. The proportion of the Middle Atlantic states fell in the ten years from 31.2 per cent to 28.7 per cent. On the other hand, the percentage of the national total of manufacturing wage earners grew in the East North Central states, where the automotive industries were located, in the South, and on the Pacific coast.

The East still remained more dependent on manufacturing than any other section, although the wage jobs per thousand of population fell drastically. In 1919, 182.6 of every thousand persons in New England had manufacturing employment against 134.5 in 1929. The corresponding figures for the Middle Atlantic states were 127.4 in 1919, and 96.6 in 1929. The East North Central states fell in the same period from 110.7 to 99.4. The region next highest in manufacturing employment per thousand was, in 1919, the Pacific states, with 78.2, but these fell to 57.5 in 1929. The South Atlantic states were barely reduced—from 59.5 to 59.2. In no other region were there as many as 40 per thousand engaged in manufacture. All showed a decline on account of the shrinking total of manufacturing employment and the rise of other occupations such as service.[9]

The composition of the labor force itself was somewhat changed. The number of women gainfully occupied, which had increased sharply during the war, remained high. In 1920, women constituted

[9] *Ibid.*, p. 316.

20.1 per cent of all gainfully occupied and in 1930 the percentage was 21.9. Omitting those employed in agriculture, 234 out of every thousand women worked for pay. The largest number were in domestic and personal service, but by 1930 1,970,000 were in clerical occupations, 1,860,000 in manufacturing and mechanical industries, and 1,226,000 in the professions. Of married women, 3,071,000, or 11.7 per cent, were gainfully occupied in 1930.[10] Employment of women made the greatest gains in transportation and communication, clerical occupations, trade, and public service. In manufacturing, the increase was very small and occurred mainly in semiskilled operations.

Negroes had gone north in large numbers during the war and many had been employed for the first time in industry—notably steel, motor vehicles, and meat packing. Many of them lost their employment during the postwar slump and returned to the South, but during the decade they came back, and by its end Negroes had regained their place in industry.

The historic trend of steady increase in the number of persons employed in manufacturing was reversed in the ten years after the war. A peak was reached in 1919, with an average number of wage earners totaling 8,403,200. Thereafter, though variation occurred between the years of higher and lower activities, the trend was slightly downward. Even in the boom year of 1929, the total of factory employment was but 8,362,200.[11] This decline was not, of course, the result of any shrinkage in manufacturing production, which, on the contrary, grew rapidly.

At the same time, the number gainfully occupied in agriculture was declining. On January 1, 1920, it was 11,439,000 and on April 1, 1930, it was 10,472,000.[12] The relative importance of agriculture in the national economy had been shrinking for some decades, but now there was an absolute fall as well. Those displaced from farms could no longer, on the whole, find work in factories, while those displaced from factories could not find work on farms. There was a shrinkage also in employment on railroads and in mining. The total employed in these two occupations at the beginning of the period had been

[10] S. P. Breckenridge, "The Activities of Women Outside the Home," Chap. XIV in *Recent Social Trends*, p. 716.
[11] Fabricant, *Employment in Manufacturing*, p. 214.
[12] Harold Barger and Hans H. Landsberg, *American Agriculture, 1899–1939* (New York: National Bureau of Economic Research, 1942), p. 231.

larger than the total of those engaged in either agriculture or manufacturing. Since the population continued to grow, unemployment
would have become much worse than it was if there had not been
a simultaneous expansion of employment in construction, trade, and
service occupations. The distribution of the gainfully occupied at the
beginning and the end of the postwar decade is shown in the accompanying table.

DISTRIBUTION OF GAINFULLY OCCUPIED
(Employees on full-time equivalent basis)

Occupational Group	1919 %	1929 %
Agriculture	21.3	18.3
Mining	2.8	2.3
Manufacturing	25.4	22.3
Construction	2.8	4.4
Transportation and public utilities	8.2	7.3
Trade	12.6	14.8
Finance	2.4	3.3
Service	12.2	15.6
Government	8.8	7.0
Miscellaneous	3.5	4.6
Total number	39,818,000	44,913,000

Source: Simon Kuznets, *National Income and Its Composition, 1919–1938*, pp. 346–347.

TECHNOLOGICAL UNEMPLOYMENT

Rapid advance in technical efficiency led not only to a growth
in the national income and an increase in the physical product of
industry, but to hardships on the part of the workers who were
displaced in the process. In the latter part of the decade particularly, complaints continually arose from the ranks of labor about
technological unemployment. Theorists who argued that the problem was not serious pointed out that in the nation as a whole, technical advance was accompanied by a growth of employment, and
that in industries where the increase of productivity was most rapid,
as in automobiles, employment also grew swiftly. No doubt men
were thrown out of work here and there, but the problem, it was
contended, was one of shifting jobs and occupations rather than of
any net decrease in the number of jobs available.

Nevertheless, the difficulties of those who actually lost their jobs were serious, whether or not technical change was the cause. A study in three industrial cities in 1928 revealed that of men who had been discharged within the preceding year, 45 per cent were still unemployed. In New Haven and Hartford, 1,190 rubber workers were displaced in 1929 by the transfer of production to more efficient plants. At the end of eleven months, 13 per cent of them were still unemployed and only 19 per cent of those who had found jobs were paid as well as before, while fully 66 per cent were earning less. Workers cannot move about freely or easily find jobs for which they are fitted, and it is not always possible to find employment while the total number of those engaged in manufacturing is shrinking.[13]

It must be remembered also that marked advances in productive efficiency occurred in large industries which, instead of benefiting from an expanding demand, like automobiles, were suffering from a stationary or declining demand, like coal mining. Between 1923 and 1929, 3,300 bituminous coal mines were forced to close and about 250,000 men lost their jobs.[14] The wages of the remainder were cut again and again. Production per worker grew more rapidly in woolen and cotton textiles than did the demand for the product, while thousands of employees were left stranded in New England by the movement of cotton mills to the South.

Workers were not only directly displaced by technological improvement in plants where the innovation was made, but might suffer indirectly in a number of ways. Production might be diverted from competing plants to the one that had installed the improvement and thus enjoyed lower costs. A cheaper or more effective substitute might reduce the output of an older industry. The elimination of waste and spoilage could affect employment in industries supplying raw material, fuel, or equipment. Improvements in the quality of industrial materials or machinery could also affect labor requirements. Better steel and machine tools made possible higher running speeds and less frequent sharpening. Improvements in the quality of steel rails reduced maintenance expense on railroads.

A period of extremely rapid technical advance thus affects the

[13] Weintraub, "Unemployment and Increasing Productivity," in *Technological Trends and National Policy*, p. 83.
[14] *Recent Social Trends*, p. 86.

volume of unemployment almost inevitably because of what economists euphemistically call the imperfect mobility of labor. This is true even though the total product might theoretically increase rapidly enough so that it could absorb all the displaced workers. In Chapter VII, estimates have been quoted of the total amount of unemployed labor time in terms of man-years. After the recovery from the 1921 deflation, this unused time varied between 10 and 13 per cent of the labor supply. How many individuals were totally unemployed it is difficult to estimate, since there were no actual counts of the unemployed and no way of keeping track of them through unemployment insurance. Naturally, the number would be smaller than the man-years of employment lost, which include the effect of part-time work by employed individuals. Figures from the National Industrial Conference Board indicate unemployment varying from minima of 400,000 in 1929 and 500,000 in 1926 to maxima of 1.9 million in 1928 and 2 million in 1924. These figures constitute about 1 per cent of the employees outside agriculture, the armed forces, and public employees in service industries in 1929, and about 6.6 per cent in 1924. How estimates may vary is illustrated by the fact that the United States Bureau of Labor Statistics, which began its series in 1929, calculated that there were 1.5 million unemployed in that year, or about 5 per cent of the total number of employees omitting agriculture, the armed forces, and federal, state, and local governments.[15]

ACTIVITIES OF UNIONS

The labor organizations, their treasuries depleted and their numbers diminished by the postwar deflation and the open-shop drive, were in no position to take full advantage of the ensuing period of prosperity. Their policies and fortunes were also deeply affected by the more fundamental economic trends of the period, such as the rapid increase in productivity, the varying fortunes of specific industries, and the failure of total manufacturing employment to grow. On the whole, the number of trade-union members slowly but steadily declined from 1923 to 1929, even after the big reduction suffered in the immediate postwar period.

[15] Calculated by the National Bureau of Economic Research from National Industrial Conference Board, *Management Almanac* (1945), pp. 18–27, and U. S. Bureau of Labor Statistics, Technical Memorandum No. 16 (July 13, 1944) and Technical Memorandum No. 20 (July 4, 1945).

One of the most interesting developments of the time was the elaboration of a new wage theory. Labor had long contended in general terms that unless employers distributed the gains of mechanical improvements in higher wages, the purchasing power of the population would not be sufficient to buy all that could be produced. During the war, attention had been concentrated on the attempt to gain increases in money wages commensurate with the rise in the cost of living. This principle, accompanied by that of a minimum wage determined by studies of family budgets, had become predominant in union contracts and the procedures of arbitration boards. When the cost of living started to fall, employers naturally attempted to apply the principle in reverse by demanding wage reductions equal to the drop in prices. To combat this argument, unions once more emphasized the necessity of increased real wages or purchasing power parallel with the advance in production per worker or per unit of the population.

The first detailed attempt to elaborate this principle in terms of statistics and economic theory was contained in a brief presented to the Committee on Labor of the House of Representatives on June 30, 1922, by representatives of employees in the United States arsenals and navy yards, organized as District 44 of the International Association of Machinists. Government workers were not supposed to strike and therefore lacked the ordinary powers of collective bargaining. Their wages had customarily been set on the basis of current wages in neighboring plants and during the war had been adjusted by the cost of living index. With widespread wage reductions in civilian plants, the employees in question were naturally in search of a more fundamental principle.[16]

Economists had recently begun to compile indexes of physical production. Comparison of these with the growth of the population or with the number of wage earners indicated a steadily increasing trend in productivity. At the same time, manufacturing wage earners had received from year to year a nearly constant proportion of the value-product of industry. It was inferred from these facts that their real earnings must have risen in direct ratio to the increase in per capita manufacturing production and that this increase had occurred without prejudice to the accumulation of capital or the

[16] Hearings before the Committee on Labor, House of Representatives, 67 Cong., 2 Sess., pursuant to House Resolution 11,956.

increase in productivity. Therefore it would be possible and desirable to increase real wages in the future in the same ratio as the trend of increase in per capita production. If this were not done, the proportionate share of wage earners in the national income would not be maintained and general economic difficulties might ensue.

The statistics then available covering productivity and real wages were incomplete, and the analysis disregarded certain important factors. It was pointed out in the union's brief that real wages had not actually kept pace with the rise in industrial productivity between 1910 and 1919, in spite of the fact that the share of the workers in the value-product of industry had not decreased. The value-product was reckoned in terms of the factory prices of manufactured articles, but real wages depended in large measure on what the workers had to pay for food at retail. At first it was suggested that the apparent contradiction between the failure of real wages to rise and their constant share of an increased factory product could be accounted for by higher costs of distribution. Further study showed that the real cause of the discrepancy was the disproportionate rise in prices of farm products, particularly food. The agricultural community had been gaining at the expense of both manufacturers and manufacturing wage earners. Since, however, after the war, prices of farm products fell much further than those of manufactured goods, real wages could rise on this account as well as in consequence of increased production per wage earner.

The general thesis that the purchasing power of the workers should be increased because productivity was rising was emphasized in many wage controversies. Later in the decade it was accepted by some employers and took a firm hold in popular discussion. It is difficult now to understand what a fundamental change was occurring in American attitudes toward the production and division of wealth.

Much has been written about the effect of the frontier on American life and the changes wrought by its passing. Whatever may have been true of the geographical frontier, the frontier period had now come to an end in an economic sense, in terms of population, and in the prevalent ideas. The American tradition had been that success was to be sought by "growing up with the country."

The markets for both factories and farms were expected to be expanded by the increase in the number of persons. The natural consequence was that most employers had looked upon their employees merely as aids in production, whose services should be obtained at the lowest possible cost. Now, however, the idea began to spread that these simple formulas were no longer operating. The opening up of new territories and the exploitation of new additions to the population had virtually come to an end. How, then, were businesses to grow and sell an increased volume of products? The obvious answer was that this could occur only through an increase in the purchasing power of the people who already existed. Wage earners began to be regarded not only as producers but also as consumers. A number of employers, among whom Henry Ford was prominent, expressed the belief that it was to the advantage of the employer to pay high wages in order to provide a market for his products. On the same grounds, the economic distress of the farmers caused some concern among those who had no direct interest in agriculture.

Thus the theory of the economy of high wages, which long before had been advanced by the unions, now became a prominent article in the creed of many business spokesmen. There is truth in the theory, but there are many reasons to doubt that it ever was deliberately practiced by many individual employers, or that it can consistently be practiced in a noncollectivist economic system, at least without strong collective action by labor. The larger part of the growth in purchasing power of wage earners that was noted at this time had actually occurred as a result of the postwar deflation, when wage rates had fallen less rapidly than the cost of living, in consequence of the bitter resistance offered by organized labor to wage reductions that employers had been doing their best to effectuate. Employers had then found it possible to maintain this new relationship between wages and prices, partly because of the wider margin between the cost of materials and the prices of manufactured products, which had occurred as a result of the unequal incidence of deflation, and partly because of the gains in efficiency of production that technology was making possible. Verbal acceptance of the economy of high wages was thus in large measure a rationalization after the event.

It will be seen from the table on page 221, showing the

average annual earnings of employed wage earners, that the big jump in real earnings occurred between 1920 and 1923. Money earnings fell during the postwar deflation and then increased again when, in 1923, employment became high. They still, however, were below the 1920 peak. The larger part of the gain was therefore attributable to the drop in the cost of living. After 1923, no further increase in earnings occurred until 1926, when upward wage adjustments brought another rise. The year 1927 registered a slight gain in real earnings because of the depression and the drop in prices, and the final stages of the boom carried wages slightly higher. The rise in real earnings in the three years from 1920 to 1923 was 13 per cent against a rise of 11 per cent for the five years from 1923 to 1928.

AVERAGE ANNUAL EARNINGS OF EMPLOYED WAGE EARNERS AND
INDEX NUMBERS OF ANNUAL MONEY AND REAL EARNINGS

Year	Average Annual Earnings (Dollars)	Money Earnings	Real Earnings
1914	613	100	100
1915	613	100	102
1916	681	111	104
1917	794	130	101
1918	997	163	104
1919	1,144	187	105
1920	1,337	218	106
1921	1,171	191	108
1922	1,144	187	113
1923	1,228	200	119
1924	1,225	200	118
1925	1,255	205	119
1926	1,375	219	126
1927	1,375	219	128
1928	1,405	224	132

(NOTE: High points of the index were reached in former years with 100 in 1892, 1906, and 1913, 101 in 1905 and 1910, and 102 in 1909.)

Sources: Paul H. Douglas, Real Wages in the United States, 1890–1926 (Boston: Houghton Mifflin Company, 1930), p. 391. Data for 1926–1928 from P. H. Douglas and F. T. Jennison, The Movement of Money and Real Earnings in the United States, 1926–1928 (Chicago: University of Chicago School of Commerce and Administration, Studies in Business Administration), Vol. I, No. 3.

By consulting the table on page 121. Indexes of Employment per Unit of Output, it will be seen that the most rapid growth of productivity in manufacturing occurred in the three years from 1919 to 1922, when the gain, reckoned in terms of man-hours, was 26 per cent. In the following seven years, the advance was 23 per cent. The greatest increase in real earnings thus came at the time that the greatest gain in productivity was realized.

The advance in manufacturing productivity for 1919 to 1928 was 40 per cent, in comparison with a rise in annual real earnings of 26 per cent. It is not, of course, to be expected that the earnings of all wage earners would rise by the same amount as increased productivity in manufacturing alone. As the table indicates, productivity followed a somewhat different course in agriculture, railroads, and mining, and on the whole did not increase so much as in manufacturing. If figures were available, a still smaller percentage of increase would be shown in trade and service occupations. Nevertheless, evidence will appear in a later chapter that business did not fully share its productive gains with wage earners and consumers by a combination of wage increases and price reduction.

The emphasis on the gains to be expected from increased productivity naturally led unions to attempt to convince employers that, instead of being a barrier to this improvement, they could offer positive assistance. The Baltimore & Ohio plan, put into effect on the railroads that recognized the union shop crafts, has been mentioned in the previous chapter. Union-management cooperation was subsequently endorsed by the American Federation of Labor. During an ineffectual organizing campaign in the automobile industry in 1926 and 1927, labor representatives spent almost as much time in trying to convince employers that collective bargaining would be to their advantage as they did in organizing the employees. A few unions, notably the Amalgamated Clothing Workers and the Full-Fashioned Hosiery Workers, successfully practiced aids to management in the establishments where they were recognized, and thus assisted union employers to compete against the nonunion.

The effort to spread organization by conciliating employers and favoring positive aids to efficiency was, of course, greatly stimulated by the competition that employee representation plans and company unions under the domination of employers were offering to the growth of the national trade-union movement. One of the earliest models of these plans was that installed by the Rockefellers in the Colorado Fuel & Iron Company, after a bitter strike had resulted in what amounted to civil war in 1914, and eleven children and two women had been killed during an attack on a tent colony of strikers by state militia, who poured machine gun bullets into it and set fire to the tents. The plan involved welfare work of various kinds, the choosing of representatives of employees by secret ballot, conferences with company officials at least three times a year, and a provision for referring deadlocked disputes to the state industrial commission. Other early plans were installed in the Philadelphia and New York transit systems.

These plans were widely imitated, with variations. In 1919, 145 companies had employee representation plans covering 403,765 workers. In 1926, the number of companies had grown to 432 and the number of workers to 1,369,078. Company unions were more common in the larger than in the smaller establishments, only 3 per cent of the employees covered working in plants of less than 1,000 employees.[17] The great majority of wage earners were unorganized and were accorded no pretense of collective representation.

Company union plans were no safeguard against labor unrest. The Rockefeller plan was undermined by a strike in 1927 led by the I.W.W., which came in to fill the void left by the exclusion of the United Mine Workers. Both the New York and the Philadelphia transit systems had labor difficulties and eventually recognized the Federation union in the field. At a later period, union organizers often found that their task had been facilitated by the existence of employee representation plans and the disappointment of the wage earners with their results.

Other methods as well were tried to bind the workers to the employers and prevent unionization. Many large employers embarked on welfare schemes including personnel departments to deal with grievances, suggestion boxes for the deposit of complaints, company housing, pensions, and the installation of more comfortable working conditions. A plan widely adopted was installment selling of stock to employees in the companies in which they worked, with the idea that ownership of stock of the company would lead them to take an interest in its profitable operation. Even a small property stake, it was believed, would discourage independent action. This stratagem had unfortunate results later, when workers lost their jobs and their savings at the same time. Many employers also took out group insurance covering their

[17] *Recent Social Trends,* p. 845.

workers, to which the insured contributed out of their pay envelopes; as a rule it provided a minor protection at an unduly high cost. The American Federation of Labor countered with an insurance company of its own.

A new venture of the labor movement in the postwar period was the establishment of banks owned by labor organizations or their members. In 1920, there was one labor bank with resources of something less than a million dollars, while at the height of the movement in 1926, thirty-five such banks had resources of $126,533,000. By 1929, however, the number of labor banks had shrunk to eighteen with resources of $78,953,000.[18] Some supporters of the labor banking movement entertained romantic ideas concerning the possibilities of labor's venture into finance. They accepted at face value the theory that bankers control the industrial system by use of the money entrusted to them by depositors. If labor would only mobilize its own surplus resources, it could, they thought, exert an important influence on the operation of the economic order. One of the pioneer labor banks, that established by the Brotherhood of Locomotive Engineers, was involved in the Florida boom and later suffered disaster largely on this account. It helped to finance a project called Venice, which at the time was intended to be a model development.

Although none of the other labor banks ventured into such uncertain fields as Florida land, most of them were so far from being conservatively managed that they disappeared during the financial crisis of the thirties when banks were closing by the hundreds. The few that survived devoted their efforts mainly to conducting legitimate banking business and as such were almost indistinguishable from banks owned by nonlabor stockholders. Their most important contribution—and it was not a small one—was their pioneering effort in extending small personal loans at moderate rates of interest. It was discovered that the losses in this business were negligible and that it could be conducted profitably with much lower charges than had been exacted by the special finance companies hitherto monopolizing it. In the course of years, many of the older and more conservative commercial banks followed the lead of the labor banks in this respect.

The ferment in union ranks for reforms in the national economy

[18] *Ibid.*, p. 383.

and in the labor movement itself persisted. Some of the labor banks were using their funds for enterprises of a cooperative nature. A vigorous movement for labor education found a permanent foothold in a number of unions and was eventually endorsed by the Federation. The conservative leadership in the older unions was blamed for many of the reverses that labor had suffered. And agitation persisted for amalgamation of the craft unions into industrial unions that would be better capable of dealing with employers in the basic industries.

The experience of the unions with both the Republican and the Democratic parties kept alive the movement for independent political action. Labor sought allies among the discontented farmers and was largely responsible for the victories of liberals in scattered Congressional districts. The Kansas Industrial Court was abolished in 1922. In 1924 the Conference for Progressive Political Action ran Senator Robert M. La Follette of Wisconsin for President, with the support of organized labor. Though it lacked funds and an experienced political machine extending down into the election districts, it polled approximately 5 million votes. Its success was not sufficient, however, to encourage continuance of the effort to build a third national party. Thereafter, progressive political efforts were concentrated on maintaining the strength of a bloc in Congress that pressed for reforms desired by labor and agricultural organizations.

Conflict on the industrial field was much diminished during the decade. In the years 1922–1925, the average number of labor disputes per year was only 37 per cent of that in 1916–1921, and only 48 per cent as many workers were involved. In 1926–1930, the number of disputes had shrunk to 23 per cent of the annual average during the war and postwar period, and the number of workers involved to 13 per cent.[19]

The most important strikes of the period were those in the coal and textile industries. Both anthracite and bituminous miners went out in 1922, beginning a long and hotly contested struggle that lasted from April until late summer. On August 15 a settlement was reached with about 20 per cent of the bituminous operators in the central competitive field, and thereafter individual contracts

[19] H. M. Douty, "The Trend of Industrial Disputes, 1922–1930," *Journal of the American Statistical Association*, XXVII (June, 1932), 169.

were signed with numerous other operators. The union was fighting against a wage reduction, but it had to surrender jurisdiction over formerly nonunion strikers who had joined its ranks, and it was unsuccessful in penetrating the nonunion districts in West Virginia, Kentucky, and Alabama.

The contracts negotiated at this time were due to expire on April 21, 1924, when a new strike was avoided by the signing of the Jacksonville agreement, which was to last three years and covered Indiana, Illinois, and western Pennsylvania. It maintained existing wages and when it was signed, 60 per cent of the output was from union mines, but a year later the union controlled only 40 per cent of the output because the nonunion fields with lower wage standards expanded their production and undercut the union operators. In 1927, another bituminous coal strike, for renewal of the Jacksonville agreement, was largely unsuccessful and led to a further decline of organization among the miners.

In the last years of the decade, labor unrest began to stir among the textile mills in the South, where the workers had hitherto been unorganized. State labor federations in the South repeatedly asked for help from the American Federation of Labor in organizing them, but until 1928 there was little response. Left-wing leaders, seeing the opportunity, stepped in to do the job. The workers objected to low pay, long hours, and the "stretch-out" system, by which each operative was required to tend more machines. Numerous small and spontaneous strikes occurred, often brought on by the discharge of active unionists. The spring of 1929 offered an opportunity for more effective action because of a revival in textiles. In protest against the discharge of active union members, strikes broke out at Elizabethton, Tennessee, and Gastonia and Marion, North Carolina. The Federation had by this time decided to respond to the calls for help.

At Elizabethton the girl employees were working 56 hours a week for 16 to 18 cents an hour. After the walkout, a verbal agreement was reached that standardized wages at the higher level paid in the locality and established a shop committee without union recognition. It was soon violated by the company. Edward F. McGrady, as official representative of the Federation, and Alfred Hoffman, president of the Full-Fashioned Hosiery Workers, went South in an attempt to patch up an agreement. They were "taken for a ride" by a mob of businessmen and local public officials, carried to the state line, and warned never to return.

In Marion, feeling was particularly bitter because strikers had been evicted from their homes, which—as was a general custom in the industry—were owned by the employer. The state intervened by sending troops, and the county sheriff with his armed deputies also arrived on the scene. In a resulting outbreak of violence, six strikers were killed and twenty-five were wounded, while there were no casualties on the side of the officers of the law. In the arrests and trials that followed, the officers involved were acquitted, but the local union leader was sentenced to prison. The irony of this outcome was not lost on the labor movement.

The decade was not a prosperous one for organized labor. The membership of American trade unions, including not only those affiliated with the Federation, but the railroad and other independent organizations, is estimated by Leo Wolman to have fallen from 5,110,800 at its peak in 1920 to 3,444,000 in 1929. The greater part of this drop had occurred by 1923, when the membership was 3,592,500, but there was scarcely a year thereafter in which a decline was not registered.[20]

The experience of unions differed according to the fortunes of their respective industries and the attitudes of the employers. Gains were registered in the building trades, where employment was relatively high because of the boom. Unions of government workers also increased, though still in their infancy. The printing trades did well because of the expansion of advertising and publishing; the established and experienced printers' unions prospered accordingly. Some advance was registered in the amusement trades and in transportation. On the other hand, the coal miners lost heavily because of the depression in the industry and the failure to make headway against the anti-union employers in the southern fields. Such incomplete organization as there was among textile workers suffered because of the competitive pressure for lower wages and the emigration of cotton mills to the southern states.

In national union headquarters the prevailing spirit of defeatism helped to prevent the extension of organization in manufacturing, and especially in the great mass-production industries like

[20] Wolman, *The Growth of American Trade Unions*, p. 119. Estimates after 1923 derived by the same author.

automobiles and steel. In spite of the upsurge of production, technological improvements continually replenished the reservoir of the jobless. Union treasuries had been depleted by the bitter struggles succeeding the war, and many officials were discouraged by the defeats suffered at that time. The legal position of unions was insecure: they had been attacked under the antitrust laws, and injunctions against strike activities were regularly invoked by anti-union employers. Many battle-worn leaders preferred to conserve their jobs and such membership as they had rather than to run the risk of aggressive action. Nor were they prepared to surrender craft jurisdictions in order to mobilize organization on an industry-wide basis, which would have been necessary to challenge success-fully the giant industries. Sixty per cent of the unions in the American Federation of Labor, representing about half the membership, either declined in numbers or remained stationary between 1924 and 1929.[21]

Vigorous and progressive leadership, however, brought better results here and there, and particularly in the union of men's clothing workers, the Amalgamated Clothing Workers of America, led by Sidney Hillman. This organization never ceased its advance into new territory; it followed the shrewd policy of unrelenting warfare against enemies of unionism, combined with effective co-operation with employers who were willing to bargain in good faith and maintain union standards. Its power and membership correspondingly increased; it was one of the first unions to win the forty-hour week and it pioneered in numerous other successful undertakings such as unemployment insurance, cooperative housing, and labor banking. Its example during the lean years of unionism prepared the way for the revival of the labor movement for which the opportunity arose after the collapse of Coolidge prosperity.

[21] Lewis L. Lorwin, *The American Federation of Labor* (Washington: The Brookings Institution, 1933), p. 279.

CHAPTER XI

Farmers after Deflation

IN THE decade before 1914, the economic position of the farmers as a whole was more favorable than it had been for many years. It has been noted above that during the war and immediately thereafter the demand for farm products was so pressing and prices rose so high that farmers' incomes rose to unprecedented levels. This, however, only made the effect of the subsequent deflation all the more severe. In 1920–1921 the average of farm prices fell to the prewar level, while other prices remained considerably above it.

An index number calculated by the Department of Agriculture to express the purchasing power of farm products in terms of the retail prices entering into farmers' cost of living stood at 75 in 1921 on the basis of 100 in 1910–1914. Comparison of farm prices with wholesale prices of nonfarm products showed a still wider disparity. During the ensuing period of industrial prosperity, the farmers suffered from a sense of grievance because the purchasing power of what they produced was less than before the war. The struggle for "parity" in price terms came to be the statistical symbol of agricultural depression. The index cited above followed a general upward trend, but never quite attained prewar parity. It was 81 in 1922, 88 in 1923, 87 in 1924, 92 in 1925, 87 in 1926, and 85 in 1927. By June, 1928, it touched a high point of 93.[1]

That the index of prices did not measure by any means the

[1] *Yearbook of Agriculture, 1928,* p. 8.

whole of the agricultural loss was emphasized by the decline in values of farm land. It had long been customary for farmers to invest their savings in land and building; rising property values represented to the farmer his accumulation of wealth. During the price boom of the war, this practice continued. Many farmers even borrowed money on mortgage to extend their holdings. Those who had incurred mortgage debt were in serious difficulties after the collapse, and many mortgages were foreclosed. Thus lifetime savings disappeared and former owners either became tenants or were forced off the land. Even those who managed to hold their farms suffered a decline in the value of their capital. Whereas in 1921 farm real estate was 57 per cent above prewar values, in March, 1928, a survey showed that farm real-estate values were only 17 per cent above the prewar level, and that in terms of constant purchasing power, they were actually about 20 per cent below that position. For the first time in the history of the United States, the acreage of land in crops decreased. Between 1919 and 1924, 13 million acres were allowed to go back to grass, brush, and woodland.[2]

In 1925, after the sharpest impact of the crisis had passed, 36 per cent of the owner-operated farms were mortgaged, and the indebtedness represented about 42 per cent of their value.[3] Through foreclosure, insurance companies and other financial institutions acquired large tracts of land that they were unable to sell without heavy sacrifice, and in many cases rented them to the former owners. Occasionally, they would install managers and operate the farms themselves. The percentage of farm tenants to farm operators —38.1 in 1921 and 38.6 in 1925—did not decrease in the succeeding years.[4] The number of farms operated by tenants declined in the Southeast because many of them simply gave up the attempt to get along and migrated elsewhere. At the same time, tenancy increased in the newer cotton-growing regions of Oklahoma and Texas, and in the West North Central and mountain regions.

These, of course, are statistics covering all the farmers in the nation, some of whom had better luck than the others. Those with the better land, good management, and better-than-average markets did not fare too badly. Some types of farming gained while

2 *Ibid.*, pp. 8–9.
3 *Ibid.*, p. 393.
4 *Ibid.*, p. 9.

others lost. Even on the average, the welfare of farmers cannot be judged wholly on the basis of price comparisons and land values. Productive efficiency grew on the farms as elsewhere, so that a smaller number of people shared the total income. As in industry, this increased productivity had unfortunate results for those who were forced off the farms, but it ameliorated the situation of those who derived the enlarged income.

Gain in efficiency was the resultant of numerous advances in different fields. Some improvement was mechanical, as in the introduction of gasoline-driven tractors at a moderate price, the small combine harvester, and other new machinery. Productivity in cotton was increased not through any mechanical improvement, but by expansion of acreage on more productive soil. Governmental research and extension work improved the stock of animals and poultry and aided the planting of better seeds, the use of fertilizer, the continual warfare against insect and bacterial pests, and better farm management in general. The result of all this was that output per worker in agriculture increased about 26 per cent between 1920 and 1930.[5]

The decline in capital value of agricultural property is reflected in the estimates of the net savings by the entrepreneurs in agriculture made by the National Bureau of Economic Research. In 1919, there had been savings of $2,275,000,000.[6] During the ensuing decade, a capital loss occurred in every year except 1925 and 1929. The figures for negative savings, or diminution in value of property, ranged between $115,000,000 in 1926 and $1,443,000,000 in 1921. These statistics exclude changes in inventory valuation and include the net savings of agricultural corporations. But the net income of those engaged in agriculture showed a steady upward trend from $5,588,000,000 in 1921 to a peak of $7,946,000,000 in 1925. Thereafter it was slightly reduced, with another upward bulge in 1929.[7] This recovery provided a gain in per capita income to the farmers as a whole. That their gain did not bring them to the level of most other occupations is, however, indicated by the fact that the share of agriculture in the national income, which had been 16 per cent in 1919 and had fallen to 10.3 per cent in

[5] Barger and Landsberg, *American Agriculture*, p. 253.
[6] Kuznets, *National Income and Its Composition*, p. 312.
[7] *Ibid.*, p. 310.

1921, continued its downward trend, ending the decade with 8.8 per cent in 1929.[8]

Per capita net income for persons on farms had fallen 62 per cent between 1919 and 1921. Between 1921 and 1929, it rose 87 per cent. Between 1920 and 1922 the per capita net income of persons not on farms had fallen 18 per cent and between 1922 and 1929 it rose 22 per cent.[9] Farmers' incomes thus fell further during the postwar deflation than incomes of nonfarmers, and rose more in the ensuing period of activity. Even at the end of the period, however, the average income per person on farms was $223 as against an average income of $870 per person not on farms.[10]

CAUSES OF DEPRESSION

The postwar deflation of agriculture had more serious consequences than that of industry and trade because farmers maintained their output and let prices fall, while business sharply contracted its operations during the crisis and was able to prevent so extensive a price decline. Farms, which are operated to a much smaller extent by hired labor and are more highly competitve than most areas of business, cannot demobilize their working force in a short time. In an effort to maintain their incomes, many farmers will raise more rather than less when prices fall. The process of forcing producers off the land is long and painful. These factors in part accounted for the more drastic depression in agriculture.

Another important element contributing to the difficulties of American farmers was the fact that the growing of many staples had been dependent largely on the export market. Foreign demand for American farm products was, of course, greatly expanded by the war, and then suffered a sudden collapse when European production was resumed and more distant sources of food came back into the market. In addition, there was a long-term trend toward the reduction of agricultural exports by the United States. This trend was the outgrowth of gradually rising

[8] *Ibid.*, p. 326.

[9] *Net Farm Income and Parity Report: 1943, and Summary for 1910–42* (U. S. Department of Agriculture, Bureau of Agricultural Economics; Washington: Government Printing Office, July, 1944), Table 6, p. 12.

[10] *Agricultural Statistics, 1943* (U. S. Department of Agriculture; Washington: Government Printing Office, 1944), Table 496, p. 406.

costs in this country and the expansion of agriculture in newer regions. It was intensified after the war by the effort of Germany and other nations to become more nearly self-sufficient.

In the year beginning July, 1919, the value of American agricultural exports reached its peak at $3,861,000,000. The total fell rapidly to $1,915,000,000 in the year beginning July, 1921. All the subsequent years of the decade were somewhat lower even than this, with the sole exception of the year beginning July, 1924, when the total rose to $2,280,000,000. Throughout the period the fall in the percentage of the value of American produce exported had been almost steady: in 1919 it had been 48.6; it ended the decade at 35.[11]

The quantity as well as the value of American agricultural exports evinced a declining tendency. Naturally, it varied from year to year according to weather conditions and temporary shifts in market demand, but the index number of exports of the 44 principal commodities involved had started the decade with 134 in the year beginning July, 1919, and fell to 117 in the year beginning July, 1928. The base of this index was the average of the years 1909–1913. Cotton, the principal export, had suffered during the war and hence showed relative gains after it. The decline in exports of all the other commodities taken together was therefore somewhat greater than this index number would indicate. Grains, cattle, and their products were the principal sufferers.[12]

Industry also had experienced a swollen demand for exports during the war and later had been compelled to readjust itself to serve mainly the domestic market. Its recovery was made easier than that of agriculture, however, by the fact that a population with sufficient purchasing power can absorb an indefinitely larger amount of industrial products, while the market for food is, in the end, limited by the capacity of the human stomach. It is true, of course, that many did not have enough to eat and many did not eat enough of the best types of food. Sales of particular foods, such as dairy products, fresh vegetables and fruit or the better cuts of meat, can be greatly increased by a rise of living levels in the cities and a more nearly equal distribution of income. Yet when such a rise occurs, it does not necessarily lead to the production of more

[11] *Yearbook of Agriculture, 1935*, p. 332.
[12] *Ibid.*, p. 635.

food in bulk, but is more likely to be registered in the substitution of some foods for others.

In the years 1910–1914, the daily per capita food consumption of the United States ranged between 5.18 pounds in good years and 5.04 in bad. In 1919 and 1920, when food prices were high, the figure fell to 4.87 pounds. It recovered during the decade, but did not reach 5 pounds until 1926, and was at no time as high as in the depression years preceding the war.[13] This reduction in food consumption during the years of prosperity for city populations naturally does not indicate any fall in purchasing power, but rather a change in eating habits. The substitution of machines for heavy manual labor probably led to less hearty appetites. The average diet contained far fewer proteins after the war than before it. It also contained a somewhat smaller quantity of carbohydrates, though consumption of fats increased—chiefly on account of the growing use of dairy products. As a consequence of this decline in per capita consumption, the growers of food products could not, as a whole, derive as much benefit from greater efficiency, reduced costs, and reduced prices as could the business community. Since the demand for food staples does not increase indefinitely with lower prices, agriculture could not profit greatly by expanding its volume of production. Its total market could grow no more rapidly than the growth of domestic population.

American farmers also produce important crops not destined to be eaten. The chief of these is cotton. It so happens, however, that the manufacturing industry using cotton as a raw material was not a rapidly expanding one and did not share in the good fortune of the newer industries of the period. It was itself subject to keen competition from mills using the nonagricultural fiber, rayon. New uses for cotton were found, as in automobile tires, and cottonseed was exploited for fats and oils. But in general, cotton was no more fortunate than the food crops. Tobacco, the next most important nonfood product, had varied fortunes in the 1920's, but succeeded in doing little more than maintaining the relatively high level of output that it had reached during the war because of the growth in consumption of cigarettes. Wool growing, an extremely small percentage of American agricultural activity, expanded only from 1927 on.

[13] Barger and Landsberg, *American Agriculture*, p. 151.

THE SHIFTING CROP PICTURE

Agriculture is not really a single industry, but a broad classification including the production of many different kinds of materials which, though interrelated with one another, follow different courses. Its practices vary according to the region and the crop, and it presents a continually shifting picture. The separation among its divisions became even more distinct in the 1920's than it had been previously, because general farming with diversified crops was diminished by the growth of specialization and the one-crop system. In the South, cotton and tobacco continued as the chief cash crops, giving way only slightly to the growing of corn, cattle, and other subordinate activities of farmers in the cotton belt and the tobacco regions. In the West and the Great Plains, mechanized wheat farming expanded. In New England and the Middle Atlantic states, increasing numbers concentrated upon dairy farming, while they bought more of their feed and raised less of it. Specialized fruit growing, vegetable growing, and poultry farms thrived in favorable locations. Beef cattle were still bred on the western ranges and fattened for market in the corn belt, but local packing houses that processed cattle bought in their immediate regions declined.

The demand for some crops fell off sharply while that for others grew. At one extreme, the production of hay was cut, by the end of the decade, to about one third of its volume at the beginning. This was a reflection of the rapid substitution of trucks, tractors, and automobiles for horses. The number of horses on farms decreased from 21,482,000 in 1919 to 14,029,000 in 1929.[14] At the other extreme, the production of truck crops more than doubled between 1919 and 1929. Growing of citrus fruit and oil crops both increased by more than one third, as did the production of milk and milk products. All these parts of the industry benefited from the larger purchasing power of consumers and their substitution of protective foods rich in vitamins for bread and other staples. Output of grain, of course, varied with the weather, but showed a marked declining tendency between 1919 and 1929. Production of meat animals remained nearly stationary, aside from its normal cycle. It was at exactly the same level in 1929 as in

[14] *Yearbook of Agriculture, 1928*, p. 967.

1918. Output of poultry and eggs, on the other hand, showed a growth only slightly less than that of dairy products. Noncitrus fruits and potatoes varied from year to year, but evinced no decided trend either up or down.[15]

While the shrinking market for wheat brought distress to many farmers, wheat acreage in the Great Plains states east of the Rocky Mountains was greatly extended. This included the semi-arid western portions of the unforested area. During the war, high prices had led to the expansion of cattle production on the plains, but many cattle ranchers were ruined in the 1921 depression. The development of gasoline tractors and small combines made possible the planting and harvesting of these level and fertile lands at less than half the cost on smaller and rougher farms. Though there was a deficiency of rainfall in this region, the weather cycle was at the time favorable enough to permit the raising of wheat. This pursuit did not always require residence on the farm. On some of the farms not a building of any sort existed. People would buy land from distressed cattlemen, invest in a few efficient machines, plant wheat, and then disappear until the time for harvest arrived. With the new type of combine, a machine that greatly reduced the work of harvest, two men could harvest between 400 and 500 acres in fifteen working days.[16]

In the thirty-eight northern counties of the Texas Panhandle, new plowing exceeded land abandonment by 2,824,000 acres. Between 1920 and 1930 only two counties on the high plains of Kansas, Oklahoma, and Texas lost population, while twenty-five counties gained more than 100 per cent.[17] The cultivated area in North Dakota, Montana, and Minnesota also expanded by about a million acres each. Colorado added a half million acres.[18] In the former grazing regions, land speculation thrived, the speculators buying from bankrupt owners at from $2 to $4 an acre and reselling to midwestern investors for $30 to $40 an acre.[19] The more arid parts of the Great Plains region subsequently became the "dust bowl" of the 1930's, when the dry phase of the weather cycle ensued, and the strong hot winds of summer blew away in great

[15] Barger and Landsberg, *American Agriculture*, p. 43.
[16] *Yearbook of Agriculture, 1927*, p. 14.
[17] Goodrich, *Migration and Economic Opportunity*, pp. 216–217.
[18] *Yearbook of Agriculture, 1928*, p. 10.
[19] Goodrich, *Migration and Economic Opportunity*, pp. 216–217.

Small Gasoline Tractors

New machinery of this kind greatly increased the efficiency of agriculture. This is a large commercial farm in New Jersey. (*Underwood–Stratton*)

Mechanized Harvester

In the broad wheat fields of the Far West, this machine, drawn by the new caterpillar gasoline tractor, was a great improvement over horse-drawn harvesters or steam tractors. (*Press Association, Inc.*)

Sharecropper's Cabin

Home of a southeastern cotton worker. Note the rock-strewn soil. (*Harris & Ewing*)

Top Soil Gone

An example of erosion, showing how the destruction of forest or other cover crops may lead to devastation of the land. Near Jackson, Mississippi, in 1920. (*Brown Brothers*)

clouds the soil that had been deprived of its grass cover. The quick profits of the wheat boom eventually led to widespread agricultural distress in the dust bowl.

Cotton acreage in the West also expanded at the expense of the older eastern farms. Between 1910 and 1920, it had grown only from 30 to 35 million acres. Between 1922 and 1926, however, cotton acreage was enlarged to nearly 48 million acres. Most of this new land was in Texas and Oklahoma. In the western region, one man could plant and care for between 75 and 150 acres of cotton, whereas in the old cotton belt in the Southeast one man, at least, was required for each 10 to 20 acres.[20]

The prevalence of tenancy and sharecropping, especially in the old cotton belt of the Southeast, continued to depress the living levels of the population and led to the deterioration of agricultural practices. Successive plantings of cotton exhausted the land, but the small farmers could grow little else because cotton was the only cash crop, and they had to pledge it in order to obtain credit for the purchase of necessities from the local merchants, who usually owned the land as well. Most were continually in debt to the merchants, and many merchants took care to keep them so. Agricultural credit even from banks was costly—interest ranging from 10 to 12 per cent—but credit from merchant-owners, on which most small cotton growers were completely dependent, cost 40 per cent or more when all charges were figured.[21]

The abject poverty of the sharecroppers prevented them from either growing or purchasing sufficient protective and nourishing food. They lived on fat pork, molasses, and corn, with little or no milk, fresh vegetables, fruit, or lean meat. They could not afford much fertilizer for the soil; lack of cleanliness in harvesting reduced the grade of the fiber; and it was nearly impossible to encourage the use of better seeds or the growing of the longer staples that brought a higher price. As a matter of fact, in the country markets the price small growers obtained for medium-staple cotton was usually no higher than that for very short-staple cotton. In Georgia, 78 per cent of the production in 1927 was of cotton seven eighths of an inch or less.[22]

[20] Yearbook of Agriculture, 1927, p. 12.
[21] Ibid., p. 21.
[22] Yearbook of Agriculture, 1928, p. 13.

The whole cotton business was highly speculative because of the wide variation of prices from year to year. It was a common joke that the spread of the boll weevil had saved the South because, by reducing the supply of cotton, it had raised the price and had forced sane diversification. Another such piece of good fortune was the great Mississippi flood of 1927, which ruined many square miles of crops, took a heavy toll of life, and gave rise to large expenditures in relief and flood control. In 1926, the cotton crop had been 17,800,000 bales, but the reduced crop of 12,955,000 bales in 1927 brought an estimated increase in income of about $325,000,000.[23]

The livestock industry also customarily experiences an alternation of low prices and high prices. In livestock, however, the variations appear in definite cycles rather than in response to fortuitous circumstances, as in cotton. At the bottom of the cycle, large numbers of animals and low prices lead to the reduction of breeding and selling off of surpluses. This trend continues until the supply is small enough to bring higher prices and encourage more breeding.

The large demands of war emphasized this alternation. Beef cattle were greatly increased in wartime, and cattlemen suffered corresponding hardships afterward in a depression lasting six years. Between January 1, 1918, and January 1, 1928, the number of cattle in the United States was reduced 22 per cent, or by 15.5 million head. The herds had then been reduced to the level of 1913. But there were 23 million more people in the population than before the war, and their average purchasing power was higher. Prices jumped correspondingly after 1926, and, since it takes three or four years to increase the herds enough to affect beef supplies, cattlemen did well for the rest of the decade.[24]

The sheep cycle is shorter, so that readjustment was completed in 1922, but after that, production expanded. During the depression in cattle, many ranchers switched to sheep. The demand for lambs, therefore, came not only from consumers, but also from cattlemen. Sheep growers flourished on account of increasing demand for wool, larger sales of lamb for meat markets, and sales to

[23] *Ibid.*, p. 12.
[24] *Ibid.*, p. 19.

ranchers. The number of sheep expanded 23 per cent from 1922 to 1928.

The hog-corn cycle—relied upon during the war to increase hog products by the fixing of the price of hogs sufficiently above that of corn to induce breeding and feeding—is normally shorter than that of either cattle or sheep. Between the war years and 1928, there were two periods of surplus hog production and low prices, with one intervening period of low production and higher prices. Another peak of the price cycle occurred at the end of the decade.

Dairy agriculture behaved during the postwar period more like one of the expanding manufacturing or extractive industries than like wheat, cotton, or cattle. Demand expanded regularly. The population not only consumed more fluid milk and cream per capita as the national income rose, but manufacturing outlets for the surplus thrived and demanded increased supplies. The ice-cream industry was booming; the evaporated-milk market grew. Feed was relatively low-priced. The industry had never depended on exports and was not threatened by imports. Although cheeses came from Switzerland, France, and Italy, and although New Zealand and Denmark shipped butter to the United States when prices were high enough, there could be no competition from foreign producers of fluid milk, except from Canada or Mexico. Tariff increases were adopted to diminish these imports, which in any case were not large in proportion to the domestic production.

Internal competition was intensified by the continued expansion of dairy production farther from the great metropolitan centers, which was made practicable by faster freight and refrigeration. Even Wisconsin and other North Central states began to ship cream to the Atlantic seaboard, while new creameries and cheese factories were established in the South. This competition was, however, a very small factor in the market for fluid milk. In 1928 the receipts at New York City were 271 million gallons from New York State; the next largest shipper was Pennsylvania, with 44 million gallons; New Jersey, Vermont, Massachusetts, Connecticut, and Maryland provided most of the rest of the supply, only 22,000 gallons coming from other states. Sources of fluid cream were much more widely distributed.[25]

[25] *Ibid.*, pp. 981–982.

Specialization made great strides in the poultry industry; the size of the individual poultry farm increased, as did the number of specialized egg and poultry producers. Industrialization of this branch of agriculture was promoted by new brooders, systematic breeding for increased egg production, improved feeding, heating the hen houses in winter, and using electric lights at night to fool the hens about the season. General farms still furnished, however, the bulk of the eggs and poultry sold in commercial channels, and in spite of increasing demand, prices experienced wide fluctuations.

Specialized truck farms, though not new, became more important, especially in warmer regions such as California and Florida, which, with the aid of improved transportation, could ship fresh vegetables out of season to the major markets. Many of these farms were strictly commercial enterprises, employing large numbers of casual workers, and producing great quantities of carefully standardized, graded, and often packaged products. Production of such crops as asparagus, lettuce, and spinach doubled in six years. The demand for potatoes did not increase, and the growth of most root crops was profitable only in especially good seasons, since freshness was not so necessary. At times gluts occurred in the vegetable markets, and the business was highly speculative.

Great expansion of the citrus fruit industry also occurred in Florida and California. Consumption of apples suffered by competition, as well as from the former overextension of orchards. The raising of prunes and raisins became a large industry. Although prohibition ruined many of the old vineyards in California and elsewhere, the growing of less choice grapes for juice was promoted by the demand for home-made vintages. Nut farming became an important specialty. In general, the specialty farmer did better than the producer of staples, though the number of them was not large enough to alter greatly the average farm fortune.

WASTING THE SOIL

Although the basic source of agricultural wealth is the fertility of the soil, most American farmers had been reckless in its use. This recklessness was due partly to ignorance of soil chemistry and of the practices necessary to retain and build fertility. To a still greater extent, it had arisen from the fact that during most of the history of the country, new and virgin soils were always available, farmers could move on from exhausted land, and those who migrated gained such an advantage in the markets that there was little incentive to remain on worn-out soil and incur the expense and trouble of restoring it. Although before the 1920's the limits of the agricultural frontier had been virtually reached, little improvement in land utilization was registered.

The general farmer, who was more likely to employ rotation of crops and to manure his fields with the nearly costless fertilizer obtained from his farm animals, was actually losing ground. Decline in the number of horses and the increasing specialization of the dairy industry reduced the available supplies of organic fertilizer in many parts of the country. Meanwhile, the expansion of wheat growing on the Great Plains, the overgrazing of western cattle ranges, and the one-crop cotton system in the South not only exhausted soils but hastened the loss of the topsoil itself through erosion by wind and water. The general agricultural depression and the declining value of agricultural land left little margin for practices that would have conserved it.

Even the seemingly inexhaustible soils of the East North Central and Prairie states, where more general farming was practiced, were rapidly being washed away by a combination of open cultivation and relatively heavy rainfall. The great Mississippi flood in the spring of 1927 gave dramatic evidence of the fact that whereas before the arrival of the white man, two thirds of the drainage area of this river system had been in forests, about half of the area had now been cleared for agriculture, so that there were no root systems in the soil to moderate the runoff of torrential rains. Neither terracing nor contour plowing was employed to check erosion.

The soil survey work of the Department of Agriculture continued, but the experts had far greater knowledge of soil resources in the United States than was put to practical use. Much experimental work was done with soil-improving crops, particularly the legumes, and their use was somewhat extended. Measures against erosion were undertaken here and there, as when a half million acres was terraced in Texas in 1927, sheep were taken off overgrazed watersheds in the drainage basin of Manti Canyon, Utah, and orange groves in southern California were protected from the erosion of the surrounding hills by measures to prevent brush fires. But on the whole, the economic situation of agriculture and the lack of organized policy prevented the knowledge of the experts from being widely applied.

Even the use of chemical fertilizers, which cannot restore soils unless accompanied by other measures, was limited by insufficient production and by agricultural distress. Both nitrogen and potash had to be imported. While production of nitrogen from the air increased from 6,000 tons in 1923 to more than 36,000 at the end of the decade, this was only a minute quantity relative to the need, even though the growing of legumes for fixation of nitrogen in the soil was widely employed. Germany was producing annually 660,000 tons of nitrogen. Production of domestic potash was less than 50,000 tons, and American consumers were dependent upon imports controlled largely by an international cartel. Even the domestic products were in large measure monopolized by private interests.[26]

CREDIT AND COOPERATIVES

Distress in the agricultural regions gave rise to vigorous protests and numerous suggestions for remedies. At the beginning, the farmer's attention was centered mainly on the disadvantage he suffered in obtaining credit. This concern was only natural, for prevalent opinion in the agricultural regions had held the banks responsible for the deflation, mortgages were being foreclosed, and, if short-term loans were available at all, farmers as a rule had to pay higher interest on them than business interests paid. In an effort to meet the credit stringency, member banks of the Federal Reserve System in the agricultural regions had reduced their outstanding loans during the deflation much less rapidly than had those in industrial districts. In addition, special credit agencies had been set up to meet the farmer's needs more adequately.

The credit difficulties of the farmers had been a subject of investigation even before the war. In July, 1916, Congress had passed a Federal Farm Loan Act, which set up a Federal Farm Loan Board as a bureau of the Treasury. Under it were two parallel mortgage banking systems. One was composed of federal land banks to supply money at cost to national farm loan associations,

[26] *Ibid.*, p. 79.

organized on a cooperative basis and composed of farmers who borrowed money on mortgages. The other consisted of joint-stock land banks, owned privately and operated for profit, to lend mortgage money directly. The country was divided into twelve districts and a federal land bank was established in each.

The system was slow in getting into operation and was not of great assistance during the postwar crisis. The federal land banks could not sell their bonds, and for a while the Treasury had to finance them so that they could operate at all. The rivalry between the public and the private branches of the system was intense. Although the ownership of the federal land banks was supposed gradually to be turned over to the cooperative associations, an effort was made to keep them under federal control because, it was charged, of the political influence of the private bankers. From the beginning the federal banks had a larger share of loans than the joint-stock banks, yet the latter made much more headway in 1925 and 1926 than the former. The situation, which was not healthy in either branch of the system, was described as follows by a banking authority: "Politics and nepotism, with their accompaniment of administrative laxness and inefficiency, honeycombed the Land Banks and the Federal Farm Loan Bureau. Three of the twelve Federal land banks and five of the joint stock land banks . . . had to undergo complete changes in their management," while "successive revelations of fraud, incompetency and laxity . . . brought about some much-needed changes." [27] The system eventually had to be reorganized.

The net value of mortgage loans extended by the federal land banks and the joint-stock land banks together increased more than 50 per cent between 1923 and the end of the decade, being in the neighborhood of $2 billion at the close of the period. Farm mortgage loans of life insurance companies showed a somewhat smaller gain, but in 1928 were about the same in volume as those of the land banks. Both together had a much larger proportion of the total outstanding farm debt at the end of the period than at the beginning. Many mortgages held by local banks or individuals were liquidated or transferred to the federal farm loan system and the insurance companies. This transfer represented a substan-

[27] G. W. Dowrie, *American Monetary and Banking Policies* (New York: Longmans, Green & Co., 1930), p. 335.

tial reduction in the farmer's interest burden, since the larger institutions charged lower rates. The rates charged by the land banks themselves were reduced from a prevailing 6 per cent to 5 per cent in July, 1928, in all districts except Spokane and Columbia, which charged 5¼. Subsequently small increases occurred.[28]

Another credit innovation was the formation in 1923 of twelve federal intermediate credit banks to provide at moderate rates the financing necessary between the planting seasons and the actual marketing of crops. The intermediate credit banks loaned money to cooperative marketing associations and rediscounted farmers' notes for financial institutions like agricultural credit corporations and livestock loan companies, as well as for local banks. By the end of 1927, 77 cooperatives with a membership of over a million farmers had borrowed from them, and they had rediscounted notes for more than 600 financial institutions. The total amount of credit involved, however, was not large in comparison with the value of American crops; it did not rise over $150 million. This type of credit was useful in supplying for agriculture the same sort of working capital that had long been enjoyed by business concerns when they borrowed from commercial banks, for it reduced the cost of the loans and facilitated orderly marketing. Farmers who made use of this service no longer had to dump their crops on the market when prices were lowest because of abundant supplies. Nor did they have to dispose of their produce to moneylenders in return for the credit necessary to see them through the growing season.[29]

Credit facilities could not, however, solve the fundamental agricultural problem. Even in the realm of credit, much improvement remained to be made. Many small farmers, particularly the sharecroppers in the South, were not in a position to utilize the new agencies. The large number of local bank failures in farm regions reflected agricultural depression, and brought hardship to thousands of depositors and borrowers.

Another remedy to which the farmers had begun to turn in large numbers was cooperation, both in the selling of crops and in the purchase of supplies. Attention was devoted mainly to the former. Information on cooperative marketing was first collected by the census in 1920, although the period of greatest increase had

---

[28] *Yearbook of Agriculture, 1928,* p. 37.
[29] *Ibid.,* p. 37.

occurred in the preceding decade. Between 1920 and 1925, if allowance is made for the price decline, cooperative business increased 85 per cent in volume. In the same period, cooperative purchasing by farmers grew 10 per cent. Thirty-one per cent of the cooperative associations reporting were handling grain or other staples, 22 per cent sold dairy products, 17 per cent livestock, 11 per cent fruits and vegetables.

The cooperative movement in the wheat regions largely took over the drive originally directed by the Nonpartisan League for state-owned grain elevators, and the number of cooperative elevators increased. In Canada, the cooperative wheat pools organized in 1923 handled over half the wheat produced in the three western provinces by 1926, but in the United States, state-wide wheat pools were unsuccessful in marketing a large percentage of the grain. Twenty-five livestock producers' cooperatives operated in nineteen terminal markets and by 1927 did $267 million of business.[30]

Conspicuous and relatively permanent success was enjoyed by the associations controlling the selling of milk and citrus fruit. Among the larger cooperatives in dairy products were the Land o' Lakes Creameries, which toward the end of the decade did a business of nearly $50 million in butter, and the Challenge Cream and Butter Association, which sold more than half the butter consumed in Los Angeles. Milk marketing associations paid special attention to the disposal of surplus milk by differential price policies, to the reduction of seasonal surpluses by variation of prices, and to the maintenance of a level of prices that would give a profit to the more efficient producers without attracting too many into the dairy business or shipment from more distant regions.

The California Fruit Growers Exchange improved practices in the selling and distribution of citrus fruit, and expanded its market by advertising and merchandising devices. The Florida Citrus Exchange and the American Cranberry Exchange were also successful. More than 150 farmers' marketing associations did an annual business in excess of $1 million each, and five or six of them had sales approximating $50 million. Still, only about one third of American farmers were members of such associations.[31] Some of

[30] *Ibid.*, p. 40.
[31] *Ibid.*, p. 42.

them were combinations of great land monopolists and were of no benefit to the small farmer.

In general, cooperative associations did not fulfill the farmers' hopes that they would remedy the excess of supply over demand or the price disadvantage suffered by the staple crops. The inability of voluntary organizations to control output in so wide a field and with such a large number of individual producers was especially apparent where the market was international. Although some of the larger and better-financed associations could hold supplies off the market temporarily and thus compensate for the part of the variation between good and bad crop years, they could not make headway against a production trend that rendered supplies continually larger than the demand at the prices they would have liked to maintain.

Minor gains were certainly possible and were registered: improvement of the quality of the products, better grading and standardization, control over the time of movement to market, better distribution among markets, advertising, and more bargaining power as against monopolistic practices of buyers. Yet cooperatives never met with more than temporary success in tobacco, cotton, potatoes, and meat animals. Some of the larger associations in other lines subsequently came to grief, partly in consequence of bitter opposition by private business interests.

On the whole, the farmers' cooperative purchasing associations, though their growth was slower, were more stable, and performed exceedingly useful services. Among the more successful consumers' cooperatives were the Cooperative Grange League Federation Exchange in New York State and the Eastern States Farmers Exchange. They concentrated, not so much upon reduction of prices to members as upon standardization and improvement of quality. About half the marketing associations also engaged in the purchase of supplies for their members, some of them doing so through separate subsidiaries.

THE FARMERS PROPOSE REFORMS

In view of the failure of credit devices and cooperative marketing to remedy the fundamental price disadvantage of the growers of agricultural staples, new and ingenious proposals were advocated to improve their status. The most prominent of these was the so-called "equalization payment" embodied in the McNary-Haugen bill.

Republican spokesmen had long commended the protective tariff as an aid to agriculture. But no import duty could be effective in raising the price of wheat, cotton, and other commodities of which more were produced than the domestic population could consume. Obviously such a tariff would not apply to the part of the crop that was exported. And if the domestic price were to rise higher than the world price, the surplus ordinarily exported would be offered for sale at home and drive it down again. Without intervention of some kind, the prices of crops of which there was an export surplus would thus be set by the world market. The McNary-Haugen bill in its various forms was a device to make the protective tariff effective on such crops. It provided a way by which exporters could sell the export surplus at world prices and still pay the higher protected price for the produce they bought. Obviously such a transaction would cause a loss to the exporter. He was to be authorized to cover this loss by charging it against the producers. The producers in turn could well afford to pay it, since the exports of grain and meat were only a small fraction of the total American output. An example is that of a wheat farmer producing a thousand bushels. Suppose that wheat was selling on the world market at $1 a bushel, that the tariff was 20 cents a bushel, and that one fifth of the crop was exported. Under ordinary conditions the farmer would receive $1 a bushel, or $1,000 in all. But under this plan he would receive $1.20 a bushel, or $1,200 for a thousand bushels. He would pay back 20 cents a bushel on the two hundred bushels exported, or $40. His net receipts would thus be $1,160. The refund he made per bushel would be the "equalization fee." This measure was passed by Congress in two successive years but each time was vetoed by President Coolidge.

Among the many criticisms leveled at the McNary-Haugen plan the most disturbing was that it would fail to improve the situation in the long run, because it would stimulate production. If farmers received higher prices, they would be certain to increase their acreage as they had done during the war. There would be a larger surplus to export, and this in turn would increase the equalization fee and depress the world price. Thus the domestic

price under protection would eventually be no higher than existing prices.

The export debenture, another scheme to accomplish the same
end, enlisted a good deal of support, and was recommended as
being simpler in operation and easier to administer than the
equalization fee. It would have provided for a higher price to
farmers, depending on the amount of tariff protection, to be paid
in cash by the processors and merchants who bought their crops.
That part of the grain or other crop which moved into domestic
consumption would be sold at a correspondingly higher price to
consumers. That part which was exported would naturally be sold
at a loss. The exporters, however, were to be allowed debentures
equivalent to the difference between the domestic and the foreign price. Those debentures were to be receivable by the government in payment of import duties. They could thus be sold at a
slight discount by exporters to importers of other goods. This plan,
which therefore involved a governmental subsidy in the form of
reduced receipts from import duties, was never passed by Congress.

Few people now remember that during the administration of
President Coolidge an economist in the Department of Agriculture,
W. J. Spillman, suggested the domestic allotment plan for restricting acreage that was later adopted during the administration of
Franklin D. Roosevelt. After its enactment this plan aroused bitter
criticism by opponents of the New Deal on the ground that it was
designed to achieve reduction of output; yet that was its main
virtue in the eyes of those who sponsored the plan. It may be
argued with much cogency that a surplus of food in relation to
the real needs of the world's population for nutrition has never existed. Yet there was little question that if the demands of the
farmers for higher prices were to be satisfied, they could not market all that they were producing. Devices to raise the prices of
crops without restricting the supply certainly ran counter to
economic law even in the days of postwar prosperity. No doubt
a better solution would have been to increase the purchasing power
both of the consumers of food throughout the world and of the
American farmers themselves, by larger production and lower
prices of manufactured products. But this solution would have
involved extensive reform in the nonagricultural sections of the

One-Room Rural School

The old-fashioned school was slowly giving way in the 1920's to the consolidated grade school. (*Underwood–Stratton*)

Radio in the Country

Early crystal sets, with earphones, began to modify rural isolation. (*Brown Brothers*)

Before Road Improvement

Soft country roads were nearly impassable by automobiles in wet weather. (*Brown Brothers*)

The Same Road after Rebuilding

Many thousands of miles of rural highways were made passable for motor cars through federal and state aid. (*Brown Brothers*)

economic structure. At any rate, the existing administration was not prepared to grasp either alternative, and none of the plans advocated in the interests of the farmers was adopted.

After President Hoover assumed office in 1929, it was thought necessary to redeem campaign promises for farm relief, and the new administration put into effect a plan of its own setting up the Federal Farm Board. An important function of this board came to be the purchase and storage of surplus crops in an effort to maintain prices in this country. The theory was that at some time in the future, when a poor crop season arrived, the board could sell its holdings. The detailed history of this plan falls outside the scope of this volume. It might have been a good one if nothing more had been necessary than to stabilize prices between years of good crops and years of bad ones.

The government did perform a number of useful services for the farmers that did not involve such drastic changes in economic institutions as the more radical proposals of the farm bloc. Many miles of rural roads were improved, thus facilitating the movement of crops to markets and bettering farm life through use of the automobile. The forecast of market conditions in the *Agricultural Outlook Reports* enabled some farmers to adjust their plans to impending surpluses or shortages.

The Reclamation Bureau of the Department of the Interior had long been engaged in irrigation projects that provided limited groups of farmers with water and electricity and, at low interest rates, sold land to them on installment payments covering a period of twenty to forty years. This bureau also proposed the establishment of a number of demonstration farm colonies in the southeastern states that would serve as experiments in a sounder type of agriculture and so might lead to better practices in the region. The powerful farm organizations were, however, so impressed with the existence of agricultural surpluses that they opposed further reclamation activities and failed to see that action of the sort recommended by the bureau in the southern states might reduce rather than expand the surplus crops.

RURAL LIFE

The life and circumstances of people on the farm were extremely varied. At the lower end of the scale were the sharecroppers of the South, and in this region and others the small family farms precariously holding to submarginal land. At the upper end were the proprietors of the great and highly mechanized wheat farms on the fertile Great Plains and the owners of large and successful truck farms or orange groves. About 8 million of the farm population lived within five miles of cities with more than 2,500 inhabitants, where they had access to hospitals, libraries, schools, and churches. About 20 million lived in greater isolation.[32]

In the middle of the decade, only 10 per cent of the farms had water piped to the house, and 7 per cent enjoyed gas or electric lighting. A much larger proportion—38 per cent—had telephones.[33] The fact that many more had radios than bathtubs was a subject of frequent comment, as if farmers enjoyed entertainment more than cleanliness. As a matter of fact, it was largely a matter of expense. A radio, complete with batteries, could be bought for a few dollars. But to put in running water and a modern bathroom was a comparatively costly plumbing job even in the city. In the country it also involved piping from the well, a gravity or pressure tank, a pumping outfit, and drainage facilities.

The backwardness of the electric utilities in extending rural electrification was an important factor in the retardation of rural plumbing as well as of other farm conveniences, since an automatic electric pump greatly simplified the problem of water supply. Pumps run by individual gasoline motors and storage batteries were available, but were costly and troublesome. The electric companies would not extend their lines in rural regions without payment of the capital cost by the consumers, either through large cash payments or excessively high rates. Even after the line was paid for, the rates were high because they were expected to cover the relatively large carrying charges while the number of customers per mile was still small. The companies, as a rule, would not incur the burden of expansion in the expectation of increased sales. Telephone companies were frequently more progressive in this respect.

During the decade, better roads and the use of motor busses made it possible to replace many of the old single-room schoolhouses with the consolidated school and thus to improve educa-

[32] *Ibid.,* p. 45.
[33] *Ibid.*

tional standards. The conservatism that impeded these changes was somewhat modified by the steadily growing influence exerted by the state agricultural colleges and the extension system of the Department of Agriculture with its county agents. In general, the greater ease of communication and transportation enabled farmers and their families to get together more readily, especially in the more thickly settled regions. Greater mechanization supplied a little more leisure, and daily hours of work were reduced for many. As a result, social life assumed a more active character and a more urban type of culture became apparent.

Such developments were more marked in the closely populated Northeast—and in Utah, where farmers lived in villages as in Europe —than in the regions of large farm acreage or in the impoverished rural South. Although farm life was becoming more urbanized, much remained to be done in the way of providing amenities for the agricultural population as a whole. Medical services in particular were sadly deficient, since good hospitals or professional nurses were seldom available and country doctors had to cover large stretches of territory. Moreover, great sections of this important part of the American population offered but a poor market for the rapidly expanding product of industry.

CHAPTER XII

International Tides

DEBTOR NATION TO CREDITOR

ONE of the most far-reaching economic developments of the war years almost escaped popular attention at the time and has never yet been fully digested in American opinion about foreign affairs. This was the shift that made the United States a creditor instead of a debtor nation.

Ever since the first colonists landed on the continent, Americans had been largely dependent on European capital for the development of their resources. Struggles between American borrowers and lenders in the mother country played a large part in the conflicts that resulted in the American Revolution. For over a century British, French, Dutch, and other European capital flowed to the new country in a steady stream. It was foreign capital that made possible the building of the great railroad system and the era of rapid development that followed the Civil War.

Although in later years American savings and the surplus of speculative fortunes played a larger and larger part in the growth of domestic industry and eventually came to dominate the scene, Americans had never before 1914 invested abroad as much as foreigners had invested in the United States. The result was that the economy early became adjusted to the position of a debtor nation. There were many defaults, of course, but the interest and dividends due the lenders across the Atlantic were for the most part paid. The nation could keep on paying them over a long period of years only by exporting more than it imported. The main part of the export surplus consisted of agricultural products and other raw materials. These sustained a large foreign market for cotton, wheat, and other staples upon which many of the farmers relied for their cash incomes.

American manufacturing before the war was not greatly interested in exports, but was intent upon securing the domestic market against the competition of British and European industries. Because of the long-accepted necessity that the United States export more than it imported, a protective tariff on manufactures fitted very nicely into the scheme of things, and the belief in its necessity was accepted by the industrial community with almost as little questioning as the Constitution or the creed of a church. It was thought that national economic health depended upon what was called a "favorable balance of trade." People seldom understood that sending more goods out of the country than were brought in meant in reality that foreigners were living at American expense, or at least that the surplus was used merely to pay debts. Naturally the cotton growers and others who had to sell in a free market while they bought in a protected one, were not well satisfied with the philosophy of protection. Many farmers, however, in spite of their unfortunate experiences, were misled by the arguments of the protectionists.

From the very beginning of the war, European financial resources, both abroad and at home, had to be utilized for military requirements. Foreign investments in the United States were sold, and it soon became impossible for Americans to borrow abroad. The money raised by the liquidation of British and French investments temporarily increased the active balance of trade of the United States because it was spent for American goods needed by the warring nations; therefore, American producers were unconscious that any change in the underlying situation was taking place. The only development of importance noticed was that now there was a pressing demand, not only for food products but for the output of many manufacturing industries as well. While many recognized that war prosperity must be temporary, few stopped to think that in so far as European investments in the United States were relinquished, the economic basis of an export surplus was being lost for the long future.

AMERICA'S INTERNATIONAL BALANCE SHEETS

(Foreign assets and liabilities in millions of dollars)

Items	1914[a]	1919[b]	1929[a]
Assets (private account):			
Securities...........................	862	2,576	7,839
Direct investments...................	2,652	3,880	7,553
Short-term credits....................	—	500	1,617
Total..........................	3,514	6,956	17,009
Liabilities:			
Securities...........................	5,440	1,623	4,304
Direct investments...................	1,310	900	1,400
Sequestrated properties and securities....	—	662	150
Short-term credits...................	450	800	3,077
Total..........................	7,200	3,985	8,931
Net assets privately held................	−3,686[c]	2,971	8,078
Intergovernment debts:			
To the United States government.......	....	9,982	11,685
By the United States government.......	....	391	—
Net assets on government account........	....	9,591	11,685
Total net assets on private and government account...........................	−3,686[c]	12,562	19,763

[a] July 1.
[b] December 31.
[c] Net liabilities (in 1914).

Source: Cleona Lewis, *America's Stake in International Investments* (Washington: The Brookings Institution, 1938), pp. 447, 450.

All together the aggregate investment of foreigners in the United States was reduced from about $7.2 billion in the summer of 1914 to about $4 billion at the close of 1919. The British government's need for dollars caused the reduction of many mortgages on American real estate, much to the discomfiture of the borrowers. About 70 per cent of British holdings of American shares and bonds were sold during the war. The French likewise disposed of about 70 per cent of their portfolio of American securities. The greater part of these sales was made before the entrance of the United States into the war. Investments by Holland in the United States were reduced from about $38,600,000 to $14,800 000.[1]

The net result of these transactions, plus the subsequent war loans, was that while on July 1, 1914, American indebtedness to

[1] Lewis, *America's Stake in International Investments,* p. 447.

foreigners had exceeded the debt of foreigners to Americans by approximately $3,686,000,000, on December 31, 1919, foreign debts to the United States exceeded the American debt to foreigners by $12,562,000,000. Before the war, intergovernmental debts had not existed, whereas after the war, the net debt of foreign governments to the United States government was $9,591,000,000. Even if the war debts had not existed, however, the shift of private investments and indebtedness would have made the United States a creditor nation in 1919 to the extent of nearly $3 billion.[2]

IMPLICATIONS FOR FOREIGN TRADE

If American private investors were to receive a return on their net foreign investments, and if interest and amortization were to be paid on the governmental war debts, enough money to meet these payments obviously had to be remitted. In order to be of any use to the recipients, this money had to be in the form of dollars rather than in pounds sterling, francs, marks, or other foreign currencies. How were the debtors to obtain the necessary dollars? Obviously they could do so only if Americans bought from them more goods and services than the debtor nations bought from the United States, or if Americans, by additional lending and investment abroad, supplied any deficiency arising from trade and services.

When nations adhere to the gold standard, international shipments of gold are supposed to balance any deficiences of payment arising from other sources. Gold shipments were temporarily suspended during the war, but the United States removed the embargo in 1919, and all the other important trading nations expected to return to the gold standard as soon as it was possible to do so. There was not enough fluid monetary gold in the world, however, to enable the debtor nations to keep on for very long making payments of the magnitude due the United States after 1919. Any attempt to meet their net obligations solely in this way would soon have driven the debtor nations off the gold standard because their gold reserves would have vanished. The fundamental necessity of achieving a balance of payments by means of trade, service, and movements of capital and credit would then have reappeared.

Axiomatically, the payments coming into a nation must balance

[2] *Ibid.*

with those going out of it, if one includes evidences of indebtedness
among the payments. This is not merely a bookkeeping convention,
nor is it anything which is in most cases deliberately contrived. It
is a necessary consequence of the fact that payments can be made
only by exchange of the currency of the nations doing the paying
for the currency of the nation receiving the payment. Of course,
actual currency is seldom transferred, since many of the items in
trade and finance arise from book entries. One nation may buy
from another more than it sells, without paying in money or gold,
but if so, the difference appears as an increase in debt.

The United States Department of Commerce has published
figures on the international balance of payments of the United
States beginning with 1919. The balance is not completely accurate,
since not all the information is available. The table does, however,
give a general picture of how the balance is achieved in any given
year. The first main classification is current transactions; the second
is gold movements; and the third is capital transactions. Current
transactions are listed under two heads—merchandise trade, and
other transactions often spoken of as "invisible" exports and imports.
The invisible items include such things as payments for shipping
and freight, interest and dividends, expenditures by travelers, personal remittances (such as gifts from immigrants in the United
States sent to their relatives abroad), and governmental grants or
payments for diplomatic expenses. It is important to note that these
invisible items are often substantial in size and make the result of
current transactions vary considerably from the payment originating from merchandise trade alone.

Nothing was more unlikely than that the United States would,
after the war, suddenly cease exporting more merchandise than it
imported. For generations the farmers had produced more cotton,
wheat, tobacco, meat, and other products than could be consumed
in the United States, and foreigners continued to need these
products, although they required less foodstuffs than during the
war. American manufacturers had started to build up exports before
the war, and their exports of war goods had been tremendous.
Most of them had insisted on protective duties against competitive
imports and when the war ended they vigorously opposed opening
the gates to more foreign competition.

The invisible current items, too, seemed likely to yield a surplus of payments to the United States. Although before the war American trade had largely been carried in foreign bottoms, the country now had a large merchant marine and a governmental policy of sustaining it, while Britain's merchant shipping had been reduced by the submarine campaign. Instead of paying more than they received, as they had done in 1914, the government and citizens of the United States were now receiving more interest and dividends than they were paying to foreign creditors.

It was equally difficult for the former creditor nations to alter their prewar structure of current transactions to accord with their new debtor status. Britain, the chief prewar creditor, did not produce half the food needed by her population, and had to import most of the raw materials used by her manufacturers. She could not suddenly start exporting more goods than she imported. Of the invisible items, she had lost much of the income from her former investments, and the prospects for increased payment for shipping services were not bright. In view of all these circumstances, the problem of maintaining an international balance of payments that would allow the debtors to meet the interest and amortization arising from the war loans was one that would seem to have merited careful attention and planning on the part of all concerned.

THE POLICY OF THE UNITED STATES

The declared policy of the United States government in its foreign economic relations was, as in the domestic economy, to withdraw from the picture as rapidly as possible and let things take their course. A letter from Secretary of the Treasury David F. Houston, dated January 28, 1920, and addressed to the President of the United States Chamber of Commerce, stated: "The governments of the world must now get out of banking and trade. . . . Such matters as the suggestion of further governmental loans by the United States, the cancellation of some or all of the obligations of European governments held by the United States government . . . are clearly not appropriate for consideration. . . . Such things as international bond issues, international guarantees, and international measures for the stabilization of exchange are utterly impracticable so long as there exist inequalities of taxation and domestic financial policies in the various countries involved; and when these inequalities no longer exist, such devices will be unnecessary. . . . The remedy for the situation is to be found not in the manufacture of bank credit in the United States for the movement of exports, a process which has already proceeded too far, but in the movement of goods, of investment securities, and, in default of goods or securities, then of gold into this country from Europe; and in order that such securities may be absorbed by investors, our people must consume less and save." [3]

It is difficult to understand how the Secretary could have expected foreigners to sell more goods to the United States if the citizens of the United States were to restrict their consumption. The government, though declaring its adherence to a laissez-faire philosophy, was soon to increase its interference with imports, first by an emergency tariff in 1921 and then by the Fordney-McCumber Tariff Act of 1922. By the high duties imposed, any possibility of a great increase in imports of manufactured goods was diminished. Moreover, the government operated large numbers of merchant ships, even though the loss in doing so was heavy, and thus reduced American payments for foreign shipping services. The Secretary of the Treasury was also somewhat inconsistent in recommending payment of foreign balances by a flow of gold to his country, for in the same statement he advocated (in a passage not quoted above) the prompt return of the debtor nations to the gold standard. Seemingly, the only way out of the dilemma was the private investment by Americans of large new sums in other countries. In fact, governmental policy encouraged this practice throughout the ensuing decade, and opinion in financial circles favored it. New York, many believed, must now replace London as the financial capital of the world.

In 1919 and 1920, United States government loans to the Allied belligerents were still being expended, and additional relief grants were made. These activities, plus the outflow of private capital both for the long and the short term, assisted in maintaining the balance of payments. In 1919, the surplus of merchandise exports was about $4 billion. The remainder of the current transactions, including governmental aid for relief, showed payments to foreigners in excess of American receipts amounting to about $2.5 billion. The United States therefore had a net active balance on current

[3] *Annual Report of the Secretary of the Treasury on Finances for the Fiscal Year Ended June 31, 1920* (1921), pp. 81–84.

transactions of about $1.5 billion. Added to this was an inflow of gold amounting to $164 million. On the other side of the ledger, the outflow of long-term capital was approximately $384 million. Although the figures are not available, it is assumed that the rest of the balance must have been achieved mainly by short-term credits from the United States to European borrowers.[4]

In 1920, also, the United States sent abroad a large export surplus of goods, though less than in 1919. At the same time its citizens received a still larger sum in interest and dividends. Foreigners were able to maintain the balance of payments mainly by the fact that American capital was freely flowing abroad at the same time. Since the need for relief was temporary, however, and a large part of the capital outflow consisted of short-term loans by the banks, this type of balance could not continue for long.

THE REPARATIONS TANGLE

No nation in Europe had been in 1914 economically self-sufficient, and Germany at its center had been of major importance both as producer and as consumer. Virtually all of western Europe, moreover, was dependent on a surplus of imports from abroad consisting of food and raw materials, for which it paid by the earnings of its foreign investments, shipping and insurance services, and the like.

War temporarily tore this delicate fabric in two, and the Peace Conference, instead of attempting to mend the rent, apparently destroyed it beyond repair. It drew numerous new national boundaries that cut across natural economic regions, and at the same time stimulated the spirit of nationalism which was to increase trade barriers.

By the cession of Alsace-Lorraine to France and of Upper Silesia to Poland, Germany lost important regions of steel and other heavy industry. It was deprived of all of its colonies, virtually all of its ocean shipping, and most of the investments and other property of its nationals that had been seized by its enemies during the war. Since the German population had been sustained in part by a surplus of imports and had paid for this surplus largely by the earnings of investments in colonies and foreign countries and by

[4] *The United States in the World Economy* (U. S. Department of Commerce, Economic Series No. 23; Washington: Government Printing Office, 1943), Table 1.

shipping services, a grave economic problem was created by these terms alone. In addition, the insistence of the Allies on indefinitely large reparation payments created even more difficult problems.

In view of Germany's obvious incapacity to pay very much at the time, the Versailles Treaty failed to fix a definite total of reparations; instead, it left the question open, and placed the whole subject under the jurisdiction of a Reparations Commission composed of representatives of the Allies.

The sum of $5 billion was to be paid before May 1, 1921, either in cash or in goods, and in addition Germany was instructed to deliver bonds with a face value of $10 billion that would pay interest at 2½ per cent annually from 1921 to 1925 and thereafter 5 per cent, plus 1 per cent for amortization. As soon as the Reparations Commission should become convinced that Germany was able to pay more than this, another bond issue of $10 billion was to be demanded, plus further issues until the total liability was met, the sum being set in April, 1921, at $33 billion or 132 billion gold marks. Any interest charge not met was to be added to the capital sum. The meaning of this provision may be seen when it is remembered that at 5 per cent compound interest, capital will double itself in fifteen years.[5]

The net effect of these provisions was that Germany was bound to pay $375 million annually from 1921 to 1925 and at least $900 million annually thereafter. If she defaulted any of this interest, the capital of her debt would increase proportionately. Though the Reparations Commission was given power to change the interest rate or to reduce the total debt, the change could be made only by unanimous consent. The Commission was instructed to collect the charges by supervision of Germany's entire foreign trade and by various other controls over her internal economy. Willful defaults were to be punished by armed occupation of German territory—a provision calculated to keep alive international animosity, and one which in fact did so.[6]

In order to pay a debt of this kind, a nation must first produce a surplus over and above the current consumption of its citizens.

---

[5] John Maynard Keynes, *The Economic Consequences of the Peace* (New York: Harcourt, Brace and Company, 1920), pp. 163–165. Also Harold G. Moulton and Constantine E. McGuire, *Germany's Capacity to Pay* (New York: McGraw-Hill Book Company, 1923), p. 60.

[6] Keynes, *The Economic Consequences of the Peace*, pp. 163–165.

The terms of the treaty showed an evident intention to collect any surplus that Germany might produce for years to come, no matter how large it might be, since the grand total was large in relation to the German national income, and the amounts currently collected were to be enlarged from time to time as the capacity to pay increased. This offered a dismal prospect to the new Weimar Republic.

Entirely aside from the difficulty that Germany might experience in producing the means of payment, an even greater difficulty was involved in transferring it to the creditors. The amount of gold in Germany available for the purpose in 1918 was shown by the statement of the Reichsbank to be $577 million.[7] This was scarcely more than a tenth of the first payment required. Germany could deliver coal and other raw materials and could also offer labor for rebuilding of devasted regions. These means of payment were utilized, but only to a limited extent, partly because they offered competition for industry and labor in the countries receiving payment. The bulk of the payment, therefore, had to be made in bills of foreign exchange that could be utilized only in the purchase of German products. But in this case also the producing interests of the countries on the receiving end of the arrangement did not wish to permit too much competition from German exporters. These difficulties served in the long run to moderate the demand for full payment. For several years, however, the transfer difficulties were obscured by the failure of Germany to create a sufficient surplus to meet the obligation, and by the efforts made to compel her to do so.

The United States was not directly a party to the reparations controversy, since she demanded no payments. It was supposed that on this account the matter was of little concern to the United States. Events proved, however, that Americans could not isolate themselves economically as they attempted to do politically.

Great Britain did not feel free to cancel reparations, even though a strong sentiment for this course arose, without the consent of the United States, the largest international creditor. The two subjects became officially connected when on August 1, 1922, Arthur J. Balfour, British Foreign Secretary, addressed a note to

[7] *Ibid.*, p. 169.

Britain's debtors laying down the principle that the British government would attempt to collect only such amounts as would equal
Britain's payments to the United States. France had borrowed large
sums from Britain during the war, and reparations were owed by
Germany to both France and the United Kingdom. The United
States was therefore to be the ultimate recipient of reparations.
The government at Washington long refused to recognize the valid-
ity of the Balfour doctrine, but in the end was compelled to admit
that debts and reparations were connected practically, if not legally.

The struggle to extract reparations from Germany proved
ineffectual for several years. Uncontrolled inflation of the German
currency had set in, and went to such extremes that price changes
occurred almost from hour to hour, and values of ordinary necessities began to be counted in millions of marks. The inflation destroyed the value of all fixed investments in Germany and reduced
the middle classes to penury, while it was pouring vast fortunes
into the hands of big industrialists like Stinnes and Thyssen. France,
under the leadership of Poincaré, in 1923 occupied Germany's
greatest industrial district, the Ruhr, because of the failure to collect
the reparations payments due.

The occupation of the Ruhr almost created an open breach
between Great Britain and France, since the British by then had
been convinced that moderation toward Germany was necessary.
The German inhabitants of the Ruhr met the occupation with
passive resistance, so that production declined sharply and great
misery ensued. Hostility between the two nations was intensified
as the conflict wore on. The occupation proved exceedingly costly
for France, which was suffering from an inflation resulting from an
excess of governmental expenditures over receipts. The time was
approaching when it would be difficult for her to float further loans,
and an indefinite expansion of the currency through the issuance
of paper money was in prospect. Not only were the expenses of the
Ruhr occupation a drain on her treasury, but, in addition, French
Lorraine, with its heavy industries and mineral deposits, was so
closely dependent economically on the Rhineland and the Ruhr
that its operations were seriously affected, with a consequent loss
in governmental revenue. In view of the opposition from Britain
and the United States and the deterioration of the fiscal situation,

the French finally changed their policy and their cabinet, and consented to a new attempt at international settlement of the reparations issue.

This settlement, arrived at in 1924, was called the Dawes plan. It scaled down the annual payments demanded of Germany, and made another change of even greater importance: it confined German responsibility to payments of marks within the Reich, and left the problem of effectuating transfer across the national boundaries to the Allied creditors themselves. It emphasized the fact that a government can pay international debts only if it has a surplus of receipts over expenditures in its national budget, and that these payments can be transferred only if its foreign trade shows an excess of exports over imports. The Dawes plan was thus an official recognition of the doctrine that leading economists had vainly urged from the beginning. It also led to the conclusion that the first essential was a reconstruction of German economic life if reparations were to be paid. Germany introduced a new currency and returned to the gold-exchange standard.

Meanwhile, the United States and the principal war debtors were engaged in negotiating a revision of the terms on which the loans had been originally extended. An agreement reached with Great Britain on June 19, 1923, funded the debt at an interest rate of 3 per cent for the first ten years and 3.5 per cent for the remainder of the term. This reduction from the 5 per cent originally charged was justified on the ground that the market interest rate had fallen. The debt was to be amortized in 62 annual installments instead of in the twenty-five years previously required. In effect, these changes canceled about 30 per cent of the debt as it stood before funding.[8] Similar settlements were subsequently made with the other debtors. France, the next largest creditor, settled on April 29, 1926. The percentage of cancellation ranged from 29.8 for Finland to 80.2 for Italy. The aggregate effective cancellation was just over half. The government of Soviet Russia alone made no settlement, since it repudiated entirely the obligations of the Czarist regime and objected to paying the costs of Allied occupation of Russian soil and warfare against the new regime—costs that had

---

[8] Harold G. Moulton and Leo Pasvolsky, *World War Debt Settlements* (New York: The Macmillan Company, 1926), p. 28.

been charged against the short-lived Russian government that the Soviets succeeded.[9]

After the adoption of the Dawes plan, transfers of the German reparations payments were regularly made, and the Allies met their debt installments to the United States. What really happened, however, was not that Germany was making any net payment, or even that Great Britain and France were now transferring to the United States, for service of their war debts, the proceeds of any German export surplus. The settlement had revived confidence in the international capital markets and led to the extension of large loans to Germany by American investors. Since the transfer of these long-term "investments" enabled Germany to fulfill the reparations payments, the money that came to the United States from the Allies was only rounding a circle to the point of its origin. This curious result was hardly the consequence of a plot or of a conscious design on anybody's part. Rather, it was an example of the way in which the conventions of finance may for a time conceal fundamental anomalies in international transactions.

THE NATURE OF AMERICAN FOREIGN TRADE

The American economy has not in recent decades been so dependent on merchandise exports and imports as have other leading industrial nations, such as the United Kingdom, Japan, and Germany. Even though during the immediate postwar boom the value of imports rose markedly, it did not at its peak reach 8 per cent of the national income. During the subsequent years of the 1920's, the value of imports fluctuated between 5 and 6 per cent of the national income. Since, in these years, the value of merchandise exports was greater than that of imports, it occupied a slightly larger percentage of the national income, but the difference was small.[10]

It is important to understand what these figures imply. In a broad sense, they indicate that American economic conditions were not so dependent on fluctuations in foreign trade as those of many other nations. They do not mean, however, that the United States could eliminate foreign trade without suffering great loss and inconvenience. In a detailed sense, the nation was far from being self-sufficient. Many industries required materials that were not

[9] *Ibid.*, p. 97.
[10] *The United States in the World Economy*, p. 38.

available at all within the boundaries of the country, and other materials were purchased abroad in large quantities because domestic sources were inferior in quality or higher in price. Some branches of agriculture, like the growing of cotton and tobacco, were dependent on foreign sales for a substantial portion of their income; moreover, the percentage of products exported was by some manufacturing industries sufficiently large so that its loss would be severely felt.

The greater part of imports by the United States during the 1920's consisted of materials or food products rather than of finished manufactures. A number of these were not competitive with American products. Raw silk in 1929 made up 9.7 per cent of the value of imports; coffee was 6.9 per cent; crude rubber, 5.5 per cent; and tin, 2.1 per cent. Other important imports were of commodities whose domestic supply was insufficient: such as cane sugar, 4.8 per cent; copper, 3.5 per cent; newsprint paper, 3.3 per cent; raw hides and skins, 3.1 per cent; wood pulp, 2 per cent; wool and mohair, 2 per cent. Imported crude petroleum in 1929 made up 1.8 per cent of the value of imports; and unmanufactured tobacco, 1.2 per cent.[11] For the years 1919 to 1939, 66 per cent of the total imports consisted of materials, foodstuffs, and semimanufactures used by industry. Another 6 per cent consisted of newsprint paper and jute, which, though classified as finished manufactures, are materials for industry. Of the consumers' goods imported, about two thirds consisted of food either in its raw state or processed, while less than 6 per cent of the total value of imports comprised finished manufactures for direct consumption, other than food. These were largely luxury products.[12]

As might be expected from the composition of imports, their total value varied, after an abnormal bulge immediately succeeding the war, in almost the same ratio as American national income. What deviations there were from the income curve were accounted for mainly by changes in the price of imported products rather than in their volume. In 1925 and 1926, the curve of imports by value rose slightly above that of the national income of the United States, but this change was due largely to the Stevenson plan, raising prices of crude rubber from British-controlled sources. The

[11] *Ibid.*, p. 43.
[12] *Ibid.*, p. 40.

physical quantity of imports followed almost exactly the same course as the curve of industrial production in the United States until 1929.

This fact is of importance not only because it throws light on the need of American industry for foreign materials, but because it shows how dependent the export trade of foreign nations was upon economic conditions in the United States. In 1929 that country bought 12.2 per cent of the total imports of the world, the only nation buying more being the United Kingdom. In 1927 and 1928, its consumption of nine principal raw materials and foodstuffs was 39 per cent of the total for the fifteen most important commercial nations.[13]

Countries most immediately dependent upon this market were naturally those producing industrial raw materials such as rubber, tin, nickel, pulp, paper, and hides, as well as those growing imported food products like sugar and coffee. They included Canada, Brazil, Cuba, and other Latin-American countries, the Dutch East Indies and Malaya, Japan, and many other nations. Since trade was multilateral, the prosperity of Great Britain and other nations that depended largely on exports of manufactures was also affected; the capacity of those who sold to the United States to buy in Britain or Europe depended largely on how much Americans bought from them.

Exports from the United States consisted chiefly of agricultural staples, petroleum, and manufactured durable goods such as iron and steel products, machinery, and automobiles. The composition of exports was much more varied than that of imports, and various classifications of exports had widely different experiences during the decade: agricultural exports had a declining tendency; non-agricultural exports, on the contrary, showed a marked rise after 1922.

Europe had long been the principal consumer of American agricultural exports. In 1921–1925, Europe absorbed 53 per cent of the total exports of the United States as against 62 per cent just before the war. The percentage fell to 45 in 1929. This drop reflected in part the decline of the United States as a source of farm products in the world market, and in part the efforts of European industrial nations to grow as much of their own food as possible.

[13] *Ibid.*, p. 29.

Europe, however, took about 32 per cent of American exports of finished manufactures throughout the period.[14] Because of the efforts to build up national industries, revived European nationalism was in part responsible for the large demand for American machinery and other durable goods.

The effect of the protective tariff on American trade is extremely difficult to estimate, because so many other factors were at work at the same time. Since it applied mainly to manufactured goods, and the rates imposed by the Fordney-McCumber Tariff Act were so high as to be almost prohibitive, it may be assumed that the United States would have imported more manufactures if this protection had not existed. Yet not all manufactured articles were protected—automobiles are a striking example—and many others would doubtless have dominated the domestic market without any governmental help whatever.

The law gave the tariff commission power to recommend changes in import duties within a limit of 50 per cent of those already in effect. Recommendations were supposed to be based upon a study of the costs of production of foreign concerns competing with American producers, and were to adjust the duties so that the cost of the imported article, after payment of the duty, would be the same to the American purchaser as the cost of the domestic product. Even if the tariff had been reduced to this point, it would have created a barrier to all competitive imports, since normally the principal incentive to buy a competitive foreign product is its lower cost. The task of the tariff commission, however, was quite impossible to perform, because it could not send accountants into foreign establishments in order to ascertain their costs. Furthermore, cost accounting is such a complex art, and costs vary so much among establishments in the same industry, that even in the United States, where such information might be obtained, the area for differences in judgment and policy is a broad one. Naturally, the commission, whose leanings were largely protectionist anyway, made relatively few recommendations for reduction of duties.

The net result of American merchandise trade was an excess of exports over imports ranging between $375,000,000 in 1923 and $1,037,000,000 in 1928. Foreigners therefore did not derive from

[14] *Ibid.,* pp. 61, 62.

this trade any balance of dollars with which to pay their debts in the United States. On the contrary, they owed more for what they bought than the amount Americans paid for imports.[15]

The invisible items in current transactions contributed little or nothing to wipe out this net deficit. Americans did pay a substantial amount for shipping services, and handed over to foreigners still larger sums in the form of the expenditures of American travelers abroad and personal remittances. These and other outgoing payments, however, were not large enough to balance the incoming payments on account of debt service and dividends between 1923 and 1929. Thus the excess of exports over imports, including both trade and invisible items, remained high year after year. The United States never developed the import excess usually regarded as the normal condition of a creditor nation.

FOREIGN INVESTMENTS, GOLD, AND EXCHANGE

In view of the continued "favorable" trade balance of the United States, the only way in which foreigners could obtain enough dollars both to pay their debts and to buy in the United States what they needed was either to obtain the money from Americans on capital account or to ship out gold. In 1919 and 1920, American foreign lending was heavy. After the Dawes plan, the restoration of international confidence prepared the way for a large and continual outflow of foreign investments. With the exception of 1923, new foreign issues increased every year from 1919 to 1927. The money went not only to Germany but to former allies, to neutrals, to new countries, such as Poland, established by peace settlement, to Canada, and to many other nations throughout the world. Between 1925 and 1929, about $5.1 billion of foreign loans were sold in the United States.

In the case of ten countries, new loans exceeded repayment by at least $100 million each. These were, in the order of their net borrowing, Germany, Canada, Italy, Australia, Chile, Argentina, Brazil, Colombia, Japan, and Poland. Together they accounted for $2.7 billion of the $3 billion net foreign borrowing in the United States during these years. In the case of twenty-nine other countries, new borrowing exceeded repayments to the extent of $685 million.

[15] *Ibid.*, Table I.

But Great Britain, France, Switzerland, and the Netherlands paid back more than they received.[16]

Many of these loans, like the majority of those to Canada, helped to increase productive capacity and could not be regarded as unsound from the point of view either of American interests or of world economic health. On the other hand, many of the loans were not used for productive purposes or were made to countries that would have difficulty in making repayments if the flow of new capital should stop, since they could not be expected to develop an export surplus. Germany was in this category.

The American investment institutions that floated the loans were often more concerned with their underwriting profits than with the probable safety of the capital. The high interest rates, in turn, tempted unwary American investors to purchase the bonds. Pressure from the lenders rather than real need of the borrowers too often was the motivating influence. Cleona Lewis offers a few examples: "Some 36 houses, most of them American, competed for a city of Budapest loan and 14 for a loan to the city of Belgrade. A Bavarian hamlet, discovered by American agents to be in need of about $125,000, was urged and finally persuaded to borrow $3 million in the American market. In Peru, a group of successful American promoters included one Peruvian, the son of the President of that republic, who was afterward tried by the courts of his country and convicted of 'illegal enrichment.' In Cuba the son-in-law of the President was given a well-paid position in the Cuban branch of an American bank during most of the time the bank was successfully competing against other American banks for the privilege of financing the Cuban government." [17]

Direct investments by American business concerns added substantially to the outflow of American capital. This practice was greatly increased after the war, the amounts being low in the earlier years and gradually rising to a peak of $602 million in 1929. Approximately $3 billion was employed for such direct foreign investments in the decade. Prominent among these ventures were the subsidiaries of such American corporations as Standard Oil Company (New Jersey), Ford Motor Company, General Motors, and International Business Machines. Other American-owned corpora-

---

[16] Lewis, *America's Stake in International Investments*, p. 392.
[17] *Ibid.*, p. 377.

tions were organized for the express purpose of doing business abroad, and though in many cases affiliated with American companies, they offered their own securities to the American public. Among these were American and Foreign Power Co., International Telephone and Telegraph, and Chile Copper Co. In addition, Americans bought heavy interests in large companies organized by foreigners.[18]

Much of this activity was merely an extension of the expanding operations in the United States. Industrial capital put aside out of the enormous profits in this country sought a return by promoting exports or exploiting foreign markets in other ways. In other cases, American manufacturers reached out for control of raw materials.

The net outflow of long-term capital was not sufficient to supply the need of the foreign nations for dollars in the first few years after the war. From 1919 to the early part of 1921 there had also been a net outflow of short-term credits amounting to more than $800 million. During the ensuing deflation, the flow was reversed. Unfunded borrowings on both sides of the ledger increased rapidly during the decade, while the direction of the net flow was not always the same. Toward the end of the period, when the boom in American securities occurred, foreign short-term funds were accumulated in the United States to finance speculative investment or take advantage of the high interest rates on collateral loans. It is estimated that by 1929, foreigners held at least $1.3 billion more short-term funds in the United States than Americans had abroad.[19] Much of this money was kept there for purposes of liquidity, on account of the apparent strength of the American economic situation and large stocks of gold. Since it could so readily be withdrawn, it represented a distinct element of danger.

Gold movements during the decade did not play their theoretical role of acting as the balance wheel in maintaining the international balance of payments. After the United States returned to the gold standard in 1919, other nations withdrew gold to build up their reserves, although at the time this country had a large export surplus. Gold export was made possible by government loans and private short-term credits. Germany returned to the gold-exchange standard in 1924 as part of her obligation under the Dawes

[18] *The United States in the World Economy*, p. 100.
[19] *Ibid.*, p. 112.

plan and, in spite of the fact that she was in a debtor position, imported gold to support her new currency. This movement was financed by a reconstruction loan. The United Kingdom restored the gold standard at the prewar parity of the pound in 1925. Other countries adopted either the gold standard or the gold-exchange standard in rapid succession. Gold left the United States in 1927 and 1928, largely on account of currency stabilization loans that made possible the restoration of the traditional system. After the middle of 1928, a heavy inflow of gold to the United States began. As will later appear, this was the period in which the American support of foreign economies by a large outflow of capital began to break down.

Since prices and costs in Britain were further above the prewar level than those in the United States, the resumption of prewar parity with the dollar constituted an overvaluation of the pound and led to pressure on its exchange value. France aggravated this situation when she achieved *de facto* currency stabilization in 1926 by a devaluation that greatly undervalued the franc in relation to both the pound and the dollar. (Legal return to the gold standard was enacted by France in 1928.) The result was that Britain suffered a competitive disadvantage in the international markets. When both the exchange value of the currency and the level of internal prices were considered, it was cheaper for many importers in other countries to buy in France than in Britain.

The natural consequence was a tendency for gold to flow from London to France and the United States, since it was extremely difficult for Britain to maintain sufficiently large exports to obviate the necessity of gold payments for part of her necessary excess of imports. According to classical theory, this situation should have been automatically corrected by an increase of the internal price levels in the countries acquiring more gold. This result was supposed to occur through the effect of a larger gold reserve on the extension of currency and credit. An expansion of purchasing power in relation to the amount of goods available would naturally lead to higher prices. American banking policy, however, fearing inflation, at times sought to prevent the growth of gold reserves from having this effect. The rapid increase in American production was a major influence in keeping prices down. French internal prices likewise did not rise so rapidly as, according to theory, they should have done. Those responsible for British financial policy were continually apprehensive about the situation and critical of American and French central banking policy.

Some American banking authorities wished, for the sake of international stability, to support the newly re-established gold standard abroad. If interest rates in the United States were above those in London, the flow of money to this country would be encouraged, and gold imports would be likely to continue. On the other hand, it was desirable to increase interest rates in the United States, in order to check the use of credit for stock market speculation, a tendency that began to be alarming in 1927. The New York Reserve Bank had cooperated closely with London in Britain's return to gold. This bank therefore wished to reduce rates. The Chicago Reserve Bank, on the contrary, believed that the ruling purpose should be to restrict credit for speculative purposes, and favored higher rates. Chicago, however, was overruled by the Federal Reserve Board.

The immediate consequence was that credit was made easier and banking policy offered no obstacle to the rapid expansion of its use for stock speculation, which was already under way. In 1928 and 1929, the federal reserve authorities reversed their policy in order to discourage speculation. This change had unfortunate effects on the international movement of short-term capital, since high interest rates were now added to the lure of the stock market and attracted both short-term funds and gold to New York, a development particularly embarrassing for Britain. In the end it led to a tightening of credit abroad and to a withdrawal of funds when banking reserves were threatened. American banking policy was thus placed in a dilemma by the unsound nature of the fundamental situation. Any course it could take seemed to be wrong.

THE COLLAPSE OF THE INTERNATIONAL STRUCTURE

After the postwar deflation and particularly after the Dawes plan, there was little sign of strain in maintaining the international balance of payments at a high level until near the end of the decade. Business was active in the United States and Americans were assisting recovery in other countries by buying large amounts of materials. At the same time, a sizable export surplus was maintained in current transactions. Payments of reparations and service on the foreign debt were being maintained. Other nations obtained the gold they needed as banking reserves. All this was made possible by the fact that the net outflow of American foreign investments was large.

WORLD SUPPLY AND USE OF DOLLARS

(*In millions of dollars*)

Type of Transactions	1919	1920	1921	1922	1923	1924	1925	1926	1927	1928	1929
Factors supplying dollars:											
U. S. merchandise imports	3,904	5,278	2,509	3,113	3,792	3,610	4,227	4,431	4,185	4,091	4,399
Other current payments..	5,727	2,437	1,467	1,269	1,290	1,394	1,484	1,466	1,633	1,819	1,962
Outflow of long-term capital...............	1,719	1,413	877	949	485	1,025	1,112	1,292	1,485	1,597	1,037
Total...............	10,350	9,128	4,853	5,331	5,567	6,029	6,823	7,289	7,303	7,507	7,398
Factors using dollars:											
U. S. merchandise exports	7,920	8,228	4,485	3,832	4,167	4,591	4,910	4,809	4,865	5,128	5,241
Other current receipts....	3,209	2,174	1,085	1,192	1,463	1,388	1,510	1,642	1,674	1,809	1,906
Inflow of long-term capital	335	581	285	134	440	325	542	566	448	750	759
Total...............	11,464	10,983	5,855	5,158	6,070	6,304	6,962	7,017	6,987	7,687	7,906
Excess of dollars used (plus) over dollars supplied (minus)...........	1,114	1,855	1,002	−173	503	275	139	−272	−316	180	508
"Balancing items":											
Net short-term capital movements (outflow −)	?	?	?	?	−33	119	−106	419	585	−348	−4
Net gold movement (Outflow −)...............	164	50	−686	−235	−295	−216	102	−72	154	272	−120
Unexplained items (outflow −)...............	−1,278	−1,905	−316	408	−175	−178	−135	−75	−423	−104	−384
Total	−1,114	−1,855	−1,002	173	−503	−275	−139	272	316	−180	−508

Source: *The United States in the World Economy* (U. S. Department of Commerce, Economic Series No. 23; Washington: Government Printing Office, 1943), Table 2.

One element of danger in this situation was the unsound character of many of the foreign loans. Toward the end of the period warnings were issued that temporarily had little effect. In October, 1927, S. Parker Gilbert, the Agent General for Reparation Payments, cautioned against further loans to Germany, and similar warnings came from South America about investments in that continent.

Even if all the loans had been carefully considered, a more fundamental peril existed. A time was likely to come when the expansion of foreign investment would slow down or cease. A tapering off of foreign lending could have occurred without damage if, at the same time, the lending nation had increased its purchases of goods and services from abroad, so that the export surplus in current transactions might diminish and eventually disappear. But if Americans were to cut off the outflow of capital without at the

same time increasing their imports, the world's supply of dollars
would be drastically diminished. Debts would have to be defaulted
and American exports would suffer.

What actually happened was that in the middle of 1928 American foreign lending began suddenly to fall off. In part, the cause
was recognition of the precarious character of many of the investments, but perhaps the main influence was the opportunity for
larger profits in the American financial markets. The effect of this
reduction was somewhat moderated by a simultaneous increase
in American direct investments abroad, which continued into 1929.
When, however, there was added, after the onset of depression, a
drastic drop both in direct investments and in American purchases
of foreign goods, the whole foundation of international economic
transactions was blasted away. The rest of the world began to
suffer from an acute shortage of dollars. A world-wide crisis became
inevitable.

CHAPTER XIII

Recession and Boom

THE last two years of the "plateau of prosperity" that followed the recovery of 1922 deserve separate analysis. These were the years that immediately preceded the great crash of 1929 and the ensuing depression. There must have been elements in them, therefore, that would have given warning of these events if only they could have been identified.

WARNINGS IN 1927

The year 1927 was marked by a slight recession. Wholesale prices showed a downward tendency, dropping nearly 3½ per cent in 1926 and 4½ per cent in 1927.[1] The upward trend of physical production as a whole was briefly interrupted, and fell 1 per cent between 1926 and 1927.[2] Though the output of factories kept on growing, it did so at a reduced rate. This recession was regarded at the time as merely a downward turn in the business cycle, which seems to occur on the average at intervals of about three and a third years. It is also frequently so regarded by subsequent writers.

The theory of business cycles is far from completely developed and involves many complex factors. It is difficult by inspection of the crude figures to identify any important cyclical factor at work in this instance. This minor slump had not been preceded, for instance, by any marked growth of inventories as were those of 1921

---

[1] *Federal Reserve Bulletin* (October, 1945), p. 1049.
[2] *Ibid.*

and 1924. While wholesale prices had risen in 1925, the increase had not been great enough to place any serious strain on currency or credit reserves, or to appear to need correction for other reasons. The interrelationship of prices was relatively stable, as indeed it had been ever since the recovery.

Whatever the cyclical phenomena, others of significance for the longer term now appear to be premonitory of the disaster that overtook the country two years later. The first of these to be noted is that for the first time since 1921, the spending of consumers decreased. The decrease was small, and reflects the fact that prices had fallen. In terms of stable prices (1929 = 100) consumers' outlay grew $1.3 billion.[3] This, however, was a much smaller expansion than in the previous year. The incomes of consumers in 1927 suffered a sharp retardation of their former advance. The annual growth of total wages and salaries, which had not been less than $1.5 billion in any previous year of the decade except 1924, and had reached much larger figures, now was measured by something less than $400 million.[4] Payment of wages and salaries showed little gain in manufacturing, a fact which is striking because manufacturing output kept on increasing. Wages and salaries actually declined in construction, trade, and mining. The main increase in payments to employees occurred in the service occupations, finance, and government. That the drop in growth of consumers' outlay must be attributed largely to limited purchases of wage earners and farmers is indicated by the fact that payments of dividends and interest both kept on increasing as usual.

Before inquiring into the causes of the retardation in growth of consumers' incomes it is well to note what form their expenditures took. In 1927 consumers actually spent more on services than in the previous year. They also spent slightly more on semidurable goods like clothing. Part of the reduction took place in the purchase of perishable goods, the most stable element of consumers' buying, and probably reflected some drop in food prices and an increase in unemployment. The largest and most striking element in the decline occurred in the purchases of durable goods such as automobiles. The output of passenger automobiles in 1927 fell 22 per cent below the previous year. In 1928, automobile production and sales in-

---

[3] Kuznets, *National Income and Its Composition*, p. 147.
[4] *Ibid.*, p. 332.

creased again, but, as noted on page 168, the average increase of
the two years together over the previous annual output was small.[5]

Consumers' purchase of durable goods is the most widely
fluctuating element in the retail markets partly because these goods
can be made to last longer when for any reason retail purchasers
wish to economize, and partly because purchases of these goods
were now being financed to a large degree by credit, the expansion
of which may be restricted for a number of reasons. At any rate, this
element in the decline probably had a significance beyond the ordinary alternations of the business cycle.

What caused the restriction of consumer income and why did
it foreshadow difficulties? Between 1925 and 1927 the continued
reduction of the number of wage earners employed by factories
was accompanied by a retarded growth in the total earnings of
those employed. The reduction in workers was not in itself a temporary development. It had been going on for several years, and
continued thereafter. If unaccompanied by a corresponding increase
in wage rates, it was bound to result in diminution of the money
available for spending by manufacturing employees.

The drop in factory employment may, of course, be balanced
by an increase of employment in other occupations, for example,
service, trade, and finance. Such an increase had in fact occurred
throughout the whole period, and had prevented a serious unemployment crisis. It continued in 1927. If nothing more had been at
work in 1927, there might have been no decrease in consumers'
outlay. Other changes that tended downward also occurred, however. Residential construction began to decline in 1926, and from
this time on the decline continued. The housing shortage had long
before disappeared, and the building of houses had passed its peak.
Business construction, which had been increasing substantially up
to this point, gained only slightly between 1926 and 1927. Employment therefore fell in the construction industry, and the building
workers had less to spend.

To make matters worse, the new investment in producers'
durable goods also dropped off. Thus private investment as a whole
began to fall. The amount of this reduction is estimated at about
$770 million. Though this sum is small relative to the total national
income, so was the business recession that occurred. In view of the

[5] *Facts and Figures of the Automobile Industry*, 1931 ed., p. 4.

theory that regards the expansion or contraction of new investment as a chief activating factor in major swings of production and employment, this development seems alarming in retrospect. At the time it might have been difficult to predict whether investment would not turn upward again. As a matter of fact, it did so for a brief period during the 1929 boom, although the large element in it represented by construction kept on falling.[6]

The stimulation of governmental spending had been withdrawn after the war. During all these years the federal government had had a surplus of receipts over expenditures, was reducing the national debt, and was cutting the interest payments. State and local governments, however, had been borrowing and spending enough so that the deflationary effect of this Treasury policy was not marked. Indeed, in all of the preceding years except 1923 there had been a small net excess of expenditures over receipts from all public sources. In 1926 and 1927, however, the surplus in the federal budget became so large as more than to counteract the spending of subordinate governmental divisions. This resulted in a decline of governmental stimulus to purchasing power of between $200 million and $300 million in each of these years. Thus the fiscal policy of the national government reinforced the restrictive tendencies that had begun to affect the private sector of the economy by the decline of new investment.[7]

WHY DID THE BOOM CONTINUE?

In view of these facts, anyone looking back over the figures is prompted to ask, not why the great depression began in 1929, but rather why it did not begin in 1927. With the passing of the peak in the long construction activity, a drop in new private investment, a decrease in employment, a slackening of consumer spending, especially for durable goods, and a deflationary fiscal policy, all the major tendencies that seem to have accounted for the previous expansion had apparently been reversed. The gain in productive efficiency, to be sure, continued, but this could not help matters unless the reduced unit costs resulted in an increase in consumers' purchasing power. In 1927 they did not appear to do so. The important

[6] Harold Barger, *Outlay and Income in the United States, 1921–1938* (New York: National Bureau of Economic Research, 1942), pp. 50–51.
[7] *Ibid.*

question seems to be why, in spite of all these depressive influences, economic activity recovered and finally exploded in the boom of 1929.

To answer this question, other elements in the situation must be examined. One of these elements was the policy of the banking system. Although in 1925 fear had been expressed that too much credit was being used for speculation on the stock market and some restriction was put into effect, the New York Reserve Bank followed an easy-money policy for a few months in 1926. It has been noted that big business was financing itself to such an extent that the need for commercial credit was reduced. This policy left bank resources free to extend a large volume of collateral loans, which helped to finance speculation. During the first half of 1927, while the business recession was occurring, the stock market kept on rising. Business needed less credit than ever, while speculation was demanding more. The net result was that during the three years 1925, 1926, and 1927, the security loans of member banks of the Federal Reserve System increased 40 per cent and their investments 20 per cent, while their commercial loans grew only 12 per cent.[8]

Conflicting motives were at work in the Federal reserve authorities at this point, and spirited controversy occurred both at the time and subsequently concerning their decisions. On the one hand, the tradition that had been built up since the inauguration of the Federal Reserve System supported the view that interest rates should be reduced and an extension of loans encouraged during the downward phase of the business cycle. On the other hand, it had become clear that a large section of manufacturing no longer depended on the banks for commercial loans since it had all the money it needed, whereas an expansion of credit would be utilized largely for speculation.

Partly on account of the tradition that favored an easy-money policy during the recession and partly on account of the desire to support the gold standard in England noted in Chapter XII, the Federal Reserve Board decided against the policy of attempting to restrict speculation by contracting bank credit. Between the middle and the end of 1927, rediscount rates were lowered from 4 to 3½ per cent and purchases of securities in the open market by the reserve banks totaled $435,000,000. Perhaps as a result of this easy-

[8] Steiner, *Money and Banking*, p. 883.

money policy, the loans and investments of the member banks increased by $1,764,000,000 in the last six months of 1927, although only 7 per cent of this increase consisted of commercial loans. Part of the money sustained speculative business building, particularly of commercial structures in the cities, which otherwise might have declined more than it did. Much of the credit flowed into stock market speculation, brokers' loans on the New York Stock Exchange rising 24 per cent.[9]

The speculative boom in stocks might have continued even if the banking system had not encouraged it. At any rate, the boom had attained such momentum that, when in 1928 rediscount rates were rapidly increased and government securities were sold in an effort to check it, stocks kept on rising and brokers' loans continued to grow. These loans by the banks were augmented by over $2 billion in 1928 and by another $200 million during the first half of 1929. Speculators for the rise were not discouraged by the increase in interest rates, because profits made in the market were far greater than the charges for the borrowed money.[10]

As the boom pursued its course, the banking authorities faced a new dilemma. They could not, they thought, further restrict credit by the general measures then available without hampering the legitimate needs of trade. Yet they could not discourage speculation without further restricting credit. Their policy in 1929 was an attempt at compromise that did not satisfy either requirement. As a matter of fact, the financing of speculation to a considerable degree passed out of their hands, since the surplus funds of large business corporations were now being lent directly to speculators. A curious commentary on the state of the American economy at the time is the fact that business could make less money by using its surplus funds in production than it could by lending the money to purchasers of stocks, the value of which was supposed to be determined by the profit on that production.

Whatever the responsibility of banking policy for the speculative boom, the state of mind of those most influential in forming American opinion had much to do with the activity on the stock market and the widespread participation of the public in it. The Republican party under Harding and Coolidge had subsidized and

9 *Ibid.*, pp. 884, 885.
10 *Ibid.*, pp. 885–886.

protected private enterprise. The country had enjoyed six years of
prosperity with only minor interruptions. Technical marvels had
greatly increased the productivity of industry. Employers were supposed to have adopted the economy of high wages. Profits were
large and increasing, not because of any rise in the price level,
which was remarkably stable, but because of expanded production
and sales. It was therefore generally concluded that the United
States had attained a "New Era" in which good times would continue indefinitely with only slight interruptions from the business
cycle, and even the latter, it was thought, was already being
brought under control by the credit policy of the banks.

Even a number of reputable economists held similar views.
These economists had concentrated their attention mainly on the
phenomena of price inflation and deflation, which had been prominent in the postwar boom and depression, and had come to believe
that the principal objective to be sought was the maintenance of
stable prices. They somewhat overestimated the influence of banking and credit policy, and thought that correct action by the banking authorities could achieve the desired result. At any rate, the
commodity price indexes had not fluctuated widely, and therefore
they saw no danger. They were confirmed in their confidence by the
long-term trend of increase in production and the large profits being made. Some of them regarded the rise in the price of stocks as
justified by the earning prospects of the corporations. Those who
were made uneasy by the Wall St. boom regarded it as a temporary
speculative madness like the Florida boom, which could be corrected in its own sphere without affecting the production and distribution of goods and services.

UNDERLYING STRAINS

The general public and the economists who supported its attitude overlooked the flaws in the internal structure of the economy
outlined at the beginning of this chapter. They held to the traditional view that free private enterprise was self-regulating, and that
any obstructions or distortions that might occur would normally be
corrected by the interplay of supply and demand, provided only
that harmful intervention from the government, the banks, or something else outside the sphere of business enterprise was avoided.
Much of the statistical material revealing the basic dangers had not

at the time been analyzed in such a way as to show what it meant. These observers, however, paid too little attention to developments that were obvious to anyone who cared to see them, and that should have given them pause.

According to traditional economic theory, equilibrium is maintained in the economic order by flexible adjustment of demand, supply, and price. When supply increases more rapidly than demand, price is supposed to fall and so to increase the demand. Alternatively, an increase in demand that raises prices will lead to an expansion of supply. A third possibility is that when supply grows more rapidly than demand, and prices fall in consequence, purchasers will not want so much as is being produced even at the lower prices, and this will lead to a curtailment of production of the article in question, with a shifting of capital and labor to other activities where the product is more needed. But for a long time the development of economic institutions had been interposing obstructions to automatic adjustments of this kind, and these barriers to flexibility were rapidly strengthened during the decade of the twenties. It is therefore possible that the very stability of average prices, which reassured the economists, gave evidence of a whole series of maladjustments arising from lack of flexibility.

Frederick C. Mills, during the subsequent depression, called attention to this possibility as follows:

The possible consequences of such a situation are numerous. Rigidity in one part of the price structure may involve excessively wide fluctuations in other parts. The variability characteristic of the prices of raw materials, and the exceptional fluctuations to which those prices have recently been subject, may be in part the result of price rigidity elsewhere. More important is the possibility of serious maladjustment among economic factors. When the nervous system of prices is functioning smoothly slight faults lead immediately to corrective action. A price system rigid and inelastic over wide areas may permit discordant and unbalanced development to proceed until the task of rectification is of major proportions.

The statistical record does not definitely establish the existence of harmful price rigidity. We have no test for distinguishing between inelasticity and stability. It is clear that during the period 1922–1929 there was a steady decline in the degree of movement occurring in the prices of individual commodities. This trend may have resulted from increasing stability. But other evidence supports the conclusion that necessary sensitivity to changing market conditions was being lost. Many of the troubles arising out of the present world depression, and out of our domestic difficulties, had their origin in the failure of the price system to preserve an efficient adjustment of the working parts of the world economy and of the national economy of the United States, at a time when there were no adequate alternative instruments of coordination.[11]

The extent of industrial concentration, both on the domestic scene and in the form of international cartels, doubtless restricted the tendency to falling prices in the industries concerned. Meanwhile, the full force of competition was felt in agriculture, bituminous coal mining, textiles, and other important parts of the economic order. Numerous other factors besides industrial concentration and monopoly price control contributed to the lack of flexible coordination. Wages, of course, respond slowly to the pressures that arise from rapid changes in other factors. This is true even when they are not fixed by collective agreement or arbitration. This rigidity is often mentioned at times when wage reductions are advocated, but it exists on the way up as well as on the way down. It is highly probable that in the period in question real wages did not rise so rapidly as increases in per capita output would have permitted, and that their failure to do so contributed to the limitation of the market for manufactured goods.

Another important element in rigidity is the difficulty, due to the immense pressure generated to sustain incomes dependent upon interest, with which long-term debt is liquidated when the need arises. This factor in turn hampers changes in taxes and creates difficulties for state and local governments that have limited borrowing power. Since local governments depend largely on property taxes, there is added an element of inflexibility in rents. The remuneration of the rapidly growing class of government employees, many of whom are subject to civil service, is even more inflexible than ordinary wages.

PROFITS AND THEIR CONSEQUENCES

One effect of inflexibilities in the long period of industrial expansion was a tremendous growth of profits for the more fortunately situated sectors of business and for the big corporations that dominated them. In part, the profits were distributed as dividends, and

[11] Mills, *Economic Tendencies in the United States*, pp. 331–332. Reprinted by permission of the National Bureau of Economic Research, publishers.

these dividends, in so far as they were spent or reinvested, were returned to the stream of purchasing power and acted as a stimulus for further production. A considerable fraction of the profits were held by the corporations and added to corporate surplus. By this means many corporations financed expansion of their productive facilities and so kept in circulation the money spent for materials and labor in construction and the manufacture of machinery.

In the table on page 122, Chapter VI, the figures showing the extraordinarily rapid growth of property income and especially of dividends are tabulated. Though the national income itself was growing, dividends increased even more rapidly, making up a percentage of the total national income, which rose steadily from 1920 on. Dividends were 4.3 per cent of the national income in 1920 and 7.2 per cent in 1929. That portion of profits which was not distributed but remained as corporate net savings naturally fluctuated more widely between good years and bad. The lowest point was $230 million in 1922 and the peak, $2.3 billion in 1926.[12] Toward the end of the period large amounts of cash remained in the hands of the big manufacturing and public-utility corporations that they did not distribute either in dividends or by means of new investment. These amounts were augmented by new security issues. As previously stated, these funds helped to supply them with working capital, so that they were no longer dependent upon commercial loans from the banks. In this way the banks were deprived of possible control over inflationary tendencies. The large corporations accumulated even more cash than they needed for their own uses, with the result that interest-bearing time deposits grew to large proportions. This money eventually spilled over into stock speculation. A reasonable inference is that the economy would have been in a more wholesome condition if these corporations had followed a policy of raising wages or reducing selling prices more rapidly and if, as a consequence of the enlarged market demand that would thus have been created, they had been led to employ their surplus profits more fully in expansion of production. Their profits presumably would have been no smaller in the aggregate, if reduced profit margins had led to larger sales.

A spectacular result of the rapid growth of profits was the activity of financial promoters in manufacturing and selling stocks

[12] Kuznets, *National Income and Its Composition*, p. 216.

and bonds themselves. Large sections of the public had been impressed by the gains reaped by owners of securities. The impression grew that there was no limit to the expansion of business. Therefore new issues of stocks and bonds were eagerly snapped up, without much regard to the underlying values they represented. Established corporations brought out a multitude of new issues, not because they needed the capital but because insiders could profit by selling to the public securities issued to them on a preferential basis. Exploitation of the capital market was pursued with great vigor by promoters of new mergers and consolidations. The era of industrial mergers in the basic industries had come to a climax before the war, but there were new opportunities, especially in public utilities, which were not subject to the antitrust laws. The issuance of new securities for the profit of the promoters, rather than because of need for new capital equipment, was particularly prevalent in utility and railroad holding companies, while the large idle funds in the possession of banks and other financial institutions stimulated the issue of real-estate bonds for speculative building.

The fact that the banks, which were employing a much smaller proportion of their resources in self-liquidating commercial loans, had become heavy investors in securities and mortgages placed them in a dangerous position when the collapse of values occurred. This circumstance later proved to be one of the most important elements of rigidity in aggravating the depression and delaying the recovery.

The large surplus funds that the huge profits were leaving in the hands of both individuals and business also flowed into foreign investment, much of which was unsound and not likely to yield a return in the long run. This constituted a danger not merely to the investor, but also to the entire economy, because the outflow of capital was what enabled foreigners to pay for the American surplus of merchandise exports. This trade was certain to be lost as soon as the volume of foreign investment should for any reason be sharply decreased.

SATURATION IN AUTOMOBILES AND HOUSES

Realistic observers of economic conditions could hardly have been ignorant of the concentration of industrial control and the rigidities of costs and prices to which it gave rise, of the profit surpluses of large corporations that were employed for speculation, of the speculative excesses on the financial markets, of the weakness in the economy represented by agriculture and "sick industries," or of the precarious situation in foreign lending and the exports that depended on it. Another question that ought to have given them pause was the doubt about the immediate future of the automobile industry. There was at the time a good deal of discussion as to whether the market for cars had not become saturated. Few, if any, would have contended that everyone who wanted a new automobile already had one. There was, however, some evidence to show that most of those who could buy cars at the prices charged had already bought them. It is true that new-car purchasers had become accustomed to turning in their old cars for new ones every few years, but even this practice could not be continued indefinitely unless a market could be found for the used cars, and the number of those who could afford to buy the used cars was not unlimited.

It is obvious that a relatively new industry of this sort must, after a period of rapid growth, become adjusted to a more stable demand. The number of automobiles on the road might go on increasing and yet, if the rate of growth in their numbers declined, the demand for new cars would actually decrease. This is what happened during the decade. The number of passenger car registrations increased every year from 1921 to 1929, the total being 9.3 million in the first of these years and 23.1 million in the last. The percentage rate of increase reached its peak at 24 per cent in 1923, and thereafter showed a downward tendency until it dropped to 5 per cent in 1927, rising slightly in the next two years, but not recovering to even the 1926 rate of 10 per cent. In 1927, the output of new cars had even decreased 22 per cent. Another evidence of the fact that sales of automobiles was approaching the saturation point of demand at the existing level and distribution of the national income is that a larger percentage of sales of new cars went to persons who were buying them as replacements and a smaller percentage to first-car owners. Replacement sales grew from 21 per cent in 1923 to 59 per cent in 1927. In 1928 and 1929, with larger incomes, the percentage fell slightly again. It was obvious, however, that the use of passenger automobiles was approaching a limit, so

The Traffic Jam

In the 1920's for the first time automobiles brought traffic jams outside metropolitan regions. Cars often stood motionless for long periods waiting for the snarl to be untangled, especially on week ends and holidays. (*Brown Brothers*)

Commercial Housing Development

Typical of row houses, with lack of planning for the whole area, erected in large numbers on the outskirts of cities. (*Brown Brothers*)

Planned Suburban Development

At Radburn, New Jersey, coordinated planning led to much better living conditions. The project of a limited dividend company. (*Courtesy City Housing Corporation, New York*)

that any diminution in the national income would cause a sharp falling off in sales.[13]

Another element in the demand for automobiles, which grew until 1927 and then started to taper off, was the export sale. In 1921, 7.5 per cent of the sales went to the foreign market. This percentage grew until it reached 18 in 1927. The same percentage was held in 1928 and thereafter the figure declined. The foreign market for automobiles was one of those being precariously maintained in large part by the outflow of capital.[14]

During the years of prosperity the market for cars and other forms of durable consumers' goods had been considerably widened by the growth of installment credit. Many more people bought these goods than would have done so if they had had to save the total price in cash before making the purchases. Installment buying could not, however, obviate the eventual retardation of expansion. There was certain to come a time when all the families who would utilize installment loans were loaded up with all the debt they could carry. In the long run the only possible means of keeping these new industries expanding would have been to augment the cash purchasing power of the consumers through sufficient increases in wages and salaries or through sufficient reduction in retail prices. Of new cars sold, 68.2 per cent were on time payments in 1925, and thereafter the percentage fell to 58 in 1927. The peak in used cars sold on time payments was reached in 1926 at 65.2 per cent, and fell to 63.1 per cent in 1927, and 60.8 per cent in 1928. This reduction in the number of cars sold on credit might have indicated that the purchasers were receiving sufficiently larger incomes so that more of them preferred to pay cash. Since, however, almost everyone who could possibly afford to buy a car did so even if he had to resort to installment purchasing, a more likely interpretation is that the limit of good risks among the population was being approached.[15]

The same logic applies to the construction of dwellings. The building of new houses, which had been increasing ever since 1921, began to decrease between 1926 and 1927, and kept on falling thereafter. This does not mean that all American families ever

[13] *Facts and Figures of the Automobile Industry*, 1931 ed., pp. 4, 11, 16.
[14] *Ibid.*, p. 11.
[15] *Facts and Figures of the Automobile Industry*, 1929 ed., p. 32.

possessed the kind of living quarters they would have liked to have. It does not even mean that the total number of houses and apartments ceased growing. What it does mean is that only a fraction of the population was able to buy or rent new houses or new apartments at the prices charged, and that the number which could do so provided an upper limit to the market. After a few years of active building this limit was being approached. There was still an actual need for better housing in large quantities, but this need could not be converted into a market demand unless either the number of those who could afford the housing was increased by sufficient enlargement of income, or the prices of the new housing could be materially decreased. Neither of these developments occurred.

THE FINAL SPURT

In spite of the growing strains and stresses in the structure of the economy, a short-lived recovery occurred in 1928 and the first half of 1929. It was most obvious in the stock market, where both prices and the volume of transactions rose to unprecedented heights. This activity, by now mainly a speculative boom and largely financed by credit, was responsible for a good deal of the renewed advance that occurred in the production and sale of goods and services.

Those consumers who were making easy money in speculation naturally spent more freely. This spending had its effect in increased sales of automobiles and other durable goods, which in 1929 rose even above the former high point of 1926. It also led to larger demand for personal services such as those supplied by barbers and beauty shops and for the professional services of lawyers, doctors, and investment counselors. A less marked gain in consumers' buying of perishable goods arose in part from a moderate increase in the numbers employed by manufacturing industry. A not inconsiderable element in the growth of demand was the fact that the activity of the stock market provided more employment and compensation for those at work in banks and financial houses. The number of employees under the general classification of finance was increased by 400,000 during the years of stock market boom between 1925 and 1929, and their aggregate compensation grew correspondingly. In 1929 their wages and salaries equaled those paid in agriculture and mining combined. The consequence of these various factors was a slight gain in consumers' outlay between 1927 and 1928 and a jump in 1929 to the highest point of the decade.[16]

No comparable expansion occurred, however, in the more fundamental activities. The amount spent for residential construction was reduced in both 1928 and 1929. The construction of business buildings was somewhat smaller in 1928 than in 1927 and then recovered slightly in 1929 under the stimulus of the speculative boom. Private investment as a whole suffered a substantial drop in 1928. While it increased sharply again in 1929, the principal element in this increase was a growth in inventories, which was larger than in any previous year since 1923. This jump was brought about by the fact that although business expected sales to keep on growing as they had done during the previous year and a half, the industrial depression actually began before the year was over. In consequence, industry was caught with large supplies of goods that it could not sell. If sales had not begun to recede during the year, the expansion of inventories would have been more moderate and the figure of increase in private investment would have shown a much smaller gain. In a sense, therefore, part of this gain in investment was a statistical accident rather than a real stimulus to employment and trade.[17]

Expenditures by government did not increase employment and production. Nor was there any marked stimulus from growth of exports. In spite of the overflow of purchasing power from the speculative boom in the stock market, the basic downward trends reasserted themselves by the middle of 1929. It is interesting to note that the curve of automobile production reached its peak and began to fall in June, while the curve of industrial production as a whole started to decline a month later. Both of these events occurred before the autumn collapse in the prices of stocks. There is little ground, therefore, for asserting that the behavior of the stock market acted as a barometer, foretelling the course of business, or that the end of financial speculation was the sole cause of the industrial depression which followed.[18]

[16] Kuznets, *National Income and Its Composition*, pp. 334–335, 332–333.
[17] Barger, *Outlay and Income in the United States*, pp. 50–51.
[18] *Federal Reserve Bulletin* (December, 1929).

CHAPTER XIV

The Crash

IN THE fall of 1929 a panic on the New York stock market caused the greatest destruction of security values and the largest capital losses to individuals that had ever occurred in time of peace. The story of this collapse and of the events which led up to it sounds so fantastic in retrospect that it seems as if it must have been a product of the imagination of a writer of romances. Those whose view of the national life has been affected by the long years of depression which followed the disaster can scarcely believe that so large a part of the population of the United States could have been as credulous and reckless as the historical record proves that it was.

OPTIMISM GENERAL

There is more in this story, however, than a monument to human folly. The course of affairs was a logical and natural development of what had gone before. True, it might conceivably have been better if those who occupied responsible positions had at the time known all that they painfully discovered in the subsequent months and years. Some of this they should have known if they had not been blinded by wishful thinking. The bitter satire directed against them after the event was in part justified. It is well to remember that what happened was not the outcome of ignorance and speculative greed merely on the part of the man in the street. The delusions that prevailed were shared by the leaders of finance,

business, government, and even many academic experts in economics. Indeed, they were not only shared but loudly proclaimed.
Rarely has a people been so misled by those who were supposed
to be its wisest and most seasoned counselors. The outcome was in
many respects comic enough to furnish material for a musical
extravaganza, but it was also a bitter tragedy to millions of innocent persons and was sufficient to destroy for years the faith of
the people in those whom they had permitted to occupy positions
of power.

Understanding of the delusion may be assisted by an attempt
to reconstruct the state of mind that prevailed in the latter part of
the decade of the twenties. The country had been turned over to
a political and industrial regime that frankly represented itself as
the flowering of private capitalism. The radical movements growing out of the war had been routed, and the ferment of opinion
demanding economic reconstruction had almost disappeared. Even
the trade unions had been declining in numbers and power. Wealth
and income had shown almost steady increase. The country was
enjoying wider and wider use of the automobile and hundreds of
other new mechanical inventions. Technical marvels were also step-
ping up the production of industry, and without any visible price
inflation the national income grew from year to year as a result of
augmented production of physical goods. The profits of business
became larger, while those who shared in them through ownership
of stocks and other securities received a steadily mounting stream
of dividends and interest. Higher real wages were paid on the
average than the nation had ever known, and the American standard of living was far in advance of that of any other country in
the world.

Spokesmen for the current order developed the thesis that it
represented genuine economic democracy. The United States was,
they declared, well on its way toward the abolition of poverty.
Americans were immune from the domestic conflicts of Europe,
where strange new doctrines and class struggles were creating confusion. Socialism and all its kin were being proved impractical by
the backwardness of Soviet Russia. Under private enterprise the
dollars spent by consumers were votes that decided what would
be produced, and business was bent on serving the wishes of the
consumers. It was true that large profits were being amassed, but

they belonged not to the few but to the many, because of the ever-widening participation in the ownership of industry. The stock market was a free institution where anyone could invest his savings by buying shares in almost any undertaking that took his fancy. Not only small businessmen and professional people but also the workers with their "high wages" were becoming partners in ownership, and therefore a better kind of collectivism was being established without disturbing the freedom and efficiency of business.

This mood received no better expression than in the annual message to Congress on the state of the nation sent by the President of the United States, Calvin Coolidge, on December 4, 1928. Composed less than a year before the crash, this document overflowed with complacency and assurance. His words were in part as follows: "No Congress of the United States ever assembled, on surveying the state of the Union, has met with a more pleasing prospect than that which appears at the present time. . . . The great wealth created by our enterprise and industry, and saved by our economy, has had the widest distribution among our own people, and has gone out in a steady stream to serve the charity and the business of the world. The requirements of existence have passed beyond the standard of necessity into the region of luxury. Enlarging production is consumed by an increasing demand at home and an expanding commerce abroad. The country can regard the present with satisfaction and anticipate the future with optimism." Mr. Coolidge, blissfully ignorant of the approaching unemployment, warned in his conclusion that Americans would "continue to be required to spend [their] days in unremitting toil." [1]

Herbert Hoover, the great engineer and the organizer of philanthropy, had just been elected to succeed Mr. Coolidge. As Secretary of Commerce in President Coolidge's Cabinet he had become the popular embodiment of the idea that standards of engineering efficiency and skillful management in the public interest were being applied in business. In his speech accepting the nomination Mr. Hoover had declared, "We in America today are nearer to the final triumph over poverty than ever before in the history of any land." [2] His campaign slogan was "A chicken in every pot and two cars in every garage." Roger Babson, a wizard who guided the

[1] *Congressional Record* (December 4, 1928), p. 20.
[2] New York *Times* (August 12, 1928), p. 1.

ventures of those who played the market, argued for his election on the ground that it would assure the continuance of prosperity, and added with unconscious irony, "If Smith should be elected with a Democratic Congress, we are almost certain to have a resulting business depression in 1929." [3] As it turned out, the Happy Warrior from the sidewalks of New York never had a chance, partly because of the fact that he was a Catholic, partly because large sections of the West and South still professed to support prohibition, which he opposed, but mainly because most of the people were overwhelmingly satisfied with the regime in power. Business leaders by the dozen confirmed the popular impression of its triumph over economic misfortune. The president of an organization of large employers engaged in economic research, Magnus W. Alexander of the National Industrial Conference Board, asserted, "There is no reason why there should be any more panics." [4] Irving T. Bush, a progressive and highly successful businessman and the owner of the Bush Terminal in Brooklyn, announced, "We are only at the beginning of a period that will go down in history as a golden age." [5]

EXTENT OF SPECULATION

There is a legend which arose at the time of the crash and has persisted ever since that every corner bootblack was speculating on the market and that virtually the whole population was engaged in a gambling spree much as formerly they might have bet on horse races or shot dice in vacant doorways. No statistics have ever been presented on the number of bootblacks involved, but while participation in the market was wide and caught up many with small incomes, the greater part of the money undoubtedly flowed in from businessmen, lawyers, doctors, and others of more substantial means.

The number of stockholders recorded on the books of American corporations was 18 million in 1928, and in 1929, 20 million. Since many individuals owned shares in more than one company, these totals must be considerably larger than the actual number of individual stockholders. A good estimate of this figure, based on income

[3] New York *Times* (September 18, 1928), p. 18.
[4] Edward Angly, *Oh, Yeah?* (New York: The Viking Press, 1931), p. 12.
[5] *Ibid.*, p. 12.

tax returns, indicates that the number was not above 9 million persons in 1929. Those with net incomes of less than $5,000 owned hardly more than one fifth of the total number of shares outstanding. Thus the major part of the activity on the market involved a minor fraction of the gainfully occupied in the United States.[6]

And while speculative fever dominated the market for many months, most of the smaller participants did not regard their ventures as a gamble at all. Many of them were investing their savings in the expectation that the market was going indefinitely higher and that they would never have another chance to buy at such low prices. Even those who were borrowing money to buy and expected to resell at higher prices did not regard the operation as one involving much speculative risk. They had seen fortunes made in the market. They or their friends had indulged in this trading for several years without substantial loss on the part of anyone. They were assured on the highest authority that they were merely sharing in the lasting prosperity of the country. Securities had become commodities valued for their own sake, with seemingly little relation to the companies that issued them. Unlike betting on horse races, stock exchange speculation apparently did not involve a balancing of losers against winners. For a long time almost everybody had been winning. Moreover, the same game was being played not merely by the ignorant many but by the well-informed few. Big bankers and businessmen with large fortunes were buying for the rise. About the only deliberate gamblers in the market were those few of the professional speculators who tried to make money by selling short, and suffered losses almost every time they counted on generally declining prices.

Some of the better-informed analysts of economic trends had, a year or two earlier, made up their minds that the market had risen too high and that a recession was due. They had therefore sold their holdings and reaped their profits in cash. When they observed, however, that prices kept on going up and that apparently the country was more prosperous than ever, many of them decided that the public had been right and they had been wrong, and began to buy again, only to be wiped out when the panic occurred.

[6] Alfred L. Bernheim and Margaret Grant Schneider (eds.), *The Security Markets* (New York: Twentieth Century Fund, 1935), pp. 50, 53, 55.

The dimensions of the long-continued boom which took place in stocks are measured by the fact that the market value of all shares listed on the New York Stock Exchange rose from $27,072,-522,000 on January 1, 1925, to $67,472,053,000 on January 1, 1929. Thus there had been almost a threefold gain in the values of these stocks before the last act began. The gain was accounted for only in part by increases in the average price per share, which rose from $62.45 at the beginning of 1925 to $89.09 on January 1, 1929. In this same period the number of shares listed increased from 433,-449,000 to 757,302,000. In part this increase in the number of shares reflected the issues of new ventures or of older companies, the securities of which had not before been sold on the stock exchange. To a great extent, however, the new securities were additional issues or stock dividends representing ownership in the same properties whose shares had been listed at the beginning of the period. If these companies had not altered their capital structures, the rise in the average price of shares would have been much higher than it was.[7]

These totals do not encompass anything like the whole volume of the increase in the market value of securities. They do not include the shares on the New York Curb Exchange, or the Consolidated Exchange, where long lists of stocks were dealt in. Nor do they include the many "over the counter" sales of unlisted shares. The totals on the stock exchange rose even higher during the year. On October 1, 1929, after some liquidation had occurred, but before the big crash, the market value of the listed stocks was $87,073,-630,000, and the number of shares listed was 1,048,359,000. In spite of the fact that nearly 300 million new shares had been listed during the first nine months of the year, the average price per share had fallen only from $89.09 to $83.06.[8]

It was scarcely to be wondered at, with such a long-continued growth in the market value of certificates of ownership, that people of all degrees were induced to buy. The activities of Wall Street had become front-page news and formed the chief topic of conversation. Changes in the prices of stocks and other market news were not only printed in the newspapers but were carried to every cross-

[7] Francis Wrigley Hirst, *Wall Street and Lombard Street* (New York: The Macmillan Company, 1931), pp. 70–72.
[8] *Ibid.*

roads and farm several times a day by the radio. Almost every bank throughout the country offered facilities for the purchase and sale of securities on the part of its depositors. Brokerage houses established branches as if they were chain stores, and hardly a small city was without its customers' room equipped with ticker and blackboard on which the most recent quotations were chalked up as they arrived. Investment counselors and statistical services multiplied, prospering on the desire of the public for predictions of the course of the market and hints as to where bargains were to be found. Theories and systems by the hundred arose that purported to forecast accurately what future prices would be. Magazines devoted entirely to stock trading attained large circulation. There was a rush to enroll in college courses designed to train securities salesmen.

SALES PROMOTION FOR SECURITIES

This expansion of the business of selling securities was not a mere response to an irresistible public demand. It was promoted by all the well-known arts of advertising and salesmanship. Old and reputable banks, whose financial strength and conservatism had been unquestioned, established affiliates for selling investments directly to the public. Their salesmen went far and wide, calling on people who had money to spare. Most of these salesmen, like their customers, possessed only the most superficial knowledge of the true financial situation and the prospects of the corporations whose shares were offered for sale. Commissions were high and inexperienced salesmen made more than they had ever dreamed of in their former occupations. In at least one case, that of the National City Company, contests were conducted, with prizes for employees whose total sales were the highest for the week or month. The mails were full of circular material describing the attractions of securities, and the newspapers printed carefully worded advertisements.

Ferdinand Pecora, who later conducted an investigation into Wall Street practices for the Senate Committee on Banking and Currency, relates the following story as typical of many experiences.[9] A small businessman with a modest amount of savings wished to retire and move to California on account of his health. He saw in his local paper an advertisement stating that anyone who was thinking of changing his residence would do well to communicate with the advertisers, who would give him advice when he no longer could consult his local banker. A reply to this advertisement resulted in a call from a salesman of the National City Company, who persuaded him that he could better provide for himself and his family if he would exchange his savings, consisting of cash and United States government bonds, for a miscellaneous list of bonds handled by the company which had higher yields and better prospects of appreciation.

He therefore invested in a group of obligations of foreign countries and domestic companies of which he had never heard, and concerning which the salesman himself had little reliable knowledge. So good did the opportunity seem that he borrowed for this purpose as well. After a time, noting that these bonds were declining in value, he again made contact with the salesman. The comment of the latter was that of course he had been foolish to put his money in bonds, but should invest in common stocks. The unfortunate customer, dazzled by the glowing sales talk, followed the salesman's advice. Shortly before the big slump on the market, he became frightened by the behavior of the prices of his stocks, and complained to the home office of the National City Company in New York. They persuaded him, however, that it would be better to shift to shares of the National City Bank itself and Anaconda Copper. The ultimate outcome was that the investor lost all he had.

The urgent demand for securities, stimulated as it was by those who made a profit in selling them, was reflected by a large increase in the supply. The traditional theory is that business corporations issue stocks and bonds only when they need additional capital, and take this method of obtaining it from the investors. During this period, however, new securities were manufactured almost like cakes of soap, for little better reason than that there was gain to be made out of their manufacture and sale. The banks and investment houses played a large part in inducing the directors of business corporations to split up into smaller fragments old shares which had become so high in price that they were difficult to sell to small investors, or to put out other types of obligations with the slightest of excuses.

Three or four series of fees or commissions were usually interposed between the original seller and the ultimate customer. An investment banking house would take over the entire issue and, acting as a wholesaler, would distribute it to other dealers for a substantial compensation. These dealers in turn would take their profit before paying commissions to their salesmen. The corporations that issued the securities were often induced to do so by the profit which could be made by their stockholders, since the companies themselves were controlled by the owners of large blocks of stock. If a stock dividend was distributed, it could be sold by the recipients. If a new issue was contemplated, "rights" would be given in advance to existing owners, which would enable them to buy the new stocks or bonds at a price lower than that which would be established on the market. These rights themselves had a market value. Investigation later disclosed that even J. P. Morgan & Co. had a "preferred list" of individuals who were permitted to buy, at prices lower than the public issue price, new issues that the firm handled. Thus a substantial share of the money "invested" by the public never found its way into the treasuries of the companies whose securities they were buying.

INVESTMENT TRUSTS, POOLS, HOLDING CORPORATIONS

One of the most prolific sources of new securities was a relatively new type of organization—the investment trust. The investment trust rested on the theory that individual investors who wanted to be secure against loss should diversify their holdings, and should rely on expert knowledge concerning what to buy and sell and when to do so. Small investors did not have enough money to command a desirable degree of diversification, and they obviously were not experts in the value of securities. They could, however, buy a few shares in an investment trust which, with its accumulated funds, could perform these functions. Numerous investment trusts were created with many different types of structure and plans of operation. Their shares were poured into the already flooded market and added to the amount of paper that the retail buyers were supposed to absorb. It was argued that investment trusts did not really increase the total market value of shares for sale, since they in turn bought stocks with the money they received. As President E. H. Simmons of the New York Stock Exchange later pointed out, however, they frequently held large amounts of cash for long periods or bought foreign securities. In his opinion, they contributed to the eventual break in the market by helping to create an excess of the supply of securities above the effective demand of the public investors.[10]

Some of the investment trusts were conservatively managed, and although they could not escape the losses of the subsequent crash, little criticism could be made of their activities. Others, however, were not so immune from attack. Their judgments about what to buy appeared to be influenced by the interest of the issuing houses with which they were directly or indirectly affiliated. An institution that was supposed to be a trustee of the customer thus became an agent of the profit-seeking seller of securities. In some instances the investment trust served principally as the device of a financial promoter to make profits for himself by the use of other people's money.

One striking case of this kind was that of Dillon, Read & Co., an investment banking house devoted to the sale of securities. In 1924 this house organized an investment trust called the United States & Foreign Securities Corporation. It had three classes of stock—first preferred, second preferred, and common. Both classes of preferred were to yield dividends limited to 6 per cent and had no voting power. The common stock, which had a minus value at the organization of the company, carried with it entire control. The bankers sold all of the first preferred to the public for about $25 million. With the shares so sold they gave as a bonus one quarter of the common stock. They themselves, with an investment of only $5 million, retained all of the second preferred and three quarters of the voting common stock. By 1928 this investment trust, after preferred dividends, had earned a cash surplus of $10 million. The price of the common stock eventually rose as high as $72 a share. Dillon, Read & Co., with an investment of about one fifth of that put into the concern by the public, eventually made between $30 million and $40 million on its own investment of $5 million. From the profits of this enterprise they established a second investment trust called the International Securities Corporation, which they controlled in the same way as they did the first one. As bankers

[10] E. H. H. Simmons, *The Principal Causes of the Stock Market Crisis of 1929,* p. 15.

they made more than a million dollars in profit out of the mere organization of this new company.[11]

In effect, this type of organization was not legitimately an investment trust at all. The bankers were merely obtaining money from the public without security, by agreeing to pay a maximum of 6 per cent if as much as that should be earned. Who would not borrow money on such terms? With the use of the funds so accumulated they gathered munificent profits in the rising market.

A potent force in increasing sales of shares to the public was manipulation by pools and syndicates composed of insiders among speculators and businessmen who had access to large amounts of money. These operations were conducted for the immediate gain of the participants and often realized huge profits in relatively brief periods. Their methods were varied and ingenious, but were of course always directed toward the ultimate goal of selling quantities of shares at prices higher than those that they paid. It was popularly supposed that a pool would begin by accumulating the shares of a given stock with the utmost secrecy and then, when it had bought enough, would bring about a rise by holding the shares off the market, and eventually distribute them at the increased price. This may sometimes have been the method of operation, but pools also took advantage of the fact that the public was avid for news of their activities and would usually try to climb aboard the bandwagon. Thus they might create the suspicion that a pool was at work on a given stock by active trading on both sides of the market, which left few shares in their hands. When outsiders bought to realize profit from the rise that they supposed the pool was trying to cause, the pool might let them bid up prices to a level that could not be maintained, and then cash in by selling short.

Tips, rumors, and skillful publicity were assiduously employed by pool operators. They had many means of increasing the sales of the stock in which they were interested whenever they wished the price to rise. Their agents in this work often consisted of customers' men in brokerage houses, who would pass on to the public word of supposed opportunities for big profits. Tipster publications played their game. Ingenious publicity methods were employed to spread the desired rumors in the more reputable financial columns. Their

[11] Pecora, *Wall Street under Oath*, pp. 207–213.

less scrupulous allies were rewarded by cash payments or by chances to participate in the profit. Large numbers of nonprofessional speculators continued for months to entertain the delusion that they could beat the pools at their own game. The fact that they were not doing so was largely concealed by the continual upsurge of the bull market.

One of the largest of these pools was that which operated for a few days of March, 1929, in the shares of the Radio Corporation of America, and extracted a profit of about $5 million from the public. Among its participants were some of the most prominent figures in industry and finance. Far from maintaining its existence a secret, it achieved widespread publicity for its intended operations. The prospects of the company itself had been so favorably featured that the volume of transactions in radio stock had been virtually quadrupled even before the pool began its work. On the first day of its activities it both bought and sold a large number of shares, but ended the day with a substantial accumulation. During the next two days it still bought and sold, but sold more than it bought. Since this distribution caused the price to sag a little, the pool went long of the market again on the fourth day, stimulated the price in this manner, and finally ended on the fifth with a substantial short position. The public, however, was not informed of the fact that the pool had ceased buying, and of course did not know what its position was on any given day. In the course of its activities in five days it had succeeded in selling at a profit 187,900 shares in radio. Radio shares never again touched the high point at which the pool sold its shares.[12]

Some of the new corporate organizations offering securities were formed for purposes of control by the promoters as well as for the profit that might be made by the use of the investors' money. One of the most amazing ventures of this sort was that of the Van Sweringen brothers in Cleveland, who were originally real-estate operators. Beginning with an investment of $500,000 of their own money and an equal amount from their associates, and without ever putting in any more cash, they eventually controlled eight Class I railroads having smaller subsidiaries, with 29,431 miles of track. The juggling act by which they achieved this miracle was too complex to be detailed here, but it involved the organization

[12] Bernheim and Schneider, *The Security Markets*, pp. 473–482.

of a number of new companies that were financed by the sale of securities to the public. The first step will indicate the nature of the operation. They bought from the New York Central System a railroad called the Nickel Plate. The purchase price was $8 million. Of this amount $2 million was paid in cash. The purchasers, however, did not dip into their own funds to pay this cash, but borrowed it from a bank by pledging as collateral the very securities they were buying. The remainder of the price was to be paid in ten years. With control of the shares of this railroad in their possession, the promoters then formed a security company, and through the sale of its issues to the public obtained the money they needed to complete the purchase. Their original and only cash investment went toward paying off the bank loan.

As the Van Sweringen empire stood on April 30, 1930, it assumed the following amazing form. At the top were Messrs. O. P. and M. J. Van Sweringen. They owned or controlled 90 per cent of a holding company called the General Securities Corporation, 40 per cent of it directly, and 50 per cent of it through the Vaness Company, of which they owned 80 per cent. This top securities corporation was the only part of the great structure in which the Van Sweringens held a majority interest. From there on down, their control was that of minority ownership, the bulk of the funds being supplied by outside investors. The General Securities Corporation controlled the Allegheny Corporation, in which the Van Sweringen equity was 8.61 per cent. The Allegheny Corporation controlled the Chesapeake Corporation, in which the Van Sweringen equity was 4.1 per cent. The Chesapeake Corporation controlled the Chesapeake & Ohio Railroad, in which the Van Sweringen equity was 0.98 per cent. The Chesapeake & Ohio controlled the Hocking Valley, in which the Van Sweringen equity was 1/25 of 1 per cent. The railroad system also embraced, through minority control, the Nickel Plate, the Wheeling and Lake Erie, the Kansas City Southern, the Pere Marquette, the Chicago and Eastern Illinois, the Erie, and, through majority control, the Missouri Pacific, which had a 50 per cent ownership in the Denver & Rio Grande.[13]

One of the largest and most complex aggregates of the times was that built up by Samuel Insull of Chicago to control public

[13] Bonbright and Means, *The Holding Company*, p. 261; also Pecora, *Wall Street under Oath*, pp. 214–242.

utilities. This, too, was financed largely by the sale to the public of stocks and bonds. So intricate was the corporate structure involved that Owen D. Young, chairman of the General Electric Company, to whom Insull came for advice, later testified before a congressional committee that he could not understand it himself. Mr. Young was, of course, a distinguished corporation lawyer who was familiar enough with finance so that he was chosen to settle the question of German reparations. Young also testified that he did not believe even Insull could understand the interrelationships and the interlocking finances of the companies he had set up. Apparently Insull was continually in fear of losing control of this lofty pyramid of holding companies, and was obliged frequently to organize new companies and sell securities to the public in order to strengthen his grasp. If neither Young nor Insull could understand what was going on, what was the plight of the innocent investor who was being asked to hand over his savings to finance the operation? [14]

Other great utility empires were built up by the holding company device, which enabled insiders to exercise control and reap huge profits with money entrusted to them by investors. The largest of the holding company structures was Insull's Middle West Utilities, with assets of over $1.2 billion and no less than 111 subsidiaries.[15]

The new securities issued rose steadily from $4,304,000,000 in 1923 to $10,183,000,000 in 1929. A rough estimate indicates that while in the first of these years the new issues represented 29 per cent of the year's saving in the nation, they equaled in 1929 nearly 50 per cent of that saving. The money available to buyers of securities, though large, was not unlimited, and this outpouring of the supply is thought by some authorities to have approached a saturation of the demand and contributed to the eventual weakness of the market.[16]

In this period commercial banks were naturally extremely profitable and prices of bank stocks soared. They were not, however, split up to the same extent as the shares of nonfinancial concerns, and their high prices were beyond the means of most of the small

[14] Pecora, *Wall Street under Oath*, pp. 225–226.
[15] *Ibid.*, p. 226.
[16] Bernheim and Schneider, *The Security Markets*, p. 66.

investors. During 1929 the largest increases were recorded by bank shares, the next largest by public utilities. Industrials were third and railroads were a poor fourth.

BROKERS' LOANS

Those who were trading in the market with the hope of making money by resale of their purchases at higher prices were encouraged to do so by the fact that they could easily borrow money for the purpose. In the early part of the year brokers' loans to their customers for margin trading required only a 25 per cent margin. This meant that the purchaser had to advance only one quarter of the cash value. In these circumstances profits in a rapidly rising market were enormous. Efforts of the banking system to check this dangerous practice were ineffectual because as rapidly as the banks reduced their own lendings in the call-money market, large corporations, individuals, or foreign lenders with surplus cash stepped into the breach.

The rates for call loans on security collateral at the end of March, 1929, were 12 per cent, and thereafter advanced rapidly in three steps to 15, 17, and 20 per cent.[17] It was no wonder that corporations took advantage of these rates to make money on their idle cash, especially when they were able to obtain almost unlimited amounts by the simple process of issuing new stock. Ironically enough, the purchasers of these shares were borrowing back, from the very corporations that issued them, more than half the money they needed with which to buy the shares, at rates that ordinarily would be regarded as usurious. This process was profitable to the borrowers as long as prices of shares rose rapidly enough, but it was too much like perpetual motion to succeed for very long.

In both February and April the Federal Reserve Board issued warnings against the volume of margin trading, but these warnings were succeeded by another increase in brokers' loans of about a billion dollars. A few months before the crash, the brokerage houses raised their margin requirements to 50 per cent. This action, combined with the large amount of money attracted to the call-loan market by the high rates, reduced these rates at the end of June to between 10 and 15 per cent, and by August to between 12 and 6 per cent. It is noteworthy that when the crash actually occurred

---

[17] Hirst, *Wall Street and Lombard Street*, p. 7.

the interest charged for loans on margin trading was relatively moderate, and therefore the collapse was not caused in the first instance by any shortage of credit, as had been the case in some previous crises.[18]

At the time many commentators sought to fix the responsibility for the ensuing collapse of prices on some force external to the market that was unnecessary or accidental. Certain authorities, for instance, asserted that the downward push came from an ill-considered effort on the part of banks to restrict credit, an action that in turn was due, they charged, to a puritanical disapproval of speculative gains. But there was in fact no scarcity of money in the call-loan market when the panic arrived. Professor Irving Fisher of Yale believed that the crisis was caused by an unreasoning terror that seized the horde of small and poorly informed speculators. Subsequent analysis showed plainly that most of these small traders held on desperately after the market began to fall. Others blamed influences from abroad.

As a matter of fact, the fundamental situation was such that a collapse was certain to come, and the actual impulse which caused the structure to topple was of relatively minor importance. The prices of many stocks had risen so high that the yield of the dividends paid was infinitesimal. Even industrial stocks as a whole were selling in January, 1929, at more than sixteen times their earnings, although according to tradition a ratio between the value of a stock and its earnings ought to be about ten to one.[19] While a person who was investing his money for the sake of the income to be derived might have been satisfied to receive 4 or 5 per cent, this was far too small a return to cover the costs of active trading in stocks, including the interest that had to be paid on brokers' loans. Such trading could be profitable only through a continuance of rising prices. But prices could not go on rising indefinitely unless earnings also did so. Those who contended that existing prices were not too high supported their argument with the assertion that profits and dividends would continue to increase and that the market was merely discounting future prosperity. Before the end of the year, however, it became evident to shrewd observers that

[18] *Ibid.*
[19] Irving Fisher, *The Stock Market Crash—and After* (New York: The Macmillan Company, 1930), p. 82.

this expectation was unjustified, because important sectors of business were actually shrinking. If the market should experience a recession from any cause whatever, the position of the margin traders would become precarious and a collapse of the speculative boom would be in prospect.

THE PANIC ARRIVES

It is probable that several influences started the decline, which began in September. A scandal on the London Stock Exchange, caused by the discovery of fraud in the operations of a promoter named Hatry, occasioned a precipitate drop and led to the recall of funds from the United States. In addition, Britain had been losing gold, although she had none too much to maintain the gold standard, and the Bank of England on September 26 raised its rediscount rate to 6½ per cent in order to discourage the outflow. The large withdrawal of funds to London which followed this action is indicated by the fact that sterling exchange, which on September 24 was slightly under $4.85, rose by October 24 above $4.88. This rise indicated that the outgoing balances must have totaled hundreds of millions of dollars.[20]

Big speculators, both in the United States and abroad, foreseeing trouble, began to liquidate their holdings. The Fisher daily index of prices of industrial stocks fell from a high of 212 on September 7 to 198 on September 30.[21] By this time there was a strong opinion among many insiders that speculation had been overdone and that some liquidation would be desirable. They looked with favor on what Leonard Ayres of the Cleveland Trust Company predicted would be a "creeping bear market." Roger Babson, the investment counselor of thousands of small traders, was almost alone when in September he forecast a fifty to sixty point break.[22]

During the early part of October, although many of the wiser insiders were still selling, general confidence buoyed up the market and there was another advance. On October 15, Irving Fisher announced that stock prices stood on "what looks like a permanently high plateau," and that he expected to see the market "a good deal

[20] *Ibid.*, p. 32.
[21] *Ibid.*, pp. 1–2.
[22] Hirst, *Wall Street and Lombard Street*, p. 19.

Skyscraper under Construction

New York Life Insurance building, Madison Square, New York City. Especially in the latter
years of the decade, commercial building of this type created a large outlet for investment
and a stimulus to employment. (*Brown Brothers*)

The Wall Street Crash

Mounted police keep crowds moving in front of the New York Stock Exchange on October 24, 1929. (*Press Association, Inc.*)

Stock Ticker

Stock broker's office.
(*Underwood–Stratton*)

higher than it is today within a few months." [23] President Charles
E. Mitchell of the National City Bank said, "I see no reason for
the end-of-the-year slump which some people are predicting." [24]
On that very day the crash began.

On October 15 prices fell five or six points a share. The next
day they dropped still further. On October 19, although trading
was limited by the Saturday half holiday, the net losses were from
five to twenty points and the number of shares turned over approximated 3.5 million. The following Monday saw the largest
volume of trading since the previous March, with more than 6
million shares dumped on the market.[25] It was on that day that
Irving Fisher, with unshakable faith, came to the rescue again with
the statement, "I believe the breaks of the last few days have driven
stocks down to hard rock." Professor Fisher referred to what he
termed "the shaking out of the lunatic fringe." [26] By this he meant
that in his opinion the break had been caused by a panic among
small speculators who did not understand the true facts.

On Tuesday, October 22, Charles E. Mitchell made another
optimistic statement and there was a slight rally. Apparently, however, many of the market traders took this as an opportunity to get
rid of their holdings before anything further happened. On the
following day occurred a loss in the total market value of stocks
exceeding $4 billion. Even the more inactive stocks declined be-
tween forty and ninety-six points.[27] Brokers clogged the wires with
calls to their customers to put up more margin in order that their
stocks might be held. This was the third call of the kind within
a few days, however, and many could not respond. Indeed, in the
prevailing confusion large numbers of margin traders were sold out
before they even had an opportunity to reply to the telegrams.

The next day, October 24, came to be known as Black Thursday. The market was completely demoralized. Before the stock
exchange closed, 12,894,650 shares were sold and prices experienced
the widest drop in the history of the exchange. At 1 o'clock the
ticker was more than an hour and a half late and it did not finish
recording the stock sales until after 7 P.M. During the day, the

[23] *Ibid.*, pp. 18–19.
[24] *Ibid.*, p. 19.
[25] *Ibid.*, pp. 19–21.
[26] *Ibid.*, p. 21.
[27] *Ibid.*, pp. 22–23.

leading bankers of New York met conspicuously at the office of J. P. Morgan & Co., and word was given out that they had decided to support the market. In the afternoon, Thomas W. Lamont, a Morgan partner, announced that the situation was sound and many stocks were already too low. An almost comic incident of the effort to renew confidence occurred when Richard Whitney dramatically walked to the trading post of United States Steel, which had been selling at 190, and shouted, "Two hundred and five for twenty-five thousand Steel!" [28]

This action of the bankers prevented the panic from being worse than it was, though even a larger number of shares was dumped on the market on October 29. It was not, however, a purely unselfish measure in the public interest. The banks themselves were heavy investors in securities and the precipitous decline was decimating the value of their assets. If the panic should go on much further at the same rate, the peril of insolvency would become real. Moreover, the banks had close business relations with many of the brokerage houses and other financial institutions on the verge of disaster. What had happened was that the nonbanking lenders in the call-money market, such as manufacturing corporations and others, had withdrawn their funds in order to avoid loss. These nonbanking lenders had been financing over half of the brokers' loans to customers. The record subsequently showed that during the one week ending on October 30, they recalled more than one third of their funds, or $1.4 billion.[29] The banks stepped in to take over a large number of these loans, and in the last three weeks of the month advanced over $1 billion to do so. In addition, they also organized a fund to support the market by buying important stocks for which no purchasers appeared.

It is difficult to imagine the confusion that prevailed in Wall Street on a day in which such an unprecedented volume of business was accompanied by imminent danger, not only to the hordes of small speculators and traders, but to the largest and most stable of financial concerns. Lights glowed all night in the tall skyscrapers while exhausted clerks and bookkeepers attempted to work their way through the mountains of records. Throughout the country the bad news brought fear and despair into millions of homes.

[28] *Ibid.*, pp. 23–28.
[29] Bernheim and Schneider, *The Security Markets*, p. 114.

This volcanic explosion set in motion a tidal wave that also over-whelmed the markets in London, Paris, Berlin and was felt through-out the world.

It was natural in these circumstances that high authorities should attempt to reassure the public. On the night of October 24, the United States Treasury announced that underlying business security remained unshaken. Two leading British economists, Josiah Stamp and John Maynard Keynes, stated that the slump would benefit the world because it would liquidate unsound speculation. Keynes argued that credit which had been absorbed by the market would now be liberated for the use of industry, and commodity prices would recover. If the financial situation in New York had been similar to that to which Keynes was accustomed in England, this might have been a valid observation. Apparently, however, he was ignorant of the fact that industry had had all the credit it needed and had actually been lending its surplus funds to Wall Street.

One negative development did encourage a great many. Al-though October 24, 1929, had been the eleventh day of genuine panic on the stock market since the Black Friday of 1869, it was the first one that had occurred without major business failures. The intervention of the banks with their large resources and their improved organization under the Federal Reserve System had at least temporarily been able to buttress most of the financial con-cerns, while large business corporations were not dependent on bank credit and actually experienced an increase in their cash bal-ances as a result of their calling of loans. The New York *World* gave voice to a generally held opinion when it wrote that this was a "gamblers' and not an investors' panic." President Hoover made a similar statement on October 25 when he said, "The fundamental business of the country—that is, the production and distribution of goods and services—is on a sound and prosperous basis." [30]

Nevertheless, both opinions were mistaken and there was fur-ther trouble in store on the stock market and in business. Although call-money rates remained low, stocks were still at a level where the yield was only one third of the interest that speculators had to pay to carry them. Unless the rise was resumed, there must be

[30] New York *World* (October 25, 1929), and Hirst, *Wall Street and Lombard Street,* p. 30.

further liquidation. The large purchasers who had been buying to support the market and had been taking over stocks held as collateral would be certain to unload their surplus holdings every time prices started to rise. This was sure to be a bearish influence until a large volume of securities was finally distributed to more or less permanent owners.

Nor was the news from production and trade entirely good. The Federal Reserve Board issued a summary of industrial production for the third quarter of the year which showed that while as a whole it was 10 per cent above the same quarter in 1928, there had been a decrease in such important industries as automobiles, tires, steel, and building contracts. Wheat fell 11 cents. Bad news came from the rest of the world. For instance, a cable from Brazil broke the news that the coffee valorization scheme had collapsed and the exchange had closed.[31]

On October 29 new selling appeared that brought stocks down to a point which cancelled the gain made for the entire year. On Black Thursday those stocks that had suffered most were the weaker speculative favorites, but this time the drop affected the strongest companies like General Electric, United States Steel, and American Telephone & Telegraph. There was another bankers' conference at J. P. Morgan & Co., but this time no banking support was announced. During the next few days occurred a number of events designed to improve the situation. Both the Bank of England and the New York Federal Reserve Bank reduced their rediscount rates. John D. Rockefeller, in one of his infrequent public statements, said that the fall in security values was unjustified and that he and his son were buying. The Ford Motor Company expressed confidence in the future and announced reduced prices on its cars and trucks. By October 31 stocks had made a small recovery.[32]

As if to give the signal for a new decline, however, Irving Fisher wrote in the Sunday issue of the New York *Herald Tribune*, November 3, that stock prices were now "absurdly low." The very next day they went down from ten to twenty points. Their average level still stood 19 per cent above 1927 and 56 per cent higher than 1926.[33] The fluctuations occurring from day to day reflected the

[31] *Federal Reserve Bulletin* (November, 1929).
[32] Hirst, *Wall Street and Lombard Street*, pp. 33, 34, 38, 39.
[33] *Ibid.*, p. 42.

struggle between the forces trying to support the market and those who were forced to liquidate. The general trend, however, continued downward, since the banks and brokers who had accumulated collateral held as security for defaulted loans disposed of some of it every time an advance began. More optimistic statements, further reduction of rediscount rates, and curtailed sessions of the stock market helped to stem the tide of selling, but in the early part of December prices drifted lower than they had been in the previous month.

DEMONS AND EXPLANATIONS

It was no wonder that in view of the many authoritative statements to the effect that stock prices had fallen too low, the prolonged decline led the public to search for a personal devil on whom to place the blame. Why should the market continue to fall unless someone was deliberately pushing it down? During these hectic weeks an agitation arose against the professional speculator engaged in short selling. The public imagined a duel of heroic proportions being conducted between the bulls and the bears. At one time the leader of the former was supposed to be a professional trader named Arthur W. Cutten, while the principal champion of lower prices was believed to be Jesse Livermore. Those who had for months profited by trading for the rise assumed that there was something immoral about trading for the fall. The stock market authorities, already under heavy fire, bowed to this criticism by attempting to curb short selling.

As a matter of fact, however, although some speculators were taking advantage of the drop in the market, the short-selling interest was too small to be a major depressant. On November 12 there was reported to be an aggregate short position of 1,691,883 shares, distributed among 681 issues.[34] In comparison with the enormous number of shares bought and sold, this total could hardly have exerted a commanding influence. The comment was later made by experts that if short selling had been more active before the crash, the need of the speculators to cover their sales would have helped to cushion the fall. During the long boom, however,

[34] U. S. Senate Committee on Banking and Currency, *Hearing on Stock Exchange Practices,* Senate Resolution 84, 72 Cong., 1 Sess. Appendix to Parts 1, 2, and 3.

those who had attempted to go short of the market had so often burned their fingers that the practice had not been popular.

The panic exerted a depressing effect on general business exactly the opposite of the stimulation that had previously resulted from the boom. Those who lost heavily could buy less in the retail markets, and even those who had not been caught in the crash felt poorer because of the decline in the values of their securities and the general atmosphere of gloom. The buying of furs, jewels, yachts, expensive country places, and other luxuries that had been so prominent was sharply curtailed. Even industries that bulked larger in the total of production and trade were adversely affected. Among these were producers of automobiles and of other durable goods. Whereas business had recently been prompted to invest in new production by the prevailing atmosphere of confidence, it was now discouraged about the prospect of expanding sales.

President Hoover tried to counteract the psychological effects of the panic by calling a national conference of representatives of finance, business, labor, and agriculture. He promised that income taxes would be reduced and public works would be expanded in order to increase spending power in the markets for goods. He asked everybody concerned to go ahead with plans for investment and production as if nothing had happened. Workers were not to be laid off and wages were not to be reduced. An account of how this effort and others to stem the industrial depression, which had already begun under cover of the stock market boom, would extend beyond the limit of the period set for this book. It suffices to say that the year 1929, which at its beginning was believed by many contemporaries to be a glorious celebration of the New Era, marked in reality its inglorious exit.

What was the actual interrelationship between the stock market and general business conditions in the last two years of the decade? During the boom in Wall Street most contemporary defenders of the business order maintained that the activity of the market was an integral part of general prosperity. After the crash, however, their estimate of it was exactly the reverse. They contended that what had occurred was a speculative inflation which was almost completely isolated from the rest of the economy and need have no depressing effect on it if people would only keep their heads. In retrospect both truth and error appear to have been in each of these positions.

The stock market boom was intimately associated with the general economy in several important aspects. It would have been unlikely to occur without the mood of optimism which resulted from the long and marked expansion of production and consumption which followed the immediate postwar depression. In its later stages, speculation for the rise was facilitated first by an easy-money policy of the banks, adopted in order to support international monetary stability and alleviate a cyclical recession, and then by the surplus funds of business itself. Given the uncritical faith in private enterprise characteristic of the period, it was natural that most people should recognize no danger in adding to profit making in the production and exchange of goods, profit making in the production and exchange of evidences of ownership. At the last, the gains derived from an active stock market gave a final impetus of demand to retail markets.

It was not true, however, that the speculative boom was an accurate reflection of business prospects. Nor does it seem in retrospect that its more violent stages necessarily had to occur as a result of what had been happening in the rest of the economic order. If, for instance, the subsequent restrictions on margin trading, brokers' loans, or other stimuli of speculation had been in effect, the security inflation of 1928–1929 might have been moderated.

The panic on the exchange undoubtedly had more influence on business than those who tried to isolate it hoped that it would. Its psychological repercussions, both on consumers and on investors, were serious. No one can tell how great an effect the shock of this experience had in strengthening the reluctance of business to expand investment in subsequent years. Nevertheless, those who contended that, taken by itself, the panic need not necessarily cause a long depression were to a large extent justified. Their mistake was in thinking that a depression in business was not already under way and had not arisen from other sources. The panic did not cause a shortage of credit for legitimate industry and trade. The funds available to business were, indeed, increased by it. Neither did it have any marked effect on the commodity price level or on costs of production. If general business conditions had been, as

President Hoover supposed, "fundamentally sound," a revival would probably have followed the panic after a relatively short interval. The behavior of Wall Street, in the sense of its speculative activities, does not seem to have been the origin of the long and disastrous industrial depression that followed. It was a dramatic symbol of the end of the New Era, but did not in itself offer the explanation.

CHAPTER XV

The Structure of "The New Era"

THE economic changes in the United States, from the time of its entry into the war in 1917 to the gloomy close of 1929, many-sided and complex though they were, constitute, on the whole, a story with some dramatic unity.

By the time the United States became a belligerent, demand for war supplies by the Allies had increased the national income to a higher level than ever before and had erased the net indebtedness of Americans to foreigners. Governmental organization for war production gave the nation its first taste of planned management of major economic processes. The immediate result of this planning was great expansion of war production and the virtual elimination of unemployment, accompanied by some sacrifice of the high living standards just previously achieved. The real national income as a whole was not increased. The war burden was borne chiefly by wage earners, especially those receiving the middle and higher incomes in nonwar industries, by salaried personnel, and by recipients of property income. The only groups who gained in real income during the war were the farmers, some industrialists and capitalists in the top income brackets, and wage earners on the lower levels, including those who previously had been unemployed. Though the war organization checked the upward movement of prices already under way, it laid the basis of future inflation by its methods of financing governmental purchases.

The incontinent abandonment of war controls immediately

after the armistice led to a brief unemployment crisis followed by a sharp inflationary boom and an equally sharp price deflation accompanied by industrial depression. The farmers lost all that they had gained, and were left at a level below that which they had occupied before the war started. Labor suffered from a large volume of unemployment, and many employers seized the occasion to attack and destroy unions. Industry as a whole emerged from the postwar depression with a wider margin than before or during the war between the cost of its materials and the prices of its-products. War profits that had been laid aside served not only to carry most of the large corporations through the depression, but greatly to augment and improve their capital equipment. More rapid gains than ever previously recorded in production per man-hour sharply lowered labor costs. Though wages had been reduced, the drop in the cost of living, and particularly in food prices, left wage earners with an increase in purchasing power when employment was resumed.

For the time being, the war and the subsequent crisis heightened the strains in the social order, brought bitter protests from labor and the farmers, and gave rise to many proposals for economic reconstruction. These movements came to little, as the majority of the population, confused, war-weary, and afraid of new ideas, returned power to those who favored isolation and virtually unlimited scope for profit-seeking private enterprise. For six or seven years this policy seemed on the whole to be justified by the results. While the complaints of the agricultural population were not remedied, and other sectors of the economy such as coal mining and textile manufacturing suffered, there ensued an era of almost unprecedented industrial expansion, increase in productivity, growth of the national income, and higher living standards.

This advance, however, concealed serious flaws, not apparent to most observers at the time. In spite of nearly universal optimism about the future, a new industrial depression set in at the end, which was to become the most serious thus far in the nation's history. Its beginning was accompanied by a wild speculative boom in securities, and by a panic of unprecedented proportions. This shock to complacency was to put an end for many years to uncritical acceptance of leadership by big business, finance, and their political spokesmen.

THE DOMINANT PATTERN

It is desirable in conclusion to pull together the threads of analysis of the New Era (1923–1929) in order to see more clearly its dominant pattern. For this purpose the statistical table on pages 318 to 323 merits careful inspection. As far as the main currents of the economy are concerned, it almost tells its own story. What is that story?

Population increased 9 per cent, less rapidly than in former decades. The growth was still slowing down, partly through exclusion of immigration and partly through a decline of the birth rate. The income of individuals grew much faster than the population, or 21 per cent. This was a genuine gain, because the cost of living scarcely rose. In no single year did total income payments fall below those of the preceding year. That this was a period of real and growing prosperity for the nation considered as a whole is no delusion.

The larger part of the income payments flowed out in wages and salaries—64 per cent in 1923 and 63 per cent in 1929. This stream of payment for services grew almost as rapidly as the income of individuals as a whole. "Entrepreneurial withdrawals"— which covers the profits that farmers and unincorporated small businessmen took out of their undertakings—shared less in the general gain, growing 19 per cent. Dividends, interest, and rent expanded more than either, or 27 per cent. Property income was thus the leading beneficiary of the advance. In 1929 it constituted about one fifth of the total sums distributed.

Advantage at the top of the income scale is revealed by the estimate that the highest 1 per cent of income recipients not only took 14.5 per cent of the national income in 1929, but had increased their share of the total 19 per cent since 1923. The highest 5 per cent of income receivers had 26.1 per cent of the income at the end; their share had grown 14 per cent. Thus, while the poor did not grow poorer, the rich grew richer more rapidly than the poor did. Federal tax policy also favored the large incomes, after 1924. For the whole period, those receiving $5,000 benefited from tax reduction only to the extent of a 1 per cent gain in income after tax; for each higher bracket the gain was larger until it reached 31 per cent for incomes of $1 million.

RECORD OF ECONOMIC CHANGES, UNITED STATES, 1923–1929

Series	Unit	1923	1924	1925	1926	1927	1928	1929	% Change
POPULATION									
Total	Million	111.9	114.1	115.8	117.4	119.0	120.5	121.8	9
Annual Increment	Million	2.030	1.941	1.642	1.603	1.551	1.366	1.288	−37
INCOME OF INDIVIDUALS									
Income Payments:									
Total	Billion $	67.9	69.1	72.0	75.0	76.1	77.9	82.4	21
Wages and salaries	Billion $	43.3	43.3	45.0	48.0	48.4	49.4	52.2	21
Entrepreneurial withdrawals	Billion $	11.3	11.9	12.5	12.5	12.6	12.9	13.4	19
Dividends, interest, and rent	Billion $	13.2	13.8	14.5	14.6	15.1	15.7	16.8	27
Relative share going to highest:									
1% of recipients	Per Cent	12.3	12.9	13.7	13.9	14.4	14.9	14.5	19
5% of recipients	Per Cent	22.9	24.3	25.2	25.2	26.0	26.8	26.1	14
Net income after federal income tax for incomes of:									
$ 5,000	Thousand $	4.949	4.974	4.992	No Change	"	"	4.997	1
10,000	Thousand $	9.658	9.859	9.917	No Change	"	"	9.960	3
25,000	Thousand $	23.14	23.48	23.87	No Change	"	24.01	24.16	4
100,000	Thousand $	77.44	77.46	83.97	"	"	84.26	85.15	10
500,000	Thousand $	304.6	300.5	384.0	"	"	384.3	389.2	27
1,000,000	Thousand $	587.1	570.5	759.0	"	"	759.3	769.2	31

RECORD OF ECONOMIC CHANGES, UNITED STATES, 1923-1929 (Continued)

Series	Unit	1923	1924	1925	1926	1927	1928	1929	% Change
Gross National Product									
Total...............	Billion 1929 $	78.8	80.3	82.9	88.5	89.5	90.6	97.1	23
Consumer outlay:									
Total...............	Billion 1929 $	61.9	66.0	64.9	70.0	71.7	73.2	76.4	23
Perishable goods........	Billion 1929 $	23.5	25.3	25.1	26.3	26.8	26.7	28.0	19
Semidurable goods........	Billion 1929 $	9.8	9.0	9.9	10.0	11.2	11.2	11.8	20
Durable goods...........	Bi'lion 1929 $	6.6	6.9	7.8	8.6	8.2	8.4	8.8	33
Services...............	Billion 1929 $	22.0	24.8	22.0	25.1	25.5	26.9	27.8	26
Gross capital formation:									
Total...............	Billion $	16.9	14.2	18.0	18.6	17.8	17.4	20.7	22
Producer durable goods....	Billion $	5.8	2.4	6.0	6.5	6.1	6.5	7.5	29
Residential construction.....	Billion $	3.8	4.4	4.8	4.8	4.5	4.1	3.7	a
Private nonresidential construction	Billion $	2.9	3.0	3.4	4.0	4.1	4.1	4.2	45
Public construction.......	Billion $	1.4	1.7	2.0	2.0	2.3	2.4	2.4	71
Labor Force									
Total, NICB............	Million	43.8	44.5	45.0	46.0	46.9	47.9	48.4	11
Total, BLS.............	Million							48.1	
Number employed:									
Total, NICB...........	Million	43.0	42.5	44.2	45.5	45.3	46.1	47.9	11
Total, BLS............	Million							46.6	
Civil, nonagricultural, NICB...	Million	30.9	30.4	32.0	33.2	33.3	34.0	35.8	16
Civil, nonagricultural, BLS....	Million							33.3	
Number Unemployed, NICB...	Million	.7	2.0	0.8	0.5	1.6	1.9	0.4	a
Number Unemployed, BLS....	Million							1.5	

a No consistent trend for period.

RECORD OF ECONOMIC CHANGES, UNITED STATES, 1923-1929 (*Continued*)

OUTPUT AND EMPLOYMENT IN MAJOR INDUSTRIES

Series	Unit	1923	1924	1925	1926	1927	1928	1929	% Change
Agriculture:									
Output..........	1929=100	92	95	96	101	98	102	100	9
Number employed........	1929=100	105	104	104	104	101	101	100	-5
Output per worker........	1929=100	87	91	92	97	97	102	100	15
Coal mining:									
Output..........	1929=100	111	98	94	109	100	96	100	-10
Number employed........	Thousand	862	779	749	759	759	683	654	-24
Hours per worker........	Per Year	1,569	1,550	1,552	1,781	1,602	1,660	1,780	-13
Output per man hour......	1929=100	96	94	94	94	96	99	100	4
Manufacturing:									
Output..........	1899=100	280	266	298	316	317	332	364	30
Number employed........	1899=100	183	170	175	179	175	175	187	a
Hours per worker........	No. per week	47.3	45.4	46.3	46.5	46.3	46.1	45.7	-3
Output per man hour......	1899=100	177	189	201	208	214	226	233	32
Steam railroads:									
Output..........	1929=100	98	92	97	102	98	98	100	2
Number employed........	1929=100	112	106	105	107	105	100	100	-11
Hours per worker........	1929=100	103	100	100	101	100	100	100	-3
Output per man hour......	1929=100	85	87	92	94	93	98	100	18
Electric light and power:									
Output..........	1929=100	50	55	64	74	82	90	100	100
Number employed........	1929=100	67	72	74	83	86	92	100	34
Hours per worker........	No. per week	45.6	45.9	46.1	44.9	45.8	45.6	46.6	a
Output per man hour......	1929=100	72	75	85	91	98	100	100	36

a No consistent trend for period.

RECORD OF ECONOMIC CHANGES, UNITED STATES, 1923-1929 (Continued)

Series	Unit	1923	1924	1925	1926	1927	1928	1929	% Change
LABOR MARKET									
Average hourly earnings:									
Manufacturing............	Dollar	.522	.547	.547	.548	.550	.562	.566	8
Coal mining............	Dollar	.832	.826	.810	.801	.774	.747	.717	-14
Steam railroads...........	Dollar	.581	.592	.599	.599	.610	.618	.630	8
Average daily wage:									
Farm laborers...........	Dollar	2.25	2.29	2.29	2.31	2.28	2.27	2.25	0
Trade-union membership...	Thousand	3,439	3,364	3,360	3,338	3,366	3,297	3,239	-6
Workers on strike.........	Thousand	757	655	428	330	330	314	289	-62
COMMODITY PRICES									
Wholesale:									
"All" commodities........	1926=100	100.6	98.1	103.5	100	95.4	96.7	95.3	-5
Raw materials...........	1926=100	98.5	97.6	106.7	100	96.5	99.1	97.5	-1
Semimanufactured goods...	1926=100	118.6	108.7	105.3	100	94.3	94.5	93.9	-21
Finished goods...........	1926=100	99.2	96.3	100.6	100	95.0	95.9	94.5	-5
Building materials........	1926=100	98.7	102.3	101.7	100	94.7	94.1	95.4	-12
Business capital goods.....	1929=100	103.5	101.4	99.5	99.4	99.2	98.0	100	-3
Cost of Living...........	1935-39=100	121.9	122.2	125.4	126.4	124.0	122.6	122.5	a
STATUS OF CORPORATIONS									
Number active...........	Thousand	381	399	411	435	454	471	486	28
New incorporations.......	1925=100	—	83	100	100	103	110	112	34
Profits—Total:...........	Billion $	4.7	4.1	5.1	6.9	5.5	6.3	7.6	62
Dividends paid..........	Billion $	3.7	3.7	4.3	4.6	4.9	5.3	6.1	65
Income retained........	Billion $	1.0	0.4	0.8	2.3	0.6	0.9	1.5	a
Depreciation and depletion..	Billion $	2.4	2.6	2.8	3.4	3.4	3.7	4.0	67

a No consistent trend for period.

RECORD OF ECONOMIC CHANGES, UNITED STATES, 1923–1929 (Continued)

Series	Unit	1923	1924	1925	1926	1927	1928	1929	% Change
Securities Market									
Prices of common stock	1935–39 = 100	72.9	76.9	94.8	105.6	124.9	158.3	200.9	176
Industrial	1935–39 = 100	60.1	62.9	79.9	90.3	107.0	139.4	171.1	185
Public utility	1935–39 = 100	86.2	92.1	110.9	116.9	135.5	173.9	274.1	217
Railroad	1935–39 = 100	190.6	203.5	237.5	265.1	315.8	340.9	390.7	105
Shares traded	Million	236	284	460	452	582	931	1,125	377
Corporate security issues	Billion $	3.23	3.84	4.74	5.30	7.32	7.82	10.03	211
Interest Rates									
Commercial paper	Per Cent	4.97	3.90	4.00	4.23	4.02	4.84	5.78	a
Customers' rate:									
New York City	Per Cent	5.19	4.60	4.47	4.67	4.53	5.15	5.98	a
Southern and western cities	Per Cent	5.94	5.71	5.58	5.61	5.60	5.70	6.14	a
Spread	Per Cent	0.75	1.11	1.11	0.94	1.07	0.55	0.26	a
Corporate bond yields:									
Moody's *Aaa* bonds	Per Cent	5.12	5.00	4.88	4.73	4.54	4.55	4.73	−8
Moody's *Baa* bonds	Per Cent	7.24	6.85	6.27	5.87	5.48	5.48	5.90	−19
Spread	Per Cent	2.12	1.83	1.39	1.14	.91	.93	1.17	−45
Supply and Turnover of Money									
Currency in public circulation	Billion $	3.69	3.71	3.62	3.65	3.63	3.58	3.59	a
Deposits	Billion $	38.5	41.0	44.6	46.7	48.5	50.9	51.3	33
Turnover of deposits	Per Year	20.8	20.7	21.7	22.2	23.4	26.2	29.9	44
Bank debits:									
Total	Billion $	685	716	820	872	952	,114	1,276	86
New York City	Billion $	281	312	369	400	463	590	712	153
Outside New York City	Billion $	404	404	451	472	489	524	564	40

a No consistent trend for period.

RECORD OF ECONOMIC CHANGES, UNITED STATES, 1923-1929 (*Continued*)

Series	Unit	1923	1924	1925	1926	1927	1928	1929	% Change
FOREIGN TRADE									
Imports............	Billion $	3.79	3.61	4.23	4.43	4.18	4.09	4.40	16
Exports............	Billion $	4.17	4.59	4.91	4.81	4.87	5.13	5.24	26
FEDERAL FINANCE									
Revenue............	Billion $	4.11	3.91	3.83	4.08	4.09	3.92	4.24	a
Expenditure........	Billion $	3.25	2.97	3.09	3.01	3.00	3.20	3.30	a
Total Debt.........	Billion $	22.4	21.4	20.7	19.8	18.7	17.7	17.0	-24

Source: Table abridged from Arthur F. Burns, *Twenty-sixth Annual Report of the National Bureau of Economic Research* (New York: 1946), pp. 30–38. Detailed notes and sources for the various series are contained in this document. Percentage of changes 1923 to 1929 calculated by me.

a No consistent trend for period.

Consumers bought 23 per cent more in 1929 than in 1923. This figure is intended to measure the goods and services they actually obtained, since the shifts in prices, minor in any case, are taken into consideration. Though the course of consumer outlay was upward as a whole, it was not a steady advance. Some years registered greater gains than others. Important changes occurred in the sorts of things consumers bought. Their spendings for perishable and semidurable articles like food and clothing grew less rapidly than their total expenditures. Their purchases of durable goods like automobiles and furniture rose 33 per cent, as compared with the 23 per cent gain in total consumer spending. The amount spent for services grew slightly faster than the total, or 26 per cent. Almost as much was spent for services—private education, domestic service, medical attention, barber and beauty shops, and the like—as for food and other perishable products. The services item does not include tax-supported services like public education.

Purchases of capital goods also gained over the period—22 per cent in all. This figure declined in the two years of cyclical recession —1924 and 1927—as well as in 1928. The slumps were particularly marked in investment in machinery and other producers' durable goods, though between 1923 and 1929 the gain of producers' investment was larger than the total, or 29 per cent. Expenditure on house building followed a course of its own, rising to a peak in 1925 and 1926, and then falling steadily until, in 1929, it was lower than in 1923. Construction of commercial buildings and public construction grew throughout the period, but not steadily. The former was retarded in 1927 and 1928, the latter in 1926, and again in 1928 and 1929. The relative instability of the broad stream of spending represented by investment is revealed by these figures. Investment was, however, less than a third as large as consumer outlay, so that smaller percentage variations in the latter were quantitatively as important. It must be borne in mind that all the figures for consumer spending and investment in this section of the table are in terms of 1929 dollars, and so represent "real product," the effect of price changes being roughly eliminated.

Figures for the labor force and unemployment in this period are open to wide margins of error. These are derived from the National Industrial Conference Board—an employers' organization. For what they are worth, they show that the total labor force grew

11 per cent—somewhat more rapidly than the population, indicating that a larger proportion of the people had the status of employees at the end than at the beginning. The number actually employed also was about 11 per cent larger in 1929 than in 1923, though its growth was spasmodic. Nonagricultural employment grew faster than agricultural. Unemployment showed no consistent trend, varying from year to year. It was, on the whole, a relatively small percentage of the labor force, if the estimates approximate the reality. It will be noted that the United States Bureau of Labor Statistics figure for unemployment, available only for 1929, is considerably larger than that of the National Industrial Conference Board.

In agriculture the physical output grew 9 per cent, while the number engaged fell 5 per cent. There was a gain of 15 per cent in output per worker. The difficulties of the coal industry are revealed by the fluctuating figures of output, with a general downward tendency, so that 10 per cent less was produced in 1929 than in 1923. Nearly one quarter of the miners lost their jobs, and their yearly hours of work were extremely irregular, not exceeding in the best year the equivalent of 224 eight-hour days. Productivity in the mines gained only slightly.

The 30 per cent gain made by manufacturing output was the backbone of the increase in the national income. At the same time, the number employed by factories had a generally declining tendency, and even in 1929 was less than .5 per cent above 1923. The weekly hours per worker were slightly reduced. Output per man-hour thus grew markedly, or 32 per cent for the six years. Steam railroads had virtually no gain in traffic, but advances in efficiency amounting to an 18 per cent increase in output per man-hour enabled them to dispense with the services of 11 per cent of their employees. Hours were also reduced slightly. The output of electric light and power doubled; output per man-hour increased 39 per cent and the number employed 18 per cent. This growth of power use made possible many of the gains in efficiency of other industries.

Gains in efficiency, other things being equal, result in lower labor costs. Was this saving neutralized by higher wages? In manufacture the rise in average hourly earnings was 8 per cent, as compared with a gain in product per man-hour of 32 per cent. An 8 per cent wage advance was also registered in railroads, against the 15 per cent gain in productivity. Coal miners' average hourly earnings fell 14 per cent, though their productivity gained 4 per cent. Farm laborers had no gain in wages.

A manufacturer who, in 1929, obtained 32 per cent more product than in 1923, from an hour of labor for which he paid only 8 per cent more, obviously saved direct labor cost per unit of product. This was the average experience. A similar though less marked saving to the employer occurred in railroads, mining, and agriculture. Probably a greater one occurred in electric power. The saving in labor cost for the average manufacturer was about 12 per cent per unit of product. Such figures can be regarded only as extremely rough estimates, since they are based on broad statistical aggregates. There can, however, be little doubt that the trend of unit labor costs was downward. It is relevant to these figures that trade-union membership declined and the number of men on strike grew progressively smaller.

What about other costs to business? Raw materials were no higher in 1929 than in 1923. Both business capital goods and building materials had a falling tendency, and did not experience even the slight upward bulge in 1925 that is shown in raw materials or wholesale prices in general. Overhead costs are difficult to calculate, but it is probable that while they increased, they did not neutralize the savings made in labor and materials.

Did the corporations pass on these savings to the consumers in lower prices? Producers of business capital goods did so only in part, since the prices of these goods showed only a minor drop. Building materials fell 12 per cent. Producers of semimanufactured goods, such as unfinished textiles, sold their product 21 per cent cheaper at the end than at the beginning of the period. These declines, however, were offset largely by the course of the prices of finished goods, which fell only 5 per cent. When the retail stage was reached, the cost of living ended the period fractionally higher than it stood at the beginning, having experienced a small bulge, as did wholesale prices in general, in the interim. It therefore looks as if business as a whole benefited by increasing profit margins during the New Era.

The figures of corporate profits reinforce this inference. Though they shrank temporarily in the slumps of 1924 and 1927, their tendency was upward, and they ended the period with a gain of 62 per cent. In large part this gain must be attributed to growing physical volume of production and sales. But the growth of income payments in the same period was 21 per cent, and that of gross national product (in physical terms), 23 per cent. This is about the extent to which the gain of profits may be attributed to increased volume. The rest of the growth in profits must have arisen from wider margins, on the average, between costs and selling prices.

The greatest advance in the income stream was registered by dividends, which rose 65 per cent, not being reduced even in 1924 or 1927. The remainder of profits, retained by corporations as additions to surplus, varied from year to year with the variation of profits, the largest savings being in 1926 and 1929. Before reckoning their book profits, corporations laid aside large and increasing amounts to maintain their capital equipment, as is indicated by the steady growth of depreciation and depletion charges, which rose 67 per cent.

The attraction that corporate prosperity offered to security buyers, as well as the large amounts of surplus income available to the recipients of profits with which to buy shares, is indicated by the behavior of the stock market. Prices of shares advanced steadily, even before the speculative fever at the end of the decade. The average of stock prices rose 176 per cent; the number of shares traded annually, 377 per cent; and new corporate issues, 211 per cent. Utilities led the procession, with industrials next and railroads bringing up the rear.

Interest rates fluctuated, but on the whole revealed no scarcity of capital funds, in spite of the large amount of financing. The credit absorbed by the stock market in 1929 is indicated by the rise of interest rates in that year, a rise felt more in New York than in interior cities. Corporate bond yields had a falling tendency, a fact that again indicates the abundance of investment funds. This is emphasized by the marked reduction in yield of the lower-grade bonds. The reversal of the downward trend of bond-yields in 1929 reveals the preference "investors" were then showing for stocks.

There was no currency inflation, the amount of circulation showing no tendency to grow. Bank deposits, however, increased more rapidly than the national income—33 per cent. The turnover of deposits increased even more, especially after 1925, the gain from

1923 to 1929 being 44 per cent. Since the quantity of purchasing power was ample to finance the payments for commodities and services at current prices, this great velocity of circulation undoubtedly reflects speculation. Speculation is also revealed by bank debits, which include, among other things, the increase in brokers' loans. Bank debits increased 86 per cent—153 per cent in New York City and 40 per cent outside. The rise was accelerated in the later years. One important development that the table does not reveal is the large extent to which banking resources were diverted from commercial loans to investments in securities and real-estate mortgage bonds, a development that may be regarded in retrospect as inflation flowing into the securities market, and as a dangerous exchange of relatively liquid assets for others that were to become frozen when the crisis depressed security and real-estate values.

In foreign trade there was a consistent and expanding surplus of exports over imports. Imports grew 16 per cent; exports, 26 per cent.

The federal budget showed a surplus year after year, and the federal debt was reduced 24 per cent. The amount of the annual surplus varied. The government was therefore not directly stimulating purchasing power or employment. It should be added, however, that local government expenditures usually exceeded revenues by enough, after 1924, to overbalance the surplus in the federal budget and offer a small stimulus to activity. These figures are not shown in the table.[1]

It is possible to infer from this table the relatively poor fortunes of bituminous coal mining and, in part, of agriculture and small business, but the table omits the figures that would show the difficulties of cotton and woolen textile manufacture, of other depressed industries, and of the technologically unemployed. It does not reveal such important influences as the growth of concentration in industrial control, the maintenance of an international balance of payments chiefly through export of capital, and the approach of saturation points in the demand for automobiles and other consumers' durable goods. All these were among the factors which indicated that there might be an end to New Era prosperity.

[1] *Public Finance and Full Employment* (Board of Governors, Federal Reserve System, 1945), p. 115.

Since all the figures are large aggregates, they do not show much concerning the important interplay of demand and supply, of costs, prices, and profits, as among industries or within industries. These factors cannot be ignored in any complete study of the causes of the subsequent breakdown.

GAINS FROM PRODUCTION

Certain broad indications, do, however, emerge. In searching for warnings of the depression that was foreshadowed in 1927 and actually began in 1929, it is possible at once to eliminate numerous factors that in popular discussion have more recently been regarded as harbingers of disaster. There was no appreciable "deficit spending"—the federal budget was in balance and the national debt was being reduced. Taxes were reduced, especially in the higher brackets. Political interference with business enterprise (except in the case of protective tariffs and shipping subsidies) was at a minimum. Business confidence and public confidence in the prevailing order were high, to say the least. The incentive of profits was not only present but had rarely been greater. Profits in the aggregate were larger than ever, and there was no visible tendency of rising costs to encroach on profit margins. The supply of capital was abundant: not only were large funds seeking safe investment but a plethora of "venture capital" was willing to take speculative chances. A steady stream of new inventions and mechanical improvements seemed to entice investment. There was no inflationary tendency in commodity prices. Labor was, on the whole, tractable and cooperative; there was no shortage in the supply either of labor or of materials, both being cheap relative to selling prices.

The substantial gain derived by the nation from the remarkable advance in productiveness stands out clearly from these figures. While the population grew moderately, the incomes and expenditures of consumers increased much more rapidly. Even wage earners as a whole advanced their levels of living almost as much as the national product grew. A contemporary document, *Recent Economic Changes*,[2] published as a result of researches under the President's Committee on Unemployment, recounted some of the general benefits that had been realized.

[2] *Recent Economic Changes in the United States*, pp. 13–28, 57, 59, 68, 69, 106, 142, 143.

The expenditure for public education had increased more than threefold since before the war. The number of hospital beds had nearly doubled. Marked increases had taken place in the funds available for libraries, recreation, public health services, charities, and mothers' pensions. The death rate from pulmonary tuberculosis, ordinarily regarded as an index of popular welfare, had fallen from 445 per 100,000 (for white males between 25 and 44) in 1914 to 148.7 in 1926. Food consumption had been diversified and improved in quality, with larger per capita production of the foods rich in vitamins and minerals.

Even greater advances had been shown in the purchase of manufactured goods, especially those in the durable category. Consumption of semiluxuries like silk goods and carpets and rugs had risen markedly. Sales of rayon, a new product, increased from 9,246,000 pounds in 1919 to 96,271,000 in 1927. There had been a substantial growth in the sales of electrical household appliances like vacuum cleaners, ranges, and refrigerators. Radio sets in use were 60,000 in 1922 and 7,500,000 in 1928. At the end of the period there was more than one car to every six persons in the country. New residential construction had more than made up the war shortage, and its square footage had materially exceeded the normal requirements of the growth of population. These homes embodied much higher standards of equipment, like sanitary plumbing, telephones, and electric wiring.

Industry had gone in heavily for technical research to develop new products and materials, improve quality, reduce costs, eliminate waste, and discover new fields of application. New products and materials rapidly came on the markets; standardization of sizes and designs of manufactured articles made rapid headway. A coordinated effort to introduce simplified practices eliminated many useless varieties and added to economies of production and distribution. Working conditions were improved by mechanical safeguards against accident and by better illumination and ventilation.

Long-term planning of future development and operations became established in the larger and more stable business concerns. Area planning also obtained a foothold in the cities, and when the report was rendered, 206 of the 287 largest cities had planning commissions. Automobile highways were planned over larger regions through the system of federal aid.

Clearly, scientific research and technical progress were having their effect. The average levels of living in the United States, always relatively high, were now indubitably much the highest in the world. Observers were sent from abroad to learn how these accomplishments had been achieved. Even the Soviet Union struggled to emulate American mass production. Little fault could be found with the skill of the engineers in enlarging the material basis of civilization.

THE PUZZLE OF PROFITS

Aside from the general gain in living levels, the other chief development was the change in distribution of income, and especially the differential growth in profits. It is essential, if one is to gain understanding of what happened, to analyze carefully the role of profits. Profits, it is generally conceded, are the mainspring of action and decision in a capitalist order. The profit incentive often leads to utilization of scientific and technical discovery. The recipients of profits either manage or hire the managers. Their decisions have much to do with the nature of production, its volume, the distribution of income, the amount of savings. Governmental policies were, in this period, largely governed by the wishes of profit seekers.

It is clear on the surface that the growth of profits was the main force behind the speculative boom in stocks. It rendered the purchase of securities attractive, and was the source of most of the surplus income utilized for that purpose. Toward the end, bank credit supported the expansion of brokers' loans, which increased the volume of margin trading and inflated security prices. But this was an accessory rather than an originating influence. Indeed, in 1929 a large part of the call money came not from banks but from the liquid assets of business itself.

It does not follow that the dangerous developments in Wall Street were an inevitable consequence of the growth in profits. If margin trading had been eliminated, if nonprofessional speculators had been forewarned of their dangers, and if other abuses had been corrected, the speculative boom and collapse might conceivably have been moderated. In these circumstances it is possible that, although the values of shares would have risen relative to their earnings, the rise would have been sufficient merely to register the abundance of the supply of money capital in relation to the demand for it for productive purposes. In any case the ensuing industrial depression itself cannot be attributed more than in part to the speculation in Wall Street.

The question remains whether the growth of profits was not too rapid in relation to the growth of other incomes. There is little question that profit margins were large enough on the whole to serve as an incentive to increase production. Nor was there any lack of funds for the purpose. As things stood at the end of the period, corporations had more money than they wished to use either for current production or for new investment. What was lacking was a sufficient market for the goods. Construction of houses had already run ahead of demand, and commercial and industrial building was showing a sagging tendency. Complaints of "excess capacity" came from many manufacturing industries. The possibility of profitable investment abroad was proving to be narrower than had been believed.

Would new lines of enterprise have appeared at home to absorb the surplus of funds if speculation had not intervened? Possibly; no certain answer can be given. In fact, they did not appear in sufficient quantity to prevent the onset of depression, even though ample capital was available until after the downward trend had begun.

As a rough judgment, it looks as if profits in the aggregate were yielding more surplus income than could be absorbed by genuine investment, *under existing circumstances*. This judgment applies both to corporate savings and to the savings of recipients of dividends. Stockholders, of course, had the alternative of spending more than they did for current consumption and "saving" less. But they were already spending freely; it is doubtful if they would have spent enough more to remedy the imbalance, even if the attractions of speculation in the stock market had not existed.

FAILURE OF INTERNAL ADJUSTMENT

When an excess of productive capital exists and labor and materials are plentiful, the economic theorist expects prices to fall. This fall in turn is supposed to stimulate demand. The purchasing power of money in the hands of consumers is thereby increased. Their wants are far from satiated—if not for some types of goods, then at least for all goods and services together. If consumer incomes do not proportionately decline, lower prices should lead to larger sales and production.

Could such a development have occurred before 1929, sufficient to increase consumer markets, thus calling forth more investment and assuring the continuance of expansion? Manufacturing profits increased 38 per cent, 1923–1929, while manufacturing output was rising 30 per cent. Profit per unit therefore grew; it looks as if prices might have been reduced, or wage rates further increased, without damage to the profit incentive. It must be remembered that 1923, from which the gain is reckoned, was itself a prosperous year. Construction profit was 56 per cent higher in 1929 than in 1923, although the physical volume of construction was only 27 per cent greater. Profits in electric light and power rose 179 per cent while output grew 100 per cent. Even railroad, Pullman, and express profits increased 58 per cent, while railroad traffic declined. Mining profits were a minus quantity in 1923 and substantial in 1929.[3]

Why did not substantial declines in prices occur when "overproduction" seemed to threaten? Why did not manufacture as a whole, electric utilities, railroads, and building behave as bituminous coal and agriculture and cotton textiles had behaved? In part the answer was the absence of as pervasive a degree of price competition in the industries benefiting from wider profit margins. In part it was a matter of industrial policy. In part (as in railroads and public utilities) it was a consequence of monopoly under public rate regulation and the forces impinging upon it. But even if it had been possible to change all of these circumstances, as well as all other causes to which is attributed the relative inflexibility of prices in important sectors of the economy, the onset of depression might not have been avoided. The trouble was probably much too complex to be capable of yielding to a simple formula like average reduction of prices to consumers, wholesome as that might have been.

[3] Figures for profits (net savings plus dividends—and entrepreneurial withdrawals in the case of construction) obtained from Kuznets, *National Income and Its Composition, 1919–1938*, pp. 578, 642, 666, 675, 665, 673, 551, 552. In these figures gains or losses from changes in inventory valuation are excluded.

The large aggregates in these statistical tables do not tell the whole story. They are reasonably accurate as far as they go, but they leave much to be said. For one thing, advances in productivity, and the consequent savings in cost, were unevenly distributed, not only among industries, but among members of the same industry. It is probable that the difference in cost between marginal concerns and those that made the largest profits was widened in a period of such rapid technical advance. Could prices have been reduced markedly without limiting production through abandonment of marginal equipment? Technically, perhaps, yes, if means had been at hand for concentrating production in the more efficient units or for subsidizing marginal producers. In an actual regime of private enterprise, who knows?

A mere redistribution of existing national income by transferring purchasing power from the few large incomes to the many smaller ones would add relatively little to the purchasing power of those individuals who received the benefits. Price reductions or wage increases at the expense of profits per unit would have produced no effect on the total national income unless they had stimulated larger production. Production was in turn limited, at the existing level of efficiency, by the total labor supply. The absorption of the unemployed—perhaps 5 per cent of the total—would have ended the process, aside from further technical improvements.

It is doubtful whether such a relatively small increase in the purchasing power of those in the lower income brackets would greatly have stimulated the sales of such expensive goods as dwellings or automobiles. Something like a revolution in the whole process of building and selling houses would have been required to bring them within the means of that large section of the population who could not afford them. Automobile production was already superbly efficient, and there seemed little chance of radical improvement in a short time. There is no sign that the economic order was fluid enough to divert quickly to other channels—assuming that more promising ones existed—the capital and labor frozen in important industries that were ceasing to expand as rapidly as formerly.

One may speculate on what society as a whole might have done to avert the fall of production and employment if the danger had been foreseen and the will to act decisively had been present. There might have been a great public housing or slum-clearance program, subsidized in part at least by taxing the surplus profits, and benefited by the low costs of cheap interest rates and large-scale operations. Or there might have been a broad movement to improve the condition of the agricultural population of the South—and so to increase its productivity and purchasing power. But no such projects were then seriously considered, and the peril of depression was not widely foreseen. It is not the function of history to examine imaginary might-have-beens.

It is sufficient here to point out that the depression that followed the Coolidge-Hoover New Era was no easily preventable accident, and that it did not result in some mysterious way from the previous war or arrive on American shores like a rocket bomb from abroad. It was the outgrowth largely of the going institutions in the United States. While it is now possible to identify certain major infections that were developing, there seems to be no simple inoculation, the injection of which into the economic body would have maintained its health. It is for the purpose of indicating this conclusion that the speculations of this chapter have been introduced. The story of the remedies actually tried during the depression belongs in the succeeding volume of this series.

CHAPTER XVI

For Further Reading

THE economic historian for so recent a period as that covered by this book has a bibliographical task somewhat different from that which would be encountered for earlier years or for a history of a different character. There is little dispute concerning the objective facts, and no present difficulty in discovering what they were. The major task is one of interpretation and integration. The records, both primary and secondary, are so voluminous, and are duplicated in so many sources, that the object should be not to present an exhaustive list, but rather to make a helpful selection.

GOVERNMENT DOCUMENTS

Although the main interest of the reader who wishes to study the subject at more length will probably lie in the interpretative books rather than in the raw material itself, it may be well to begin by listing briefly the main documentary sources. Statistical or other economic material is to be found in a large number of governmental publications. Among these the more important are the following:

The Census Bureau provides in its decennial *Census of the United States* exhaustive facts about population and occupation. This bureau also issues a *Census of Manufactures,* which at the beginning of the period was taken every five years, and later was changed to a biennial basis. The Census Bureau also publishes valuable monographs on special subjects. Its figures on unemployment and the distributive trades were not gathered until after the end of the period covered by this book. Those who wish census information in abbreviated form may find it for any particular census period in the *Statistical Abstract of the United States.*

Aside from the figures obtainable from the census, the most valuable source for income data is the Bureau of Internal Revenue of the Treasury Department, which regularly publishes *Statistics of Income.* This material is abstracted from the income tax returns of individuals and business concerns. It is therefore limited by the coverage of the income tax and is subject to correction for possible errors in the returns.

The figures on the receipts, expenditures, and the financing of the federal government are contained in the *Annual Report* of the Secretary of the Treasury. Similar figures for states and local governments are found in the reports of the proper authorities in each case.

The records of the banks, in so far as they are represented by the Federal Reserve System, are published in the *Annual Report* of the Federal Reserve Board. In the *Federal Reserve Bulletin,* published monthly, may be found an exceedingly valuable summary of current banking and fiscal data, both for the United States and for other countries, as well as summary indexes of economic activities in general. The *Federal Reserve Bulletin* also contains useful interpretative comment on the current economic situation, particularly as it is affected by financial affairs, and occasional special articles.

For most of the years here covered the largest collection of current economic data in summary form is contained in the *Survey of Current Business,* issued monthly by the Department of Commerce. In this publication may be found more material on individual industries than in the *Federal Reserve Bulletin.* The Bureau of Foreign and Domestic Commerce of the Department of Commerce publishes regular figures on foreign trade and the international balance of payments of the United States. An excellent discussion of international economic relations is contained in the monograph *The United States in the World Economy* (U. S. Department of Commerce, Economic Series No. 23; Washington: Government Printing Office, 1943).

The Bureau of Labor Statistics of the Department of Labor is the original source for official figures on the course of wholesale prices and the cost of living. The *Monthly Labor Review,* published by this bureau, contains not only these figures, but others which are available pertaining to labor matters. Its data on wage rates and the changes in them are, for the period under consideration, less inclusive and reliable than those for prices, because of the difficulty in obtaining information. It publishes extensive data on hours of work, labor turnover, and labor productivity as well as special articles on numerous subjects in the field.

The Department of Agriculture, in its annual *Yearbooks* and in the publications of the Bureau of Agricultural Economics, presents exhaustive material concerning acreage and production of crops, crop prices, the relation between prices paid by farmers and prices received by them, farmers' incomes, agricultural exports and imports, and other matters.

The Interstate Commerce Commission is the major source of financial and operating statistics concerning the railroads. Because of the nature and extent of railroad regulation, these figures are probably more detailed and accurate than those reporting any other branch of the nation's economy except the figures for banking and government finances.

From reports of the Tariff Commission may be obtained all official figures about import duties and the changes in them.

Among the most valuable public documents are the numerous reports of special investigations by committees of the United States Senate and the House of Representatives. Some of these reports are pertinent to currently pending legislation and some are concerned with the results of investigations, pursued in conformity with resolutions of the Senate or House. Particularly fruitful are the reports of the Senate Committee on Manufactures, the Senate Committee on Banking and Currency, and the Senate Committee on Labor and Education. Outstanding reports during the period covered were those on the Teapot Dome and Elk Hills scandals, the steel strike of 1919, and stock exchange practices. The results of an investigation into war profits are contained in "Profiteering," *Senate Document* No. 248, 65 Cong., 2 Sess.

An extensive investigation into the nature and operation of the American economy was conducted by the Temporary National Economic Committee. Its voluminous and controversial hearings mainly relate to a period subsequent to that recorded in this book, but many of the subjects are relevant to those here discussed. One of the most pertinent of these monographs (No. 16) is the study by Walton Hamilton, *Antitrust in Action* (Washington: Government Printing Office, 1940). Monographs No. 6 and No. 21 contain information on cartels.

Other valuable government monographs containing statistical information and analysis are Leonard P. Ayres, *The War With Germany* (Washington: Government Printing Office, 1919); *Technological Trends and National Policy*, National Resources Committee (Washington: Government Printing Office, 1937); *Housing after World War I*, National Housing Agency (Washington: Government Printing Office, 1945); *Net Farm Income and Parity Report: 1943, and Summary for 1910–42* (U. S. Department of Agriculture, Bureau of Agricultural Economics; Washington: Government Printing Office, July, 1944); *Public Finance and Full Employment* (Board of Governors, Federal Reserve System, 1945).

STATISTICAL STUDIES

Much of the important statistical material cannot be obtained directly from government documents or other original sources, but is the result of interpretation and combination of figures by individual economists or private research foundations. One field of central significance concerning which this is true, at least for the earlier years of the period, is the national income. Willford I. King, Oswald W. Knauth, Frederick R. Macaulay, Wesley C. Mitchell, (editors of), *Income in the United States, Its Amount and Distribution, 1901–1919* (New York: National Bureau of Economic Research, 1930), were pioneers in this field. Probably no better figures exist for that period. Willford I. King, *The National Income and Its Purchasing Power* (New York: National Bureau of Economic Research, 1930), carries the study to a later date.   The standard work in the field since 1919 is Simon Kuznets, *National Income and Its Composition, 1919–1938* (New York: National Bureau of Economic Research, 1941). Other studies use approximately the same basic data, but their results differ largely as a consequence of the different concepts employed. Simon Kuznets, *Commodity Flow and Capital Formation* (New York: National Bureau of Economic Research, 1938), is a valuable by-product of the above study, covering an aspect of it that is theoretically of high importance. I have made extensive use of Harold Barger, *Outlay and Income in the United States, 1921–1938* (New York: National Bureau of Economic Research, 1942). This study depends mainly on Kuznets' material, but presents it in a more convenient form for those who are particularly interested in the fluctuations of consumers' purchases for various types of goods and services, investment, and net governmental expenditure. Barger also presents an attempt to trace the movements of components of the national income by quarters instead of merely by years, as is customary in income studies. Although his results do not embody a high degree of accuracy, they are useful for students of the business cycle.

Next to figures on the national income, the most important statistical series are those dealing with physical production. The logical obstacles inherent in the construction of production indexes and the consequent difficulty of deriving precise meaning from the results are well discussed in Arthur F. Burns, *Production Trends in the United States since 1870* (New York: National Bureau of Economic Research, 1934).

Solomon Fabricant, in *The Output of Manufacturing Industries, 1899–1937* (New York: National Bureau of Economic Research, 1940), and in his *Employment in Manufacturing, 1899–1939* (New York: National Bureau of Economic Research, 1942), provides excellent statistics of trends of physical production and of productivity. Figures of gains in productivity for agriculture, mining, manufacturing, and public utilities are conveniently summarized in Fabricant, *Labor Savings in American Industry, 1899–1939* (New York: National Bureau of Economic Research, 1945). Harold Barger and Hans H. Landsberg, *American Agriculture, 1899–1939* (New York: National Bureau of Economic Research, 1942), is a recent economic study of long-term agricultural tendencies, laying special stress on shifts in demand and increases in productivity. A similar study of mining is contained in Harold Barger and Sam H. Schurr, *The Mining Industries, 1899–1939: A Study of Output, Employment and Productivity* (New York: National Bureau of Economic Research, 1944). A special analysis of production and income in the two world wars is offered by Simon Kuznets, *National Product in Wartime* (New York: National Bureau of Economic Research, 1945). A highly specialized contribution is that of Geoffrey H. Moore, *Production of Industrial Materials in World Wars I and II* (New York: National Bureau of Economic Research, 1944).

One of the best of the analyses of prices is Frederick C. Mills, *The Behavior of Prices* (New York: National Bureau of Economic Research, 1927). A later period is covered by the same author in

Prices in Recession and Recovery (New York: National Bureau of Economic Research, 1936); in his *Economic Tendencies in the United States* (New York: National Bureau of Economic Research, 1932) he analyzes not only prices, but also costs, production, productivity, and other basic factors before, during, and after World War I up to the end of the period of prosperity.

Factual studies of important subjects, making full use of statistical material, are Harry Jerome, *Migration and Business Cycles* (New York: National Bureau of Economic Research, 1926) and his *Mechanization in Industry* (New York: National Bureau of Economic Research, 1934); Leo Wolman, *The Growth of American Trade Unions, 1880–1923* (New York: National Bureau of Economic Research, 1924); Paul H. Douglas, *Real Wages in the United States, 1890–1926* (Boston: Houghton Mifflin Company, 1930); and Imre Ferenczi, *International Migrations* (New York: National Bureau of Economic Research, 1929).

A trade association publication appearing annually is *Facts and Figures of the Automobile Industry*, National Automobile Chamber of Commerce. *Lloyd's Register of British and Foreign Shipping* (London), also published annually, is the chief source for shipping statistics.

SPECIFIC PERIODS AND PROBLEMS

On World War I, one of the best general histories is Frederic Logan Paxson, *American Democracy and the World War* (Boston: Houghton Mifflin Company, 1939), especially Volume II. John Maurice Clark, *The Costs of the World War to the American People* (New Haven: Yale University Press, 1931), summarizes the monetary and the real costs and their distribution. Ernest Ludlow Bogart, *War Costs and Their Financing* (New York: D. Appleton-Century Company, 1921), is a more narrowly limited fiscal study.

A relatively brief but comprehensive factual review of the war administration is contained in William Franklin Willoughby, *Government Organization in War Time and After* (New York: D. Appleton-Century Company, 1919). Probably the most extensive work on the subject is Benedict Crowell and Robert Forest Wilson, *How America Went to War* (New Haven: Yale University Press, 1921). Its six volumes are both detailed and discursive, and while they omit little of any importance, they represent a special point of view, since one of the authors was Assistant Secretary of War in charge of production and the other was an Army officer. Grosvenor B. Clarkson, *Industrial America in the World War* (Boston: Houghton Mifflin Company, 1923), is a detailed and somewhat laudatory account of the War Industries Board and the activities which came under its jurisdiction. The standard work on the Food Administration is William C. Mullendore, *History of the United States Food Administration, 1917–1919* (Stanford University: Stanford University Press, 1941). This contains an introduction by Herbert Hoover and in general represents the attitude of the administration itself. It is, however, an accurate and scholarly record of facts and statistics. The same may be said of Walker D. Hines, *War History of American Railroads* (New Haven: Yale University Press, 1928), which presents the activities of the Railroad Administration from the point of view of the administrator. An excellent account of one of the more important international agencies is I. A. Salter, *Allied Shipping Control* (Oxford: Carnegie Endowment for International Peace). This is one of the series issued by the Carnegie Endowment for International Peace under the general title, *Economic and Social History of the World War*. Other volumes in this series contain valuable material, although many of them do not refer directly to the United States. A complete list of all the war agencies with their subdivisions, and summaries of their functions, is provided in the official *Handbook of Federal World War Agencies and Their Records, 1917–1921*, issued under the auspices of the National Archives.

H. J. Tobin and Percy W. Bidwell, *Mobilizing Civilian America* (New York: Council on Foreign Relations, 1940), is a relatively brief summary. Gordon S. Watkins, *Labor Problems and Labor Administration in the United States during the World War* (Urbana: University of Illinois, *Studies in the Social Sciences*, September, 1919), is a critical and descriptive discussion. *A Report of the Activities of the War Department in the Field of Industrial Relations during the War* (Washington: Government Printing Office, 1919) contains the official report on the subject. See also Kuznets, *National Product in Wartime*, cited above, and the Senate document on profiteering, listed under governmental publications.

Paul A. Samuelson and Everett E. Hagen, *After the War—1918–1920* (Washington: National Resources Planning Board, 1943) is a brief but excellent analysis of the demobilization and postwar inflation. E. Jay Hovenstine, Jr., "Lessons of World War I," *American Academy of Political & Social Science, Annals,* CCXXXVIII (March, 1945), also deals with demobilization. *Recent Economic Changes in the United States,* Report of the Committee on Recent Economic Changes (New York: McGraw-Hill Book Company, 1929), assesses the postwar decade as it was viewed before the onset of depression. *Recent Social Trends* (New York: McGraw-Hill Book Company, 1933) contains a wealth of material by numerous authorities written in the early years of the depression. See also Mills, *The Behavior of Prices* and *Economic Tendencies in the United States,* listed above.

Walter M. W. Splawn, *Consolidation of Railroads* (New York: The Macmillan Company, 1925), discusses the problem in considerable factual detail. Julius Grodinsky, *Railroad Consolidation* (New York: D. Appleton-Century Company, 1930), presents a special thesis concerning the motives and results of consolidations which were proposed or which took place, in the decade following the Transportation Act of 1920. Walton H. Hamilton and Helen R. Wright, *The Case of Bituminous Coal* (New York: The Macmillan Company, 1925), offers a relatively brief but discerning analysis of the difficulties of the coal industry. A later book by the same authors, *A Way of Order for Bituminous Coal* (New York: The Macmillan Company, 1928), presents suggestions for a solution. Edward E. Hunt, F. G. Tryon, and Joseph H. Willits, *What the Coal Commission Found* (Baltimore: The Williams & Wilkins Co., 1925), summarizes the studies and recommendations of the United States Coal Commission in the immediate postwar years.

Lawrence H. Seltzer, *A Financial History of the American Automobile Industry* (Boston: Houghton Mifflin Company, 1928), is an outstanding account of the development of a single industry which led the expansion in the 1920's. *The Dynamics of Automobile Demand* (Detroit: General Motors Corp., 1939) contains, among other things, a highly technical study by Roos and von Szeliski on the problem of saturation at a given national income. Ralph C. Epstein, *The Automobile Industry* (Chicago: A. W. Shaw Co., 1928), is an authoritative history. The same author's *Industrial Profits in the United States* (New York: National Bureau of Economic Research, 1942) contains the best available, though necessarily incomplete and unsatisfactory, study of profits for various manufacturing industries, including automobiles. See also *Facts and Figures of the Automobile Industry* noted above.

INTERNATIONAL ECONOMIC RELATIONS

The best single source on the role played by the United States and the international balance of payments after 1919 is *The United States in the World Economy*, referred to above under government documents. John Maynard Keynes, *The Economic Consequences of the Peace* (New York: Harcourt, Brace and Company, 1920), contains an analysis of the reparations problem before any revision occurred. Its chapters describing the personalities and attitudes of Clemenceau, Wilson, and Lloyd George are brilliantly written. Carl Bergmann, *The History of Reparations* (Boston: Houghton Mifflin Company, 1927), is a narrative of negotiations on this subject by a prominent German participant. Harold G. Moulton and Constantine E. McGuire, *Germany's Capacity to Pay* (New York: McGraw-Hill Book Company, 1923), presents a systematic analysis of the reparations issue, as of a somewhat later date than Keynes's book, but before the adoption of the Dawes plan in 1924. Harold G. Moulton and Leo Pasvolsky, *World War Debt Settlements* (New York: The Macmillan Company, 1926), summarizes the revisions agreed upon up to 1926. Cleona Lewis, *America's Stake in International Investments* (Washington: The Brookings Institution, 1938), is an excellent study of the history of America's debtor and creditor position, with detailed figures. An earlier and less exhaustive treatment of the same subject may be found in James W. Angell, *Financial Foreign Policy of the United States* (New York: Council on Foreign Relations, 1933).

A standard exposition of the traditional economic theory of international trade is Frank W. Taussig, *International Trade* (New York: The Macmillan Company, 1927). William Adams Brown, Jr., *The International Gold Standard Reinterpreted, 1914–1934* (New York: National Bureau of Economic Research, 1940), a thorough history of the gold standard, sets against the abstract theory of the subject a study of the institutions, controls, and functions through which it operated. A briefer treatment, written to answer a specific question, is Charles O. Hardy, *Is There Enough Gold?* (Washington: The Brookings Institution, 1936). Paul Einzig, *World Finance, 1914–1935* (New York: The Macmillan Company, 1935), presents an interpretation of the disturbances and distortions from an international rather than a purely American point of view. *International Currency Experience, Lessons of the Inter-War Period* (New York: International Documents Service, Columbia University Press, 1944), a document of the League of Nations, presents what is perhaps the best interpretation of the currency and exchange controls both before and during the Great Depression. Benjamin Bruce Wallace and Lynn Ramsay Edminister, *International Control of Raw Materials* (Washington: The Brookings Institution, 1930), contains a fairly complete account of cartels and valorization schemes in operation before the crisis of 1929. A handy summary of specific cartel activities is *Canada and International Cartels*, Report of Commissioner, Combines Investigation Act (Ottawa: Edmond Cloutier, 1945).

For a scholarly discussion of cartel problems, and one which also contains historical material pertinent to the period of this book, see Irvin Hexner, *International Cartels* (Chapel Hill: The University of North Carolina Press, 1945). A contemporary official report is William Frederick Notz, *Representative International Cartels, Combines and Trusts* (Washington: Government Printing Office, 1929). Wendell Berge, *Cartels* (Washington: Public Affairs Press, 1944), represents the point of view of the Antitrust Division of the Department of Justice under the last term of Franklin D. Roosevelt.

LABOR AND AGRICULTURE

An exhaustive and illuminating study of postwar population movements within the United States as they affected industry, labor, and agriculture is Carter Goodrich and others, *Migration and Economic Opportunity* (Philadelphia: University of Pennsylvania Press, 1936). *The Problems of a Changing Population,* Report of the Committee on Population Problems to the National Resources Committee, May, 1938 (Washington: Government Printing Office, 1938), is another good study including consideration of general population problems. Harry Jerome, *Migration and Business Cycles,* previously referred to, deals mainly with international migration in relation to a specific problem.

John R. Commons and associates, *A History of Labour in the United States* (New York: The Macmillan Company, 1935), Vols. III and IV, contains much pertinent material on this period. A good source for trade-union history is Lewis L. Lorwin, *The American*

Federation of Labor (Washington: The Brookings Institution, 1933). Edgar S. Furniss and Lawrence R. Guild, *Labor Problems* (Boston: Houghton Mifflin Company, 1925), offers a discussion of many of the questions that seemed important to contemporaries in the first part of the postwar decade. David J. Saposs and Bertha T. Saposs, *Readings in Trade Unionism* (New York: The Macmillan Company, 1927), contains a collection of articles and documents illuminating the union programs, problems, and point of view. A more theoretical treatment of labor problems in their broader setting is offered in Solomon Blum, *Labor Economics* (New York: Henry Holt and Company, 1925). Summaries of actual wage arbitration cases in the period immediately after the war are contained in George H. Soule, *Wage Arbitrations: Selected Cases, 1920–1924* (New York: The Macmillan Company, 1928). Here may be found the union presentation of the case for the economy of high wages, as well as other union arguments.

The Interchurch World Movement of North America, *Report on the Steel Strike of 1919* (New York: Harcourt, Brace and Company, 1920), presents the results and conclusions of the investigation of this upheaval by a central organization of Protestant churches. A history of the same strike by its active leader is contained in William Z. Foster, *The Great Steel Strike* (New York: B. W. Huebsch, 1920). Another book by a union leader on the problems of his organization, and one that devotes particular attention to the war and postwar periods, is John L. Lewis, *The Miners' Fight for American Standards* (Indianapolis: Bell Publishing Co., 1925). Harry W. Laidler, *A History of Socialist Thought* (New York: Thomas Y. Crowell Co., 1927), is an extensive and well-documented treatise. Otto S. Beyer and others, *Wertheim Lectures on Industrial Relations, 1928* (Cambridge: Harvard University Press, 1929), contains accounts of the Baltimore & Ohio plan and other aspects of industrial relations after the war. Savel Zimand, *The Open Shop Drive* (New York: Bureau of Industrial Research, 1921), is a contemporary research pamphlet. Hearings before the Committee on Labor, House of Representatives, 67 Cong., 2 Sess., on House Resolution 11,956 (1922), offers probably the first economic study presented by a labor organization to support the theory that real wages should increase as national productivity rises.

Several studies listed above also contain much information on labor developments and problems. Among these the more important are *Technological Trends and National Policy*, which examines the facts of technological unemployment; Fabricant, *Labor Savings in American Industry;* Douglas, *Real Wages in the United States;* Leo Wolman, *The Growth of American Trade Unions, 1880–1923* (New York: National Bureau of Economic Research, 1924); and H. M. Douty, "The Trend of Industrial Disputes, 1922–1930," *Journal of the American Statistical Association,* Vol. XXVII (June, 1932).

There is a voluminous literature on agriculture and agricultural problems, especially in the period following 1917. Bibliographies of this material may be found in Everett Eugene Edwards, *A Bibliography of the History of Agriculture in the United States* (U.S. Department of Agriculture, Miscellaneous Publication No. 84; Washington: Government Printing Office, 1930), which covers documents and monographs, and in the *Agricultural Index* (New York: H. W. Wilson Co., 1916–), a cumulative monthly listing by subjects. For the years covered by this book, a mine of statistical and historical material may be found in the *Yearbooks of Agriculture* issued annually by the Department of Agriculture.

Three books of special usefulness for analysis of the outstanding events of the period are Edwin G. Nourse, *American Agriculture and the European Market* (New York: McGraw-Hill Book Company, 1924), which contains an analysis of agricultural supply, demand, and prices during and immediately after the war; John D. Black, *Agricultural Reform in the United States* (New York: McGraw-Hill Book Co., 1929), a thorough contemporary treatment of agricultural problems, agencies, and proposals, published just before the depression; and Barger, *American Agriculture, 1899–1939,* mentioned above, which lays special stress on shifts in demand and increases in productivity. An abundance of further references may be found in the bibliography of Fred A. Shannon, *The Farmer's Last Frontier* (New York: Rinehart & Company, Inc., 1945), which, although it deals with a period earlier than that covered by the present volume, lists many sources bearing on the problems of agriculture during and after the war.

EFFICIENCY AND SCIENTIFIC MANAGEMENT

C. Bertrand Thompson, *The Theory and Practice of Scientific Management* (Boston: Houghton Mifflin Company, 1917), is an excellent presentation of this subject as it stood just before the United States entered World War I. A report which had a wide influence in the postwar period was that on *Waste in Industry* (New York: Mc-Graw-Hill Book Company, 1921), sponsored by the Federated American Engineering Societies. It described numerous prevalent sources of waste and inefficiency and attempted a quantitative evaluation of the waste attributable respectively to management and labor. Its conclusions were much more favorable to labor in this respect than those offered the public during the "open-shop" drive, which was in full course at the time of its publication. Ordway Tead and Henry C. Metcalf, *Personnel Administration* (New York: McGraw-Hill Book Company, 1920), presented the more advanced and scientific view of labor management existing at the time of its publication in 1920. Relevant to this subject are the books cited above concerning productivity and technological change such as Jerome, *Mechanization in Industry;* Fabricant, *Labor Savings in American Industry;* and *Technological Trends and National Policy.* Elizabeth Faulkner Baker, *Displacement of Men by Machines* (New York: Columbia University Press, 1933), also offers a careful economic analysis of the effects of mechanical progress on unemployment during the postwar decade. Thorstein Veblen, *The Engineers and the Price System* (New York: B. W. Huebsch, Inc., 1921), states Veblen's thesis that the function of the engineers and the commercial incentive are in fundamental opposition, which exerted influence in the postwar period.

BANKING AND MONETARY PROBLEMS

Paul M. Warburg, *The Federal Reserve System* (New York: The Macmillan Company, 1930), is a long and detailed history of that institution by a man who was intimately connected with its formation and operation. It is valuable not only for the facts it records but for its personal reminiscences and its strong opinions. The book was published after the crisis of 1929, but before it was evident that a long industrial depression would ensue. Harold G. Moulton, *The Financial Organization of Society* (Chicago: University of Chicago Press, 1921), is a text book covering banking, the capital markets, and governmental fiscal policy. The edition listed is an early one valuable for the present purpose because it describes financial institutions as they existed immediately after the war and typifies the analysis current at that time. William Howard Steiner, *Money and Banking* (New York: Henry Holt and Company, 1933), a comprehensive text published after the end of the postwar decade, contains much historical material. B. H. Beckhard, *The New York Money Market* (New York: Columbia University Press, 1932), describes the processes and customs in the country's financial capital. An interesting and apparently conclusive proof that variations in interest rates do not affect stock speculation is contained in Richard N. Owens and Charles O. Hardy, *Interest Rates and Stock Speculation* (New York: The Macmillan Company, 1925). Esther R. Taus, *Central Banking Functions of the United States Treasury, 1789–1941* (New York: Columbia University Press, 1943), analyzes the relations between the Treasury and banking from the foundation of the United States to the present. A collection of studies of the behavior of the security markets containing much factual material made with the purpose of obtaining a basis for recommendation of reforms after the Great Depression is contained in Alfred L. Bernheim and Margaret Grant Schneider (eds.), *The Security Markets* (New York: Twentieth Century Fund, 1935). John H. Williams, *Postwar Monetary Plans and Other Essays* (New York: Alfred A. Knopf, Inc., 1944), contains critical essays on international banking and monetary problems, international trade, and the Keynes theory of unemployment.

THE CRISIS OF 1929

Probably the best single account of the 1929 crash is offered in Francis Wrigley Hirst, *Wall Street and Lombard Street* (New York: The Macmillan Company, 1931). Irving Fisher, *The Stock Market Crash—and After* (New York: The Macmillan Company, 1930), presents the view of an economist who did not expect the collapse of the market and regarded it as unnecessary. It contains, however, a number of interesting facts and figures. An entertaining and illuminating summary of the revelations obtained by the Senate committee investigating the stock market, by the attorney who conducted the investigation, is Ferdinand Pecora, *Wall Street under Oath* (New York: Simon & Schuster, 1939). The original document on which this book is based is the report of the U. S. Senate Committee on Banking and Currency, "Stock Exchange Practices," 72 Cong., 1 Sess. Two contemporary documents of interest because they represent the view of stock exchange officials are Edward Henry Harriman Simmons, *The Principal Causes of the Stock Market Crisis of 1929* (Pamphlet) and Richard Whitney, *The Work of the New York Stock Exchange in the Panic of 1929* (Pamphlet). An amusing collection of contemporary optimistic prophecies during the stock market boom and even after the beginning of its deflation is contained in Edward Angly, *Oh Yeah?* (New York: The Viking Press, 1931).

INSTITUTIONS AND THEORY

A generally recognized authority on industrial concentration and the control exercised through corporate organization is Adolph A. Berle and Gardiner C. Means, *The Modern Corporation and Private Property* (New York: The Macmillan Company, 1933). James C. Bonbright and Gardiner C. Means, *The Holding Company* (New York: McGraw-Hill Book Company, 1932), is the standard work on this subject. Alfred L. Bernheim and others, *Big Business, Its Growth and Place* (New York: Twentieth Century Fund, 1937), presents a convenient factual study with interpretative discussion of the size of establishments and of the companies that own them. A formal discussion of the legal and economic implications of monopoly may be found in Henry R. Seager and Charles A. Gulick, Jr., *Trust and Corporation Problems* (New York: Harper & Brothers, 1929). *Trade Associations, Their Economic Significance and Legal Status* (New York: National Industrial Conference Board, 1925) is a research study presented from the point of view of business. A detailed and critical analysis of the work of the Federal Trade Commission from the time of its foundation through the early postwar years is contained in Gerard C. Henderson, *The Federal Trade Commission* (New Haven: Yale University Press, 1924). A later study evaluating the work of the commission through the decade of the 1920's is T. C. Blaisdell, *The Federal Trade Commission* (New York: Columbia University Press, 1933). See also *Antitrust in Action* (Monograph No. 16 of the Temporary National Economic Committee), cited above.

The problem of the control of the business order for socially desirable ends, as it appeared in the middle of the period of prosperity, is carefully analyzed in John Maurice Clark, *Social Control of Business* (Chicago: University of Chicago Press, 1926). In contrast, a more recent book by Abba P. Lerner, a student of Keynes, *The Economics of Control* (New York: The Macmillan Company, 1944), deals principally in abstract theory by the method of marginal analysis. Edward Chamberlin, *The Theory of Monopolistic Competition* (Cambridge: Harvard University Press, 1933), broke new ground by a rigorous theoretical treatment of the price incentives operating in industries dominated by a few large competitors. An essay presenting a broad view of the important institutional changes that have taken place in the modern economy is Karl Polanyi, *The Great Transformation* (New York: Rinehart & Company, Inc., 1944). This book argues that the market economy has never prevailed except when enforced, because it is too individualistic. Fred Rogers Fairchild and Ralph Theodore Compton, *Opinions on Economic Problems* (New Haven: Yale University Press, 1927), is a collection of reprinted essays appearing during the postwar decade. A contemporary effort to present a comprehensive picture of the institutions and operation of the economy is contained in Sumner H. Slichter, *Modern Economic Society* (New York: Henry Holt and Company, 1928).

A preliminary report on extensive quantitative research into the phenomena of business cycles is contained in Wesley C. Mitchell, *Business Cycles* (New York: National Bureau of Economic Research, 1927). An interesting attempt to present a theoretical analysis of the same type of material may be found in John Maurice Clark, *Strategic Factors in Business Cycles* (New York: National Bureau of Economic Research, 1934). It was this book that set forth in its most precise form an explanation of the theory that a slackening of the growth in consumer demand is likely to result in an actual diminution of new capital investment. The theory of unemployment that underlies the recommendation of a compensatory fiscal policy was first presented in extensive and rigorous form in John Maynard Keynes, *A Treatise on Money* (New York: Harcourt, Brace and Company, 1930). The book is highly technical and depends to a large extent on mathematical analysis. Keynes subsequently revised this theory in *The General Theory of Employment, Interest and Money* (New York: Harcourt, Brace and Company, 1936), now regarded as the standard exposition of the school of which Keynes was the founder. Joan Robinson, *Introduction to the Theory of Employment* (New York: The Macmillan Company, 1937), is a shorter and less technical summary of the theory, which differs from Keynes's point of view in minor details. An application of this body of thinking to recent American economic history is presented in Alvin H. Hansen, *Fiscal Policy and Business Cycles* (New York: W. W. Norton and Company, 1941). Hansen makes certain contributions of his own. It is not necessary to refer in detail to the extensive list of books and articles that have carried on the controversies about the Keynes theory. One should not overlook in this connection, however, the pertinent quantitative material in Kuznets, *Commodity Flow and Capital Formation* or in Barger, *Outlay and Income in the United States, 1921–1938*, listed above. Arthur F. Burns, *Twenty-sixth Annual Report of the National Bureau of Economic Research* (New York: 1946), offers a penetrating though brief criticism of the adequacy of the Keynes analysis.

Probably the best advocacy of the theory that insufficient consumer demand, leading to unemployment, occurs when industry does not reduce prices as technical progress lowers costs is contained in Edwin G. Nourse, *Price Making in a Democracy* (Washington: Brookings Institution, 1944). An earlier book, Zenas Clark Dickinson, *Economic Motives* (Cambridge: Harvard University Press, 1922), offers a contemporary critique of the psychological premises of the classical theory concerning incentives in the economic order. The record of the hearings of the Senate Committee on Manufactures on "Establishment of a National Economic Council," (S6215, 72nd Congress, Washington: Government Printing Office, 1931) contains a valuable summary of economic statistics for the postwar decade and argument for and against the proposal to install national economic planning. Friedrich A. Hayek (ed.), *Collectivist Economic Planning* (London: G. Routledge & Sons, 1935), presents essays by himself, von Mises, and others attacking the concepts and results of economic planning, and defending laissez faire. Wassily W. Leontief, *The Structure of the American Economy, 1919–1929* (Cambridge: Harvard University Press, 1941), uses the method of equilibrium analysis to study the economic events of the decade.

Index

Underwood Act, 131
Unemployment, increase of, 125
  and increased production, 130
  in 1921, 96
  postwar, 83, 93, 104
  prewar, 57, 64
  technological, 215
  (*See also* Employment *and* Labor)
Unions, 65
  activities of, 217
  in building industry, 68
  in clothing industry, 68
  company, 202, 223
  fines against, 134
  membership of, 188, 227, 321
  in mining industry, 177
  postwar position of, 187
United Mine Workers, 195, 223
United States Coal Commission, 178
United States & Foreign Securities Corporation, 299
United States Employment Service, 71, 82
United States Steel Corporation, 139, 143, 192, 310
Utilities, 182
  employment in, 215, 320
  regulation of, 143

Van Fleet, V. W., 137
Van Sweringen operations, 162, 301
Vaness Company, 302
Varnish industry, gains in, 61
Victory loans, 49, 76, 86, 88

Wage Adjustment Commission, 68
Wages, average earnings, 113, 200, 221, 318, 321
  and cost of living, 74, 218
  fixing of, 203
  from 1923 to 1929, 122
  taxes on, 48
  wartime boost in, 65
Wall Street boom, 275
Walsh, Frank P., 70
War, cost of, 47
  economic planning for, 8
  economy during, 46
  labor during, 64
  postwar boom, 81
  prewar economics, 7
  reparations, 259
War Finance Corporation, 42
War Industries Board, 12, 14, 44, 56, 60, 81, 141
  Clearance Division, 16
  Requirements Division, 16
War Labor Board, 67, 193
War Trade Board, 15, 39
Watson, James A., 137
Webb-Pomerene Act, 139, 145
Weintraub, David, 130
Wheat industry, decline of, 99
  gains in, 77
Wheeling and Lake Erie Railroad, 302
White-Jones Act, 164
Whitney, Richard, 308
Wilkerson, James H., 204
Willard, Daniel, 11, 12
Wolman, Leo, 227
Women, employment of, 73, 213
Wood, Leonard, 10
Wool industry, decline of, 99, 178
  gains in, 61, 77
Working conditions (*see* Labor)

Yellow dog contract, 205
Young, Owen D., 303